Emmaus High School Library
Emmaus, Pennsylvania

W9-AWR-315

WITHDRAWN

ALSO BY E. J. DIONNE JR.
Why Americans Hate Politics

They Only
Look Dead

*Why Progressives
Will Dominate
the Next Political Era*

E. J. DIONNE JR.

SIMON & SCHUSTER
*New York   London   Toronto
Sydney   Tokyo   Singapore*

320.973
Dio

 SIMON & SCHUSTER
Rockefeller Center
1230 Avenue of the Americas
New York, NY 10020

Copyright © 1996 by E. J. Dionne Jr.
All rights reserved,
including the right of reproduction
in whole or in part in any form.
SIMON & SCHUSTER and colophon are
registered trademarks of Simon & Schuster Inc.
Designed by Edith Fowler
Manufactured in the United States of America

10   9   8   7   6   5   4   3   2   1

Library of Congress Cataloging-in-Publication Data

Dionne, E. J.
   They only look dead : why progressives will dominate the next political era / E. J. Dionne Jr.
      p.   cm.
   Includes bibliographical references (p.   ) and in-
dex.
   1. United States—Politics and government—
1993–   2. United States—Economic policy—1993–
3. United States—Social policy—1993–   4. Conservatism—United States.   5. Liberalism—United
States.   6. Progressivism (United States politics)
I. Title.
JK271.D56   1996
320.973'09'049—dc20   95-40224   CIP
ISBN 0-684-80768-8

43.38(17.84 (147 9/96

FOR MARY
with love

Contents

"A blind and ignorant resistance to every effort for the reform of abuses and for the readjustment of society to modern industrial conditions represents not true conservatism, but an incitement to the wildest radicalism; for wise radicalism and wise conservatism go hand in hand, one bent on progress, the other bent on seeing that no change is made unless in the right direction."

THEODORE ROOSEVELT, 1908

PREFACE

The Coming of the Second Progressive Era

THIS BOOK describes the recent past in order to make an argument about the future. Its central assertion is that the United States is on the verge of a second Progressive Era. The approaches to politics that Americans are likely to find most relevant in the coming years are rooted in the aspirations of Theodore and Franklin Roosevelt, Woodrow Wilson and Harry Truman, not in the ideas of William McKinley and Calvin Coolidge. Beneath all the rhetoric and posturing, it is this battle between two serious political traditions that now lies at the heart of American politics.

The 1994 elections and their aftermath radicalized American politics. After years of circumlocution and evasion, the Republicans have set out to overturn not only the Great Society but also the New Deal and the Progressive tradition. One only has to listen carefully, especially to Newt Gingrich, to realize that the Republicans are entirely serious and candid in describing this ultimate purpose. The boldness of their choice has endowed the Republican Party with a new political and intellectual energy. But the particular brand of radicalism the choice embodies carries large dangers for the Republicans and for the country. The Republicans have enjoyed great success over the last two years in casting themselves as the party of the future and their anti-government program as the logical pathway to the liberation of the new, high-technology information age.

11

In fact, the new Republican philosophy looks *backward* to the late nineteenth century, seeking to revive the radical, unregulated capitalism of the Gilded Age and that era's belief that material progress depends on the fiercest forms of unchecked competition. In doing so, this new philosophy marks a break not only with the Progressive tradition that was once so powerful in the Republican Party, but also with many of the communitarian currents of traditional conservatism. It is the central argument of this book that the Republican attack on Progressivism will lead to its revival by forcing its advocates to an open defense of their first principles and to a modernization of their program.

The dynamism of the New Republicanism has left the Democratic Party confused and divided. The radicalism inherent in the Republican program has confronted Democrats with a fundamental choice: As the carriers of a Progressive tradition that once found a home in both parties, Democrats can either revitalize it for the next century or watch as their party collapses into incoherence and irrelevance.

This book will argue that a wager on a New Progressivism is sound as politics and essential as policy. Our time combines social change with moral crisis, enormous economic opportunity with great economic dislocation and distress. It most closely resembles the period 1870 to 1900, which led to the Progressive Era. Then, as now, Americans were looking to forge new rules to realize a new era's potential while containing its threats. Progressives have always understood that while governments in authoritarian societies oppress, governments in democratic societies have the capacity to liberate. Unlike state socialism or pure, unregulated capitalism, the American Progressive tradition takes a pragmatic view of the possibilities of both government and the economy.

Progressives believe that the vast economic transformation now under way could confer large benefits and they do not seek to stop economic change in its tracks. They accept the freedoms and disciplines of the marketplace; they do not believe that government has infinite capacities, and respect an American business system that Progressivism itself helped to build, save and nurture. But neither do Progressives believe that government can simply get out of the way, ignore the declining living standards of so many American families or expect the free market to solve problems that the market has never been able to solve in the past. Progressives believe that government can ease the economic transition, help preserve a broad American middle class and *expand* the choices available to individuals. That is what Progressives did in the era of Theodore Roosevelt's Square Deal and Woodrow Wilson's New Freedom, and during the age of the New and Fair Deals. As the twentieth century closes, the Progressive project is more relevant than ever.

This book attempts to build on *Why Americans Hate Politics,* a book in which I argued that contemporary liberalism and conservatism had cast American politics as a series of false choices. Many of those false choices are still with us and, as I shall be arguing in Chapter One, so is the trivialization of politics that has left so many Americans cynical and apathetic. In particular, Americans are as impatient as ever with the false choice over the country's moral crisis that would make the agenda of the Christian Coalition or an indifference to family breakup and the coarsening of our culture the only available options. Contrary to so much of the current vogue, Americans are also dissatisfied with a debate that casts "big" and "small" government as all-encompassing and exclusive options. Buried in recent election returns is a broader message: Voters are angry at government not just for what it has done, but also for what it has *failed* to do. The current political upheaval can thus be defined less as a revolt against *big* government than as a rebellion against *bad* government—government that has proven ineffectual in grappling with the political, economic and moral crises that have shaken the country. This book is very tough on Democrats for squandering the opportunity they were given during the first two years of the Clinton presidency to demonstrate both their own capacities and the possibilities of reformed and modernized government. Voters will almost always pick small government over ineffective government. But those are not, and ought not to be, the only choices.

Bill Clinton's 1992 victory and the large vote given to Ross Perot reflected public frustration with the retreat from practical government. Clinton was elected not only in reaction to the failures of George Bush but also because he seemed to promise a plausible approach to the problems that most troubled the country: He pledged to use job training and education to ease the transition of individuals from the old economy to the new, to reshape the health care and welfare systems and to reform the political system to reduce the influence of special interests and expand the public's democratic capacities.

But in the two years after the 1992 election the Democrats failed fundamentally. Health care, welfare and political reform all fell victim to divisions within the party. Budget constraints never allowed the Clinton job-training and education initiatives to get off the ground. The Republicans, of course, played a large role in killing all these initiatives, but it was Democratic failure that gave the Republicans the opening they needed. To many Americans, the Democrats seemed to have become a dysfunctional party.

This failure and not some sudden popular surge to the right explains the Republican victory in 1994. Republicans brilliantly took advantage of the public's sense that Democrats had broken their promises by offering a "Contract with America." The genius of the contract lay not in its content but in the very notion of a contract itself. It implied a promise of accountable government oriented to action. The Republicans mobilized the country's deepest democratic yearnings by leading a revolt against distant congressional power and promising a new era in which power would be wielded by individuals and local communities.

Because of the substantial renovation that has occurred inside the Republican Party, some of the false choices described in *Why Americans Hate Politics* have been swept off the political agenda. A good deal of the new clarity in politics is the result of Newt Gingrich's audaciousness and the behind-the-scenes work of Republican intellectuals who have sought to resolve some of the contradictions in the conservative creed described in the earlier book. By moving boldly on budget issues, Gingrich has taken large steps toward bringing Republican policies into line with the party's anti-government (and anti-deficit) rhetoric. One can disagree with Gingrich's choices, as I do, while still recognizing their sweeping nature. At the same time, Republican thinkers and strategists have tried to resolve many of the philosophical conflicts between their traditionalist, religious wing and their small-government libertarian wing in favor of the libertarians. This effort at synthesis has, as I shall be arguing, grave weaknesses. But it does represent a significant change that is part of the radicalization of the choices American voters now confront.

President Clinton has also sought renovation within the Democratic Party, and for all of the Democrats' failures, it has gone forward. Whatever the voters' verdict in 1996, Clinton is likely to get credit in the long term for beginning a process through which Democrats and liberals began to update their program to match the demands of a radically new economy and to make peace in the cultural civil war that tore the party apart during the 1960s. The radicalization within the Republican Party has given the Democrats new openings. It will speed the process of change, as will, of course, the Democrats' confrontation with the reality of the 1994 election returns.

But the future, in 1996 and beyond, hangs largely on whether Clinton and the Democrats meet the challenge put to them by the radicalized Republicans and take up the task of ushering in a new Progressive period. If the Democrats fail, the calls for third and fourth parties will grow as the country seeks alternatives to Republican policies premised on the idea that government can almost never do good. The nation's most thoughtful conservatives are arguing that the central political question before the country is whether America's Progressive tradition—involving the careful but active use of government to temper markets and enhance individual opportunities—is dead. The conservatives say that it is. To their credit, they are asking exactly the right question. This gives conservatism an energy and coherence that liberalism lacks. But the conservatives' answer to their question is exactly wrong for the country. This should give liberals hope and purpose.

A Progressive response to both the promise and the dangers of new economic times is logical and in some sense inevitable. The policies of pure laissez-faire cannot solve the problems Americans are experiencing from economic change because the pure anti-government creed tries to define those problems out of existence. If the private market is not creating rising living standards, access to health care and pathways out of poverty, devout believers in the anti-government view presume that the problem cannot possibly lie in the market—and that the solution, or even parts of it, cannot possibly lie with government. Their response is thus to resist popular efforts to get government to act. Voters are asked to accept as "natural" and "inevitable" whatever outcome the market happens to produce. They are scolded to "stop whining" and to "work harder." They are lectured that it is "unrealistic" to expect anything better.

Eventually, voters tire of this response. In the United States, they have historically turned to Progressive politicians for practical remedies designed "to get the country moving again."

But if Democrats and liberals take on the task of bringing about a Progressive renewal, they will need to change some deeply ingrained habits. By turns, Democrats and liberals have been too timid in defending government's legitimate role, and too reflexive in resisting efforts to renew government and reformulate the Progressive approach. This is the paradox of Progressivism: Progressives lose if they fail to defend government's capacities to improve society; they also lose if they pretend that government *on its own* can improve society, or that government can escape the innovation Progressives would prescribe for every other part of society.

It will do no good for Democrats to pretend that they are an anti-government party, to suggest that they, like the Republicans, will tear government down, albeit in a kinder and gentler way. To the extent that Democrats have joined Republicans in delegitimizing government, they have prepared the way for their own crushing defeats.

But even as they mouthed anti-government slogans, many Democrats and liberals also tenaciously resisted efforts to change government and to overturn their own programmatic handiwork. Far from being associated with innovative efforts to solve new problems, liberalism has come to be seen as a defense of the governmental status quo, the preservation of old programs and the defense of bureaucracy for its own sake. This made it easy for Gringrich and other conservatives to begin speaking of a "reactionary liberalism." The authentic Progressive tradition is emphatically *not* reactionary. It is resolutely experimental rather than reflexively ideological, in constant search of new methods and insistent on continuous reform.

To succeed, a New Progressivism must be genuinely and not simply rhetorically *new*. Its task is to restore the legitimacy of public life by renewing the effectiveness of government and reforming the workings of politics. Its purpose now is what it always has been: to remind Americans that politics in a democracy is open to anyone and confers power—the responsibilities and satisfactions of self-rule—on everyone.

Part One

THE PROBLEM

WHY POLITICIANS DON'T GET RESPECT ANYMORE:

The Politics of Moral Annihilation

IT'S ANOTHER press conference at one of those conclaves of activists that seem to take place almost daily in Washington. Such gatherings, whether conducted by liberals, moderates, conservatives or radicals, often amount to one running press conference punctuated occasionally by the convention itself. Much of the point of these things, after all, is to get the movement's message out. Unless they can buy infinite amounts of media time, activists usually must rely on reporters to put their message out for them.

But this conservative press conference was different. It was called not to denounce taxes or socialized medicine or prayerless schools or pornography. Its purpose was to allow a young woman named Paula Jones to let loose a charge against the President of the United States. And not just any charge. Ms. Jones was accusing Bill Clinton of having harassed her sexually when he served as governor of Arkansas. Arkansas state troopers, she said, had invited her up to Clinton's hotel suite wherein, she insisted, the state's married governor made "unwelcomed sexual advances." Conservatives who only a few years earlier had denounced the very idea of sexual harassment as a feminist invention cooed sympathy for Ms. Jones. In describing Bill Clinton, these conservatives did a passable imitation of Kate Millett decrying the exploitative habits of the American male. And, later, on the day the statute of limitations on the president's

19

alleged offense was about to expire, Ms. Jones sued the president for something that supposedly happened in that Little Rock hotel room. The governor, she claimed in her suit, even dropped his pants and propositioned her in a way that can be charitably described as crude.

So much for the nobility of America's experiment with self-government. Each time Americans watch attacks on their top officials and declare, "It can't get worse than this," it does. The fact that so many seemed to take the charges at face value was President Clinton's problem. And sexual harassment, as the case of Bob Packwood showed, is a real issue. Still, one must ask: Is this era's collection of politicians much worse and more corrupt than those of an earlier era; or is the political climate now meaner, the press more unforgiving, the public more inclined to believe the very worst of public officials?

If one operates on the reasonable assumption that human nature is rather constant, it's hard to believe that today's politicians are demonstrably more venal than those of a generation or a century ago—especially since formal ethics codes are stricter now, and politicians have to live by tougher rules. Whatever their real failings—and politicians *do* have real failings—something more profound is going on. American politics is mired in recrimination, mistrust and accusation. The accusatory tone is not limited to charges of being unfaithful or on the take. Nor is the coarsening of politics limited to *A Current Affair* or *Hard Copy*. It crosses over into what is sometimes, albeit less and less, called the respectable press and respectable television.

The United States has fallen into a politics of accusation in which the moral annihilation of opponents is the ultimate goal. It is now no longer enough simply to defeat, outargue or outpoll a foe. Now, the only test of victory is whether an adversary's moral standing is thoroughly shredded and destroyed. A political rival or philosophical adversary cannot be simply mistaken, foolish, impractical or wrongheaded. He or she has to be made into the moral equivalent of Hitler or Stalin, the Marquis de Sade or Al Capone. This trend especially hurt Bill Clinton, but it did not start with him. On the contrary, conservative Clinton bashers were motivated in part by a desire to avenge the wrong done to their own heroes. Democrats had been happy to engage in moral annihilation when it suited their purposes: against Robert Bork and Clarence Thomas, Elliott Abrams and Ed Meese. "Remember Clarence Thomas!" has now assumed the same power on the right as "Remember Madrid!" did for anti-fascist veterans of the Spanish civil war. The result, across the spectrum, is a political war of all against all.

II

The late Senator Sam Ervin of Watergate fame once offered some sound advice for lawyers facing difficult cases. If the law is against you, he said, pound the evidence. If the evidence is against you, pound the law. And if they're both against you, pound the table.

Politicians have come up with their own version of Ervin's law: When you cannot satisfactorily explain your positions or offer solutions, pound one another. Politicians are the people with the most to lose from today's accusatory political climate. Yet paradoxically, they play the largest role in creating it. The personal attacks routinely used in political advertising are the most obvious manifestations of the politics of moral annihilation. Politicians rightly sense the depth of the public's disenchantment and yet also know the difficulty of selling solutions that might unsettle the status quo. As an alternative, they have transformed campaigns and the policy debate itself into an exercise in continuing invective. If you know the public is so mad that it will discount your proposed solutions, your best tactic is to denounce what the other guy is suggesting—and, of course, the other guy himself.

That is now the conventional wisdom among political consultants of all stripes. During the 1994 campaign one consultant after another declared that the public was simply too cynical to listen to anything good about a politician's life, or to anything positive a candidate might offer by way of solving problems. "We found people are unwilling to believe the best of a candidate and are willing to believe the worst," said Mark Mellman, a Democratic pollster. "You need someone with a substantial gut like me to sit on them and say, 'You've got to point out the faults of your opponent or you'll get creamed.'" So in 1994, "negative information" was served up in huge gobs. Opponents were attacked not only for their views, which is fair enough, but also for their *spouses'* finances, for every intricacy in their tax

returns, for lying, for cheating on their wives, for simply being incumbents—in effect, for any sin, real or imagined, serious or trivial,
that the negative researchers could come up with.

In perhaps the most vicious campaign of the year, the battle for
one of Virginia's U.S. Senate seats, a campaign commercial for Republican Oliver North had this to say about Senator Chuck Robb:

> Why can't Chuck Robb tell the truth? About the cocaine par-
> ties where Robb said he never saw drugs—then four of his
> party friends were sent to prison for dealing cocaine. Or
> about a beauty queen in the hotel room in New York. Robb
> says it was only a massage. "Chuck Robb lived a lie and
> violated his oath of good faith to the people," writes the
> *Richmond Times-Dispatch*. Character counts, and North has it
> all over Robb.

Lest anyone miss the point, the television screen filled with the
cover of the *Playboy* magazine featuring Tai Collins, the former Miss
Virginia/USA, who is described on the coverline as "the woman
Charles Robb couldn't resist." Robb replied quickly with an ad of his
own, charging that North had lied not only to President Reagan but
even in an address to "schoolchildren." The ad concluded: "Oliver
North—people are starting to wonder if he knows what the truth
is." It must be said that negative ads do not automatically reduce
voter turnout—Virginia voters cast ballots in droves, though a great
many of those ballots appear to have been cast more *against* one of
the main contenders than *for* either of them.

The imperatives of the contemporary political campaign were
well described by Joseph Gaylord, a close aide to Newt Gingrich
and one of the architects of the 1994 Republican victory. As *The Wall
Street Journal* reported, Gaylord's "how-to" textbook for Republican candidates urged challengers to "go negative" early and "never
back off." Candidates often do well to *avoid* the voters' main concerns because, Gaylord said in a remarkable passage worth italiciz-
ing, *"important issues can be of limited value."* Gaylord cited the
Willie Horton campaign run by George Bush against Michael
Dukakis to demonstrate the usefulness of a "minor detail" against
an opponent. Gaylord allowed that positive proposals by candidates
can be useful, but warned candidates to consider the political implications of any proposal they offered: "Does it help, or at least not
harm, efforts to raise money?" Gingrich called the book "absolutely

brilliant." Gaylord's suggestions are notable not because they are unusual, but precisely because they are *typical* (if rather candid) examples of the advice candidates in both parties receive all the time. Gaylord's compendium of campaign tips suggests that the things so often bemoaned about the political process are not simply the product of a few evil geniuses, but *systematic* characteristics of the modern political campaign.

The game of negative campaigning is open to right, left and center alike. But more than liberals may realize, the overall impact of the foul atmosphere the ads create is toward the anti-government right, because the most obvious target of the public's anger (as the Republicans demonstrated in 1994) is the government. If things are going wrong in society, it's far easier to blame government, a big, obvious institution, and politicians, whom no one much likes anyway, than to talk about important but rather vague forces such as "the global economy" or "the decline of community." And because democracy gives people control over the government, they can use elections to boot out the politicians in a way they cannot boot out most of the other people in society with whom they are unhappy. So all discontent comes to focus on politicians and government. As conservative writer David Frum notes in his fine book, *Dead Right,* "Listen to Rush Limbaugh or read the editorial columns in the *Wall Street Journal* and you will hear politicians described in language that we once applied only to the most hardened criminals."

The campaign ads themselves echo this view, sometimes almost literally. Consider an ad run by Republican Jeb Bush against Governor Lawton Chiles of Florida in 1994. A mother whose daughter was murdered says: "Her killer is still on death row and we're still waiting for justice. We won't get it from Lawton Chiles because he's too liberal." Or take another mother, this one in an ad for victorious New York Republican gubernatorial candidate George Pataki against Mario Cuomo: "I blame it all on Cuomo and his policies," she says. "Cuomo does not care about the victims of crime. He cares about the criminals."

It should be noted that even liberal candidates carrying liberal messages can end up discrediting the very government on which they propose to rely for achieving their ends. In Michigan, for example, the Democratic Party ran an ad against Republican Governor John Engler in 1994 accusing him of throwing ailing people onto the street. "It was a moment of horror and shame," the announcer said. "State troopers forced to close a mental health clinic, evicting dozens of terrified patients." The footage, in black and white, showed patients, their belongings in garbage bags, being led onto buses. Some of them were crying. One woman fell out of a wheelchair. Whatever other messages the ad sent, one of them surely was that government programs for the mentally ill—which Democrats want to strengthen—are an abysmal, inhumane failure. And the ad itself was extremely deceptive, as Howard Kurtz noted in *The Washington Post:* "While the eviction was bungled, most of the 37 patients were transferred to other facilities and the rest released to their parents." As for Governor Engler, Kurtz reported that he had "actually increased funding for mental health."

But if Democrats send anti-government messages against their own principles, Republicans spent years contradicting their own anti-government rhetoric with their performance in office. Frum, as honest in his assessment of conservatism as he is ardent in support of its ideas, has argued convincingly that while they talked a good game against government, conservatives actually oversaw its growth during the years they held the White House. The big programs grew big time: The cost of Medicare rose an average of 12 percent per year between 1980 and 1993. But smaller programs, even the ones Republicans claimed to oppose, went up a lot as well. In his 1980 campaign Ronald Reagan promised to abolish the Department of Education. Not only didn't he keep his promise, he actually let the department get bigger than ever—its spending rose from $14.7 billion in 1981 to $21.5 billion in 1989. Farmers usually vote Republican, and they were paid off, too. Farm assistance went up from $9.8 billion in 1981 to $29.6 billion in 1986. As Frum is candid enough to point out, the $20 billion increase was "nearly three times the entire federal contribution to Aid to Families with Dependent Children that year." Republicans hate welfare, unless it's going to one of their constituencies.

There is nothing dishonorable about supporting various federal programs. Elderly Americans would rightly revolt if Medicare were suddenly repealed, a fact Republican politicians know well, which is why they insisted that their proposed cuts in 1995 were designed only to "save the system." But there was something entirely dishonest about claiming to be the anti-government party in public speeches, then focusing budget cuts mainly on programs for the poor, who are not politically powerful and don't vote for your side anyway. Worse still is knowing that much of the structure of the government you've denounced will remain standing after all the talk is over.

The effect of the continuing rhetorical war against government is to discredit not simply this or that bad program, but the entire political enterprise. Because so many Republican politicians wanted to sound anti-government while pledging not to disturb anyone's favorite program, they opted for a rhetoric of accusation. They insisted that they would not harm a single elderly person on Medicare, but railed against "entitlement programs" and "big government" and "bureaucracy" and "big spending." The high cost of government became the product of some sort of liberal conspiracy.

In fact, it is nothing of the sort. The deficit itself, which adds over $100 billion a year to the cost of government in interest payments alone, is the product of four conscious decisions taken in the 1980s (with the support of Republicans). These included the Reagan tax cuts, the big increase in military spending at the beginning of Reagan's first term, the failure to make large cuts in the big programs for the elderly (Medicare and Social Security) and changes in the laws on savings and loans which raised the cost of the subsequent S&L bailout. All these things happened at once, thus red ink. Moreover, the most important upward pressures on government spending are the product of trends we actually welcome as private individuals: steady improvements in medical technology and much longer lifespans. The improvements in medical technology come at a high cost, and the government (mainly because of Medicare) pays over 40 percent of the country's health bills. We could, of course, say no to all sorts of medical procedures for the elderly. But no one—neither younger people nor their elderly parents— wants to do that. Longer lives also mean higher spending on Social Security. Some fiscal conservatives have been honest enough to acknowledge this reality and have called for later retirement and trims in Social Security expenditures, especially for the wealthy among the elderly. But most self-described fiscal conservatives don't want to touch Social Security, knowing, as Jack Kemp and Irving Kristol have argued, that Social Security is the third rail of American politics.

Voters were thus left with vituperation against big government that was, finally, empty. This fed popular cynicism twice over. Government was described as being large not because it paid for a lot of programs that people actually wanted, but because of some big government plot. Yet from 1980 to 1992 the Republicans only deepened the cynicism by being unwilling and unable to contain the size of government—again, except where government assistance to the poor was concerned. George Bush, so attacked on the right for raising taxes, did so not out of a political death wish or because he was a closet liberal, but because the numbers of big government and low taxes simply didn't add up. Yet Bush, eager to appease a restive right, went on assailing big government when it suited his purposes.

The problem for Democrats is the inverse of that facing Republicans. Beginning in the late 1970s, Democrats sensed that government was becoming increasingly less popular—and that taxes were anathema to many of the middle-class voters who had once been loyal Democrats. In truth, Democrats really *did* support expansive government, and were more than happy to bash Republicans when they even hinted at cutting social security or when they trimmed the school lunch program. The Democrats did it again on Social Security and Medicare in the 1994 campaign, though with far less effect than in the past.

Because their self-confidence was utterly destroyed in the Reagan period, Democrats have repeatedly put themselves in the untenable position of being for and against big government at the same time. In the early 1980s a new wave of politicians, popularly known as Atari Democrats, began their assault on "old New Deal ideas," "big spending," "redistributionism" and the party's alleged refusal to accommodate "new realities." These Democrats heaped praise on the private sector, fashioned their own tax-cut proposals and generally tried to sound like Republicans. "Democrats have been concerned for too long with the distribution of golden eggs," wrote Paul Tsongas in his influential 1981 book, *The Road from Here*. "Now it's time to worry about the health of the goose."

The Democrats' reassessment of their attitudes toward government action was by no means fruitless or foolish. The rise in taxes on the less-well-off sectors of the middle class—especially through payroll levies and rising state and local taxes—was an issue of vital concern to Democrats. The increase in middle-class taxes made the financing of government less progressive and led many rank-and-file Democrats to new doubts about activism in Washington. And since they were widely identified as "the party of government," Democrats had a larger interest than anyone else in reforming the workings of the bureaucracies. The public's perception that government could be unresponsive and ineffective—that civil servants were not always civil to the citizens they served, that public schools did not always teach, that the criminal justice system did not stop crime—had substance. Ignoring the public's worries meant ignoring the central challenge to the liberal Democratic project.

But by fleeing to their own version of empty anti-government rhetoric, Democrats consistently undermined voter confidence in the very programs they were trying to enact. Democrats fell into double-talk: In thirty-second spots, many declared themselves fierce enemies of "waste," "inefficiency," and "needless government spending." But who isn't? The Republicans' attacks on government so spooked the Democrats that they only rarely tried to defend what had been, since the New Deal, their main reason for existence. Worse, many of the candidates who used anti-government talk in their commercials then battled against *substantive* efforts to make government work more efficiently, such as Vice President Al Gore's undervalued "reinventing government" initiatives.

Faced with an anti-government party that was unwilling to reduce the size of government and a pro-government party that only periodically defended its role, voters came to be cynical about the entire political enterprise. There could be no honest talk about the deficit because so few politicians were willing to say that the deficit was big because of *popular* big programs. Since so few politicians were straight about where the deficit came from, most voters presumed it had been created by government "waste." Why weren't politicians cutting it? Presumably because they were rotten, corrupt and self-interested. As cynicism deepened, voters themselves often became complicit in a politics that involved the evasion of choices.

With politicians unwilling to engage in a frank debate over just how big government should be and how it should be paid for, the politics of moral annihilation became inevitable. The costs of being constructive were too high; destroying an opponent worked much better. Thus, campaign commercials came to revolve around petty

concerns such as the attendance record of a member of Congress—
missing even trivial roll calls or meaningless quorum calls became
a high crime. A single vote on a controversial piece of legislation,
often misdescribed in the commercials, could bring a candidate
down. Given where most politicians had to raise their campaign
money, every candidate for office could reasonably be characterized as "a tool of the special interests" or of "the big developers" or
of "big business" or "big labor." Making such charges was far easier
than explaining where you would trim social security or why a
modest tax increase might be necessary to pay for programs voters
said they wanted.

III

There were other costs that arose from the refusal of politicians
to talk substantively about government. If what government actually
does is not taken seriously, then those engaged in government and
politics are not taken seriously, either. When they are not seen as a
band of criminals, they are viewed as being no more than ordinary
celebrities. If a president is just a more boring version of Madonna
or Michael Jackson, then his (or, someday, her) private life is no less
the subject of gossip and prurient public interest than theirs. Moreover, if citizens no longer feel they have some measure of control
over government, they will not have a large stake in what politicians
do. They become mere spectators watching with growing fury and
detachment what "those politicians" are doing at the public's expense. Why spend time following the details of health care? It's
more fun to scoff at Bill Clinton's love life and question his old real
estate dealings—and, for his opponents, much more effective. Rush
Limbaugh candidly noted during a 1994 *Nightline* interview that
conservatives assailed Clinton's integrity on personal matters partly
to undermine his health care proposal. Trashing aspects of his private life was surely easier than arguing the intricacies of modern
medicine.

What has been lost is all distinction between the public and the
private realm. The flip side of turning public business into a matter
of private foibles is the tendency of the culture to view anyone's
private life as appropriate for public discussion. When people are

willing to go on *Oprah* or *Sally Jessy Raphaël* to reveal their most intimate secrets and their most frightful childhood experiences, and when the public in large numbers wants to watch, the barriers between public and private life have truly been torn down. This is deeply harmful to democratic politics. The political philosopher Jean Bethke Elshtain refers to this as "the politics of displacement" and describes this displacement as having "two trajectories."

> In the first, everything private—from one's sexual practices to blaming one's parents for a lack of "self esteem"—becomes grist for the public mill. In the second, everything public—from the grounds on which politicians are judged to health policies to gun regulations—is itself privatized, the playing out of a psychodrama on a grand scale. That is, we fret as much about a politician's affairs as his foreign policy. . . .

If what a politician does as part of his or her public life is not regarded as important or comprehensible, and if citizens become entirely cynical about democratic politics, then public purposes recede and all that is left are the private failures. It's true, of course, that voters have always paid a good deal of attention to the personal "character" of candidates, especially candidates for president. Character surely matters in a leader, which is why interest in Colin Powell as a potential president mushroomed. But the definition of "character" has become ever narrower. We focus more and more on sex and money, and less and less on a constancy of belief, a commitment to public purposes, a capacity to lead.

Electoral campaigns have also affected the press by creating a largely artificial sense of intimacy between politicians and voters. For decades campaign advertisements have depicted candidates in warm and loving scenes with their families. By using intimacy for their own purposes, candidates have encouraged the media to use intimacy against them. Reporters have decided, not entirely without reason, that the public now deserves to know: What lurks beneath that happy family scene? Is this politician a hypocrite? Whom does he (or she) really sleep with?

The politics of accusation and moral annihilation reflect a deep and fundamental polarization of opinion among political elites. When every fight is regarded as fundamental, when differences are regarded as unbridgeable, all-out political warfare becomes inevitable. Civility requires some basic agreement and mutual respect. That has been lacking in American politics since at least the early Reagan years, and arguably since the 1960s.

It has become easier to accuse political foes of disabling moral flaws precisely because so much of what is at issue in politics involves competing understandings of morality itself. The "culture wars" described so well by sociologist James Davison Hunter (and declared by Pat Buchanan at the 1992 Republican National Convention) involve battles between camps that neither understand nor particularly respect each other. Viewed from within, each of these worlds is attractive. On the one side are the upholders of tradition, religion, the two-parent family, personal responsibility and hard work. On the other side are the upholders of tolerance, openness, diversity, freedom and creativity. Yet neither world sees the other exactly that way. The upholders of tradition are often seen by their foes as bigoted and narrow-minded, repressive and moralistic. The upholders of openness are often seen by their enemies as immoral and irresponsible, libertine and decadent.

This extreme polarization is alien to the many Americans who find themselves sympathetic to tradition but also well disposed toward advances in tolerance. Yet on a large list of issues, from abortion to school prayer to welfare to gay rights, the battle lines are often drawn by the fiercest antagonists. And fierce antagonists on moral questions feel morally bound to give no quarter. For those who most strenuously opposed Bill Clinton's proposal to end the ban on gays in the military, it was axiomatic that his "permissive" attitudes toward homosexuality must be of a piece with the "permissive" way in which he led his personal life. Likewise, for abortion rights advocates, if Clarence Thomas proposed to roll back the advances made in this area, it was axiomatic that his private attitudes toward women left much room for sexual harassment.

All-out wars over public morality easily spill over into all-out assaults against the moral character of the individuals who play the central roles in these conflicts. It becomes harder and harder to draw lines between public and private when so much of the political debate is over the public meaning of private moral acts and the consequences of publicly proclaimed moral codes. If the personal is political, the political gets very personal.

There is one more reason the politics of accusation has arisen, and it is the most important of all. In a democracy, the public itself, whether consciously or unconsciously, sets the political agenda. Its anxieties and hopes are always on the minds of politicians. Its pulse is taken often. Its confusions are dealt with honestly or exploited.

The American public is now gripped with a quiet anxiety rooted in worries about real things. It senses social and moral breakdown, as evidenced by high rates of violent crime and family breakup. It senses chaos and disorder in the economic sphere, even in the midst of periods of high economic growth. It is as uncertain as the foreign policy makers are about what the country's role in the world should be after the Cold War.

The honest confusion among citizens is reflected constantly in the seemingly contradictory answers voters offer to journalists and polltakers. Ask Americans whether they think their government is competent to accomplish much of anything and they respond with anti-government tirades appropriate to the most fervent anarchist. Yet for all their polemics about lousy government, they consistently express a longing for government that does more and does it more effectively. Americans will almost always call for cuts in their own taxes (a fact Republicans are especially aware of) and increases in taxes on the rich (a point the Democrats are happy to note). In this climate, it's easier to convince voters that your opponent will hurt them than that you will somehow help them.

The marriage of vehemence to ideological eclecticism has created huge instability in the body politic. Sensing the confusion and anxiety, politicians often resort to accusation simply because candor about what government should do in the new situation carries such a high risk. It is far easier to replay the old debates—about big and small government, about abortion and gay rights, about public versus private schools, about which politician is truly crooked—than to be honest about what it will take to make this transitional era more stable, productive and fair. Yet that is now the central question in American politics.

IV

Against this background it is easy to understand why, in only a few years, the United States has gone through one of the greatest political upheavals in its history. Widespread cynicism and disaffection weakened the already frayed bonds of party allegiance. In 1992 a Republican president suffered a disastrous defeat that left his party with its smallest share of the popular vote in eighty years. That year also saw the rise of Ross Perot and the largest number of votes for a third party candidate in American history. Then, in 1994, a Democratic president presided over midterm election losses that were the worst for an incumbent party in nearly half a century. Republicans took control of both houses of Congress for the first time since the early 1950s.

In their search for answers, the voters seemed to be veering from one set of convictions to another. In 1992 the Democrats promised that a more active government could resolve the country's anxieties through reforms in health care, welfare, job training and education. In 1994 the Republicans said they would resolve the country's anxieties with a sweeping program to *shrink* the federal government.

The radicalization of American politics now under way becomes explicable when it is seen as a response to a political situation saturated in both cynicism and uncertainty. After fifteen years of running against government, Republicans faced the choice of either making good on their pledge to shrink it or abandoning what had been the heart of their electoral appeal. Some moderate Republicans had hoped in the wake of the Reagan era to ease the party toward acceptance of a kind of Eisenhower conservatism, now exemplified by Colin Powell, that would consolidate the achievements of the Reagan years but accept stewardship of a substantial federal establishment. But the most active forces in the party, and especially Newt Gingrich, rejected this view. And so with the "Contract with America" in 1994 and the party's budget proposals in 1995, they launched an attack on government far broader than anything attempted in the Reagan years.

The Democrats, for whom presidential defeat was a habit until 1992, were shaken to their foundations with the loss of their congressional bastion in the House. They were forced to confront the emptiness of a politics of incumbency which asserted confidently that no matter what large changes might be taking place in the country as a whole, their position in the House would be saved. It could be done with large expenditures of political action committee money, clever campaign commercials and, wherever necessary, tactical feints to the right. That formula failed in 1994. For the House Democrats, suddenly, all the seminars on "recasting the Democratic message" and "reinventing the Democratic program" were no longer academic exercises carried out for the benefit of those poor souls who would carry their party's banner in presidential elections. Now, their own long-term future was at stake.

The angry churning in American politics had not been caused by a single recession or the failure of a single administration. Nor could it be ascribed simply to Ross Perot's agitation, Bill Clinton's troubles or Newt Gingrich's strategizing. Its underlying causes were deeper. They encompass the four crises of American politics.

□ 2 □

POLITICIANS ADRIFT:

The Four Crises
of American Politics

THE CURRENT CHAOS in American political life arises from possibilities
and insecurities created by a new economic and moral order. But
for the United States, what seems very new is not entirely novel. Our
times bear a striking similarity to the period between the Civil War
and the turn of the century, which culminated in the original Progressive achievement. That era of upheaval is described brilliantly
by the historian Robert Wiebe in his classic work *The Search for
Order*. It was, Wiebe writes, a time when "Americans everywhere
were crying out in scorn and despair." In the post–Civil War period
the small town was losing its central role in American life to the big
city. The shop was being replaced by the factory, craftsmen by
factory workers, local elites by powerful national elites. State legislatures came under the influence of lobbyists for the railroads and
the other trusts. Public expenditure came under suspicion. Reformers demanded change, though their programs were as often as not
backward-looking. Sounding much like Ross Perot does today, the
Illinois Grange issued a call in the late 1870s for continuous reform
"until every department of our government gives token that the
reign of licentious extravagance is over, and something of the purity, honesty and frugality with which our fathers inaugurated it, has
taken its place." Wiebe notes that there was even a revolt against a
congressional pay raise, routinely labeled a "salary grab" by its

34

critics—the same phrase invoked by Ralph Nader and other opponents of congressional pay raises a century later.

The dissident and reform impulses of that time, like this one,
were rooted not simply in a sense of economic injustice but also in
a fear that old values were being undermined or ignored in the rush
of industrialism. Thus was the late nineteenth century awash in
movements to restore American morality and a sense of the "purity"
of its community, seen under threat from immigrants who poured
into the factories of the big cities. The drive for the prohibition of
alcohol began in that era, spawning organizations such as the Woman's Christian Temperance Union. The cause of prohibition was
perfectly suited for a time of rapid change. "Uneasy people could
turn here, as they had for generations," writes Wiebe, "with assur-
ance that in attacking liquor they fought beyond question for the
Lord and the sanctity of the hearth." The chaotic era of the late
nineteenth century also saw the rise of movements for school reform—including calls for teaching religious values in the schools—
and for social and moral uplift in the slums. There was also, Wiebe
notes, "a hectic campaign to instill patriotism through worship of
the Constitution, the flag and America's heroes." All these movements—no less than today's battles over abortion, prayer in school,
immigration, drugs, the Pledge of Allegiance, illegitimacy and gay
rights—bespoke the country's acute sense of passing through a
period of moral crisis.

The turn-of-the-century Progressives arose to bring order to
both politics and the economy, but their quest was at least as much
about morality as about political economy. The values of the Progressives were rooted in the old virtues, even as they accepted that
the tide of industrialism could not be turned back. The new trusts
and corporations might be regulated or—for the more radical Progressives—brought under government control, but they could not
be abolished. Government could be run more efficiently, but in the
new era, inescapably, it would be bigger and run according to
predictable bureaucratic rules.

The parallels between now and the period leading to Progressivism go beyond pay raises and the Perot movement. "There is,"
writes Hugh Heclo, an acute student of American politics, "something familiar in the Progressives' deep worry that, despite living in
an era of relative peace and prosperity, something had gone seri-

ously wrong in the internal life of the nation." In the 1990s the country is again seeking what it looked for in the earlier rounds of Progressive reform: new arrangements that would preserve older values under radically new circumstances and create a sense of opportunity for those anxious about losing out in a period of chaotic change. Those demands grow out of the four crises in American politics—the economic crisis itself, a political crisis, a moral crisis and a crisis over how Americans view their country's role in the world.

"Crisis" is surely one of the most overused words in politics. It is usually better discarded in favor of the more modest word "problem." In our times, so many crises have been announced (and televised) that one humorist was drawn to describing "The Crisis Crisis." So it is with some trepidation, but also as a conscious choice, that I offer a description of the four crises. I use the conventional dictionary definition of the word "crisis"—"turning point" or "decisive or crucial time." I accept as well the dictionary's qualification that the word is also usually used to refer to "a time of great danger or trouble whose outcome will decide whether possible bad consequences will follow."

Because of this last meaning, my use of the term will be especially controversial when applied to the rise of the global economy. Lurking beneath almost every other argument in American politics is a debate over whether the steady economic integration of the planet should be viewed primarily as benign or menacing. This question divides people who had once been allies, and will not be settled on the basis of "the evidence" alone, since attitudes toward the global economy depend so heavily on the assumptions brought to the evidence.

The argument about the global economy is difficult because so many different things can be said about it that are true. It is true, for example, that the world as a whole is getting richer. In Asia generally and in China in particular, economic growth goes forward at staggering rates. Technological progress over just the last two decades has revolutionized the ways things are made, problems are solved, information is exchanged and spread, and individuals interact with one another. Because increases in technical capacity have been so enormous and the opportunities for wealth creation are so vast, defenders of the global economy question not just the judgment but also the very sanity of globalism's critics. To impede this process, say its champions, would be to block a great leap forward. For the United States to do so would be particularly foolish in light of its strong potential to dominate in the information age economy. Far from doing badly, the United States was meeting the competition splendidly, they argued, with its output increasing more rapidly than in any other industrial country, including Japan. Conservative economist Alan Reynolds was explicit in warning of the dangers of "crisis-mongering." On the basic measures of living standards that actually matter to citizens, he said, Americans were doing very well. Between 1970 and 1990 the average size of houses increased from 1,500 to 2,080 square feet. The proportion of homes with air conditioning rose from 34 to 76 percent, of families with two or more cars from 29 to 54 percent. And a strong case can be made that the future will be even better. A wide spectrum of economists has argued that the period of slower economic growth that began around 1973 may be ending and that the United States is within sight of a far more dynamic economic period akin to that of the 1950s and 1960s. "Here's how it could happen," wrote *Wall Street Journal* reporters Bob Davis and Lucinda Harper:

> Changes in technology, trade and education would boost the fortunes of most Americans. Growing global markets would create big opportunities for dynamic U.S. companies and their employees. Broader computer use would make workers more productive, more in demand and able to command higher salaries. And growing college enrollment would shrink the gap between the wealthy and the middle classes.

Davis and Harper cited the view of Harvard University economist Jeffrey Sachs. "If we play our cards right," Sachs said, "we're at the beginning of a period of significant long-term prosperity. We are in the midst of one of history's greatest expansions of market capitalism."

But is this globalism such a leap forward, and, more particularly, *who* is leaping forward and *who* is falling back? For it is the central fact of the global economy that individuals who even a generation ago felt secure in an economic competition largely confined by national borders are now competing with hundreds of millions of people willing to work for less, under conditions that

American workers would regard as barbaric. For those caught up in the bottom rungs of this competition, argue the critics of globalism, it can't be progress to see hourly wage rates decline year after year. It can't be progress, they say, to watch as companies cut back benefits for full-time workers, or to witness the largest explosion in employment occurring among temporary workers for whom companies need not provide health insurance, pensions or paid vacations. Can it be progress, they ask, if there is a steady widening of inequalities in both income and wealth? Americans have never minded the rich getting richer, as long as everyone else gets richer, too. The new economy, however, seems to break the link between the success of the affluent and the well-being of everyone else. And in the new circumstances, legislated social gains struggled for over generations—laws on the environment, workplace safety, child labor—are steadily eroded by international competitive pressures. In this telling, globalism is not merely a crisis, it is a disaster.

Thus the outlines of the great debate. Its contours will be defined not by traditional labels such as liberal and conservative but by the expectations of individuals: Those who are doing well in the new economy (or hope to) will have large differences with those who are doing badly (or fear that they might). My purpose in using the word "crisis" to describe the impact of the new economy is to preserve a certain neutrality, because either description of the new economy—optimistic or pessimistic—is a potentially accurate portrait of the future. Taken as a whole, the world is indeed far richer now than it was a decade or a half century ago. Global integration combined with technological progress holds the potential Sachs described, of a historic expansion of wealth and opportunity. Unbridled pessimism about the coming period is not only alien to the American tradition, but also unsupported by the facts. But it is just as undeniable that the process of global integration creates large new problems, which make it harder and harder for national governments to exercise authority. This process creates a sense that things are out of control. It simultaneously fosters new economic growth and new inequalities. It creates both new classes of economic winners and new classes of losers. The bitterness of those on the edge is heightened by a sense of moral betrayal, since most of those losing out do so despite their commitments to the rules, values and aspirations the society claims to revere.

II

The first crisis is defined by the economic transformation itself. The increasing ease with which money, equipment and whole factories can be moved to anywhere in the world has created all manner of dislocations. Blue-collar jobs, once the keystone of what we (and, under different labels, the Western Europeans) thought of as a middle-class standard of living, can be shipped off at a moment's notice. When factories are mobile, national labor, safety and environmental regulations are increasingly difficult to enforce. If employers don't like certain regulations, they can just pick up and move. Competition in the world market forces many of them to do just that.

The most obvious result of globalization is perhaps the best known: the movement of production jobs from the United States to low-wage countries overseas. Workers in the United States with few skills are in direct competition with workers in other countries where pay and workplace and living standards are much lower. Richard Rothstein, a brilliant analyst of the labor movement, has referred to this as the rise of "the global hiring hall." The global hiring hall has affected not just older industries such as textiles and cars, but also newer endeavors such as computer key-punching and the assembly of sophisticated electronics. As Rothstein has reported, Malaysia, with 85,000 electronics workers, became the world's largest exporter of semiconductors. Wages there run to about 45 cents an hour for unskilled production work. Many of the American workers who lost their old jobs found new ones, but often at significant cost to their standards of living. Robert Reich, who became President Clinton's Labor secretary, cited Bureau of Labor Statistics estimates that of the 2.8 million manufacturing workers who lost their jobs in the early 1980s, one-third were rehired in service industry jobs paying at least 20 percent less. Even industries that recovered successfully from recession and intense foreign competition—steel and auto, for example—made do with many fewer workers. The ranks of the "aristocrats" of blue-collar work thinned notably. As Reich reported, the number of all routine steelmaking jobs in the United States dropped from 480,000 to 260,000 between 1974 and 1988. The United Auto Workers union, he noted, lost a third of its membership—500,000 people—during the 1980s.

Service workers, though generally paid less, are presumed safer from global competition and, in many ways, they are. The person who serves you a Big Mac at a McDonald's in Chicago cannot do that job from China or Mexico. But because of advances in computer and communication technology, many jobs characterized as being in the service sector can be done abroad. Insurance claim forms can be processed as easily in Ireland as in Peoria, and even consumer-assistance telephone banks can be located in any country where there are people who speak English (or, in some cases, Spanish).

One consequence of the global hiring hall is that those with more skills and knowledge to bring to the marketplace do far better than those without them. In all of the debates over the rise of inequality during the Reagan years, much attention was paid to the impact of tax policies that benefited the well-off and to the "predators' ball" on Wall Street where junk bond specialists and takeover artists made big scores. Less noticed then (but increasingly commented upon now) is the far more pervasive impact of the "education gap," whereby those with college and advanced degrees found a share of prosperity while most of those with less formal education found themselves falling fast.

Between 1980 and 1990 the median income of all households in America rose slightly in constant dollars—from $28,115 to $28,906. Women continued to lag well behind men in their incomes, but while the average man working full-time, year-round *lost* more than $1,000 in real annual income between 1980 and 1990, the average woman gained $1,800.

But these figures concealed exceptional differences by levels of education. Male college graduates saw their inflation-adjusted incomes rise by $1,560 over the decade to $37,553. Men who only graduated from high school saw their incomes skid by $4,266 to $21,650. And men who didn't graduate from high school dropped $3,904 to $14,439—they lost over a fifth of their incomes.

Women posted income gains at every educational level. But again, the college educated gained the most. The income of women college graduates rose by 30 percent over the decade, to $21,659. Women who did not go to high school gained a measly $154, to earn a subpoverty-level annual wage of $6,752.

The entry of women into the workforce helped many families

to improve their living standards, or at least hold them steady. But this option works only for one generation. Additional spouses cannot be acquired and sent into the workforce, and there are limits on how many additional hours a husband and wife can work.

To underscore how income disparities have grown across the lines of education, imagine two couples, one in which both partners graduated from college, another in which neither graduated from high school. The median college-graduate couple saw its income rise from $52,500 to something over $59,000 in the decade of the 1980s. But the income of the median non–high school couple dropped from about $25,000 to $21,000, the loss in male income far outweighing the tiny gain in female income. In other words, in a decade the earnings of the family without a high school degree fell from about half those of a college family to just a little more than a third. Is there any wonder why there was so much publicly expressed resentment of "yuppies"?

The recession of the early 1990s and the continued restructuring of companies during the subsequent recovery complicated this picture. There was substantial unemployment among well-educated professionals and middle managers. The recession aggravated income disparities by creating new forms of inequality within the educated class, without producing any upward changes for the less educated. Indeed, even highly skilled Americans found themselves in competition with similarly well-educated workers from Third World nations, such as India, where salaries for highly technical jobs were much lower. Frank Luntz, a Republican pollster who worked for Ross Perot in 1992 and for Newt Gingrich's House Republicans in 1994, has called the new cohort on the road to downward mobility "the underachievers." They are an angry group whose income and status do not match what they had reason to expect that their levels of education would earn them. The recovery in the early Clinton term continued to distribute economic benefits in a distended way. In 1993, 72 percent of the growth in income went to the top one-fifth of households, and 40 percent went to the top 5 percent.

Not all of the economic changes that produce new anxieties can be explained simply by the rise of a global economy. It is the global economy *combined* with other factors that is so explosive. The economist Paul Krugman argues that the export of jobs and

industries to other countries is far less important in explaining
these economic changes than the growth of new technologies that
can replace large numbers of unskilled or semi-skilled workers
with smaller numbers of very skilled workers. Krugman says that
"the overwhelming evidence is that the demand for unskilled workers has fallen not because of a change in *what* we produce but
because of a change in *how* we produce." As an anecdotal example,
he cites economist Jagdish Bhagwati's observation of the "computer
with a single skilled typist that replaces half a dozen unskilled typ-
ists." In this telling, well-paying jobs disappear not because they are
sent abroad, but because technology renders them obsolete.

Rising inequality would not necessarily breed such political
turmoil if living standards were rising across the economy. But that
is not what is happening. Even excluding the very top, there have
been new inequalities within what we like to think of as the broad
middle class. An especially revealing account of the human effects of
these changes was a report by David Wessel that appeared in *The
Wall Street Journal* in the summer of 1994. Wessel visited Cedar
Rapids, Iowa, a city that by conventional standards was doing very
well indeed. Unemployment there at the time was only 3.6 percent,
well below the national figure. Wessel reported enormous economic change in what had once been a town with a large blue-collar
workforce. Many of the manufacturing jobs had disappeared, replaced by service jobs that were a mix of rather well-paying positions at the top and even more less-well-paid service jobs at the
bottom. The economic recovery, Wessel reported, was not easing
income inequalities. "The gap between the jobs that pay well and
those that don't is persisting despite a growing economy and an
influx of new employers," he wrote. "In this city of 100,000 and
elsewhere in the U.S., good jobs are still scarce, and they require
training that many workers lack. Meanwhile, there is an abundance
of low-skill, low-pay jobs."

Wessel quoted Federal Reserve Board chairman Alan Greenspan, hardly a critic of capitalism, underscoring the economic insecurity abroad in the country. "Somewhat surprisingly," said
Greenspan, "despite the recent unambiguous evidence of recent
economic improvement, there continues to be a deep-rooted fore-
boding among a number of American families that current and
future generations will not live as well as previous ones." He went

on: "The most likely cause is the clear evidence that . . . a significant part of our population is lagging behind the improved standards of living of the majority of our families."

Underlying the public's jitters is the steady erosion of economic growth since the 1950s and 1960s. Broadly speaking, the American economy grew at an annual rate of 3 to 4 percent in the 1950s and 1960s. It grew by 2.8 percent per year in the 1970s. The annual growth rate in the 1980s was around 2.5 percent and seems likely to stay in that range in the 1990s. In a multitrillion-dollar economy these sorts of declines involve huge amounts of lost national income. The political stability and social harmony of the 1950s and early 1960s were due to many factors, but one of them surely was unprecedented growth. The issue here, it should be underscored, is not that the economy has done terribly in recent years; it has, after all, *grown,* which means that many people were getting richer. But slower growth meant that fewer people were doing as well as they expected to. The great middle class had certainly learned to expect more in the 1950s and 1960s. A rising tide does not always lift all boats, but when the tide rises as fast as it did then, all boats tend to rise higher. Inequalities tend to seem harsher when the experience of growing prosperity is not shared so widely.

Other factors may have been contributing to inequalities. Derek Bok has argued that greater political and moral acceptance of inequality, combined with a tendency to value material incentives over all others, increased some income disparities. This created a climate in which it was possible for the chief executive officers of the two hundred largest corporations to win annual compensation 150 times the salary of the average American production worker; in 1974, CEO compensation was "only" thirty-five times higher.

Economists Robert H. Frank and Philip Cook point to the rise of what they call the "winner-take-all society" in which "a handful of top performers walk away with the lion's share of total rewards." We are accustomed to this in sports and movies, but they see the phenomenon as spreading to many other sectors of the economy. Frank and Cook note that this change is not the product of some conspiracy among the highly talented. Rather, it is "developments in communications, manufacturing, technology and transportation costs that have enabled the most talented performers to serve an even broader market, which increased the value of their services." The best entertainment lawyer in Los Angeles can—thanks to airlines, telephones, computers and fax machines—quickly become the best entertainment lawyer in Bombay, New York, Paris, London and Moscow, displacing many other lawyers in the process. In different areas of expertise, companies all over the world compete for the services of the best in their professions, no matter what country they call home. Frank and Cook observe that "changes in implicit and explicit rules . . . have led to much more open competition for top performers" and "made it more likely that they will be paid their economic 'value' as determined by the marketplace." In the winner-take-all economy, as in professional sports, small differences in skill, talent and (one presumes) luck among those at the top can create huge gulfs in earnings and success generally. Frank and Cook offer the instructive lesson of professional tennis, where the top ten players tend to win virtually all of the television and endorsement revenues. A twentieth-ranked tennis player is still very good, but his or her income is usually nowhere close to that of the player who is number one. This pattern is now repeating itself, they say, in law, investment banking and many other endeavors. And of course, this phenomenon has a global dimension, since the tops in almost every field compete not simply at home, but all over the world. Krugman offers a similar lesson with this powerful example. "Television does not take the place of hundreds of struggling standup nightclub comedians," he writes. "It allows Jay Leno to take their place instead."

It should be stressed that one need not conclude that all of these developments are "bad" to accept that the new global and technologically advanced economy creates a crisis by sowing economic life with new forms of disorder insecurity and unpredictability.

Working Americans are not worried about inequality as an abstraction. But they are concerned about the impact of downsizing, wage stagnation and declining benefits on their own lives. Uncertainty about the future seemed built in, even to good times. Layoffs seemed to become a fact of life even when the economy was improving. The Census Bureau, for example, reported that in 1994, after more than two years of recovery, the median household income was still 6 percent below where it had been in 1989.

Even those who are doing well are affected by the chaos and the costs of the new inequalities. The rise of a visible class of homeless people and the disproportionate crime rates in impoverished inner-city areas are only among the more obvious symptoms that even the well-to-do cannot ignore. As for those who are doing badly, or those whose standards of living are slowly deteriorating, there is anger and impatience. These Americans combine an intense desire to have the government *do something* about their economic circumstances with a disbelief bordering on cynicism that government will actually do anything worth doing. There is even a suspicion among some especially angry Americans (including the right-wing militias, but not limited to them) that the government is in collusion with dark international banking forces to achieve globalization explicitly at the *expense* of American workers.

What makes it especially hard for government to respond to these attacks is that the new circumstances really do put it in a weaker position than ever to deal with the discontents. Thus does an economic crisis feed into a political crisis.

III

The great achievement of American politics in the Progressive Era and the New Deal was to create a framework in which the new industrial economy could coexist with democratic government and the values of personal independence and mutual assistance. When corporate giants began to displace local businesses as the dominant economic form between the 1870s and the 1890s, Americans saw democracy and the values they associated with it as in peril. Angry and threatened, they blamed their woes on the new trusts and the new class of millionaires. "There were no beggars till Vanderbilts and Stewarts and Goulds and Scotts and Huntingtons and Fisks shaped the action of Congress and moulded the purposes of government," said a Texas congressman, offering a typical complaint during the 1870s. "Then the few became fabulously rich, the many wretchedly poor ... and the poorer we are, the poorer they would make us."

The Progressives sought to bring some order out of the chaos created by the new economy. Franklin Roosevelt continued this work with new federal regulatory mechanisms, and extended the Progressives' project to include a variety of protections for workers, the elderly, widows, orphans, farmers and the unemployed. After World War II, under the influence of the economic theories of John Maynard Keynes, diplomats and economic planners constructed a new economic order rather different from the "new order" Hitler had in mind. The new system involved stable currencies and largely open trade (though not "free trade" by the strict definitions). The system presumed that the industrial countries would be democratic.

At home, the governments of the wealthy countries pursued what Walter Russell Mead has called the "social democratic bargain." The bargain was a marriage between the market economics preached by capitalists and the welfare and worker protections preached by socialists. Most economic decisions remained in private hands, but national governments used the tools at their disposal—notably spending—to take the edge off economic downturns and hasten the return to prosperity. Labor laws guaranteed workers the right to organize, which boosted their share of the economic largesse. Governments also helped citizens of modest means to secure housing, educate their children and enjoy a decent retirement. In most democratic countries, health coverage was also part of the deal—in the United States, this was largely though not entirely taken care of by employers—and many countries (especially France) guaranteed decently long vacations.

It was a good deal, and it was possible to make it because market economics delivered the goods and because national governments had it in their power to tax and spend and regulate pretty much as they and their electorates wanted to. Especially until 1973, the United States depended on world trade for only a small fraction of its wealth. But as the one great power to survive World War II far more prosperous at the war's end than at its beginning, the United States profited from that trade and could afford to be lenient with its more protectionist trading partners. There were large trade flows across Western European borders, but it was trade among nations all pursuing their own versions—some more and some less successfully—of the social democratic bargain. Words like "outsourcing" and "downsizing" had not entered the vocabulary.

The global bargain struck after World War II began to break down, symbolized by Richard Nixon's cancellation of the postwar agreements on currency in 1971. Since then, rising trade flows, the opening of the poorer countries to investment and job shifts made easy by changes in transportation and technology have left the social democratic bargain in tatters. It should be recalled that this bargain was designed to *preserve* market capitalism by protecting citizens from some of its more extreme unpredictabilities. The Great Depression was very much on the minds of those who struck the bargain. The idea, which worked, was that people would accept the risks created by capitalism if they were provided with a basic level of security.

New economic trends have made that security far more tenuous, which is what underlies the moodiness of electorates throughout the democracies. (If anything, the voters in Italy and Japan have been even more insurrectionary than Americans, and large political swings have taken place in, among other places, France, Spain and Sweden.) Voters sense that big changes are taking place and that their own national governments have less power than ever to deal with them. Foreign currency traders have more control over the value of the money in citizens' pockets than their own governments. Economic policies pursued halfway around the globe by a foreign politician most Americans have never heard of can cut American exports and destroy jobs. The comfort Americans might feel over U.S. laws against child labor is diminished by the knowledge that some of the products in American stores may have been made by children in some other country. The American government's efforts to enforce decent environmental standards can be undermined if a company closes its doors here and starts up again in a country with less demanding standards—one reason many American businesses have asked either for a loosening of American rules or a tightening of environmental agreements with other nations.

These changes add up to a major decline in the power of democratic governments all over the world. Much as local governments saw their influence crumble in the 1880s and 1890s, so now do national leaders feel constrained and, in some cases, helpless. Yet voters still hold politicians responsible for the state of the economy. Who else, after all, can they blame? The average voter cannot elect a president of General Motors or Mitsubishi, but he or she can elect a president, a senator, a member of parliament—and also throw the bums out. For politicians in the democratic countries, this marriage of ever-higher levels of accountability with less actual power is a nightmare. And the worldwide economic squeeze combines with regular voter rebellions against government and taxes to give politicians everywhere less money to spend, depriving them of the universal lubricant of democratic consent.

The new global economy has also produced a complicated set of conflicting loyalties among the citizens of democratic nations. The views of American Toyota dealers about what constitutes our true national economic interest might differ substantially from those of workers at Ford or GM. And the rise of the international class of high earners and high performers in a global "winner-take-all" economy described by Frank and Cook further weakens ties to "national" economies.

As the economic moorings of politics have decayed, so have its philosophical underpinnings. This is true on the right as well as the left. The crisis of the left is the more visible. The collapse of the Soviet Union has been widely interpreted as the end of the socialist promise. The democratic, anti-communist left had ample grounds for feeling libeled, since social democrats and democratic socialists had been among the most committed foes of the Soviet dictatorship. Still, the damage done by the Soviet failure to the credibility of state economic management and planning has hurt even the most democratic elements of the left. There was, it turned out, more to say for market economics than the left allowed. Not all experiments with government ownership of companies failed, but the state companies that worked best tended to be those that behaved most like capitalist firms, leading many, including many socialists, to question whether state ownership was worth the trouble. Moreover, government itself—the primary vehicle for both social democrats in Europe and liberal reformers in the United States—became increasingly unpopular. The bureaucratic forms introduced at the turn of the century to prevent favoritism and corruption came under criticism as unnecessarily rigid, unresponsive and painfully slow for the age of microtechnology. As Ralf Dahrendorf argued, democratic citizens came to see government bureaucrats as a new democratic *nomenklatura,* a class apart from the people with its own interests and priorities.

As a result, the left has become more cautious in its claims and less utopian. In the process, it has lost much of its emotional appeal.

The philosopher Richard Rorty, a friend of the left, suggests that former socialists give up on system-building and occupy themselves with the basics. "The best we can hope for," Rorty writes, "is more of the same experimental, hit-or-miss, two-steps-forward-and-one-step-back reforms that have been taking place in the industrial democracies since the French Revolution." That is perfectly sensible, but as Rorty points out, it's a long way from the "world historical romance" that characterized the left for generations. The left still has a lot to say—especially about the impact of globalization—but its grander themes and promises lack the power they once enjoyed.

Having sent the Reds packing, the right ought to feel triumphant—and especially in the United States after the 1994 elections, it certainly does. It is true, as the Republicans have shown, that conservative anti-government promises can win elections. Economically pressed voters can be counted on to unite with the better off and try to vote themselves a less taxing and intrusive government when the party of active government fails. But the right's answer to the disruptive effects of the global economy—to urge patience and to insist that it will all work out well eventually—has already tried the patience of voters in the other industrialized nations. The forces of pure free market conservatism are on the decline outside the United States, notably in Britain, which has seen a collapse in support for the Conservative Party and the rebirth of a Labour Party that rebuilt itself along American Progressive lines; and in France, where Jacques Chirac was elected president as the "conservative" candidate, but on a platform that promised large-scale government intervention to fight unemployment.

The decline of ideological illusions, left and right, is no bad thing. Vaclav Havel, the prophet of the post-ideological age, had it right when he praised the retreat from a "universal theory of the world" as a victory over intellectual arrogance. But as the big ideologies lose their intellectual authority, they also lose the capacity to mobilize popular loyalties. The result is an impulse to fragment. Thus, one recent development that liberals, socialists, capitalists and conservatives alike mostly failed to predict was the rise of nationalism, ethnicity and regional separatism in the world after the Cold War. As the old ideologies lost their power to explain everything, individuals and small groups turned inward. On the left, concerns over class and economics gave way to a focus on race, gender and culture. On the right, there was a renewal of nationalism, religious fundamentalism and xenophobia. Such movements are not confined to the Balkans, as the rise of anti-immigrant feeling in the United States demonstrates. Voters mistrustful of central governments are opting for regional movements, often built on old forms of nationalism. Such impulses can be seen in Italy and Quebec, in Scotland and Wales—and also in the various militia and anti-regulatory movements in the American West, which seek to use the power of county governments to nullify the enforcement of federal regulations.

But in this rise of particularisms, one of the most important in the American case has been the growing influence of the religious right. Far from suffering from the 1992 Republican defeat, as many expected they would, the Christian conservatives grew stronger and better organized. Their power reflected the sense among many voters that the central issues in American politics concerned, as the Christian Coalition's "Contract with the American Family" puts it, "the coarsening of the culture, the breakup of the family and a decline in civility." The growing role of moral issues in politics pointed to America's third crisis.

IV

It is common, especially among conservatives, to see the country's moral crisis as arising from the vast changes in values and attitudes bred by the "counterculture" of the 1960s—changes that they say must be reversed. As Newt Gingrich put it, "We have to say to the counterculture: Nice try, you failed, you're wrong." The effects of the 1960s on American politics remain large, and they are even felt in many parts of the conservative movement which, for all its attacks on "permissiveness," has come to accept—certainly in deed, and often in word—new roles for women, the irreversibility of the civil rights gains of African-Americans, and a somewhat looser and more tolerant attitude toward sexuality. But the causes of the current moral crisis go well beyond the sixties counterculture. They relate not just to changed "values," but also to an economic revolution that is altering family life, attitudes toward the work ethic and the popular sense of which sorts of behavior are rewarded in society.

The basic components of the moral crisis are clear enough. Assumptions about the division of labor between men and women have already been drastically altered. The rate of out-of-wedlock births has risen steadily and the toll of family breakup has been large: In 1994 roughly 40 percent of all children in the nation did not live with their fathers. Economic pressures continued to disrupt even the strongest families. Social scientists, moralists and politicians alike mourned the decline in the number of hours each day that parents spent with their children. Parents spoke often of the guilt they felt at having to choose between defending their children's standard of living by working more, or having enough time to spend with the children themselves. And crime was the most visible, violent and pervasive sign of social and moral breakdown. It affected virtually everyone, while also compounding the misery of those in the country's poorest neighborhoods.

The welfare debate has demonstrated how hard it is to keep our values straight. Traditionalist conservatives are usually insistent on the need for mothers to spend more time with their young children. The whole point of Aid to Families with Dependent Children, the welfare system, was to provide enough relief to needy single mothers—usually widows—so they could rear their children properly. There was little popular resentment against this, since the old image of a "single mother" involved a decent woman whose misfortune was that her husband had died young. Of course society had an interest in easing her burdens.

Yet the same conservatives who speak of the imperatives of motherhood are now the fiercest critics of "welfare." Supporting single mothers is seen by many as morally indefensible. The very phrase "single mothers" refers not to widows but to women who have children out of wedlock. The AFDC program, which once held families together, is now seen as encouraging family breakup and dysfunctional child rearing.

Moreover, the original moral case for AFDC rested on the assumption that most mothers would not and should not work as long as their children were young. Yet with so many mothers, married and single, now working outside the home, the old moral case for AFDC began to collapse. The great welfare debate of 1995 brought home other moral contradictions. When the House Republican leadership proposed cutting off welfare benefits to single

Emmaus High School Library
Emmaus, Pennsylvania

mothers under the age of eighteen, the strongest support for the measure came from one wing of the "pro-family" movement—which sought to discourage the formation of new households headed by teen mothers—while the strongest opposition came from *another* wing of the pro-family movement—which feared the provision would encourage young women to have abortions. Representative Chris Smith, a New Jersey Republican and a leader of right-to-life forces in the House, denounced his party's welfare plan as "inhumane" for punishing children for the mistakes of their parents and for using "the child as a pawn in trying to influence the mother's behavior."

The moral crisis gets trickier still with the breakdown of traditional views of sexuality. The debate over former Vice President Dan Quayle's criticism of *Murphy Brown* during the 1992 presidential campaign seemed unedifying or just plain silly. Yet this debate caught the popular imagination because it reached so many issues on which the public is divided or confused. Murphy Brown herself was what might be thought of as a classic post-modern character: Candice Bergen as a television character *playing* a television character, in this case a TV newswoman. Brown got pregnant by an old boyfriend and decided to have the child without marrying the father. The ensuing debate raised almost every imaginable issue at the nexus of sexuality, morality and economics. White House spokesman Marlin Fitzwater wondered if Murphy Brown should not be *celebrated* as a pro-life heroine who bravely chose to have her child. Feminists suggested that Quayle was attacking working single mothers who, after all, took responsibility for their children in ways single fathers rarely did. Quayle himself subsequently insisted that his main thrust was not against Brown but against "deadbeat dads" who abandoned their kids. But he was also arguing that well-to-do women like the Brown character were setting a bad example for the rest of society—and especially for poorer single mothers who might not be able to provide for their children as Brown could for hers.

Enter class issues, with conservatives seeking the populist high ground by contending that the licentious rich were living immoral lives that set poor examples and undermined the values on which social stability depends. Little was said about the growing economic inequalities on which the allegedly licentious well-to-do depended for the wherewithal to engage in those acts of immorality. Here again did economic, moral and political crises produce strange controversies and alliances. It's worth noting that the Republican attacks on "permissiveness" and "the cultural elite" largely failed in 1992. Many who were worried that the decay of the old values had created a "spiritual vacuum"—the words are Hillary Rodham Clinton's—nonetheless drew back from a full-scale rollback of cultural liberalism. Even the young conservatives who cheered Dan Quayle's speeches wanted their MTV.

If family and sexuality are at one pole of the moral crisis, the work ethic is at the other. Richard Cornuelle, a libertarian writer, once noted that one of the many tricks America played on Karl Marx was to produce "a working class with proletarian status but with middle-class means." But for many among the unskilled—including many who decidedly did *not* think of themselves as "proletarians"— middle-class means are increasingly elusive. Americans who worked longer hours for stagnant or declining wages wondered whether the proclamations of the country's public creed about the value of hard work bore any relationship to the country's treatment of those who worked hard.

At bottom, American politics was roiled over moral issues because the old-fashioned virtues the society claimed to celebrate were being less and less rewarded—which is why during the 1992 presidential campaign Clinton spoke repeatedly of the unhappiness felt by those who "worked hard and played by the rules." The values we said we honored included loyalty and commitment, long-term painstaking effort and patience, generosity and community-mindedness. Yet the marketplace seemed to reward speed and impatience, sudden fame and rapidly made fortunes. It punished excessive loyalty, whether by the companies to employees or by employees to their employers; whether by investors to the firms they financed or by the managers of those firms to their stockholders. Employers were under increasing pressure to cut expenses, which encouraged "downsizing." Employees sensed less employer loyalty and returned less. The financial marketplace encouraged quick moves in and out of company stocks—"investor loyalty" was also weakened. Inevitably, corporate managers felt little loyalty to stockholders, who were, in any event, mostly represented by those who ran the large pension and money market funds. Why not seek golden parachutes and huge salaries? How could a manager know when he or she might be tossed out by angry stockholders or by the buyout specialists who took over their firms?

All of these developments, of course, were viewed by many as positive, leading to greater efficiency in labor and financial markets and to leaner and more competitive companies. But there could be no denying that these developments reshaped and transformed moral attitudes. For those caught up in the wrong end of "downsizing" (or, in a word particularly offensive to those thrown out of work, "rightsizing"), the social contract seemed broken.

The political debate on moral issues was degraded by the refusal of so many of the participants to speak candidly about crisscrossing currents that defied easy ideological classification. The Murphy Brown debate was typical—each side staked out ground mostly to make itself feel good. Conservatives could feel righteous in defending young children against the instability bred by irresponsible fathers and the burdens of single motherhood. Liberals could enjoy their own righteousness by defending a brave working woman against the bigotry of a narrow-minded minority. The debate rarely reached the issue of whether there might be a large contradiction in our public creed—whether virtues that made for good parents or neighbors or citizens might not be at odds with the characteristics that made for success and celebrity. Many aspects of the economy that conservatives celebrated seemed to undermine the very virtues that conservatives claimed to revere.

The confluence of economic, political and moral crisis has been made all the more difficult by the rise of a fourth crisis involving widespread confusion over the U.S. position in—and responsibilities to—the rest of the world. The piling up of anxieties took much of the joy out of victory in the Cold War. Many Americans, as the historian Charles Maier put it in a broader context, had the "gnawing conviction" that a great cause might simultaneously have been achieved and betrayed, since the fruits of victory did not seem sweet.

V

Much has been made of the Cold War "consensus" involving broad agreement among both elites and ordinary voters about the need to contain the Soviet Union. But consensus on America's world role has not been the pattern of American history, and it did not even hold throughout the Cold War. Arguments over engagement and detachment have divided Americans since the founding of the republic. The Mexican War, which vastly expanded the country's territory, was a deeply divisive conflict. Opposition to the war was one of the early public acts of a young politician named Abraham Lincoln. The Progressive Era began with an explicit argument over the merits of "imperialism" during and after the Spanish-American War. The Progressives themselves, along with the rest of the country, were divided between those who favored forceful American intervention to spread democracy to "backward" lands and those who saw imperialism as antithetical to the democratic idea. Intervention in World War I was divisive; until Pearl Harbor, engagement in World War II was even more so.

The rise of the Soviet threat in the late 1940s temporarily settled the debate by swinging a large segment of traditionally isolationist conservative opinion behind a global crusade against communism. For roughly two decades, until the Vietnam War, an interventionist consensus dominated both political parties. Vietnam legitimized political argument over foreign policy again. But if that war proved unpopular, there was still wide and general support for the idea that a strong United States was needed to counter Soviet power. It's worth remembering that in the elections in which an assertive foreign policy was up for debate—1972, 1980 and 1988—the supporters of assertiveness (Nixon, Reagan and Bush) won.

But the 1992 election, the first of the post–Cold War world, represented a striking setback for this view of America's role. Although Americans cheered their country's military triumph in the Gulf war, the war had little political afterlife. For a substantial majority of Americans, the collapse of communism and the breakup of the Soviet empire made foreign policy much less important. Bill Clinton and Ross Perot disagreed on many issues, but both were running implicitly against George Bush's vision of a "new world order" underwritten by American power. Both argued that it was time for the United States to turn its attentions and energies homeward. In this, they echoed a surprising victor in a 1991 special election in Pennsylvania. Harris Wofford won a Senate seat—which he subsequently lost in 1994—partly because most Pennsylvanians agreed with him when he said that "it's time to take care of our own."

The final result of the 1992 presidential election showed opponents of the new world order winning 62 percent of the vote. Polls showed that Bush won overwhelmingly among those who said foreign policy concerns had been important in determining their choice. But only about one voter in ten cared enough about foreign policy to say that. The point was not that George Bush's management of foreign policy was unpopular—for the most part, voters liked what Bush did. Voters simply didn't accord foreign affairs the *importance* that Bush seemed to. When George McGovern spoke the words "Come home, America" in 1972, he was mocked as an isolationist. Twenty years later many Americans seemed ready to make the trip.

Yet the negative verdict on Bush by no means settled the foreign policy debate. On the contrary, it simply showed how unsettled the debate was. Barely four years after the fall of the Berlin wall, the seemingly solid foreign policy coalitions that set in during the Vietnam War had been disrupted beyond recognition. Longtime doves who had opposed American intervention in Vietnam and Central America found themselves demanding that the United States go to war to defend Bosnian Muslims and send troops to save starving Somalis. Many Cold War interventionists who had been willing to pay any price to stop communism argued that no clear American interest was at stake in either conflict. The labels liberal and conservative were useless as clues to where anyone stood on any particular conflict. Former adversaries found themselves standing together on both sides of new foreign policy divides.

The deep splits affected not only the public but also the foreign policy establishment. On the one side were those who saw the United States as having expansive world obligations as "the only remaining superpower." Partisans of this view argued that world order—and the expansion of democracy and human rights—depended on vigorous American engagement. Opposed to this view were those who insisted that the United States was, if not exhausted by the Cold War, then at least obligated to tend to new economic and social problems on its own shores. For the United States to assert itself as the last superpower was not worth the price except in a sharply defined number of circumstances (such as preventing

Russia from veering toward an assertive nationalism). Early in Clinton's term, one administration official was widely rebuked for advocating a less militarily assertive America and emphasizing the priority of economic relations over diplomatic issues. "We simply don't have the leverage," said Peter Tarnoff, undersecretary of state for political affairs. "We don't have the influence, we don't have the inclination to use military forces, we certainly don't have the money." Yet the rebuke from the administration to Tarnoff was more for the provocative form of the speech than for its content. What was said actually reflected the views of many inside the administration, including, to some degree at least, the president himself.

The very existence of this argument told much about how Americans felt about their country and its potential at the end of the Cold War. A United States fully confident of its economic position would no doubt have been less reluctant to assert itself. Under those circumstances, the end of the Cold War might have been experienced as the great victory which it was. But Americans were more inclined to insist that tending to the troubles of Bosnian Muslims, starving Somalis or slaughtered Rwandans placed a distant second in importance, behind dealing with economic dislocation and criminal disorder at home. If the United States could not keep its own streets safe, many asked, how could it dare attempt to impose order on nations thousands of miles away?

These questions point to a central reality: that arguments over America's world role were in large part a reflection of domestic disagreements. They were arguments about how the United States should view itself. Americans were, as Garry Wills observed, a people who had lost a sense of mission. The fragmentation of opinion on these matters was especially visible on the right. Ronald Reagan's rhetorical skills combined with the existence of a common enemy in Soviet power to bridge the gap between nationalist and internationalist camps on the right. Internationalism, the view that the United States had special responsibilities to be engaged in the world, was a particularly strong sentiment among elites. Nationalism was stronger at the grass roots, among Americans proud to chant "U.S.A.! U.S.A.!" during the 1984 Olympics and to cheer Lee Greenwood's Reagan-era anthem, "God Bless the U.S.A." The nationalists were uninterested in balance-of-power politics, but their instinctive patriotism was aroused by the dangers of the Soviet

Union and threats from the Middle East. This patriotism was harnessed by the internationalists to broader policy objectives, though not always with success. Reagan's Central American policy, for example, was never popular, because Americans were never convinced, even by President Reagan, that the Sandinistas in Nicaragua really posed a threat to Texas.

With Reagan out of power and the Cold War over, the alliance between internationalists and nationalists blew apart. Conservative commentator and two-time presidential candidate Pat Buchanan represents a particularly bold, even extreme form of nationalism, and he explicitly used the old isolationist slogan "America First!" in his 1992 campaign. Nationalists of the Buchanan stripe threw overboard a whole series of conservative commitments from the Cold War era—to free trade, to large defense budgets, to efforts to spread democracy abroad. But the nationalist impulse in conservative politics was not limited to Republicans of Buchananite sympathies. It took more moderate forms in the foreign policy of Republicans such as Senator John McCain of Arizona. McCain, a widely respected former prisoner of war in Vietnam, is understandably skeptical of the use of the American military in conflicts where the U.S. national interest is not unmistakably engaged. McCain was thus a vocal opponent of intervention in Bosnia and a skeptic about the U.S. mission in Somalia. Colin Powell was another reluctant interventionist.

But old-fashioned internationalism was far from dead on the right. Its leading spokesman before his death was Richard M. Nixon, whose last book includes some sharp criticisms of President Clinton for his failure to take action in Bosnia. Senate Republican leader Bob Dole also spoke boldly for intervention in Bosnia—and he did so consistently, his criticisms of Clinton's Bosnian policies only echoing his attacks on those of George Bush.

Nor did the splits on the right end with the nationalist-internationalist feuds. There were divisions within these camps, too, particularly among internationalists. Not all internationalists, for example, favored intervention in Bosnia. Syndicated columnist Charles Krauthammer, who coined the phrase "The Reagan Doctrine," was sharply critical of those who urged intervention in Bosnia, arguing that the United States needed to preserve its power for fights that mattered, such as preventing North Korea from becoming a nuclear power. Most conservative internationalists opposed military intervention in Haiti. Many conservatives backed President Clinton's decision to grant most-favored-nation status to China despite the Chinese regime's human rights abuses. But others on the right clung to the principle that dictatorships—especially communist ones—should pay a price for oppression.

The right, however, had one great advantage after 1992: It no longer controlled the presidency. This meant that whatever their weaknesses and divisions, conservatives could go on the attack. Circumstances and, especially in his first two years, President Clinton himself gave the right a great deal to attack.

The roots of Clinton's early problems on foreign policy lay, first and foremost, in the very lack of any national consensus on America's world role. Clinton could not fall back comfortably on some set of popular assumptions, a luxury all presidents had during the Cold War. Clinton literally had to invent a new vision, a new set of priorities. And he had to make a series of very hard decisions in specific conflicts. The decisions were hard because in none of these conflicts—Haiti, Somalia, Bosnia—was there anything like a unified national view of what was at stake for the United States. Only where Saddam Hussein was involved could it be said that Americans broadly agreed on the need for strong action, and Clinton's tough moves against Saddam did win widespread, bipartisan applause.

But if Clinton was handed very complex problems, he also created some of his own difficulties. His central problem lay in a contradiction between what he had said during the 1992 campaign and what he appeared willing to do once in office. Clinton was acutely aware that Democrats had lost election after election because they had been perceived as "weak," "irresolute" or "isolationist" in foreign policy. He also knew that the country, while unhappy with the priority George Bush placed on foreign policy, generally accepted that Bush understood these issues well, certainly better than a governor of Arkansas. So Clinton's goal during the 1992 campaign was twofold: to make sure voters saw him as tough—more as Harry Truman than as George McGovern or Jimmy Carter—and to neutralize foreign policy as an electoral concern. As long as voters were casting ballots on the basis of domestic issues, Clinton knew he was home.

Clinton's way of achieving these goals was, in electoral terms, ingenious. He embraced most of Bush's foreign policy, strongly

supporting the Gulf war (albeit in retrospect) and generally praising the content of Bush's policies toward Russia (though occasionally criticizing him for moving too slowly). But where Clinton chose
to disagree with Bush, he sought to position himself to Bush's
activist side. He tried to look *tougher* than Bush.

Clinton thus denounced Bush for "coddling" the Chinese dictatorship and called for a firmer and more consistent approach to
human rights. He criticized Bush's handling of Bosnia and Croatia,
suggesting that he would be more willing than Bush was to come to
the defense of those facing Serbian aggression. He attacked Bush's
policy toward Haitian immigration, arguing that the United States
needed to be more sympathetic to the victims of the Haitian dictatorship.

The problem for Clinton was that if he carried through on the
implications of his various promises, pledges and criticisms once he
took office, he would become a very aggressive foreign policy president. He would have needed to turn or defy public opinion to take
bold early action in the Balkans or to admit all the fleeing Haitians.
His campaign policy on China won broad sympathy from human
rights groups but it defied the dominant view within the foreign
policy establishment, which opposed linking trade and human
rights. Clinton had an additional problem: If there was a signature
Clinton foreign policy idea, it was that economics should now be at
the center of America's international dealings. Economic power had
overtaken military power as the test of a nation's strength, he argued, and raising the standard of living of average Americans was
the overriding issue in American political life. What did Bosnia,
Somalia or Haiti have to do with economics? How could trade
sanctions against China help American business?

Clinton was not able to hold all these commitments together.
He was unwilling to let bold activism abroad get in the way of his
domestic priorities, especially in his first two years, when he seemed
to have a chance of passing a big domestic program through a
Democratic Congress. So one by one, he altered his campaign commitments. First to go was his promise to Haitian refugees. He returned to Bush's policy even before he was inaugurated, fearing an
influx of refugees as soon as he had taken the oath of office. He
continued to talk tough against Serbia, but until 1995 the tough talk
was only sporadically matched by action, and the Americans and the

Western Europeans feuded regularly about whose failures had mattered most in allowing a bad situation to worsen continually. Clinton eventually arranged an American withdrawal from Somalia. He reversed his human rights policy on China.

It must be said that in other areas of foreign policy Clinton himself regarded as important, there was a consistency of purpose, often in the face of substantial opposition. Ultimately, he was bold in his intervention in Haiti, moving despite almost unanimous opposition from Republicans and deep skepticism among many Democrats. Clinton battled for free trade agreements—NAFTA and GATT—against substantial opposition within his own party, and then took forceful steps to try to open the Japanese market against well-organized opposition from many in the free trade camp. Toward Russia he pursued a consistent policy of general sympathy for Boris Yeltsin and sought to avoid moves that might strengthen nationalist feeling in Russia. This policy, too, was undertaken despite substantial criticism—that he was banking too much on Yeltsin and was too ready to draw back from any moves that might offend Russian sensibilities. But the policy did seem to prevent the worst from happening, which in foreign policy is no small matter. The Republican takeover of Congress forced a certain coherence on at least some aspects of policy, if only in opposition to Republican initiatives. Although his administration itself did not always present a unified front, Clinton did try to preserve executive authority, the possibility of action through the United Nations and other multinational forces, and a substantial foreign aid program.

The Republicans were most effective in their critique of Clinton when they centered on problems in the Clinton policy-making process. Clinton's critics particularly enjoyed contrasting an image of the United States astride the globe after the Gulf war with the apparent confusion and reduction in American influence that seemed to characterize the Clinton period. "We might say that Clinton has taken a good situation and made the least of it," wrote conservative Joshua Muravchik in a typical criticism, "squandering a time of unparalleled American preeminence. . . ."

In fact, Clinton's foreign policy making became more confident as his administration moved forward. After two years of uncertainty, the administration moved forcefully in the Balkans—with both air strikes and a diplomatic offensive—and pushed the Serbs toward the bargaining table. It was widely said that Clinton did not want to enter the election year with the slaughter continuing in Bosnia, and congressional sentiment became increasingly sympathetic toward the plight of the Bosnians. Those who had long urged action said that Clinton's intervention had come much later than necessary, and that many lives had been lost in the interim. Nonetheless, the administration did act, and made clear that, as in the case of Haiti, it was willing to live with congressional opposition to its course. Similarly, the administration continued to mediate negotiations between Israel and the Palestine Liberation Organization. It helped win important agreements that, despite continuing tensions, gradually transferred control over parts of the West Bank to Palestinian authorities. Speaking on National Public Radio after the Bosnian and Middle East breakthroughs, one French diplomat only half-jokingly echoed a slogan of the Reagan years and declared, "America's back!" The alleged "squandering" of American power may not have gone as far as the administration's critics claimed.

Indeed, the Bush administration itself had shown—despite the Gulf war victory—that foreign policy in the post–Cold War world was a hit-and-miss thing. The Bush policies in the Balkans could hardly be called successful. Clinton early on may have lacked a clear sense of direction in foreign affairs, but in this he was far from alone.

For beyond criticisms of Clinton, the Republicans were not in the least united as to which policies they would install in place of his. Particularly revealing was the growing role that attacks on the United Nations played in Republican rhetoric. For the far right, the anti-UN rhetoric of the 1990s was no different in form and content from the "US Out of the UN" talk of the John Birch Society and others on the radical right in the 1960s. On the right, the United Nations was, and always would be, an impediment to American sovereignty, an organization whose purpose was imposing the will of a globalist elite on an unwilling American people. But criticism of the United Nations was by no means confined to the far right. Many mainstream conservative internationalists also came to be mistrustful of the United Nations as a body dominated by Third World opinion and incapable of mounting a coherent and effective military response anywhere. These "global unilateralists," as they were sometimes known, did not buy into any of the anti-UN conspiracy theories. Nonetheless, they shared with those well to their right a suspicion of limiting American foreign policy options by relying too much on the United Nations or any other multilateral body. For political purposes, many kinds of Republicans could agree to make "multilateralism" an enemy and to pass provisions and resolutions insisting that American troops never be placed under the command of foreign generals. But this was hardly the basis of an alternative foreign policy and underscored the lack of real consensus even where apparent consensus existed.

Where it came to America's role in the world, the mid-1990s were characterized by fragmentation and uncertainty on the right, the left and in the center, among nationalists, isolationists and internationalists, within the Clinton administration and among Republicans in Congress, in the foreign policy establishment and among Americans themselves.

VI

The existence of four simultaneous crises in American politics gave politicians and ideologues a great deal of ammunition to use at election time and many opportunities to shift the focus of the public debate to wherever the terrain was most favorable. In a sense, parties to the debate could use one crisis to evade another.

For example, Republicans could point to the moral crisis as the core problem facing the country, and define the moral crisis in a way that played down its economic components. One of the most forceful expositions of this view came from William Bennett in a speech before the Christian Coalition. "Our problem is not economic," he said. "Our problems are moral, spiritual, philosophical, behavioral ... crime, murder, divorce, drug use, births to unwed mothers, child abuse, casual cruelty and casual sex, and just plain trashy behavior." If "just plain trashy behavior" is the core problem—and not the global economy or the economic pressures on the family—then the answers lie in cultural changes that are beyond the reach of government, or perhaps in changing the cultural messages sent by "big government liberals." The answer to this is not government activism, but less government linked to a moral and cultural revolution carried out in the country's churches and neighborhoods. Thus did the Republicans constantly seek to redefine what voters might experience as an economic crisis into a moral one.

Liberals, in the meantime, could point to all the economic factors causing distress and to the few rewards accorded by the economy to those Americans who worked hard for modest incomes. *This* was the predominant moral issue. Liberals could thereby downplay the problems that were explicitly "moral, spiritual, philosophical, behavioral" and play up the imperative of an active government that would pass laws giving everyone health insurance or requiring employers to give leave time to the parents of newborns. The moral crisis was thus constantly redefined as an economic one.

The political crisis, in the meantime, could be ascribed by opponents of free trade to the tyranny of the global market; by reformist liberals to the tyranny of money in the campaign finance system; by Republicans and fiscal conservatives to the tyranny of government that did too much, taxed too much, regulated too much; and by many of Ross Perot's supporters as a combination of the three. Any of these arguments was plausible, and each served particular interests and purposes.

As for the international crisis, most Americans freely vented their uncertainties, and political activists tended to link events abroad to their pet theories and domestic obsessions. The far right could link the United Nations and free trade to a globalist conspiracy. Clinton haters of all stripes could point to any confusion in foreign policy as yet more evidence of the president's "fecklessness" and "incompetence." Liberals could see Jesse Helms's efforts to seize control of foreign policy from the administration as another in a long series of devilish tricks. Longtime internationalists could mourn the rise of "know-nothing isolationism." Critics of the foreign policy establishment could talk of those who cared about the affairs of every country in the world except their own.

Within each party, the four crises sowed discord. Republicans were divided between internationalists and nationalists, Christian conservatives and libertarians, those who sought to moderate Clinton's social and economic reforms and those who wanted to block them. Democrats were split asunder on the proper stance toward the global economy. Almost all Democrats agreed that some government action was needed to counter its harsher effects, but the consensus ended there. Some in the party, led by Clinton, urged an embrace of the global economy as the key to prosperity, while many others (including a majority of House Democrats) bitterly resisted Clinton-backed trade initiatives that, they were certain, would lead to lower living standards and degraded working conditions. Democrats split as well on moral issues (such as gays in the military), on the extent to which government action was needed to shore up living standards (the health care battle being the premier case) and on all manner of governmental reforms (including changes in the campaign finance laws).

All this maneuvering was for the benefit of an electorate that was certain something was wrong, but was neither clear nor united on just what it was. In fact, millions of Americans understood that all four crises were central to their discontent. These voters alternately responded to angry ideological arguments and drew back from them, knowing that something was missing. These voters constituted America's Anxious Middle. The story of the last two elections is the story of how each party appealed to the Anxious Middle by minimizing the problems created by the four crises for their own worldview and maximizing the disorder they created for the other side.

□ 3 □

THE POLITICS OF
THE ANXIOUS MIDDLE:

*From Republican Disaster
to Democratic Calamity*

THERE COULD NOT, it would seem, be two elections more different than those of 1992 and 1994. The first was a Republican debacle, the second a Democratic disaster. The first seemed to herald a new wave of government activism and the end of a conservative era. The second was widely interpreted as marking the resurrection of conservatism and perhaps more: the birth of a more hard-edged, anti-government political alignment with commitments going well beyond the soothing verities of Ronald Reagan's American morning. The first election suggested potential Democratic strength everywhere in the country, even in the staunchest Republican bastions of the South and West. The second suggested that 1992 was an aberration, that the steady march of Republicanism through the states of the Old Confederacy and the Rocky Mountains would continue and affect every level of government.

What the two elections demonstrated above all was the instability of the American body politic in the 1990's, the intense impatience of the electorate and its vague but powerful sense of crisis and unraveling. The large swings back and forth between 1984 and 1994—and especially the enormous shifts in just the two years after 1992—can be traced to the emergence of a large new group at the heart of the electorate that has abandoned traditional ideological and partisan loyalties. This group feels pressed by economic change and worries that the country is experiencing a moral and social breakdown. Its members are angry at government but uneasy over the workings of the economic system. They crave self-reliance—and honor this virtue in others—but fear that both the government and the economy are blocking their own paths to self-sufficiency. *Newsweek* columnist Joe Klein has referred to "the Radical Middle," a group that includes many of these voters but may also go beyond it. Labor Secretary Robert Reich has spoken specifically of these hard-pressed Americans as "the anxious class." Marrying aspects of both formulations, one might refer to the Anxious Middle as the group that holds the future of American politics in its hands.

The Anxious Middle set the terms for the 1992 and 1994 elections. It destroyed a Republican presidential coalition that had seemed invulnerable only a few years earlier. It made Ross Perot possible, ended George Bush's political career, sent Bill Clinton to the White House—and then rebuked Clinton and helped make Newt Gingrich one of the central figures of American politics. Perot spoke instinctively for the Anxious Middle. Bush never understood it. Clinton saw it coming long before most politicians, shaped his campaign to respond to its concerns—and then confronted its ire after only two years in office. Gingrich sought his own radical language to speak to its anxieties.

II

The Anxious Middle first found its power in 1992, reducing a Republican president's share of the vote to a little more than a third and giving Democrats full control of the elected part of the federal government for the first time in twelve years. The Democrats, moreover, seemed ready to lead. In Bill Clinton, they had a candidate who had thought through the causes of the party's earlier failures and catastrophes. He understood the weaknesses of the party's liberal wing and accepted the need for a substantial renovation of the Democrats' public philosophy. Yet he was uncompromisingly a Democrat in a way Jimmy Carter had never been. He spoke of a new party, but was at home with its old constituencies. He understood, in principle, that if the Democratic Party did not deliver for the more threatened part of the middle class, it would not survive. Thus,

a hymn to "the forgotten middle class" became his electoral anthem. Clinton knew that the middle class was torn—between hope
for what government might do and skepticism over whether (and
how) it would do it; between acceptance of many recent social
changes and a strong streak of traditionalism. The middle class did
not want to outlaw abortion, yet most of its members lived family-
centered lives and respected Ronald Reagan's famous trilogy of
"family, work and neighborhood."

Clinton and those who gathered around him seemed determined to end a period in which, it was said, all the ideas were on
the right. Clinton offered voters a host of specific programs. He
proposed welfare reform, offering recipients new training and education programs but requiring them to take jobs after two years on
the rolls. He promised a Kennedyesque national service program,
under which those who sought to go to college could earn tuition
aid by serving their country—a harkening back to the GI Bill, one
of the most successful programs for upward mobility in the country's history. He suggested a mix of tax increases on the rich and tax
reductions for middle-class families with children. He had a plan for
national health insurance, proposals to help high-tech companies,
ideas for expanding enterprise in the inner city, suggestions for
improving the public schools, youth apprenticeship programs to
help young people find their footing in a new economy. All these
initiatives were united under a rubric few could argue with: opportunity, responsibility, community. It sounded like a very activist
program—and it was—but Clinton insisted it was "neither liberal
nor conservative," but new and better. "No more something for
nothing" was a constant Clinton refrain that surely did not remind
people of their worst fears of liberalism.

The core political problem Clinton sought to solve was the
defection of white voters of moderate incomes from Democratic
ranks. Since Richard Nixon, Republicans had won by making heavy
inroads in this group, which included the overlapping constituencies of blue-collar and lower-middle-class voters, northern Catholics and southern evangelicals. In a broad sense, being a "New
Democrat" meant being a Democrat who would be more acceptable to these voters than, say, George McGovern or Michael Dukakis.

Clinton's decision to take over the presidency of the Democratic Leadership Council in 1990 was part of his effort to distance

himself from this part of the Democratic past. The DLC had been formed after Walter Mondale's 1984 defeat to pull the party to the political center—and, specifically, to make it more acceptable to moderate and conservative white southerners. The DLC's earliest incarnation as a home for the party's white southern wing won it the instant and enduring enmity of many Democratic liberals, including Jesse Jackson, who routinely referred to the organization as Democrats for the Leisure Class. The DLC was also consciously and conspicuously pro-business—it received substantial contributions from business groups—and critical of organized labor. And it was decidedly on the Cold War (read: anti-McGovern) side of the post-Vietnam foreign policy debates, criticizing the party for sending a message of "ambivalence toward the assertion of American values and interests abroad."

But if the DLC's early phase made it appear to be little more than a redoubt of southern Tory Democrats, its intellectual efforts after the 1988 election were more far-reaching and complex. The organization set out to distinguish its views not only from those of liberal Democrats, but also from those of conservative Republicans. It started its own think tank called the Progressive Policy Institute, the choice of the word "progressive" being significant for its implicit contrast to the word "conservative." Unlike conservatives, the DLC took a stand in favor of active government in a host of spheres, including welfare, job training, national service, education and housing. But it sought to distinguish its version of activism from earlier Democratic versions. "We believe the purpose of social welfare is to bring the poor into the nation's economic mainstream, not maintain them in dependence," its 1990 New Orleans declaration asserted. "We believe the right way to rebuild America's economic security is to invest in the skills and ingenuity of our people, and to expand trade, not restrict it." The DLC was especially conscious of the Democrats' problems on social and cultural issues. "We believe in preventing crime and punishing criminals, not explaining away their behavior," the New Democrats declared. "We believe in the moral and cultural values that most Americans share: liberty of conscience, individual responsibility, tolerance of difference, the imperative of work, the need for faith, and the importance of family." The DLC's turn toward a broader message coincided, it might be noted, with Clinton's assumption of its presidency.

The DLC's achievement was to understand that basic Democratic themes of economic equity would not even penetrate the electorate unless the party made clear its commitment to certain basic, popular values. William Galston, an intellectual architect of the DLC strategy, made this point explicitly. Only by gaining "credibility on defense, foreign policy and social values," he said, could the party get a hearing for "a progressive economic program."

Despite the immense importance of DLC ideas to Clinton's rise, it is a mistake to see the 1992 Clinton campaign as a pure reflection of the DLC's outlook. The journalist John Judis noted two other crucial elements of Clinton's 1992 message: economic populism and an "anti-establishment economic nationalism developed largely in response to Ross Perot's campaign." Clinton, as Judis observed, assailed the Republicans as the party of "the rich and special interests" who had foisted "trickle-down economics" on a country that was thereby burdened with a huge deficit and falling real wages. Large numbers of Americans, Clinton said, were "working harder for less," even as business executives pulled down "outrageous salaries." Clinton's economic nationalism was somewhat more equivocal. Judis is correct in stating that Clinton promised to end tax breaks for companies that "ship American jobs overseas" and to bar "trade negotiators from cashing in on their positions by serving as representatives for foreign corporations and governments." Rhetorically, Clinton constantly tried to be tougher than Bush when he spoke of how he would deal with Japan and other American trading partners. But he also tried to preserve his free trade credentials. When he spoke of the United States falling behind other countries, he would declare that his goal was not to shut others out of the American market, but to compete and win everywhere, within a fair trading system. In keeping with his desire to avoid being labeled protectionist, Clinton delayed taking a stand on the North American Free Trade Agreement with Mexico until near the end of the 1992 campaign. When he did take a stand, it was *for* NAFTA, but with hedges about the need to add protections for American labor and environmental standards. Clinton was thus to the free trade side of Perot, but unlike the purer free traders in the DLC and elsewhere, he accepted the political importance of carrying at least a tinge of economic nationalism. This stance spoke precisely to the mood of economic insecurity that played such a large part in Clinton's election.

As we shall see in subsequent chapters, the issue of whether Clinton had been true to the New Democratic creed and to the persona he established in the campaign became important as his presidency became more controversial. The point here is that the campaign itself was, as Judis put it, more "eclectic and expansive" than is usually allowed. Clinton very consciously appealed to very different wings of a potential Democratic coalition, all at the same time. This would cause him problems as president, but it worked very well indeed in 1992.

Measured by his 43 percent share of the popular vote, Clinton's was not a famous victory. But his triumph was bigger than it looked. Polls of voters after they cast their ballots made clear that if Ross Perot had not been a candidate, Clinton would have been a majority president with a share of about 53 percent. He scored break-throughs everywhere, sweeping New England and becoming only the second Democrat after 1936 to carry the three big midwestern states of Illinois, Michigan and Ohio. He regained Democratic votes in the South and won Rocky Mountain states that had only recently seemed permanent Republican strongholds.

The numbers of the 1992 election tell the story of drastic trans-formation. Bush's vote declined by fifteen percentage points be-tween 1988 and 1992. His 37.4 percent was the lowest share for a Republican presidential candidate since 1912. Bush received nearly 10 million fewer votes in 1992 than in 1988. Moreover, Bush got *15 million* fewer votes in 1992 than Ronald Reagan did in 1984. This happened even though more people voted in 1992 than in either of the previous two elections. Bush's 39 million votes were the lowest Republican total since 1968. In the meantime, Ross Perot's 19 mil-lion votes were, in raw terms, the largest outpouring of third party support in the country's history, and Perot won the second-highest third party percentage ever. All this paved the way for Clinton, whose 44.9 million votes represented the largest number ever won by a Democratic presidential candidate.

Bush lost ground for the Republicans everywhere, but most alarming for his party were its shrunken margins in its suburban strongholds. In 1988 it was said frequently—and not just by Repub-licans—that since the 1992 election marked the first time that a majority of the votes would be cast in the suburbs, the election would herald a new round of ineluctable Republican victories. Like many predictions predicated on a strong Bush presidency, this one misfired badly. Bush's suburban returns ran from disappointing to terrible. In 1988, Bush carried rapidly growing San Bernardino County in California by 84,000 votes over Michael Dukakis. In 1992, Clinton (with help from Ross Perot) carried the county by 7,000 votes. In Du Page County, where Chicago suburbanites provided Bush with his Illinois victory margin in 1988, Clinton (and Perot) cut Bush's margin in half—from 124,000 votes to just 64,000. In Macomb County, the virtually all-white Detroit suburbs where many ethnic Reagan Democrats live, Bush's margin dropped from 63,000 to 17,000. In the meantime, Clinton increased the Democratic total vote in many of his party's traditional urban strongholds such as Cook County (Chicago) and Wayne County (Detroit), proving that it was possible for a Democrat to win the inner cities and appeal to suburbanites as well. In Wayne County, to pick a particularly dramatic example, Clinton increased the Democratic margin from 158,000 in 1988 to 281,000 in 1992.

Finally, Clinton won back millions of white southern votes. This seemed to mark the destruction of one of the most important building blocks of Republican ascendancy—what had seemed to be a Republican "lock" on the South. In the eleven states of the Old Confederacy, Bush had defeated Dukakis by 4 million votes, 13.6 million to 9.5 million. In 1992, Bush's margin in these states shrank to 390,000 votes: 11.73 million for Bush, 11.34 million for Clinton, and 4.2 million for Perot.

Almost as important as Clinton's candidacy, of course, was Perot's, and his rise proved to be an essential component of Clinton's victory. In the spring of 1992, as discontent against Bush was growing, Perot's sudden availability as a candidate shook loose millions of previously Republican voters. Before he dropped out of the contest, Perot had risen to first in the polls and had driven Bush down to about a third of the potential vote. In his withdrawal statement in July—in the midst of the Democratic National Convention—Perot gave Clinton a large boost when he explained that his candidacy might no longer be needed "now that the Democratic Party has revitalized itself." Clinton soared in the polls.

More importantly, Perot fundamentally altered the *content* of the debate in a way that hugely benefited the Democrats. He trumpeted the fact that the end of the Cold War should force a large change in the behavior of government. This was, among other things, a direct attack on Bush's orientation toward foreign policy. "The people are concerned that our government is still organized to fight the Cold War," Perot said when he got back into the race in October. "They want it reorganized to rebuild America as the highest priority." Indeed, Perot was the true economic nationalist in the contest, arguing that Japan was now America's foremost adversary. He linked this message to an assault on the governing elites, whom he charged with corruptly aiding America's economic competitors. "If you wonder why international trade is not played on a level playing field," he said, "don't point a finger at the Japanese or the British or anyone else. Look first to our own political elites who enter government to gain expertise and personal contacts while on the public payroll, then leave to enrich themselves by taking inside knowledge to the other side." Washington, Perot insisted, was a corrupted place. His attack was as much against a Congress led by Democrats as against a Republican president. But in 1992, Perot was running for president, and his charges hurt Bush most. Only later would he take on the Democratic congressional majority.

Perot, moreover, excoriated the Republicans' handling of the economy, reinforcing Clinton's argument that the United States faced deep structural problems in the new global system. "A disturbing trend has emerged from the decade of greed, the era of trickle-down economics and the period of capital gains tax manipulation," Perot declared. "We are headed for a two-class society." Finally, he argued that closing the budget deficit was a central moral and political imperative. Here again, Perot's attack was directly against the Republicans, but his language was redolent with the oldest of Republican commitments. Perot's was the Main Street balance-the-books Republicanism of Robert Taft, not the Easy Street Republicanism of Ronald Reagan. "In your family, when you can't pay the bills, you either get a raise or you start cutting back to the necessities," Perot would say. Finally, as historian Sean Wilentz pointed out, Perot almost perfectly captured the country's own ambiguities on the cultural issues. On the one hand, he effused what Wilentz called "a no-nonsense morality." No one would ever consider Perot "a counter-culture McGovernik." Yet his actual stands on cultural matters, particularly on abortion, were moderate or even liberal. What Perot understood above all, as Wilentz argued, was "the mounting public frustration at how the social issues, especially abortion, have tended to dominate the economic issues that many consider the federal government's primary responsibility."

The power of the Perot synthesis rested on its ability to appeal simultaneously to very different constituencies that only rarely voted together. His focus on the budget deficit appealed strongly both to very conservative Republicans, outraged generally at unbalanced budgets and government spending, and to upper-middle-class moderates, including many Democrats, outraged at the fiscal imbalances of the Reagan years. But his message about America's economic decline along with his nationalistic assaults against Japan and its paid minions in Washington appealed to the heart of what had once been the Democratic Party's blue-collar base. Finally, his more general critique of Washington as a failing and corrupt political culture appealed to the angry and alienated across the political spectrum.

The broad nature of Perot's appeal was reflected in the extraordinary diversity of his supporters. On the one hand, Perot's was a classic revolt of the middle: He did best among moderates and independents—and actually ran ahead of Bush among the 14 percent of voters who described themselves as *both* moderate and independent. These were the voters most detached from the dominant organizing forces in American politics, Republican and Democratic, liberal and conservative. His was a movement of "the middle middle" in other respects as well. Perot voters were educated, but not overly so. One of his strongest groups in the electorate consisted of men (he did better across the board with men than women) who had attended college but didn't get a degree. Perot's support crossed class lines, but he did better in the heart of the middle class than among either the best or worst off.

Perot's strength in the middle sectors was, in part, a reflection of Clinton's weakness. Ruy Teixeira, a political analyst at the Economic Policy Institute, noted that Clinton's share of the vote among lower- and lower-middle-income whites was remarkably low, given his victory and the focus of his strategy. Among whites earning between $15,000 and $30,000 a year, Clinton won only 40 percent. Whites earning between $30,000 and $50,000 a year gave Clinton only 37 percent. Clinton's difficulties in these middle strata would come back to haunt Democrats in 1994. Teixeira also found two other major differences between Clinton voters and Perot voters that would have long-term significance. Perot voters were far more skeptical than Clinton supporters of government activism and government spending. The Voter Research and Surveys 1992 exit poll for the major news organizations asked whether voters preferred a government that would provide more in services but cost more in taxes, or a government that would cost less and provide fewer services. Among Clinton voters, 61 percent picked the bigger government option; among Perot voters, just 28 percent did. Teixeira's other important finding was based on his own analysis of which groups in the electorate had suffered the most severe wage losses, based on their age, education, gender and race. According to Teixeira, when all other factors were held constant, "the greater the wage loss experienced, the more likely a voter would choose Perot over Clinton." Clinton may have captured the electorate's unhappiness, but Perot was the channel of the angriest sentiments of the angriest constituencies.

Perot's constituency was a catchall coalition that included voters who disagreed on almost everything except their willingness to use a Texas billionaire as a vehicle for saying a loud "no" to both parties. Perot's 1992 voters included Paul Tsongas–style liberals and George Wallace–style conservatives. In casting ballots in congressional contests, Perotians split evenly between the Republicans and the Democrats. Perot called his political organization United We Stand, but united is exactly what his supporters were not. He did well in areas of New England and the Pacific Northwest that had been hospitable to George McGovern and Michael Dukakis. But he also did well in Rocky Mountain counties where the deep anti-Washington conservatism of the Sagebrush Rebellion had nothing in common with the polite fiscal responsibility of the Boston and Seattle suburbs.

Perot himself may have no future in American politics. His quirky personality and his tendency toward conspiracy theories may prevent him from ever achieving the broad support (and trust) he would need to reach the presidency. But his ability to win so many votes by harnessing so many different streams of anxiety and unhappiness pointed to a deep instability in the political system. Perot's candidacy suggested that something fundamental was afoot in American politics. It was not clear what was being born, but an old politics—the politics of American triumph in World War II and the Cold War—was in the process of dying.

It is therefore a mistake to limit the meaning of the 1992 election by pointing only to Clinton's less than overwhelming share of the vote. It would have been a similar mistake to downplay Richard Nixon's far narrower triumph over Hubert Humphrey in 1968. The 1992 election heralded the end of the Republican era that began with Richard Nixon and reached high tide under Ronald Reagan. Even a revived Republican Party would need to find new themes and to resolve deep philosophical and electoral tensions. The Republicans emerged from the election divided, dispirited and at a decided intellectual disadvantage. Republicans, mourned Bush aide Jim Pinkerton, "lost the driving energy of the Reagan years in a fog of issueless indirection."

III

The fog cleared with remarkable speed. Just two years after their disaster, the Republicans stood astride Washington, confining the Democrats to what looked like a White House bunker. The Republicans not only recaptured the Senate, which they had controlled as recently as 1986, but also seized control of the House of Representatives. The parallels with 1992 were striking—and dispiriting for Democrats, who now seemed to be caught in an issueless fog of their own. The Republican campaign was relentlessly negative against Clinton, of course, but the Democrats had hardly been kind to George Bush two years earlier. What made 1994 so different was the extent to which the intellectual energy had again shifted back to the right. The Republicans, and particularly Newt Gingrich, tossed off ideas as if the Bush experience had never happened.

The House Republicans' "Contract with America" was a carefully drawn document aimed at putting together the pieces of a Republican majority while also giving the party a platform from which to govern. As Ronald Brownstein of the *Los Angeles Times* put it, the Republicans' contract and overall strategy was one part Reagan, one part Perot and one part William Bennett. It combined Reagan's overall anti-government, anti-tax message with Perot's anti-system, anti-Congress appeal and Bennett's call for a revival of traditional morality.

For Perot's partisans, there were term limits, congressional reform and a balanced budget amendment. For average families, the Republicans offered a tax credit for parents with children, an idea that Clinton embraced in 1992, cast aside when he assembled his first budget and then came back to, albeit only after the Republican triumph. The children's tax credit not only had general appeal, but spoke specifically to cultural conservatives who wanted government policy to be pro-family. The Republicans' contract had other goodies for traditionalists, including an end to the "marriage penalty" in the tax code, tougher enforcement of child support decrees on absent fathers, adoption assistance, and new penalties against sexual offenses and child pornography. For another kind of social conservative, the Republicans put together a draconian welfare reform program and a series of very tough-sounding anti-crime measures. For the wealthy, there was a cut in the capital gains tax. For business, there were other tax breaks and a reform of the product liability laws that would weaken the ability of consumers to bring suit. This was part of what the Republicans called the "Common Sense Legal Reforms Act," a series of measures directed against lawyers—always a good political target—and designed to reduce the number of lawsuits. For hawkish nationalists, the Republicans promised to ban the use of American troops in multinational forces under foreign command. For senior citizens, there was a repeal of the tax on higher-income Social Security recipients passed in 1993, and a lifting of the ceiling on what seniors could earn without losing their Social Security benefits.

To a remarkable extent, the Republican program was a political mirror image of Clinton's 1992 program. In effect, the Republicans were trying to recapture both the electoral and the intellectual ground they had lost to Clinton (and Perot) two years earlier. Clinton had proposed a "new" welfare system based on the "old" values of work, family and personal responsibility. But Clinton failed to get welfare reform passed. The Republicans jumped to his right by embracing the same values but arguing that they would be best achieved by a smaller and cheaper welfare system. Clinton profited from Bush's decision to break his "read my lips" pledge not to raise taxes. He sought to trump Bush by proposing a middle-class tax cut aimed at families with children. But here again, Clinton failed to act—he abandoned his own pledge in his first budget—and the Republicans again jumped to his right with their own tax package.

Clinton had promised political reform and failed to deliver. Republicans first made sure through obstruction that the outgoing Democratic Congress did not have reform achievements to bring to the voters. (The Democrats, as we shall see, made this easy by delaying the reform package until the end of the congressional session.) Then the Republicans offered their own political reforms, including many on Clinton's list plus some harder-edged stuff such as term limits.

In a sense, both the 1992 Clinton program and the 1994 Republican program were aimed at the same broad group of voters—those who were unhappy about the performance of government, doubtful that government actually operated in their interest and concerned that the country was in moral decline. And the Republicans' 1994 program worked as well as Clinton's had two years earlier.

The breadth of the Republican gains was staggering. The Republicans picked up eight seats in the Senate, a remarkable accomplishment since just thirty-five seats were being contested. True, the Democrats lost five of those eight because some of their most popular incumbents had retired—among them, majority leader George Mitchell of Maine, David Boren of Oklahoma, Howard Metzenbaum of Ohio and, earlier, Al Gore of Tennessee and Lloyd Bentsen of Texas. But two incumbent Democrats also lost, Harris Wofford of Pennsylvania (narrowly) and Jim Sasser of Tennessee (decisively). And Democrats proved unable to pick off any Republican seats, even in Minnesota. A state long hospitable to liberals and Democrats, Minnesota gave its open seat to a Republican, and a right-wing Republican at that.

The shifting political mood may have been captured best by the rise and fall of Pennsylvania's Wofford, elected to the Senate in a 1991 special election that proved to be a harbinger for 1992. Wofford started as a decided underdog against Republican Richard Thornburgh, a moderate who had been a popular governor and then went to Washington to serve as George Bush's attorney general. Thornburgh ran as an experienced insider who could deliver for his state—which turned out to be exactly the wrong approach in the face of rising anti-Washington feeling. Wofford became the outsider who would shake up the capital. His message was directed to middle-class voters who felt left out. His argument was *not* that government was oppressing the middle class, but that it was failing to deliver what the middle class wanted.

In 1991, Wofford captured middle-class anxiety with perfect pitch. His promise to fight for universal health coverage resonated even though some 92 percent of Pennsylvanians already had health insurance. As Robert Shrum, Wofford's 1991 media adviser explained, the health care issue was not simply powerful in itself but also served as a metaphor for the broader economic insecurities experienced by voters. Many who were confident that they would find another job if they lost their current one were still worried that the new job would pay less and carry fewer benefits, such as health coverage. Wofford's talk about health care spoke directly to those insecurities. And the language Wofford used in discussing health care presaged Clinton's success in casting himself as someone who shared the middle class's sense that those who lived by the rules were not being rewarded. "If criminals have the right to a lawyer," Wofford would say, "I think working Americans should have the right to see a doctor."

By 1994, just three years later, the political landscape had changed dramatically. The voters were still angry, and they were still directing much of their anger at Washington. But now, the Democrats held the White House and both houses of Congress, and Wofford was the Man from Washington. Congress, moreover, had failed in a very public way to pass the health reform measure Wofford had pledged to deliver. It thus fell to Republican Rick Santorum, a thirty-six-year-old conservative congressman, to capture the public's disaffection and retarget it. Santorum's argument was not that the government was failing to deliver to the middle class, but that government itself was the enemy of middle-class aspirations and a barrier to middle-class freedom. Santorum's orientation was toward the anti-system, anti-Congress message perfected by Newt Gingrich. That turned out to be the grammar of protest in 1994. This time, Democratic consultant Edward Mitchell told *The Philadelphia Inquirer*, it was Santorum "whose sails were being carried by the wind moving through the country." But in another sense Santorum was riding exactly the same tide of disaffection that had sent Wofford and Clinton to Washington in the first place. "In electing Harris Wofford and Bill Clinton, voters were in an anti-incumbent mode," said Tony May, former executive director of the Pennsylvania Democratic Party. "Then they turned around and elected Christie Whitman [as governor] in New Jersey and others. There is no reason to assume voters will be satisfied turning out two or three incumbents and think they are finished with their task."

But even more remarkable than the Republicans' capture of the Senate was their success in taking over the House. The Republicans picked up fifty-two seats. Their gains were national in scope, and the ranks of the defeated Democrats included representatives of every wing and style in the party. Dan Rostenkowski, a perfect symbol of the old Democratic House barons, was defeated, but he was under indictment. Jack Brooks, another fixture, lost even though he had no legal problems. Young and able freshmen reformers such as Karen Shepherd of Utah and Eric Fingerhut of Ohio went down to defeat even though so much of what they stood for squared well with an electorate clamoring for cleaner government. Southern conservatives such as Don Johnson of Georgia were sacked, but so were thoughtful moderates such as North Carolina's David Price and liberals such as Virginia's Leslie Byrne and Washington's Jay Inslee. And of course, symbolizing the entire election, House Speaker Tom Foley was ousted from a seat he had held for three decades.

The Republicans' gains were particularly dramatic in the South, and these are likely to be their most enduring. The year 1994 was the one when the Republicans' fifty-year campaign to break the Democratic "Solid South," so successful in presidential contests, came to fruition at the congressional level. For the first time since Reconstruction, the Republicans enjoyed a majority of the congressional seats in the states that had made up the Old Confederacy. In the House, they picked up sixteen seats in these states, giving them a 64–60 edge. Twenty years earlier these states had given the Democrats an 81–27 margin; forty years earlier these states had sent ninety-nine Democrats to the House and only seven Republicans. In 1992, Clinton had made the South genuinely competitive for the Democratic Party. In 1994, Republicans used southern unhappiness with Clinton to win back what they had lost—and much more. True, some of the Republican pickups in the South could be ascribed to reapportionment plans designed to increase the number of African-Americans in the House. These plans packed African-American voters, who are overwhelmingly Democratic, into a small number of districts, creating new overwhelmingly white (and conservative) districts that inclined heavily toward the Republicans. But reapportionment was only one of many factors working in the Republicans' favor in the South.

The results in the South reflected a true nationalization of American politics. In the recent past, Democrats had held onto Congress despite repeated Republican presidential victories because so many voters split their tickets. Many voters backed congressional Democrats either out of loyalty to individual politicians or as a sign of their residual faithfulness to the Democratic Party itself. What made it likely that the congressional Republicans would hold many of their 1994 southern gains over the long term was the fact that most of them came from districts that had recently voted Republican for president. This meant that their victory in the South was not a one-shot protest, but a confirmation of long-term trends.

Going into the election, Democrats held fifty-one House seats from districts that had voted for George Bush in both 1988 and 1992. Most of them were in the South or the border states. The Democrats lost twenty-seven of these fifty-one in 1994, holding on to only twenty-four. The Democrats were further hurt by their performance in "swing" districts that had voted for Bush in 1988 but Clinton in 1992. Democrats held seventy-seven of these seats before the polls opened in 1994; they had lost twenty-one of them when the votes were counted. On the other hand, the Democrats lost only eight of the 128 seats they held going into the election in districts that had voted Democratic in both 1988 and 1992. Oddly, then, a country that is often described as being tired of partisan politics was more rigidly divided along partisan lines after the 1994 elections than it was before.

Finally, the Republicans scored decisively in state contests, not only for governorships but also for seats in state legislatures. The Republicans won twenty-four of the thirty-six governorships at stake in 1994 and took over ten statehouses that had been in Democratic hands. The Republicans emerged with thirty statehouses, compared with nineteen for the Democrats. (Maine elected an independent.) The Republicans ended up with the governorships in eight of the nine largest states; only Florida eluded their grasp. After the election 70 percent of the country's population lived in states with Republican governors. In the meantime, the Republicans had their best showing in elections for state legislatures since 1968—and in many ways, the 1994 results were more impressive. The Republicans took control of legislative chambers in the Deep South for the first time in the century, capturing the House in North Carolina and the Senate in Florida. The Republicans' state legislative triumphs were particularly promising signs for the GOP and disturbing portents for the Democrats. As political analyst Michael Barone has pointed out, one of the Democrats' major advantages in past congressional elections had been their ability to groom gifted candidates at the grass roots. Even when the partisan trends were moving in the wrong direction, skilled and savvy Democratic politicians often managed victories against Republican amateurs. The 1994 elections gave the Republicans much greater depth, bequeathing the party a class of younger politicians with a chance of continuing the crusade for long-term majority status over the next generation.

IV

The conventional view of the 1994 results contained some large truths. The vote was obviously symptomatic of fundamental failures by Clinton and the Democrats in the two years they controlled the elected branches of government. Democrats had not only failed to enact their own program; they also failed to transform the terms of political debate.

The collapse of Clinton's health care initiative, which will be discussed in more detail later, was particularly instructive. In political terms, Clinton's intent had been to demonstrate to the middle class that the federal government could establish new programs that reflected its interests. In so doing, he hoped to reverse the anti-government trend in public opinion that began in the 1970s. Instead, that very trend ultimately undermined the proposal's chances of passing. The core argument of the plan's opponents—that a larger government role in health care would mean worse care for most people—struck a powerful chord. Stanley Greenberg, Clinton's own polltaker and a prime proponent of the view that universal coverage could cement middle-class support for government activism, wrote after the 1994 elections that a key force behind the Republican triumph was the public's feeling that "government spends too much and wastes taxpayers' dollars." Greenberg went on: "For the majority of independents who felt disappointed in Clinton, the biggest reason was the dependence on big government solutions, *particularly in health care*. The concern about Clinton and big government solutions was particularly marked for key swing groups, such as Perot voters and those who shifted toward the Republicans this year." [Emphasis added.]

Greenberg's study and virtually all the other post-election polls made clear that the public clearly heard the Republicans' anti-government, anti-tax message and responded to it.

But it is also important to understand the limits of the Republican victory. For example, the Republicans secured a little over half the vote in House races (the only contests held in all fifty states). This was a major improvement over the past, but not a landslide. The Republicans, moreover, gained many seats, but emerged with only a narrow, 230–204, House majority. Many of the Republican gains came in extremely close races. Thirty of the victorious Republicans were elected with 52 percent of the vote or less—meaning that control of the House hung on a very small number of popular votes. None of these figures takes away from the Republicans' achievement or eases the rebuke experienced by the Democrats. In fact, twenty-six Democrats *also* won seats with 52 percent of the vote or less, giving the Republicans many opportunities for expanding their majority. But the numbers do show that the 1994 elections, far from being a landslide, were actually very close. In other words, the fact that the Republicans' victory had great historical significance does not mean that it represented a permanent realignment, except, perhaps, in parts of the South. That awaits future electoral confirmation.

The need to put the Republican victory in perspective is underscored by the findings of the exit polls. They suggested that four large factors were responsible for the Republicans' victory. First, the Republicans were enormously successful in uniting their own party, in significant part in reaction against Clinton. In the 1990 midterm elections, according to the exit polls, about a quarter of voters who called themselves Republicans actually voted for *Democratic* House candidates. In 1994, by contrast, only 7 percent of self-identified Republicans voted Democratic in House races. This represented a shift of some 3.5 to 4 million votes out of 75 million cast and accounted for many of the Republicans' close victories. Party unity of this sort is certainly essential for future Republican victories, but it is not sufficient. There are still not enough Republicans—and too many independents—for Republicans to win elections on their own.

The second big movement toward the GOP came among Perot voters, reflecting the shrewdness of the Republicans' strategy. In 1992, Perot voters had split their ballots evenly between Republican and Democratic House candidates. In 1994 those Perot voters who went to the polls backed the Republicans by about two to one. This shift was worth another 2 million or so Republican votes. The Perot shift is important to the GOP because so many of Perot's 1992 supporters were actually defectors from the Republican ranks. Perot himself urged his supporters to favor Republicans in congressional races. Perhaps more significantly, the Democrats were no longer in a position to capitalize on Perot's themes. Having failed to institute political reform, Democrats were easily attacked as the party now *entirely* responsible for what voters saw as Washington's corruption. Clinton's embrace of free trade with the NAFTA and GATT agreements made it impossible for him to use the themes of economic nationalism with any credibility. And while the economy had improved substantially since 1992, many of the most economically distressed voters remained unhappy about their economic state after 1992. They demonstrated their willingness to punish Republicans in 1992 and Democrats in 1994. They are likely to remain in a punishing mood for some time to come. In the wake of the elections, the Republicans were well positioned to address the concerns Perot voters had about the deficit and their skepticism about government programs. They were less well placed to address the deep sense of economic grievance felt by so many in his constituency.

The other critical group in the 1994 elections overlapped with the Perot constituency. They were voters without college degrees, particularly white voters and especially white males. This group had experienced a long-term decline in its economic fortunes, and it is in this group that Democrats suffered their sharpest losses in 1994. Among white males, the Democratic share of the House vote dropped ten points between 1992 and 1994 among high school dropouts; it dropped a staggering twenty points—from 57 to 37 percent—among white male high school graduates who did not go on to college. The Democrats also fell fifteen points among white males who attended college but never got a degree. But among those doing rather well, white male college graduates, the Democrats lost only five points.

Among white women, the patterns were the same, if less dramatic, suggesting that something more than a rebellion of "angry white men" explained the 1994 results. The Democratic share among white female high school graduates dropped by four points; it dropped by nine points among both high school graduates and those with some college education. But among white women who attended college, the Democratic share actually *went up*, albeit marginally, by two percentage points.

Broadly put, the Democrats did very well indeed in holding onto their share among college graduates; they did very badly among voters without college degrees. As we shall see shortly, the Democratic loss among non–college-educated whites is hugely important. This group, the most fluid in the electorate, has suffered the sharpest economic declines and is therefore potentially the angriest portion of the electorate—it lies at the heart of the Anxious Middle. Like the Perot constituency with which it overlaps, this group is quick to punish.

Finally, Democrats suffered from a drop in voter turnout among groups that had voted for Clinton in 1992. According to Greenberg's study, the voters who stayed home in 1994 were "mostly younger, non–college-educated voters who leaned strongly Democratic but who remained disengaged, largely because of their ambivalence about the President." Overall, voter turnout (at about 39 percent) was higher in 1994 than in 1990, the year of the previous midterm elections. But the polling suggests that almost all of the increase came from angry Republicans and other constituencies (gun owners, Christian conservatives, opponents of abortion, critics of tax increases) motivated to cast ballots against Clinton. The voters who went to the polls in 1992 but stayed home in 1994 were disproportionately the very voters Democrats needed to hold their own. The 1994 earthquake was caused by the energy of Motivated Republicans and the indifference or outright hostility of Demoralized Democrats.

The 1994 elections might be seen as the natural result of the voters' unrequited rebellion of 1992. The angriest constituencies were the quickest to move away from George Bush, the most likely to embrace Ross Perot and the most eager to punish Bill Clinton. By the end of George Bush's presidency, voters had decided that Republicans were disengaged from their problems. A large majority rejected Bush, and a majority of those who did so were prepared to listen to Democratic arguments that active government could work. When they decided that the Democrats' version of active government had not done the job, enough of the angry voters were prepared to give the Republicans a chance to prove their claim that *less* government would work better. The edgy, pragmatic voters willing to punish politicians quickly and shift allegiances suddenly constitute the Anxious Middle.

V

The Anxious Middle is as peculiar a political formation as its name implies. It is radical in its disaffection with the status quo, in the depth of its worries about the future, in its desire for far-reaching change, and in its critique of current political and economic arrangements. It is "middle" because it lacks the rigid definition usually associated with the words "left" and "right," "liberal" and "conservative." It is also "middle" because its longings are not utopian. The Anxious Middle does not expect a New Jerusalem, a world without sin, pain, conflict or injustice. It hopes simply for a return to the sort of economic growth that characterized the twenty-five years after World War II. It looks to greater fairness, a modicum of job security, a sense that hard work will be rewarded, and that violent crime will be punished. The fact that such demands can be seen as radical in the context of our current uncertainties is a sign of how disorderly the world of the 1990s has become.

The Anxious Middle is "middle" in another sense: It tends to be quite moderate or pragmatic on the issues that so excite liberals and conservatives. On questions of culture and morality, the Anxious Middle is neither repressive nor permissive. It senses the moral crisis, but is inclined to see both its cultural and economic sides. Its attitude toward the power of government is contingent on how effectively the government performs. On economics, the Anxious Middle is in favor of what works. It is in love neither with the market nor with government. It trusts the market and the government only so far.

The issue of "fairness," derided by the right for so long, is very much on the mind of the Anxious Middle. But its sense of "unfairness" is not quite the same as the version that had animated liberals for years. It does not seek government programs involving wholesale redistribution. Indeed, it is often so skeptical of what government can accomplish that it is, as often as not, inclined to vote Republican in the hopes of getting at least some tax relief. The Anxious Middle is often of the view that if government cannot be expected to lend a hand, the least it can do is hand back some money to taxpayers who are working hard simply to stay even. It can be skeptical of the wealthy, but it is not, on the whole, anti-business. As Louis Uchitelle noted in *The New York Times*, "business is seen also as a victim, caught in a global competition that forces cost-cutting and layoffs." This was among the findings of a study of the attitudes of 2,400 workers conducted by Joel Rogers of the University of Wisconsin and Richard Freeman of Harvard University. "They tell us, 'My boss is trying hard, but there is nothing he can do either,' " Rogers said. "That does not mean they don't see their employer as often unfair and cruel. But then they say he does not have the ability to protect them, which is much different from saying, 'He could protect me if he wanted but he chooses not to.' " This makes today's Anxious Middle rather different from the working class of the 1930s and 1940s, which had a class consciousness defined more pointedly against "the bosses" and "the rich" and cheered Franklin Roosevelt's attacks on "economic royalists."

In its attitude toward politics, the Anxious Middle is often ambivalent or divided. Many in its ranks long for a more democratic and participatory political system. It was this desire that helped force the 1992 campaign toward substance: All three candidates issued "plans" for the economic future. It also transformed the way the mass media covered the campaign. To the shock of the networks, putting a presidential candidate on the air to answer phone calls from voters actually *boosted* ratings.

At the same time, the Anxious Middle seems to long for a strong political leader who will "fix" things. This approach to politics can have an authoritarian tinge. The 1992 revolt against "gridlock in Washington" could be viewed as reflecting an impatience with a system of separated powers and the often leisurely workings of democracy. Democrats certainly suffered in 1994 from impatience with inaction. Newt Gingrich's Republicans spoke directly to this impatience with their promise of fast action on the "Contract with America." Ross Perot seemed to have an especially sensitive grasp of both sides of the Anxious Middle's view of politics. His calls for "electronic town meetings" appealed to its democratic instinct, while his attacks on gridlock and his promise to "get under the hood" to fix the nation's problems appealed to its desire for decisive leadership.

The authoritarian side of the Anxious Middle may yet become its stronger instinct, especially if the economy should take another tumble. For the moment, however, it is the longing for a stronger democracy that seems the dominant tendency. Far from representing an authoritarian impulse, the revolt against Washington's inaction could also be seen as a simple demand that democratic government produce measurable accomplishments.

The Anxious Middle shares the moral unease abroad in the country. It mistrusts government and doubts its capacity. But more than anything, it is economic change that motivates the Anxious Middle. Among the many mistakes made by George Bush and his lieutenants in 1992, the fatal one was underestimating the level of economic anxiety in the country. The Bush camp made what seemed a reasonable calculation—that given the relatively low unemployment rate reached at the bottom of the 1990–91 recession, the downturn would have a limited political impact. But the unemployment rate turned out to be a poor measure of unhappiness. Voters, as the Wofford campaign demonstrated, were worried at least as much about falling incomes and lost benefits as they were about not working at all. As Clinton put it repeatedly, Americans sensed that they were "working harder for less."

But the same forces that helped elect Clinton came back to haunt him and the Democrats in 1994. Democrats presumed that the lowest unemployment rate in four years, and nearly two years of steady growth, would save them from a midterm catastrophe. Yet many Americans in the middle and lower reaches of the economy sensed, correctly, that the recovery had not affected them at all. The unemployment rate once again proved to be an unreliable guide to the country's sense of economic well-being. On election day 1994, only a quarter of the voters said their financial situation was getting better, another quarter said it was worsening, the rest sensed no change—and change, of course, is what Clinton had promised.

Few understood the relationship between the political and economic forces better than Labor Secretary Reich, whose 1994 pre–Labor Day address on the problems of "the anxious class" eerily (for Democrats, at least) presaged what was about to come at the polls. "In an astonishingly short time," Reich declared, "the old middle class has splintered. The erosion of a sense of shared prospects poses what may be our nation's most critical challenge of the post–Cold War era." He went on:

> Broad trends that have converged and accelerated since the middle 1970s have split the old middle class into three new groups. An underclass largely trapped in center cities, increasingly isolated from the core economy; an overclass of those who are positioned profitably to ride the wave of change; and in between, the largest group, an anxious class, most of whom hold jobs but are justifiably uneasy about their own standing and fearful for their children's future.

Reich had long been arguing that differentials in skill and education levels explained a good deal of the growing inequality in the country. In his Labor Day speech he extended his analysis to show how the education gap was also producing large disparities in basic benefits such as health coverage. Between 1979 and 1993 employer-based health coverage declined for all workers. But for the college educated, the decline in the proportion receiving such coverage was slight, from 79 to 76 percent. For high school graduates, the share with employer-based health coverage dropped from 68 to 60 percent. And for high school dropouts, the proportion with coverage dropped catastrophically, from the already-low 52 percent level in 1979 to a mere 36 percent in 1993.

After the election Reich drew the logical conclusion from his own analysis, describing the vote as "The Revolt of the Anxious Class" and noting that "tens of millions of middle-class Americans continue to experience what they began to face in the 1970s: downward mobility.

"They know recoveries are cyclical, but fear that the underlying trend is permanent," he went on. "They voted for change in 1994 just as they voted for change in 1992, and they will do so again and again until they feel that their downward slide is reversing." And Reich was careful to link the economic trends to the underlying moral message:

All the old bargains, it seems, have been breached. The economic bargain was that if you worked hard and your company prospered, you would share the fruits of success. There
was a cultural bargain, too, echoing the same themes of responsibility and its rewards: Live by the norms of your community—take care of your family, obey the law, treat your
neighbors with respect, love your country—and you'll feel
secure in the certainty that everyone else would behave the
same way.

Reich concluded that the core question—for Democrats and for the
country—was: "How can we get it back?"

That, of course, had been the animating question of Bill
Clinton's 1992 campaign. Rewarding those who "worked hard and
played by the rules" was supposed to be the central point of the
Clinton presidency. But that is not how matters worked out, especially in Clinton's troubled first two years when Democratic majorities in Congress were supposed to make things easy.

Part Two

THE PLAYERS

□ 4 □

THE CLINTON EXPERIMENT:

The Democrats' Hopes and Nightmares

BILL CLINTON was elected president for many reasons. Chief among them was an economic downturn and the perception among a majority of voters that George Bush was either responsible for it or indifferent to the problems it had caused. Take away the recession—and, more broadly, the perception that living standards were skidding sharply—and it's highly likely that Bill Clinton could not have won. "It's the economy, stupid," became a cliché for good reason. Like many clichés, this one was broadly true.

But it's also true that Bill Clinton could not have taken advantage of the recession and unhappiness with Bush if he had not substantially shifted the message of the Democratic Party and— perhaps as importantly—the *perception* of what the Democratic Party stood for. The Clinton Experiment thus had far-reaching implications that transcended the president's troubles (and personal history) because what underlay it was a large project involving ideas and an attempt to shift the country's philosophical leanings. Riding on the Clinton presidency was more than the fate of a single politician with his own unusual mixture of virtues and flaws. If the Clinton Experiment failed, it would be a sign that the deep factional splits in the Democratic Party were close to unbridgeable. It would demonstrate the difficulty of forging a new synthesis to revive the popularity and coherence of American liberalism.

Clinton's 1992 campaign was effective because implicitly and, at times, explicitly, it directed itself to the sense of crisis that Americans felt about the economy, their living standards, the efficacy of government and the country's moral unease. Clinton argued repeatedly that the United States confronted a situation novel in its history. Not only had the Cold War ended, but the economic challenges facing the nation had changed because of technological transformation and global competition. Clinton, it should be recalled, did not base his campaign simply on reducing unemployment or restoring economic growth. He spoke often and quite clearly about the decline in *living standards* and *income* experienced by a large segment of the employed middle class. He also spoke of the specific problems confronted by an underclass whose difficulties were quite different—and much deeper—than those faced by the traditionally employed.

But Clinton's troubles in office arose in significant part because the problems were far more easily described than resolved. It cannot be stressed enough how much the budget deficit he inherited from the Reagan-Bush years impeded his ability to govern and build a sustainable political coalition. The need to deal with the deficit sharply restricted the administration's ability to create new programs. It also forced Democrats to enact a tax increase that was bound to be controversial even if almost all of it was levied on the wealthy. And the deficit repeatedly created deep conflicts inside the Democratic coalition. Again and again, factions of the party faced off against one another to battle over which constituencies would have to bear the largest burdens of deficit reduction. Gone were the days when Democrats could resolve their conflicts by spending just a little bit more money.

Similarly, the administration's ability to intervene in rapid fashion to lift the living standards of those whose wages were skidding was constrained by its firm embrace of the global economy. Clinton argued, plausibly, that an open economy would grow more quickly and that protectionism—specifically, opposition to the North American Free Trade Agreement and the General Agreement on Tariffs and Trade—would harm the nation's long-term position. But having embraced global competition, Clinton had to live with the sometimes chaotic change it could impose. Clinton's answer, in office as during the campaign, involved Labor Secretary Robert Reich's core ideas: that only a more skilled and educated workforce could count on growing affluence. But once he accepted the constraints of deficit reduction, Clinton could not finance the Reich program to an extent that would make it a visible answer to economic anxieties.

It was also easier for Clinton to recognize the need for a substantial renovation in the Democratic Party's public philosophy than to put a reformed philosophy into practice. By the beginning of the 1990s, it was clear that Democrats needed to address three large worries that had weakened the party's links to some of its traditional constituencies. These concerned cultural breakdown, the practical failures of government and public doubts about the nature of the welfare state. Clinton moved forcefully on all three fronts during the 1992 campaign. He was less successful in office because these questions were far easier to resolve in word than in deed, verbal formulations being easier to coin than policy, and because the matters at stake involved not just the intellect but also the passions.

It was, in other words, far easier to unite the Democratic Party for the purposes of a single election than to convince its factions to work together, let alone to work with the Clinton White House. The lines of division within the Democratic Party were infinitely more complex than the New Democrat versus Old Democrat shorthand description so popular in analyzing the Clinton years. Many New Democrats held views on taxes and social policy that were quite consistent with the views of some of the party's strongest liberals. Yet many other self-styled New Democrats, especially southern conservatives in Congress, voted to defend a slew of old programs in agriculture, rural electrification and veterans affairs that the Democratic Leadership Council was, in theory, committed to abolishing. Many liberals with reputations as "big spenders" supported cuts in these programs. Issues such as gun control, abortion and the death penalty crisscrossed the dividing lines. So did free trade. And on issues involving the reform of campaign spending and lobbying laws, many of the most conservative and the most liberal old-timers ganged up against younger Democrats to delay action. On issue after issue, Clinton found himself struggling for votes as one faction or another abandoned his favored position. Increasingly, neither New nor Old Democrats fully trusted Clinton precisely because he refused to side permanently with any faction—on the theory that the Democratic Party could not prosper unless it harmonized its wings. Yet his attempts to achieve harmony often bred yet more division—and his own clumsy efforts in the fall of 1995 to disavow some of his record made matters worse.

What's important to recognize about the Clinton presidency is that its problems went beyond both the "trust issue" and the manifest failures of organization, "focus," salesmanship and day-to-day decision making that have received so much attention. Clinton could ill afford these failures because the task he set for himself—and that the times set for him—was large, and very difficult. If Clinton often seemed indecisive, that was, in part, because almost any decision he made carried substantial political risks.

The focus of this chapter and the next is far more on how ideas and policies moved people and shaped events than it is on Clinton the man, his character or his organizational style. It concentrates on the two years between Clinton's triumph and the Republican congressional victory of 1994 by way of exploring why Democratic factionalism and simple incoherence created the conditions for the Republican triumph. I look especially at budget issues, the health care battle and welfare reform to show how hard it was for Democrats to translate good (and largely popular) intentions into action.

There have already been some fine accounts of the internal workings of the Clinton White House (by Bob Woodward and Elizabeth Drew, for example) and some excellent portraits of Clinton (notably by David Maraniss). My purpose is to suggest that it is impossible to understand the difficulties Clinton encountered apart from the intellectual challenges that confronted Democrats and the deep divisions in the party that Clinton was trying to heal or transcend. These divisions affected the behavior of the congressional party and the attitudes of Democratic thinkers and strategists outside Congress and the White House. The congressional factions and the strategists often found more to fight about with one another than with the Republicans.

None of this absolves Clinton from his mistakes. Nor is a full analysis of his administration complete without attention to the intensely personal reactions Clinton aroused, including the deeply negative response to him from a significant segment of the electorate. As we shall see, some of what have been politely called Clinton's "personal problems" made it more difficult for him to address issues related to the country's sense of moral crisis. Nonetheless, my approach differs some from the earlier accounts in the emphasis it puts on the practical, political and intellectual constraints under which Clinton governed. These constraints gave him little room for error. Even an error-free Clinton administration would have encountered fundamental problems—problems deeply rooted in the Democratic Party and in contemporary liberalism, and also in the challenges of the four crises of American politics themselves.

II

To understand the nature of the innovation Clinton was proposing, it's important to look first at the ways in which he sought to alter the Democratic Party's message in the areas of culture, government performance and welfare. It is on these matters that Clinton sought—at first mostly successfully—to put a New Democrat stamp on his party.

Especially after Michael Dukakis's 1988 defeat, as we saw earlier, it was clear even to the most loyal and liberal Democrats that the party needed to send a number of new messages: that tolerance and open-mindedness were not the same as a rejection of traditional standards; that opposition to bigotry against gays and lesbians did not entail a denial of the importance of the two-parent family; that embracing civil liberties did not translate into permissiveness toward violent crime. Since one of the significant crises facing the country was a moral one involving fears that the nation's social and cultural fabric was unraveling, it was impossible for the party even to get a hearing in the public debate if it did not address these issues.

Clinton's single greatest achievement was to reposition the Democrats on these questions—and to bring along many, if not all, in the party's liberal wing. The single most important, and the best received, speech of his first year in office was an address to a group of black ministers in Memphis in which he sounded all of the traditionalist themes about family breakup, violence and personal responsibility. Clinton invoked Martin Luther King Jr. to make his case, thereby trying to assure his audience that an appeal to white backlash did not lurk beneath his words. "The freedom to die before you're a teenager is not what Martin Luther King lived and died for," he

declared. Nor, Clinton said, had King died "to see the American family destroyed" or "to see thirteen-year-old boys get automatic weapons and gun down nine-year-olds just for the kick of it." The speech
also included a lengthy section on civil rights and the need to bring
jobs to the inner city. It was one of the clearest statements of the inner
balances of Clintonism, and these themes quickly became common
currency in the party as a whole. In the 1994 midterm elections, many
Republicans giggled over Democratic campaign commercials that
seemed to have been written by the moralists of the Christian Coalition. In one particularly well-publicized example, Democratic Senator Jim Sasser expressed his commitment to family and church and
even prayer in the public schools. It was clear that the Democrats had
substantially transformed themselves from the days when they were
charged with being the party of "acid, amnesty and abortion," no
small achievement.

Still, Clinton's ability to address the moral issues was limited by
public doubts about the way he had conducted his own life. Paradoxically, one of the Democrats' most eloquent spokesmen on
moral themes found his own voice muffled on the issues to which
he assigned such importance. At the same time, certain conflicts
between tolerance and tradition could simply not be wished away.
Clinton fell into difficulty within days of the 1992 election when he
renewed his not-much-noticed campaign pledge to end the military's ban on gays and lesbians. The issue took on far greater importance than Clinton had ever intended. It was highlighted by the
press in the early post-election days in significant part because
Clinton did not have much else to announce in that period. Gays in
the military was, for a while, the only "news." And it became even
bigger news when military leaders who had nothing to do with the
Moral Majority or the Christian Coalition—notably General Colin
Powell—resisted Clinton's initiative. In Clinton's view, allowing gays
to volunteer for military service in no way vitiated his commitment
to strengthening families. But for many traditionalists, Clinton
moved from being a peacemaker in the culture wars to becoming
an active participant on the side they abhorred.

The second large shift that was required of Democrats concerned the public's impatience with government failures and
bureaucracy. During the civil rights period attacks on federal "bureaucrats" came to be associated with opposition to the govern-

ment's role in promoting black advancement. George Wallace was at the forefront with his signature attacks on "bureaucrats with thin briefcases full of guidelines." But over time it became clear that the public's criticisms of government were more than simply a reaction to civil rights. People were unhappy because many public institutions seemed to be failing at basic jobs—to educate kids, to keep the streets safe and clean, to buy the things the government needed at reasonable prices, to respond efficiently to citizen complaints and requests. Clinton's answer was to embrace the ideas of David Osborne and other reformers who proposed to "reinvent government"—that is, to bring government institutions up to date and, where useful, to use market principles to foster efficiency within the public sector. The theory went—and it was right—that Democrats who hoped to use government to accomplish certain desirable ends could not convince voters to embrace this idea unless they first believed that government knew what it was doing. Clinton's message on the cultural issues reinforced the notion that his was, for a Democrat, a "new" approach to government. Repeatedly, Clinton stressed that government on its own could not solve social problems—that many would only be solved at the level of the family or the neighborhood.

Here again, Clinton enjoyed more success in the first part of his term than he was commonly given credit for. Vice President Al Gore's "reinventing government" project promoted administrative change across the government. It led to the passage of a series of bills in 1994 that, among other things, changed the government's buying practices and substantially reorganized several federal agencies. On the other hand, the reinvention program received minimal attention once the administration became embroiled in the battle for health care reform. If anything, Republican successes in branding the Clinton health proposal as a "bureaucratic, big government" program eviscerated the administration's claims to having broken with old-style bureaucracy. Still, the long-term political impact of the reinvention initiatives within the Democratic Party is likely to be large. Their influence can be measured by the fact that many liberals initially hostile to the New Democrat strategy came around to embracing reinvention as a necessary task. "A dollar liberated by efficiency gains buys just as much as a dollar borrowed or taxed," wrote Robert Kuttner, the editor of *The American Prospect,* a liberal journal, and a leading DLC critic. "It is all government has when borrowing or taxing are foreclosed. This part of the 'New Democrat' agenda makes sense. It also steals the Republicans' clothes that are worth stealing."

Finally, Clinton sought to ease the problems Democrats faced because the concept of the "welfare state" had been so radically redefined in the public mind. Once, the welfare state was associated with a broad array of popular programs that benefited large and heterogeneous groups of Americans—Social Security, Medicare, unemployment compensation, assistance to widows and veterans benefits. Beginning in the 1960s, and again partly in response to the politics of race, the word "welfare" developed decidedly negative connotations. Less and less was it associated with help for the deserving elderly or assistance to tide families through bad times. More and more, "welfare" came to be viewed as a system of subsidies for idleness and for families headed by young, nonworking single mothers. For some Americans, "welfare programs" were "programs for blacks"; racism surely explains some of the backlash against welfare. But the reaction against welfare, like the reaction against bureaucracy, was not simply about race. It was also intimately linked to the country's sense of social and moral breakdown, to the idea that rewarding work was no longer at the center of government social policy. To win—and to rehabilitate the welfare state, albeit under another name—Democrats had to show that their support for assisting the poor embraced a concern for reinforcing the value of hard work.

Clinton's approach to this problem was more complex than is usually allowed. Welfare reform was seen as the central element of this effort, and it was certainly important. In a phrase he must have repeated hundreds of times, Clinton declared that "welfare should be a second chance, not a way of life." As he promised in the campaign, he proposed a welfare reform plan built around the idea of limiting recipients to two years on the rolls. During those two years they would receive training and education. At the end of the period they would be expected to take jobs. Clinton proposed the plan too late to get it enacted before the 1994 elections, a major political mistake. But the plan itself was certainly in keeping with his overall promises and strategy.

But the other side of Clinton's project of rehabilitating the compassionate state rested on measures that had nothing to do with welfare as such. Clinton also proposed—and got passed—a large increase in the Earned Income Tax Credit. This program uses the tax system to funnel money to the working poor, either by reducing their federal taxes or, if they are too poor to pay income taxes, through direct payments to lift their incomes. The EITC, historically popular on both the left and the right, is a central element to any program to "make work pay." Lifting the incomes of poor people who work is clearly the most powerful incentive available to keeping people off welfare. Clinton pursued this part of the program early, avidly and successfully. (In 1995, however, many Republicans who had supported the EITC in the past called for cuts, raising questions about whether there were *any* programs for *any* class of poor people to which they were willing to commit themselves.)

Health care reform was also a central element of Clinton's welfare strategy. On the one hand, the availability of health coverage through Medicaid has been one of the most powerful magnets drawing people to welfare, since so many low-paying jobs carry no health insurance. Universal coverage would vastly increase the incentives for the low-paid to stay at work. At the same time, as we have seen, the hope was that a universal national health program explicitly geared to easing middle-class anxieties would relegitimize government and the welfare state for voters who had been drifting to the anti-government side of the political debate. In the end, of course, health care reform failed badly because of the public anxieties that Clinton had set out to ease. It was a large irony: A program designed to reduce public mistrust of government fell victim to that very mistrust.

Clinton's new message in all these areas was, in theory, highly popular across most of the Democratic Party because it promised to solve so many electoral problems at once. As Ruy Teixeira argued, the elements of the party "most hostile to the image makeover" that Clinton proposed had already been "thoroughly marginalized" by the time of the 1992 Democratic Convention. Yet when it got down to specifics, much of what Clinton proposed was resisted by one or another wing of his party, heightening the factional warfare among them.

Theoretically, for example, New Democrats accepted the need for health care reform (if only to curb spiraling costs) while Old

Democrats understood that welfare reform was a necessity after the campaign Clinton had run. But throughout 1993 and 1994 the two wings of the party fought a kind of shadow battle that focused on whether health care or welfare reform should come first. Not surprisingly, the New Democrats argued that welfare reform would be easier to pass and more popular and should thus take the lead. More liberal Democrats argued that welfare reform, opposed by many in the Congressional Black Caucus, would split a Democratic Party that needed unity if it were ever to win the health care battle.

This debate was just one of many debilitating battles that created the catastrophic breakdown at the end of the 1994 congressional session. A Congress that had begun its work with such energy—passing a mandatory family leave law, a measure to make voter registration easier, a national service plan, a large deficit-reduction package and the North American Free Trade Agreement—deadlocked at the end and left a large pile of legislative business undone. Reforms in health care, welfare, lobbying laws and campaign finance were only the more prominent victims of the end-of-session slaughter, the focus of the next chapter. The Republicans had much to do with this, consciously pursuing a strategy of obstruction that paid off brilliantly at the polls. But it was Democratic division that made that strategy possible.

III

The factional divisions that characterize Democratic politics in the 1990s owe something to the older lines of demarcation in the party that are now so familiar—"McGovernites" versus "Scoop Jackson Democrats," southern conservatives against northern liberals, well-to-do "reformers" versus working-class "regulars." But the truth is that those categories are in large part obsolete. The split between the military doves who rallied to George McGovern and the hawks who gathered to the late Henry Jackson was entirely a product of the Cold War. The battles between them had lasting effects—many Scoop Jackson Democrats are now Republicans—but are largely irrelevant to current policy disputes. Differences between southern conservatives and northern liberals remain—witness the converts the Republicans won in the Senate and House after the 1994 elections—but they are vastly narrower than the splits in the 1940s and 1950s between northerners who strongly advocated civil rights and southerners who were militant segregationists. Ardent conservatives are becoming rare indeed in the Democratic Party; many southern districts that once sent conservative Democrats to Congress are now electing Republicans. And the battles between "regulars" and "reformers," the product of machine politics and the reaction against it, are a thing of the past. All the large Democratic machines are dead. In Chicago, a Democratic mayor named Richard Daley governs with wide support among some of the very reformers who spent decades fighting his father. Indeed, it can be argued that insofar as anything resembling machine politics still exists, it lives on in suburban *Republican* bastions, in places such as Nassau County in New York and Du Page County in Illinois.

But the end of these old conflicts has not brought peace to the Democratic Party. The differences now may be more subtle, but they can be just as agonizing. Indeed, the new factionalism can be *more* difficult to manage than the old because many of the splits crosscut each other.

In Congress, for example, one can distinguish at least five discrete groupings of Democrats: southern moderates and conservatives; suburban centrists; urban, labor-oriented white liberals; black and Hispanic members from cities and parts of the rural South (who are also mostly liberals); and a diverse group of western and midwestern Democrats from rural areas. These five groups can produce an almost infinite variety of coalitions, depending on the issue at stake. The suburban centrists tend to be at odds with the pro-labor liberals on trade issues, with the suburbanites favoring free trade on grounds of both conviction and interest. The southern and rural members often split on trade issues, while the black and Hispanic members tend to side with their pro-labor white allies (though not uniformly). Gun control often casts suburban and urban Democrats against their southern and rural brethren, as do farm subsidies. Abortion splits almost all these groups, but the suburbanites tend to be the most pro-choice, while the southerners and urban whites (especially Catholics) provide the right-to-life movement with most of its support in the party. The same division tends to replay itself on other social issues as well.

These categories, of course, are not absolute. Many of the Dem-

ocrats' suburban constituencies are "suburban" by formal definition, but in fact include many of the blue-collar whites who form the
base of union-oriented politics in the cities. House Democratic whip
David Bonior represents just such a district in the Macomb County
suburbs just outside Detroit. He is pro-life, strongly critical of free
trade and very liberal on bread-and-butter economic issues. Democrats who represent the more affluent suburbs are almost uniformly pro-choice on abortion, but can vary a good deal in their
attitudes toward economic questions. Some are old-fashioned economic liberals; others are cautiously moderate on issues involving
taxing, spending and business regulation. What is most striking is
the growing role these suburban representatives are playing in
Democratic congressional politics. As recently as forty years ago, the
congressional party was dominated by southerners and urban machine politicians. Today, no faction has control but the suburbanites
are gaining power and are increasingly important in setting the
party's tone.

The divisions among congressional Democrats would be difficult enough for the party. In theory, at least, they might be man-
ageable because they are based primarily on differences of interest.
Interests can split the differences, especially where money is involved. But money is scarce because of the budget deficit. A few
extra billion for farmers, a few billion for suburban schools and
another few billion for the inner cities might buy a lot of political
peace. Now those "few" billion are hard to find.

But even if the deficit did not lurk to make buying peace so
difficult, the Democrats would still face fierce feuding over ideas,
principles and objectives.

There is always a danger in overplaying the role of ideas in
explaining political outcomes. Democrats lost most of the presidential elections after 1964 for practical and quite specific reasons that
had little to do with philosophy or ideology. Lyndon Johnson (and
Hubert Humphrey) suffered because of a reaction to the Vietnam
War and to civil rights. Jimmy Carter lost in large part because of
high inflation, rising unemployment and an apparent weakening of
the U.S. position in the world, symbolized by the hostage crisis in
Iran. Walter Mondale lost not only because he said he would raise
taxes but—much more importantly—because the economy was
booming in 1984 and many Americans had reason to believe that it

really was "morning in America." George Bush ran to succeed Ronald Reagan in 1988, which just happened to have the second highest growth rate of any year in the 1980s (1984 ranked first). Similarly, many of the low points of the Clinton presidency can be traced to the controversies surrounding Whitewater, the White House travel office, haircuts on Air Force One and an early uneasiness with Clinton's handling of foreign policy. As Michael Dukakis might put it, these controversies owed far less to matters of ideology than to questions about competence.

But Clinton's success ultimately depended on whether he could manage to forge a new intellectual synthesis within the Democratic Party, and this was not easily achieved. As we have seen, Clinton had four stratagems in 1992 that offered practically everyone within reach of the Democratic coalition a piece of what it wanted. For New Democrats, there were social moderation, welfare reform, attacks on "tax-and-spend" policies and "reinventing government." For liberals, African-Americans and urban voters generally, there was a commitment to higher levels of "public investment" (which, for other ears, didn't quite sound like "spending"). For those in the middle class who felt threatened—by government and by foreign economic competition—there was a tax cut and a tempered but emotive economic nationalism. And for almost all of the Democratic groups, there was economic populism that blamed the Reagan-Bush years for advancing the rich at the expense of everyone else. The very breadth of the agenda suggested the diversity of the constituencies to which Clinton was appealing. Their differences reemerged after the election.

In part, the differences owed as much to past loyalties as to substantive issues—the old divisions in the party might have become largely irrelevant, but they still enlisted passions. Democratic liberals were not willing to toss overboard their commitments to the trade union movement, to civil rights organizations and to liberal government as an honorable calling. For the New Democrats around the Democratic Leadership Council, these old commitments were precisely the problem of the Democratic Party—it was being strangled, they argued, by its refusal to challenge unions, civil rights groups and public employees. "Unfortunately," said Will Marshall, the president of the DLC's think tank, "for many Democrats, solidarity, not adaptation, remains the overriding imperative."

   Defenders of the unions and the other traditionally Democratic
groups did not take attacks on their roles lightly. Jeff Faux, president
of the pro-labor Economic Policy Institute, argued that New Democrats

> indulge in the conceit that they alone reside somewhere in
> the cosmos beyond liberalism and conservatism where the
> "national" interest lies. This is humbug. The sanctimonious
> position that *my* interests are "national" while *your* interests
> are special stops common sense political discussion. But per-
> haps that is the point.

Whatever the point was, conversation often was stopped between
the New Democrats and their foes—even if both kinds of Democrats had voted for Clinton. Those on either side of the argument
insisted resolutely that Clinton's triumph had been a victory for *their*
wing of the party and *their* strategy. Faux, speaking for many liberals, argued that Clinton had surely not won because he was "a
credible commander-in-chief," and noted acidly that Clinton had
"spent the campaign avoiding George Bush's call for debates on
morality." Faux asserted that had the unemployment rate in 1992
been 5.5 percent instead of 7.5 percent, "there is little doubt that
George Bush would be president today." Moreover, Faux maintained, "Clinton's message on the economy was unmistakably liberal." Faux went on:

> And after outbidding George Bush with the promise of
> middle-class tax cuts flopped in the early primaries, Clinton
> overruled his DLC advisers and shifted to an emphasis on
> more government investment spending both as a way of jump-
> starting the economy and to create more good jobs in the long
> run. He even argued that closing the investment deficit was
> every bit as important as reducing the fiscal deficit.

   Nonsense, said the DLC Democrats. In an exchange with Faux
in *The American Prospect* magazine, Marshall argued that what had
been crucial to Clinton's victory was his willingness to break with
Democratic orthodoxy and to reach out to groups that felt excluded
by liberalism. "Left-liberals," Marshall contended, dream "of a rain-
bow coalition that pointedly excludes white males." Clinton, by
contrast, "refuses to sentimentalize the poor or condescend to black
Americans by treating them as a monolithic group with one set of

opinions." Clinton, Marshall went on, "stressed economic mobility rather than wealth transfers, took a tough-minded line on crime, welfare dependency, and international security issues, and called for a new ethic of personal responsibility to temper demands for entitlements."

The difficulty with this argument is that fundamentally, both Faux and Marshall were right. Clinton had, indeed, as Faux asserted, run a campaign infused with economic populism and had stressed the importance of public investments. At the same time, he had been careful, as Marshall said he was, to be "tough-minded" on the social issues. It is certainly true, as Faux said, that Clinton could not have won without the economic discontent that made his economic message appealing. But it is also true, as Marshall asserted, that people listened to Clinton because they thought he was accept-able—more acceptable, anyway, than past Democratic nomi-nees—on issues related to "culture" and "values."

Beneath this argument, however, lurked another and more substantive difference that split Democrats: their attitude toward globalism and the new economy. Democrats of the DLC stripe, along with a variety of other interests in the party, asserted strenu-ously that free trade was in the U.S. interest and that there could be no escaping the world economy. Al From, the president of the Democratic Leadership Council, felt so strongly about this that he registered as a lobbyist in order to battle in Congress for the North American Free Trade Agreement. Faux, on the other hand, saw NAFTA as contributing to the long-term erosion of the average American's living standards. The agreement, he said, provided hun-dreds of pages of protections for "those who invest," even as it left defenseless "the interests of those who work." And Faux argued that he and other NAFTA foes were clearly on the side of the very "forgotten middle class" on whose behalf Clinton (and, for that matter, the DLC) claimed to speak. The polls, Faux noted, showed that those who earned under $50,000 a year and had not gone to college had opposed the treaty. The DLC (and Clinton himself) contended, plausibly enough, that the interests of those displaced by freer trade could be protected through aggressive job-training and placement programs. Faux retorted that the DLC fought for NAFTA first, while spending for the training programs had been postponed "to the indefinite future."

The split on trade was not about some small and easily compromised matter. It reflected fundamental differences in view inside
the party over which stance toward the global economy and which
set of policies would most benefit its constituencies. To make matters worse, there was also disagreement over just who would make
up the party's constituency of the future. This disagreement divided
the DLC itself. Whatever his differences with Faux, Marshall broadly
agreed with him that the Democrats needed to target struggling
middle-class constituencies whose interests would surely not be
represented by the pure laissez-faire economics preached by the
Republicans. But Joel Kotkin, another DLC thinker, argued that
Democrats were mistaken in basing their future on those losing out
in the new economy and on their allies in the government. This, he
maintained, was the central strategic mistake of Kathleen Brown's
1994 campaign for governor in California. Brown had started the
campaign with a huge lead over Republican Governor Pete Wilson,
only to lose in a landslide. Her problem, said Kotkin, was that she
had spoken far more for those who feared economic change than
for those who hoped for and anticipated growth and better times.
The future, for the Democrats and the country, continued Kotkin,
lay with "the most affluent baby boomers working in the new
information-age economy, particularly in metropolitan urban regions." Noting that since the late 1980s the number of business
owners had eclipsed the number of union members, Kotkin argued
that the Democrats' new target constituency "is made up largely of
people whose experiences have been shaped in the post-
bureaucratic economic environment of the late 1980s and early
1990s." These voters would be "natural supporters of a program
built around political decentralization, deregulation, free trade and
public secularism." Kotkin's was a minority view within the Democratic Party—and, to a significant degree, within the DLC itself. But
his views illustrated the breadth of the argument within the party,
and thus the depth of the divisions.

Kotkin aside, there certainly was (and is) common ground on
which both New and Old Democrats might stand. It was ground that
Clinton desperately searched for in the second part of his term.
Even if they disagreed on free trade, the two wings of the party
broadly agreed that economic change could, as the New Democrat
Marshall himself put it, have "jarring effects . . . on some US work-

ers, industries and communities." Both sides agreed on the need for far-reaching intervention in the economy to enable workers to switch to better jobs and acquire more education and new skills. Similarly, although Faux cast the DLC as being opposed to Clinton's "investment" program, the truth was more complicated. Rob Shapiro, a DLC vice president and a Clinton economic adviser during the 1992 campaign, had been skeptical of some of the more expansive plans of his candidate's most liberal advisers. But he, too, advocated substantial new government spending. After the election Shapiro pushed what he called a "cut and invest" program to reduce government subsidies and tax benefits to business that both distorted the market and primarily benefited the well-to-do and the established. His list of cuts (especially of tax loopholes) won cheers from many liberals. And Shapiro suggested that some proceeds from his cuts should be spent on new programs to help those displaced by economic change.

But to have even a chance of working, this strategy required a unity of purpose within the administration and among Democrats in Congress. While Democrats controlled both houses of Congress, that unity was simply not there.

IV

President Clinton had a hellish time winning enactment of his 1993 budget because Democrats were divided on both the fundamental issues it raised and the niggling particulars it involved. As the 1992 Democratic primaries demonstrated, the party was torn asunder over the central matter of whether deficit reduction was the most important priority of the moment. Paul Tsongas answered an emphatic "yes!" and organized an entire presidential campaign around this proposition. His success was both surprising and important. At the start of his campaign political professionals universally rated Tsongas as having no chance whatsoever of winning the Democratic presidential nomination. He was helped, to be sure, by the fact that the first major primary took place in New Hampshire, where he was relatively well known because of his service first as a congressman from a Massachusetts district that bordered New Hampshire and later as a United States senator. But Tsongas re-

ceived strong support both in New Hampshire and in later primaries from well-educated, upper-middle-class voters who fully shared
his view that the large deficits of the Reagan years were not simply
bad policy but also "immoral." Many of Tsongas's supporters, it
should be noted, were well-to-do social liberals who were not looking for much in the way of government benefits. His combination of
a hard line on fiscal issues and liberalism on abortion, gay rights
and assorted other social questions suited them perfectly. When
Tsongas declared, "I'm not Santa Claus," those who had no need for
Santa Claus were especially inclined to cheer.

The most vociferous challenge to Tsongas's overall approach
came from Bill Clinton. Clinton, of course, was careful to agree with
Tsongas that the deficit mattered. But it was not, he insisted, the only
thing that mattered. Clinton argued that his support for a middle-
class tax cut, a "down payment on fairness," was the clearest difference between himself and Tsongas. He also asserted that taking
steps to improve middle-class living standards was as important as
balancing the federal books. As Tsongas's position strengthened
after the New Hampshire primary, Clinton's attacks sharpened.
Clinton, the New Democrat, pulled out the oldest weapon in the old
liberal arsenal, accusing Tsongas during the Florida primary of wanting to impose cuts on Social Security.

Three things are notable about the Clinton-Tsongas clash. The
first is that Clinton won, suggesting that while Tsongas's arguments
about the deficit had the ability to mobilize a substantial chunk of
the electorate and win respectful attention, they did not represent
the dominant view inside the Democratic Party. Tsongas often
charged that Clinton's economic ideas "came out of the polling
data." But this was a revealing criticism: It suggested that while
Tsongas might win admiration for candor and courage, the ideas he
was proposing were not necessarily popular. Also significant was
the fact that although Clinton was, in many respects, running to
Tsongas's "left"—Clinton, as the "populist," often defended government and argued that fiscal prudence was not all that mattered—
Tsongas tended to do a little better among self-identified "liberals"
and Clinton a little better among "conservatives." In the main, however, those labels had very little predictive power in the 1992 primaries because they were largely irrelevant. This was not George
McGovern against Hubert Humphrey and George Wallace. Many

voters who called themselves liberal were defining themselves in terms of cultural issues on which Tsongas was certainly very liberal, arguably more so than Clinton. Many voters who said they were conservative were really populists with traditional views on cultural issues but rather expansive in their views of what government should do, especially if the subjects were Social Security and Medicare.

But a third factor in this contest proved significant in the long run. Clinton himself was much bothered by Tsongas's criticisms of him as a "pander bear." He resented that editorial writers and others cast Tsongas as a "truth teller" while he was characterized as a politician searching for votes. Clinton complained to his political advisers that the middle-class tax cut (which probably helped him win votes) was hurting him because Tsongas had been so successful in using it to portray him as an opportunist. Clinton's reaction at the time made him very open—once he was elected—to arguments from deficit hawks that he should junk the middle-class tax cut in favor of a full-scale assault on the deficit.

It should be noted that the other Democrat to survive through the primaries, former California Governor Jerry Brown, was not much involved in the fiscal debate between Clinton and Tsongas. His themes were quite different. Brown attacked the corruption of the political system and limited the size of contributions to his campaign to $100 or less. He also struck chords of economic nationalism, especially during the Michigan primary, warning of the impact of the global economy on American workers and their hopes for the future. In a sense, Brown was Ross Perot with a leftward tilt, a more consistently egalitarian message and a more culturally liberal persona. He shared Tsongas's view of Clinton as a political opportunist, but shared Clinton's suspicion of Tsongas's agenda as too pro-business and too little concerned with the costs of inequality. The power of both the Tsongas and Brown messages presaged Perot's influence. Perot effectively married Tsongas's concerns about the deficit with Brown's attacks on politics as usual. It proved to be a potent mix.

Clinton won the fight with Tsongas, and later with Perot (and Bush). But the battle over the priority of deficit reduction was not over at all. Indeed, the early post-election battles within the Clinton inner circle might be seen as a replay of the Clinton-Tsongas debate.

Clinton's appointees were far more centrist and deficit-conscious than Clinton's campaign advisers. The deficit hawks included Leon Panetta, Clinton's budget director and later his chief of staff; Alice Rivlin, Panetta's deputy and, later, his successor; Treasury Secretary Lloyd Bentsen; and Robert Rubin, who led the White House economic team and later succeeded Bentsen. They insisted that much of what had been said in the campaign had to go, including the middle-class tax cut. New spending programs would be hard to finance. Unpopular measures such as an energy tax needed to be considered. It was striking that the main proponents of a more "populist" alternative, with less pain for the middle class and perhaps even some tax cuts, were the president's political consultants. Indeed, Bob Woodward reports that Rivlin was openly critical of the stance Clinton had taken during the campaign, discounting the president's claim that the deficit estimates had suddenly mushroomed after the election and that this had come as a surprise to him. "Bill Clinton knew where this deficit was going," Woodward quotes her as saying during a meeting with campaign adviser Paul Begala. She added, according to Woodward's account, that "the campaign" had been "dishonest" and its statements on the deficit "untrue."

Ultimately, the arguments inside the administration were resolved largely in favor of the deficit hawks, though deficit reduction still did not go as far as many of them would have liked. Clinton's first and critical budget was a peculiar mixture of boldness and caution. Its boldness lay in an outright repudiation of the central premises of Reaganomics. Reagan's approach had been based on the idea that prosperity stemmed primarily from the savings and investments of the entrepreneurial class. What was distinctive about Reaganomics had to do not with tax cuts in general, but with cuts in the marginal tax rate—that is, the top rates on the rich. Reward the wealthy with tax cuts, the supply-siders said, and prosperity would follow.

Just as recession and inflation under Jimmy Carter discredited Democratic economics with much of the public, so did recession and high deficits discredit Reaganomics in the early 1990s. This was one area in which Clinton seized his opportunity. Almost all the tax increases in the Clinton plan came from higher levies on the wealthy, with the biggest burden falling on those earning more than $250,000 a year. Nothing else Clinton did so enraged the economic wing of the Reagan right. Oddly, however, Clinton's willingness to raise taxes to close the deficit proved reassuring to a different kind of traditionally Republican constituency—the bond traders, who, initially at least, brought long-term interest rates down. They were especially appreciative of Clinton's support for an energy tax. The bond sellers made Clinton's willingness to support some sort of levy on the middle class a test of his "seriousness" about deficit reduction. Clinton's budget included some of his "investment" programs for Head Start and job training. It also included the big boost in the Earned Income Tax Credit for the working poor. But the need to make deficit reduction such a high priority forced Clinton to be less generous in financing his new initiatives, which made them less visible.

The divisions within the administration on deficit reduction were revealing of the large difficulties Clinton faced. The president had three priorities on taking office, and they were at odds with one another. He needed to cut the fiscal deficit. He needed to reduce the "social" or "investment" deficit—that is, to spend considerable sums on social programs and infrastructure improvements to make up for the decline in such spending during the Reagan-Bush years. And he needed to close the "fairness deficit" by providing some relief to a middle class that felt it was bearing an increasing share of the government's fiscal burden.

No one disputed the need at least to control the deficit. In political terms, Ross Perot's candidacy had suggested that there was a sizable political constituency for deficit reduction. In policy terms, even economic liberals for whom deficit reduction was not a priority acknowledged that continuing streams of red ink would endanger the liberal project by impeding the government's ability to spend money on worthy programs in the future. But many of these economic liberals and self-styled populists argued that the deficit itself was most assuredly *not* the major problem facing Clinton or the country. Far more important were stagnating living standards and social breakdown in the inner city. Public spending, in this view, was desperately needed to solve both sets of problems. The deficit hawks countered that nothing else could get done until the deficit was brought down and that the financial markets would punish the president and the economy if the administration did not take deficit reduction seriously.

This was a novel debate in the Democratic Party, the product of quite new conditions. The party had been split in the past, of course, between fiscal conservatives and big spenders. It had been divided at the beginning of the Kennedy administration between those who wanted to stimulate the economy with tax cuts and those who preferred the stimulation to come from government spending. But the overwhelming balance of opinion among Democrats had been in favor of Keynesian solutions emphasizing economic growth and discounting the impact of modest deficits. What changed, of course, was the *size* of the deficit. Many Democrats who had been comfortably Keynesian two decades earlier argued that even Keynesian doctrine could not justify continuous deficit spending during *good* economic times. Ronald Reagan did many things to damage the Democratic Party. By creating such a big deficit, he guaranteed a running, divisive argument within its ranks.

It's worth pausing for a moment over the importance of Clinton's decision to abandon the middle-class tax cut and his subsequent decision (after the 1994 debacle) to revive it. When Clinton announced his rejection of any tax reductions, the response among commentators, editorialists and opinion leaders was largely positive. Broadly, their view was akin to Tsongas's and Rivlin's: that Clinton's tax-cut promise had been irresponsible in the first place and that deficit reduction needed to be his top priority. Stan Greenberg, Clinton's polltaker, argued that abandoning the tax cut might not be so politically damaging, since few voters had actually expected Clinton to keep his promise.

But even accepting for the sake of argument that abandoning the tax cut was the more "responsible" course, those who urged Clinton to do so were ignoring central elements of the politics of the 1990s. First, precisely *because* of the public's cynicism about politics and government, it was more than ever important for politicians to keep high-profile promises (and voters always remembered what politicians said about taxes). House Republicans showed they had learned this lesson when they cast their 1994 promises as "a contract" with the voters and set out on the first day of the 1995 congressional session to begin passing it. If anything, cynicism about government was even more dangerous to Clinton than to the Republicans, since he proposed to use government so aggressively. Rather than using voter cynicism ("he's not going to do it anyway") as an excuse for abandoning the tax cut, Clinton needed to strike a strong blow against such cynicism.

Moreover, Clinton's overall task of rebuilding a national consensus behind Democratic objectives was crucially concerned with shifting the way middle-class voters viewed the party's attitude toward taxes. Clinton's campaign commercials, after all, hammered repeatedly on the theme that he was not a "tax-and-spend" liberal. Clinton's program was designed to tell middle-income voters that he understood their sense that they were paying too much for too little. As a matter of tax justice, it was also true that the largest shifts in the tax burden had fallen precisely on middle- and lower-middle-income voters. In the late 1970s and early 1980s, inflation had driven those with modest incomes into ever higher tax brackets. During the rest of the 1980s and early 1990s, increases in regressive federal payroll taxes and in state and local levies wiped out any relief these voters got from the Reagan tax breaks—and in many cases, left people paying more than they had under Jimmy Carter. Democrats would never sell government to such voters until they had begun to deal with their legitimate anxieties about taxes.

Finally, few in the administration realized that Clinton assumed a special burden to keep his middle-class tax-cut promise after he reaffirmed his campaign pledge to end the ban on gays in the military. The battle over gays in the military was bound in all events to create controversy and to cost Clinton some political support. But it should be recalled that the main element of Clinton's tax pledge had been a promise to create a tax credit for children in middle-class families. The tax pledge had combined fiscal policy with elements of a "pro-family" policy. By at least trying to keep his promise to gays while almost cavalierly breaking his pledge to middle-income families with children, Clinton inadvertently sent exactly the wrong signal about his priorities to the middle-income voters whose support he had once courted so ardently. His task of coalition management was already difficult enough without this added burden. It was inevitable that Clinton would have to revisit the tax cut, though doing so only after the Republican landslide vastly reduced its political benefits and yet again raised questions about Clinton's constancy.

But the tax cut seemed the least of Clinton's problems as he battled in 1993 to forge a consensus on budget issues. For if divisions within the Clinton ranks on fiscal questions were bad, splits among Democrats in Congress were worse. Many self-described deficit hawks who in theory sided entirely with their allies inside the administration rejected many of their proposals in practice. Interest group and regional politics turned out to be far more important than theory. For example, Senator David Boren of Oklahoma was a stout fiscal conservative who had supported Tsongas during the primaries. Yet deficit reduction was not so important to Boren, who represented an oil-and-gas state, that he was willing to support the administration's energy tax. He fought it and won. Many southern and rural legislators also touted themselves as friends of deficit reduction. They were not, however, particularly friendly to reductions in farm programs or in subsidies to rural electric cooperatives or in help for veterans. In principle, all deficit hawks (and many liberals) could agree that Clinton was quite right in suggesting that the well-off among the elderly should pay slightly higher taxes on their Social Security checks. This, after all, was the sort of cut in "entitlement spending" that all deficit hawks claimed to support in theory. But in practice, many Democrats (and almost all Republicans) resisted any steps that might offend a large constituency that also turned out at election time in disproportionately large numbers.

One could multiply examples of where the rhetoric of self-described deficit hawks was belied by their behavior on specific issues. The point was that no matter what voters and politicians said about the deficit, any Democratic president who sought to confront it was bound to discover that almost any specific policy that inflicted loss on any important constituency would create many enemies. Even at the heart of the anti-deficit constituency (one thinks here, for example, of Boren and some of the southern conservatives), there were always particular interests that trumped the general interest in balancing the books.

For a Democrat who had run on promises to expand government in certain areas, the problem was all the greater. Voters who supported Democrats tended to do so because they wanted government to do *more* about social and economic problems. Yet the deficit wars forced Clinton to do much less than he had promised by way of government "investment." Clinton's opponents saw him raising taxes and not cutting the deficit enough. His supporters saw him as not delivering on the spending programs he had made sound so attractive. Worse still, any move toward either objective—more deficit reduction or more spending—might create yet more peril for Clinton. There was no evidence that Republican-inclined voters would ever give Clinton much credit for cutting the deficit. There was little evidence that hard-core deficit hawks (in the electorate or in Congress) would be satisfied with anything less than a wholesale assault on Social Security and Medicare. Yet neither could advocates of a spending (or, as they preferred, "investment") program demonstrate that the country had the political will for new, large-scale government activism. When Clinton proposed an economic "stimulus" package of new spending ahead of his budget, all the pressures were to defeat it. There were no mobilizations, no mass marches to urge Congress to vote the spending up. It was said at the time that the stimulus was too small to have much effect or win much support, yet big enough to seem like "big spending." That may have been true. But there was little evidence that a bigger stimulus plan would have fared better—and much evidence that it would have fared worse. The problem Clinton faced with both the stimulus plan and the budget was that the country wanted the government to act and didn't trust it to act well or competently. It wanted "change," but feared change if change meant higher taxes or cuts in important programs. There was, to be sure, a constituency that might support a wholesale assault on federal spending. But that constituency was precisely the one that had *not* elected Clinton. To have hopes of creating a political majority, he needed support from some in the anti-deficit ranks. But every overture he made to these voters threatened to alienate those who had sent him to the White House in the first place.

Clinton had some ideas about how to solve this problem. They involved big reforms—in health care, in welfare, in trade and in the way politics and public life were carried out. With the exception of trade, all of Clinton's big ideas fizzled, defeated by a Congress that was, nominally at least, in the hands of his own party.

□ 5 □

THE FAILURE OF REFORM:

Health, Welfare and the Political Education of Bill Clinton

GUARANTEEING HEALTH COVERAGE for every American was supposed to solve the Democrats' core political problem. The idea was simple, seductive and, it seemed, sensible.

To the extent that middle-income Americans were turned off to government, their alienation could be explained by government's failure to do much for them. The big federal spending programs, for Social Security and Medicare, went to the elderly. That was fine, but such programs were of little immediate benefit to middle-class people not yet of retirement age. Moreover, Americans now *expected* these benefits and thought their parents were *entitled* to them. Here was the paradox: Precisely because Americans thought these entitlements were legitimate, they refused to see them as entitlement programs. The polls made clear that the public thought of entitlement programs as programs to which *other* people felt entitled, and weren't. Mostly, they thought of people on welfare. So those polled were all for "entitlement cuts" until they learned that these were largely reductions in programs for the elderly. Then they turned against them.

The result was that members of the middle class came to believe that almost all government spending went to someone other than themselves. This had not always been the case. During the Great Depression so many Americans were in need that it was

118

relatively easy to build support for government spending (though it's worth noting that even in 1940, Roosevelt and the New Deal secured only 53 percent of the popular vote). After the war the GI Bill helped confer middle-class status on millions of returning soldiers. Eisenhower, though fiscally quite conservative, launched a huge and popular public works program (by building the Interstate Highway System) and ushered in student loans (through the National Defense Education Act). But during and after the 1960s—and despite the enactment of Medicare—middle-class Americans felt they were paying more to the government and getting less.

Having the federal government ensure that all Americans would have health care coverage seemed a perfect step toward reconnecting middle-class voters with Washington. After all, many in the middle class—and even in the upper middle class—feared that they were in danger of losing some or all of their health benefits. While universal coverage would be especially beneficial to Americans with lower incomes, the benefit promised was, literally, "universal"—it would go to the wealthy, the middle class and the poor alike. And the program was one designed precisely *not* to offer new benefits to welfare recipients, since people on welfare were already covered by Medicaid. This put Democrats on the right side of the welfare debate: Why, they could ask, should welfare recipients get health coverage when so many working people could not afford it? The Clinton inner circle was broadly (though not universally) united behind this proposition, but the main architect of this view was Stan Greenberg, Clinton's pollster. He was much taken by the arguments in favor of "universal" programs offered by sociologists Theda Skocpol and William J. Wilson. The evidence of American history was that programs designed for the poor alone were poor programs that quickly lost political support. Programs offering general benefits to wide populations—Social Security was example number one—were both good policy and politically sustainable. Universal health coverage would be the next step. It would represent the logical completion of the New Deal project and also the beginning of a new effort to relegitimize government in the eyes of "the forgotten middle class." Health care reform could also be seen as fitting into Clinton's broader concept involving government's obligation to respond to changing economic circumstances. With the global economy and technological change threatening the

living standards of so many families, government could at least
ensure that those who worked achieved certain minimum levels of
security, including medical security.

The logic seemed impeccable, and many conservatives were
afraid that the gambit would work. In declaring that Republicans
should resolutely oppose Clinton on health care, Republican strategist William Kristol argued against the plan not so much because
it wouldn't work, but because, at least as a political matter, it might
work all too well for the Democrats. "It will relegitimize middle-
class dependence for 'security' on government spending and regulation," Kristol wrote in one of his widely circulated memos. "It
will revive the reputation of the party that spends and regulates, the
Democrats, as the generous protector of middle-class interests. And
it will at the same time strike a punishing blow against Republican
claims to defend the middle class by restraining government." Kristol's memo accorded so closely with Greenberg's overall strategy
that the pollster quoted it at length in his book. The opportunity for
the Democrats and the danger for the Republicans lay in the fact that
once enacted, a universal health program would almost certainly
prove to be widely popular, as it is in Canada, Great Britain, Germany and virtually every other industrial democracy. But the program would have to be enacted first.

II

Many things went haywire once Clinton embarked on trying to
fulfill the promise of the Greenberg theory. Much of the discussion
since the death of the Clinton plan has focused on faulty strategy, the
complexity of the proposal's design, the ungainly task force that set
about writing it, the failure to deal early on with potential congressional allies and make compromises when they were achievable, the
problems raised by Hillary Rodham Clinton's role and the like. From
the Clinton side, there were complaints about the large sums spent
by interest groups on advertising that distorted the proposal; the fact
that promised Republican filibusters in the Senate meant the plan
would need an unachievably high sixty votes to stop the talking and
secure passage; and the failure of moderate Republicans and conservative Democrats to respond to compromise proposals that em-

bodied much of what they had once embraced. There was certainly raw politics: Republicans, sensing a chance to win the 1994 elections, were increasingly disinclined to hand Clinton any legislative victories as the voting got closer. Even before that, Clinton had begun to lose the popular confidence he needed to sell the plan because of the incessant attention given to the Whitewater land deal at the beginning of 1994. And as the recession ebbed in 1993 and health-cost inflation declined, interest in reform dropped among voters, business leaders and opinion makers alike. Had Clinton been in a position to push a plan through in 1993, as Senate Majority Leader George Mitchell and many of the plan's architects wished, some version of health reform might have passed.

All these factors were important, and the weight given one or another of them depends on one's perspective, political proclivities and attitudes toward Clinton himself. It is undoubtedly true that the decision of the Republican Party leadership not to cooperate with Clinton on behalf of any proposal was decisive in preventing even modest steps forward. The Republicans knew that even if they were the prime movers in defeating reform, the Democrats and especially Clinton would take the blame. In a brilliant and candidly self-critical article on the death of the health care proposal, Paul Starr, an author of the Clinton plan, argued that "the Republicans enjoyed a double triumph, killing reform and then watching jurors find the president guilty. It was the political equivalent of the perfect crime."

But what deserves particular attention here are the difficulties *Democrats* had in reaching anything like consensus behind a coherent health proposal. Their failure was certainly fatal to their chances in the 1994 elections. And the factional interplay on the issue offers yet another example of why the Democratic Party and liberalism face such difficulties in sustaining a governing majority.

On health, as on budget policy, the Democrats confronted crisscrossing lines of conflict. While a majority of Democrats in Congress and within the Clinton administration backed the idea of comprehensive reform and universal coverage, their view was by no means universal. As important a figure as Treasury Secretary Lloyd Bentsen, for example, had long favored what came to be known as "incremental" reforms aimed first at rationalizing the insurance markets. Such measures, which in theory at least had broad Republican support, included proposals to bar insurance companies from denying individuals health coverage because of "preexisting conditions" and to permit people to hold onto their health insurance when they switched jobs. Some incrementalists also proposed linking insurance reforms to subsidies that would permit more Americans with modest incomes to buy insurance.

Critics, however, noted that such reforms did little to control the cost of insurance and by no means guaranteed that individuals could continue their coverage. For example, insurance companies that wrote policies for those with preexisting conditions might charge so much for them that few would be able to afford coverage even if it was available. If the government put ceilings on what the companies could charge for the already sick, this would spread the cost to other policies. That, in turn, would raise the general cost of insurance high enough that many among the young and healthy would decide to take their chances and drop out of the system. This had been the experience with such reforms in states that had tried them, such as New York. Nor did guaranteeing "portability" guarantee coverage. A $30,000-a-year worker who moved from a job with employer-paid health insurance to one with no such coverage might simply not be able to afford the $4,000 (or more) annual tab that buying private insurance for his or her family involved.

Other incrementalists argued that the primary problem with health care concerned the overall cost of the system, which was rising far more rapidly than other prices. This camp contended that the government's first job was to find ways of clamping down on health care inflation. Only after this was done could the country hope to afford universal coverage. Many in the business community, especially large businesses with generous health plans, were interested in reform primarily for what it might do to curb increasingly prohibitive expenses. Chrysler's Lee Iacocca often pointed out that the cost of workers' health care per car amounted to more than the cost of all the steel that went into making it. It was a line Clinton often used.

Allied at times with these incrementalist camps were the New Democrats at the Democratic Leadership Council. As we have seen, the DLC's partisans believed that passing welfare reform and "reinventing government" measures needed to take priority over comprehensive health care reform. For the DLC, Clinton's overriding need was to demonstrate early on that his approach was different from that of an earlier generation of liberals. Clinton could do this by changing welfare and slashing the bureaucracy. He would then have the credibility and public support to grapple with the health care problem. For the DLC Democrats, health care reform looked like a quintessentially Old Democratic program. Was it not, after all, Ted Kennedy who had championed this cause throughout his political life? The DLC also noted, accurately, that health care reform had not been an original Clinton priority during the 1992 campaign. He was pushed into offering an initial version of a health care plan only after Senator Robert Kerrey, one of his rivals for the Democratic nomination, made health care his central issue during the New Hampshire primary. Ironically, Kerrey later abandoned Clinton when the going got tough during the health care battle of 1994.

The dominant view in the party was closer to Kennedy's than to the DLC's. Universal health coverage had been a central Democratic cause since the days of Harry Truman. Democratic veterans such as Representative John Dingell of Michigan had been pushing for universal coverage since their earliest days in Congress (and, in Dingell's case, his congressman-father had done so even before his son had arrived on Capitol Hill). Those who supported comprehensive coverage guaranteed by government had strong arguments to make on both policy and political grounds. They noted that only by including all Americans "inside the system" could there be any hope of getting a real handle on costs. As it was, hospitals and doctors caring for uninsured patients often shifted the costs of doing so onto the insured, raising the price of both care and insurance. The way to stop cost-shifting was to cover everyone. Politically, voters were less concerned with the intricacies of health care financing than with making sure that they and their families had coverage and care that they could afford. Reform would be a complicated and at times painful process. Getting popular support for the cause required that consumers/voters get something out of it, and that "something" would be "health care that can never be taken away."

But agreeing on the principle of universal coverage was quite different from winning agreement on how it would be done, what procedures would be covered, how it would be paid for and how costs would be controlled. Optimistic reformers failed to realize going into the fight that there were good reasons universal coverage had eluded the grasp of even the nation's strongest and most skilled Democratic politicians. The American health care system, partly because of its strengths and partly because of its size, had created a dizzying array of competing interests. The constituencies that generally supported reform—organized labor, big business, hospitals, nurses, some physicians' groups, managed care providers, the elderly and the uninsured—had radically different goals and concerns going into the debate. Absent the most careful coalition management, almost any plan committed to paper was bound to split potential allies. On the other hand, those most skeptical of reform—small-business organizations, many insurance and drug companies, the majority of physicians and individuals who could afford the best coverage—needed only agreement on killing off any proposals that were not to their liking.

Making a difficult situation even worse was the fact that the politicians and policy specialists who supported a comprehensive approach were sharply at odds over how best to proceed. Broadly, the reform camp was divided into three groups: those who essentially favored a government takeover of health care financing through a "single payer" system similar to Canada's; those who favored "managed competition" under which the government would guarantee universal coverage through private insurers and allow market competition among insurers and providers (mostly health maintenance organizations) to force down prices; and those who supported a mixed system. Some in this last camp favored managed competition generally but saw a need for a substantial government role to control costs and guarantee that consumers (and not just employers) would have some opportunity to choose among health plans. Others favored what they called a "pay or play" system under which employers would be given a choice of providing coverage directly or paying into a government plan that would offer it.

Overlapping these differences were disagreements over how expanded coverage should be paid for. There were only four basic choices: Individuals would pay for their own insurance; employers would pay; the government would pay; or, as in "pay or play," there would be some combination among these three. The single payer advocates were willing to shift the cost of health care onto the government and pay for the plan with new taxes. Some advocates of the various approaches to managed competition were also willing to see the government pay a large share of the costs. Others argued that given the country's anti-tax mood, it was unrealistic to expect that a big tax-increase measure could be passed. Since a majority of Americans already had most of their health costs paid by their employers, why not simply enact an "employer mandate" that would require all employers to contribute something toward the coverage of their employees? This would build on the current system and create fewer incentives for employers to slough off their costs to the government or to individuals. But many Democrats in Congress had close ties with local businesspeople (especially those who owned smaller businesses). Many responded to the fears of small business that mandates would put too big a burden on them and might force layoffs. It must also be said that—at least until the 1994 elections— many Democrats raised substantial sums from small-business owners and business groups to finance their campaigns.

But if the government did not pay and if business would not pay, then the burden of universal coverage would fall back on individuals. And part of the problem health reformers were trying to solve was the increasing difficulty so many individuals and families were having in affording health insurance coverage.

The Clinton plan was designed to split as many of these differences as possible. It can thus be argued that the Clinton proposal itself was both brilliant and fatally flawed from the outset. The designers of the Clinton proposal thought theirs was the ultimate "centrist" approach because it took into account the criticisms that each camp in this miasma of ideas and interests directed against the others. Clinton rejected the single payer approach as too radical and politically unsustainable. Total government financing of health care was simply not possible in the current climate and might not, in any event, be the most practical approach at a time when many European governments were searching for alternatives to their state-centered systems. This led the administration to embrace the concept of managed competition. Insurance would continue to be provided by the private sector, and the move away from "fee for service" medicine and toward health maintenance organizations would be given a modest push forward. But individuals would still have the right to "fee for service" coverage if they were willing to pay a little more (which, after all, was the system many private companies were already adopting). Some narrow tax increases (for example, on tobacco) could be sold politically to finance expanded coverage. But broad-based tax increases were out. That meant that the administration would rely on the employer mandate—plus cuts in Medicare and savings in Medicaid—as the primary way of financing reform. But to prevent the burden on business from rising too high, individuals would have to kick in a share, and small employers would have their obligations limited through subsidies. Because managed competition on its own was an untested idea, the competition would take place under a cap on insurance premiums imposed by government so that costs were held down. And to expand individual choice and not simply leave it to employers to pick a health plan, the design created purchasing "alliances" among employers and individuals that would broadly pool costs and offer individuals at least three options for coverage.

As Starr, one of the authors of the Clinton plan, has pointed out, the administration made other crucial choices. For example, it was decided that the plan would offer a large package of benefits and not simply minimal coverage. The idea here was twofold: to make the plan as attractive as possible, especially to those who already had reasonable health coverage, and to create room for bargaining. If the costs of the plan had to be pared down, there would be much to cut without endangering a basic package of benefits. Because the plan was partly financed by cuts in Medicare, the administration decided it needed to offer some new help to senior citizens. So it included a new prescription drug benefit for seniors and a program for home-based health care.

On paper, the plan had a lot going for it. Single payer advocates would eventually come around because the plan did what they most wanted done: create a national system of coverage for everybody. Managed competition advocates would certainly appreciate the central role the plan accorded to their concept. The elderly would rally to new benefits. Business would see how the creation of a more rational market would cut down costs—and the majority of businesses that already provided their employees with coverage might see their costs drop. The employer mandate meant that labor unions would no longer have to bargain for employer-paid health coverage; the right to such coverage would now be enshrined in law. The uninsured would finally have coverage and the already-insured would have the security of knowing that they would never go without it.

So much has been made of the administration's mistakes on the health care issue that it's important to understand that the choices it made were, in principle at least, rooted in rational policy and political logic. The fact that the administration made tactical blunders should not obscure the fact that it was at least trying to bridge the gaps among potential allies.

In the end, its largest single mistake was precisely the assumption that those gaps could be bridged easily. Far from embracing Clinton's design, advocates of managed competition (notably represented in Congress by then-Representative Jim Cooper) came to see the Clinton proposal as involving too much government and not enough competition. Moreover, as Starr pointed out, advocates of a more market-oriented approach such as Cooper and Rhode Island's progressive Republican Senator John Chafee were reluctant to come up with enough financing to pay for their proposals, which required large government subsidies. At the other end of the spectrum, single payer advocates alternated between criticizing Clinton for timidity and praying that his gambit would succeed. True, the Clinton calculation about where the single payer supporters would end up proved largely right—single payer champions such as Senator Paul Wellstone of Minnesota were largely loyal to the president at the end. But supporters of a single payer plan never had enough votes to offer. Clinton was always going to be forced back to the center (as at least some single payer supporters such as Wellstone understood from the beginning). To make matters even more difficult, some liberals in the party (notably Representative Pete Stark of California) sought a different halfway house from the one proposed by Clinton, based on the old "pay or play" idea. They suggested that many of the uninsured could be picked up by a new government program which they labeled "Medicare, Part C." This resembled a single payer plan in that it would be a program totally organized by the government—and critics of the proposal such as Republican Representative Dick Armey saw it as "an intermediary step to socialized medicine." But the "pay or play" proposal would not, at least initially, have enrolled anything close to a majority of the country.

The inability of the forces represented by Cooper and those

represented by Wellstone to come together behind the Clinton plan pointed to the deep ambivalence within the Democratic Party about markets and government. In theory, all Democrats agree on the basic proposition that markets work, but need to be tempered by government intervention. But one Democratic camp is so skeptical of the marketplace that it is inclined to see market-oriented innovations (such as managed competition) as inimical to the party's philosophy and interests. Wellstone, for example, teamed up with the American Medical Association in support of legislation designed to limit the ability of private health maintenance organizations to regulate the practice of doctors. The ability of HMOs to impose such regulation was essential to their ability to control costs. But Wellstone and many on the party's left feared extending such power to private corporations and hoped for a time when doctors would opt for a government single-payer program to escape the exactions of Prudential and Aetna. At the other end of the spectrum, Democrats such as Cooper were so skeptical of government that they came to see the Clinton effort to balance the competing interests as a wholesale sellout to the forces of state coercion. The competitive aspect of Clinton's plan did not loom nearly as large to Cooper and his allies as the parts that relied on government. As the health debate reached a conclusion, Cooper moved away from his own ambitious design toward increasingly fragmentary and cautious efforts to cut deals with quite conservative Republicans.

Clinton, of course, also scaled back his hopes at the end, but his efforts at compromise came too late. Large forces outside his party had already moved against reform. In the early stages of the fight, interest groups that supported reform spent more of their time lobbying to make sure that their particular benefit was included in the package than in fighting for the general principle of universal coverage. The Clinton effort to buy their support with a generous coverage package bought little until it was too late.

Big business fell off the reform bandwagon, fearing the Clinton plan might end up doing little in the way of cost-cutting while obstructing corporate efforts to shed health expenses and move toward HMOs. The behavior of business groups was revealing. As political analyst John Judis pointed out in an important article, businesses that provided coverage for their employees—and most did— had a large interest in reform along at least the general lines Clinton proposed. They had much to gain from a plan designed to curb health care inflation and to spread the cost of coverage more broadly. As it was, businesses that paid for insurance were subsidizing businesses that did not. Many business leaders and their organizations—importantly, the National Association of Manufacturers and the Chamber of Commerce—were initially prepared to work with the president. But the politics of health care shifted rapidly. The voices opposed to all reform, from large and small business that provided little or no coverage for their employees and from parts of the health industry itself, came to dominate the business side of the debate. In an odd role reversal, conservative Republican leaders *lobbied* the business *lobbyists.* They successfully brought much pressure to bear that ultimately forced even business groups sympathetic to reform to back off. The Clinton administration made the work of these Republican foes of health care easier by failing early on to build a bipartisan alliance for action. The lack of Republican support only highlighted the fears of even reform sympathizers in business that the final product would prove too bureaucratic for their taste. The lessons here for a longer-term Progressive project are important. As Judis argued, "without a business community moderately supportive of social reform, little is possible."

In the end, small-business groups and smaller insurance companies led the fight against the plan and won an audience from many average voters who no longer understood in the midst of all the combat just what Clinton was trying to do—and what his proposal might end up doing to them. In particular, many Americans came to see a plan that was consciously designed to *expand* their health choices as restricting them. The notion that government might actually give people more rather than fewer options was simply not credible in an age when government was so mistrusted. The administration may also have inadvertently hurt itself on this score. By focusing so much on "universal coverage," it deemphasized its efforts to increase choices and control costs.

Finally, it can be argued that the Clinton plan foundered on the one issue that is so crippling to any sort of government innovation in the 1990s: Who pays? What became clear as the health battle ground to its sad end is that *all* the options for financing health care reform were closed off. Given the deficit, piling new and unfunded

costs onto the federal treasury was out of the question. New revenues generated by economic growth (the way Democrats had financed many innovations in the past) were needed simply to lessen
the *increase* in the federal debt. New taxes (except on unfashion-
able tobacco consumption) were deemed a political impossibility.
And in the end, the employer mandate was killed not just by Republicans, but also by moderate and conservative *Democrats.* They
judged that an ambivalent public's appreciation for a health bill
would be far less potent at election time than the anger a mandate
would arouse among business leaders.

But when counting time came during the 1994 elections,
moderate-to-conservative Democrats such as Cooper and Oklahoma's Dave McCurdy suffered from the general loss of confidence in
the Democrats no less than their more liberal colleagues who had
been willing to support taxes or mandates to get a health care bill
passed. In the end, the health care issue hurt the Democrats twice
over. As Stan Greenberg argued, the Republicans' success in por-
traying the Clinton plan as a "big government" enterprise played
directly into their overall strategy and undermined Clinton's efforts
to reshape the Democrats' image. But at least as significant is the fact
that the failure to enact a health care bill demonstrated that the deep
fissures within the Democratic Party—divisions heightened by the
constraints of the deficit—made it difficult for the party to deliver
on what it promised. Clinton overcame these divisions, barely, on
the budget, salvaging a one-vote victory. On health care, he never
even got a vote. And on welfare reform, he did not put forward a
plan in time for it to get serious consideration.

III

Hopes that Clinton could deliver welfare reform before the
1994 elections foundered early. It might be argued that the program
died in Clinton's first budget, offered in February 1993, when
Clinton's emphasis on deficit reduction led him to slash funds des-
ignated for his welfare project. This meant that once Clinton's welfare task force went to work, it could not simply devote its energies
to fashioning the new welfare system. It spent months searching for
budget cuts to finance the training and job creation that Clinton had

promised as part of his effort to move welfare recipients to work. Many of the cuts the task force examined were in existing programs for the poor. Each proposed reduction aroused intense opposition within the heart of the Democratic Party. Liberals charged that Clinton was putting new burdens on the backs of the poor in order to finance a program that was putatively designed to help them. Most of the cuts were rejected in the end, but the lengthy process of finding adequate funds pushed introduction of the plan into 1994, which turned out to be too late for it to have any chance of passage.

Even without this delay, welfare had already lost out to health care as a top administration priority. There is a certain irony to this, since in the grand design of Clintonism, as we have seen, health and welfare reform could be seen as fitting together in a neat package. Both proposals appealed to middle-class voters, the first aimed at serving their interests, the second at embodying their values. Both sought ways for the government to reinforce the value of work and especially to try to strengthen the standing of the working poor and the lower end of the middle class. But the fact that both proposals ended up as weapons in the factional strife inside and outside the administration spoke mountains about the difficulties confronting the Democratic Party. Liberals in the party argued that health care reform would be impossible if welfare reform came first. Moderates and conservatives said health care reform would not happen if welfare reform were *not* done first. The administration sided with the liberals, including most of the party's congressional leadership. And in the end, of course, Clinton won *neither* welfare reform nor health reform. The health care crack-up took so long to play out that almost nothing else happened by the time the 103d Congress closed shop.

Despite the priority given the health bill, some in the administration still harbored slim hopes in the spring of 1994 that welfare reform might slip past the health care wreckage. This would have required a unity of purpose that was utterly lacking on the issue within the Democratic Party. Democrats disagreed with one another on both political and substantive grounds. Many party liberals saw welfare reform as dangerous because it would arouse the anger of the party's poorest constituents, especially African-Americans and their representatives in Congress. The Democrats could not hope to

sustain themselves if they attacked their own political base. Advocates of reform, on the other hand, saw it as essential both to
securing the tentative support Clinton had received from white
middle-class swing voters and to expanding his coalition to include
many who had voted for Ross Perot. In their hearts, many liberals
really did see the Clinton welfare proposals as pandering to popular
hostility to poor African-American single mothers. Advocates of reform—including some in the party's liberal wing—insisted just as
passionately that the existing welfare system was such an obvious
failure that reforming it was, quite simply, the only option. It should
be noted that for all the fears of liberals that Clinton was pandering
to anti-welfare sentiment, the major architects of his proposal included two of the most important *liberal* advocates of a reformed
system, David Ellwood and Mary Jo Bane, both assistant secretaries
at the Department of Health and Human Services. It was symptomatic of the crossfire in which the administration found itself that
Ellwood and Bane were frequently under simultaneous attack from
their old liberal friends for pushing reform at all and from conservatives for allegedly undermining the cause of "real" reform.

The difficulties on this issue were underscored by divisions
even within the Democratic reform camp itself. When Clinton took
office, Senator Daniel Patrick Moynihan, the party's long-standing
expert on welfare, cheered the president's interest in and knowledge of the subject. True, he had qualms about Clinton's approach.
Having pushed the last effort at pro-work welfare reform in 1988,
Moynihan preferred to build on the 1988 act, which included work,
job-training and education requirements but no two-year cutoff. But
what ultimately infuriated him was the low priority he saw the
administration giving the issue he cared about most passionately.
Having finally reached the chairmanship of the Finance Committee
with Lloyd Bentsen's appointment as Treasury secretary, he had
reason to look forward to the culmination of his lifelong effort to
change the welfare system. He had particular reason for satisfaction,
since many liberals had come around to his view, especially on the
role of family breakdown in creating a "tangle of pathologies." This
satisfaction dissolved into anger when the administration assigned
welfare reform a lower priority.

There were also fierce fights within the administration itself.
Some allies of the Democratic Leadership Council—represented on

the welfare task force by Bruce Reed, who had played a major policy role during the 1992 campaign—worried that the plan's work requirement might turn into a large guaranteed jobs program. But more liberal members of the task force such as Ellwood feared that unless long-term job guarantees were included in the plan, the basic covenant it embodied—continued assistance in exchange for work—would be broken. But Reed and Ellwood agreed, and insisted, against other administration antagonists, that the two-year cutoff could not be compromised. Only this would send the signal that Clinton had kept his promise to "end welfare as we know it" and establish a new moral basis for public assistance.

This idea did not go over well with many liberals in Congress, led on this issue by Representatives Bob Matsui and George Miller of California. Ironically, Matsui emerged as one of the administration's leading critics on welfare after leading the way for Clinton in the battle for the North American Free Trade Agreement. Matsui and Miller introduced their own welfare reform proposal which, like Clinton's, included substantial new spending for education and training, but pointedly did *not* include the mandatory cutoff of recipients after two years on the rolls. At the heart of Matsui's argument was that Clinton's plan, like the even tougher Republican proposals, threatened the living standards of the children of welfare mothers. "My goal is to make sure that we don't come up with a piece of legislation that will hurt children," Matsui said at a congressional hearing in July 1994. He sharply criticized administration officials for engaging in "hot rhetoric" in discussing reform and was particularly harsh in his treatment of Ellwood. Ellwood had recently argued that the problem with the welfare system was that it did nothing for the poor but give them checks: "We have a welfare system that is basically in the check-writing business." Matsui said at the hearing, "I don't think David Ellwood would have gone before a group of senior citizens and said Social Security is a big check-writing machine. That's politically incorrect. But it's easy to attack welfare recipients that way."

In fact, *the whole point* of Social Security was to write checks—to pensioners who had already done a life's worth of work, and contributed to the system. The welfare system, in principle at least, was never intended to be a permanent benefit or pension plan. It was supposed to offer temporary help to people in their

working years who were facing hard times. But Matsui's anger reflected a fear, widespread among liberals, that Clinton's rhetoric
had opened the way for more radical proposals from the Republicans. The president also faced challenges from his right, both from
within his party and from the Republicans. Representative Dave
McCurdy and a group of conservative Democrats, for example, introduced an alternative to the Clinton bill that resembled it in many
respects but was somewhat more stringent.

As things worked out, these intramural debates among Democrats proved academic. Since welfare reform did not come close to
passage in the 103d Congress, the initiative fell to the Republicans.
The Republican proposals of 1995 were breathtakingly radical when
seen in the context of the 1994 debate. The bills passed in the
House and Senate slashed federal spending for the poor and ended
the federal government's "entitlement" guarantees. Liberals who
opposed Clinton would have been overjoyed to pass his plan as an
alternative to the Republican proposals of a year later. Clinton himself moved steadily closer to the Republicans on the issue, to the
fury of Moynihan.

Few issues were more revealing of the difficulties inherent in
Clinton's balancing act. Clinton came to office with a clear sense of
where he was seeking to move liberalism and his party. Democrats,
he insisted, would not abandon their commitments to the poor.
Programs to give the welfare poor a chance to enter the workforce
would be expanded. These commitments were in keeping with the
party's liberal traditions and would, presumably, satisfy its liberal
constituencies. But Clinton accepted the middle class's moral critique of existing welfare policy—that it was insufficiently conducive
to work and had helped sustain (if not create) a multigenerational
class of impoverished young mothers and children raised in one-
parent households.

In light of Clinton's failure during his first two years to get this
message across, it is striking how closely his view correlated with
where most Americans stood. A bipartisan study of public attitudes
toward welfare conducted in November 1993 concluded that Americans were disgusted with the welfare system, rating its performance
well below that of the country's systems for education, health care
and taxation. (Welfare was seen as on a par with, and as bad as, the
criminal justice system.) But the poll also found that Americans

were critical of the welfare system not only because it "encourage[d] dependence" but also because it "fail[ed] to provide sufficient help for people to make the transition to self-reliance." The poll, conducted jointly by Peter D. Hart Research Associates, a Democratic firm, and American Viewpoint, a Republican research company, found that by a better than five-to-one margin, Americans were willing to spend *more* money on a reformed system if doing so would help move people off the welfare rolls. Had a public debate on welfare policy been fully joined, Clinton would have had a decent chance of winning. But that public consensus was not reflected in Washington, and Clinton later fled some of his own principles by embracing Republican proposals he had rejected earlier. The Democratic debate was haunted by old ghosts, real worries, divergent electoral calculations and genuine philosophical differences. On welfare, as on health care, the party gridlocked itself. It therefore opened the way for a sweeping new Republican approach whose purpose was not to improve and strengthen the federal welfare safety net, but to abolish it altogether.

IV

Three other issues—one involving success, the second involving failure and the third a success that amounted to a failure—complete the portrait of Democratic disarray during the first two Clinton years.

The big success story of 1993 was congressional approval of the North American Free Trade Agreement, which tore down trade barriers with Mexico and opened up a new market that included the United States, Mexico and Canada. Victory on the agreement won Clinton acclaim that went far beyond popular concern with the NAFTA itself. At the beginning of the battle, most Americans knew little about the agreement and were not much interested in whether it passed or not. The agreement did, however, greatly concern organized labor, which feared it would lead to a flood of jobs to Mexico and put downward pressure on American wages. It was of great importance to businesses, which saw Mexico as a large potential market and had already begun building factories there under earlier agreements easing import rules near the border. The issue also mattered to policy elites who saw the struggle over NAFTA as a test of the U.S. commitment to free trade. For free traders, victory on NAFTA was essential. For critics of NAFTA, the issue was one of whether the country would put open markets for business above the interests of its workers and the environment.

Precisely because the issue mattered so much to policy elites, Clinton's willingness to take a strong stand gained enormous attention. Because the elites overwhelmingly favor free trade, his stand against some of the constituencies that had elected him—primarily organized labor—won him the sort of extravagant praise to which he was unaccustomed. Typically for his first two years, Clinton had earlier found himself under sharp attack from the same elites for *failing* to make NAFTA an important enough priority. NAFTA enthusiasts said that Clinton had allowed support for the accord to slip, especially within the Democratic Party. But this only made Clinton's victory on NAFTA seem all the more significant. He had "bucked the odds" and "come from behind" to win this triumph for open markets.

It also helped—in the short term if not the long—that the administration decided to take on Ross Perot, the champion of the Anxious Middle. In a debate on CNN's *Larry King Live,* Vice President Al Gore dispatched Perot, whose clichés about the "giant sucking sound" of jobs flowing south to Mexico were not an answer to Gore's carefully framed arguments about the specific benefits of the agreement. Perot, it's true, spoke for many Americans in expressing fears that American companies would take advantage of the accord at the expense of American workers. But on these points, he preached mostly to the converted. And Gore did himself a world of good with free traders when he pulled out his picture of Messieurs Smoot and Hawley, the architects of a protectionist tariff during the Hoover administration. Standing against Smoot and Hawley was, for the free trade camp, to stand on the side of the angels.

Clinton's position on NAFTA was part of what at least in theory was a coherent approach to the issues of globalization and maintenance of American living standards. The president argued that protectionists and small government Republicans alike were wrong about the emerging economy. The protectionists pretended that the United States could escape the global marketplace. Sharp restrictions on world trade, he contended, would simply hurt living standards in the United States and around the globe. Slower global growth would come back to haunt the United States. But the administration in fact made a kind of double argument aimed at appealing not just to free traders but also to those who hoped the United States could win an edge in global markets. The deal with Mexico, many in the administration insisted, was a response to the rise of trading groups in Europe and Asia. If the Europeans were to have an integrated market, America needed a counter. In the long run, a prosperous alliance with Canada and Mexico could give the United States a new advantage. But unlike the Republicans, Clinton promised protections for American workers through training and transition programs that would let those whose jobs might be lost to NAFTA move to *better* jobs. Clinton's outline was of a happy and wealthy "win-win" world.

For opponents of NAFTA, this was all nonsense. They were especially mindful that the administration was appealing simultaneously to free traders and to those who might be convinced that NAFTA would strike a blow against Japan and Europe. How could both arguments be true at once? But far more important to NAFTA opponents was the fear that the accord would lead to an export of well-paying jobs to a country with low wages and an intimidated trade union movement. Mexico's lower environmental standards would become a magnet to companies seeking to escape the stricter rules of the United States. Clinton had pledged to add stricter environmental and labor standards to the agreement negotiated by President Bush. Clinton, said his critics, had settled for flimsy improvements. He had been quite willing to use appeals to economic nationalism in the campaign when they might win him votes. He had abandoned them, said his foes on the left, once he was in power.

It can be plausibly argued that NAFTA was not as important as either its supporters or opponents claimed. It was never clear that the movement of jobs to Mexico, already substantial before the accord, would accelerate significantly after it was approved. The agreement did include certain protections for the North American market. It was reasonable to contend, as NAFTA supporters did, that the global market was destined to draw lower-skilled jobs from the United States in any event. Better that such jobs go to America's neighbor than halfway around the world—especially since that neighbor, if its standard of living remained low, was destined to ship workers, legal and illegal, across a long border that would always be hard to patrol. But this modest view of NAFTA's impact flew in the face of the large moral and rhetorical investment that each side made in the battle. It was entirely understandable that the issue provoked such passion.

The voting on NAFTA crisscrossed party lines. In the crucial voting in the House, some conservative Republicans responded to the nationalist arguments of Perot and commentator Pat Buchanan, creating a strange alliance against NAFTA—parts of the right wing, organized labor, environmental groups and Ralph Nader and his organizations. Clinton, in the meantime, won over a mix of conservative Democrats and mainly suburban liberals to the cause of the agreement. But the central fact is that a large majority of Republicans, led by Newt Gingrich, voted *for* the agreement, while a majority of Democrats voted no. Included in the anti-NAFTA camp were some of the Democrats' most important congressional leaders, notably majority leader Richard Gephardt and majority whip David Bonior.

The NAFTA vote was indeed a victory for Clinton, but the battle underscored the deep chasm the global economy had created within the Democratic Party. The Republicans, historically the protectionist party, were in the main comfortable with embracing free trade and the global market. This was the logical view for the party of free markets and limited government. The Democrats, on the other hand, were badly torn precisely because their faith in the market went only so far. Anti- and pro-NAFTA Democrats, including Clinton, broadly agreed that free trade and free markets without some worker protections were unacceptable. But pro-NAFTA Democrats made the calculation that the global market was inescapable and ultimately a promoter of growth. The anti-NAFTA Democrats took a kind of "slippery slope" view: that free trade could not be given a priority, in this or any other agreement, over the more tangible issues of living standards and environmental rules. The point here is that Clinton's position, though defensible and lying within the Democrats' free trade tradition, was in fact divisive for his party. Republicans were torn to some degree by trade issues, but they were broadly committed to the same *system,* the largely unregulated free market, which logically entailed free trade. Democrats were committed to a *goal,* an expanding living standard for low- and middle-income workers. But there were wide differences within the party over how that goal could be reached, where and how much the government should intervene, and whether the whole globalization process was primarily benign or menacing. Trade issues brought all these arguments to the surface.

Many of the same arguments (and alignments) were reproduced when Congress finally ratified the General Agreement on Tariffs and Trade at the end of 1994. On the GATT agreement, Gingrich played matters cagily, holding up a vote until after the election to make sure he did not alienate the protectionist and nationalist rump of his party. But he ultimately sided again with Clinton and the forces for free trade, once again helping the president score a "victory." Here again, it was a victory that broadly advanced the Republicans' free market agenda while sowing divisions in Democratic ranks.

The sad irony for the Democrats is that both NAFTA and GATT were issues left over from the previous Republican administration. On many trade issues, the party stood united. Indeed, in 1995, Clinton won loud applause from critics of free trade (and even from some Republicans) for threatening tough sanctions against the Japanese auto industry in an effort to pry open Japan's markets. But while particular trade fights might give the president a chance to stand up for American interests in a visible way, the broad battle over GATT and NAFTA forced a general declaration of principle, and it was on principles that the trade issue divided Democrats. For the longer run, these could prove more important than divisions on welfare or health care—to the party itself and to the prospect for a new Progressive program. Ultimately, the shape of economic strategies aimed at lifting living standards at the middle and bottom of the economy depend on fundamental choices about America's relationship to the global market. Clinton has placed his own bet on freer trade, but a large part of his party has not.

V

The Democrats might have limited their losses among Perot's supporters on trade had they delivered on the other set of issues that so animated this constituency: reform of the way Washington worked. But the Democrats were again torn, this time less along the lines of ideology than of interest and seniority.

As a practical matter, Democrats ought to have welcomed political reform—meaning primarily the reform of lobbying and campaign finance laws. To the extent that the Democrats are, to one degree or another, committed to the interests of the less-well-off and to the idea that the marketplace needs to be tempered and regulated by government, theirs is the party that in the long run will always come up short in the contest for campaign donations. The Republicans are committed to the interests of the well-to-do *on principle,* meaning that they believe that higher taxes on the wealthy and heavy regulation of business are morally unsound—violations of personal liberty and antithetical to rapid economic growth. One need not be a Marxist to see that a party with such views is bound to do well in raising money.

But partly by historical accident (and also through the hard work and skill of some political entrepreneurs), the Democrats—particularly in the House—found themselves doing very well in the race for political money throughout the 1980s and early 1990s. By managing to hold onto control of the House of Representatives in the 1980 Reagan victory, Democrats created a beachhead of power which they converted into a mighty money machine. Under the leadership of then-Representative Tony Coelho, the Democratic Congressional Campaign Committee became expert at shaking money from nearly every interest group and business that needed favor and protection—or even mere neutrality—on Capitol Hill. As Brooks Jackson documented in his fine book, *Honest Graft,* Coelho had a valuable commodity to sell: the idea that Democrats, having held onto the House in the worst of times, were likely to maintain control there forever. Anyone who hoped to do business with the permanent Democratic majority needed to get right with it by contributing to the DCCC and to needy Democratic candidates. To the bounty they traditionally raised from organized labor, the Democrats added millions from business groups that, under other circumstances, would have been giving to Republicans. This system worked not only for the "D-triple-C," as the Democratic Congressional Campaign Committee was known, but also for individual candidates, especially but not exclusively committee and subcommittee chairs.

House Democrats were reluctant to tamper with a system by which they had done so well. Younger members, closer to the anti-Washington mood in the country and further from the chairmanships that carried with them so much fund-raising power, pressed for action. They argued that Perot supporters and other fed-up voters needed a tangible sign that Democrats were willing to break with business as usual. But older members thought they understood their own interests better. Clinton, who strongly attacked special interests, lobbyists and the ways of Washington in 1992, decided against pushing hard for early passage of political reforms. Democratic congressional leaders asked him not to, and he decided that their support for the rest of his program took priority.

The death of campaign reform was yet another striking example of how Republicans took advantage of Democratic problems to kill a bill they didn't like while leaving Democrats responsible for the crime. Democrats had long argued that the true test for campaign reform would be the partial replacement of privately raised contributions with public (i.e., government) money. A public financing system has long been used in presidential campaigns, and it has worked rather well. The Republicans said this amounted to "taxpayer-financing of politicians." Their real test for reform involved curbing or eliminating political action committees. Organized labor had pioneered PACs, but they were now the norm for most large companies, many small ones, and a slew of trade associations and interest groups. The Republicans had never liked labor PACs—Thomas E. Dewey made the CIO's PAC a major issue in his 1944 campaign against Franklin Roosevelt—and increasingly disliked the tendency of business PACs to give disproportionately to Democratic House incumbents. PAC reform became the Republican bottom line.

This proved important, because under the Senate's filibuster rules, it takes sixty votes to shut off debate and the Democrats were short of a filibuster-proof majority. To win over a crucial handful of votes from moderate and progressive Republicans, Senate Democratic leaders agreed to severe restrictions on PACs as part of a reform package. House Democrats were initially unwilling to take this step and passed a different bill. The two competing Democratic reform bills languished for most of 1994 as House Democrats re-

jected serious compromise on the PAC issue. By the time a compromise limiting the PACs was reached near the end of the session,
it was too late. Democratic delay and gleeful Republican obstruction
had produced an end-of-session train wreck. Nothing passed. Killed
in similar fashion was a bill severely limiting the amount lobbyists
could give members of Congress in gifts—a measure that enjoyed
almost universal support in the electorate. By failing to reach agreement in time, Democrats let the Republicans kill a popular proposal
that would have subjected Congress to the same rules it imposed on
private employers. Having worked to defeat the measure to deny
Democrats credit for it, Republicans were pleased to make essentially the same bill a first order of business when they took over
Congress in January 1995.

The ironies of the Democrats' failures on political reform were
multiple and large. The young reform Democrats who had struggled so hard against the older members to pass these bills were,
disproportionately, the victims of the Republican victory in 1994.
These younger members, such as Shepherd and Fingerhut, had well
understood the dangers they would confront if the Democrats failed
to act as a reform party. The fact that they were proven right was
little consolation when they lost their seats.

And the very political action committee system the Democrats
had worked so hard to preserve was transformed by the 1994 results
into a bulwark for the new *Republican* majority. The Coelho strategy,
after all, was premised on selling the notion that Democrats would
be in power in the House forever. Business groups that had far more
in common with Republicans had given to Democrats for self-
protection. But once the Republicans assumed congressional dominance, incumbency and self-interest worked to reinforce the natural
Republican leanings of these groups. Even before the 1994 results
were known, Gingrich and other Republican leaders showed what
the new world would look like, bringing Coelho-style pressure to
bear on the PACs and other established Washington givers. They argued that Republicans were on the verge of winning and would remember who had been with them before the votes were counted—
and who came later. Much of the "late money" in 1994 went
Republican, giving them a crucial edge in the close races that determined who would control Congress. The trend against the Democrats accelerated after the election. A study by the weekly Washington

newspaper *The Hill* in May 1995 found that since the election the ten most generous business political action committees had contributed four times as much to the Republicans as to the Democrats. In 1994 these same corporate PACs had tilted toward the Democrats. "Before, business gave to the party in power," said Craig Veith, a spokesman for the National Republican Congressional Committee. "Now these PACs are giving to the party that reflects their own philosophical underpinning."

By failing to enact political reforms, Democrats thus lost all around: They handed a crucial campaign issue to the Republicans, they helped defeat some of their most promising younger members, and they worked to preserve a system of political finance that would work against the party's long-term interests.

VI

But of all the issues Clinton sought to confront in the 103d Congress, the matter of crime proved to be the most agonizing. The president, in fact, did sign a crime bill in 1994. But the Republicans were enormously successful in compromising even this victory. It can be argued that the Republicans' success in temporarily derailing the crime bill was crucial to everything else that led to their 1994 victory. By pushing the battle for the crime bill into the late summer, the Republicans jammed up the rest of the legislative agenda and hurt Clinton on every other issue, including health care. And by muddying the public's perception of what the crime bill did, the Republicans robbed the president of a large chance to transform the Democrats' image on an issue that had been hurting them since the 1960s.

The crime bill was, in many ways, *the* classic Clinton-style New Democratic compromise. On the one hand, it contained severe new penalties—including a large new list of crimes that would be punishable by death. But it also contained a ban on assault weapons and a great deal of spending. In its final version, the bill contained $30 billion in new federal spending over five years that gave a little to every constituency. Just under $9 billion of that went to putting 100,000 new policemen on the streets in "community policing" programs, involving more cops walking neighborhood beats. There was also $7.9 billion for building new prisons and boot camps. Another $4.4 billion went for drug treatment and crime prevention programs, especially for youth programs in inner cities. ("Midnight basketball" became the Republican shorthand for all of the prevention programs.) Feminists won provisions from what had been called the "Violence Against Women Act." Included in this section were $1.6 billion, the largest sums going to assist prosecutors in establishing units to take action against family violence and sexual assault.

Clinton put much rhetorical muscle behind the crime bill, on the theory that one of his central tasks was to still public fears that Democrats were "soft on crime." But he also sought to shift the crime debate away from Republican terrain. Yes, he would say, the country needed to be "tough" on crime, but it also needed to be "smart." The "smart" part of the bill spent money—on the cops and prisons and prevention programs. Crime was ultimately a state and local responsibility, the president would say, but the federal government could surely help by providing resources. The bill itself might be seen as an embodiment of the balance of political forces Clinton was trying to achieve. Conservative Democrats were pleased with the tougher penalties, including the expanded use of capital punishment. Liberals who opposed the new death penalties strongly supported the prevention package, especially since so much of the money in it would likely help inner-city neighborhoods.

The final product was easily parodied as a politically inspired mishmash. Noting that Clinton had often criticized "the brain-dead politics of both parties," *Newsweek* columnist Joe Klein called the bill a *compendium* of brain-dead notions. Most of the new federal penalties would do little to affect street crime. The death penalties were there more for emotive than rational reasons. And the "prevention package" included a mix of sound ideas and untested programs, many of them added to satisfy various constituencies and individual members of Congress. Still, the bill did keep a central Clinton campaign promise—to pay for 100,000 more cops—and sought to balance punishment with prevention. Politically, Democrats figured the bill could only help them.

But in the first two years of the Clinton administration, even seemingly foolproof ventures managed to fall victim to accident and miscalculation. The crime bill might have passed long before the summer of 1994 but for a controversy involving the Congressional Black Caucus. Members of the caucus had long insisted that the death penalty was not only wrong but also unfairly applied, with African-Americans receiving a disproportionate share of the death sentences. The facts were actually less clear. Black defendants were subjected to the death penalty in about the same proportion as they were defendants in murder cases. So critics of the death penalty took their case one step further, arguing that the identity of the *victim* influenced death sentences unfairly, with black-on-white murderers receiving a disproportionate share of death sentences. Even the figures on this were equivocal. But members of the caucus insisted for months that the crime bill include the provisions of the "Racial Justice Act" which permitted defendants to use sentencing statistics to challenge whether state or federal death sentences were being imposed in a racially discriminatory way. The proposal was easily parodied as "death penalty quotas" and never had a chance of enactment. But negotiations between the administration and the caucus dragged out, pushing off action on a bill that was seen as a political necessity. The controversy over the Racial Justice Act suggested that even when Democrats were in overwhelming agreement on a course, some line of division would emerge to stop action.

With the election nearing, the Republicans seized new openings to stop the Democrats from establishing a muscular image for crime fighting. Their attack was two-pronged and, in electoral terms, very sophisticated. On the one hand, they argued that the bill was insufficiently tough, spent too little on new prisons and was larded with "pork" and "social programs." In fact, it was hard to imagine a more draconian set of penalties, and some of the programs the Republicans attacked as "pork" (such as "midnight basketball") had actually proven effective in communities around the country. But there surely was pork in the bill, and, in any event, the public was already inclined to doubt the Democrats' toughness but not their dedication to pork. The charges stuck enough to deflate the Democrats' claims about the bill, even though polls showed that most of its provisions were popular.

At the same time, the Republicans assailed the bill's gun-control provisions, guaranteeing that gun control would play a large role in the fall campaign. The Republicans thereby ensured that the Na-

tional Rifle Association and the rest of the gun lobby would make it
its business to teach the Democrats a lesson. Large majorities favored gun control, but supporters of gun control rarely used the
issue to determine how they would vote. But for many of gun
control's opponents, it was the only issue that mattered.

The crucial event was the 225–210 House vote on August 11,
1994, blocking the bill on a procedural motion. All but nine Republicans voted to kill the measure. The defeat was played widely in the
media as a triumph for the Republicans, and it was. But it would
have been impossible without the defection of two streams of Democrats. Ten African-Americans voted the motion down, most of them
arguing that the bill's death penalty provisions had rendered it
unacceptable. Their votes alone could have saved it. A larger contingent of conservative and rural Democrats also voted against it,
mostly to oppose gun control.

Democrats had put in years of work to write and pass a bill that
would cure them once and for all of the deadly "soft on crime"
disease. Clinton and leading congressional Democrats had invested
hugely in the measure. In the end, the president compromised on
the bill's spending provisions to win enough moderate Republican
votes for passage. But for the purposes of the 1994 elections, it
didn't much matter. Democrats had known for years that they
needed to change their party's image on crime. But when the time
came, they just couldn't get the job done right.

VII

The 1992 elections had offered the Democrats a historic opportunity to prove that they could govern. The economic cycle had
blessed them in 1992 as it had not in 1980. This time the Democrats
could use a Republican recession to discredit Republican economic
ideas and then claim credit when the economic cycle turned upward again. In Bill Clinton, the party had a leader who had thought
more clearly and creatively than most about how the party needed
to change. He would ensure that Democrats were seen as representing the "mainstream" values of hard work, family, personal
responsibility and public order. And he would deliver tangible benefits to the crucial constituencies in the working and lower middle

classes. In shorthand, he would pass welfare reform and a crime bill, institute a national health system and reform a corrupted Washington.

But he and the congressional Democrats did not deliver welfare or political reform—and his crime bill "victory" meant little. To the extent that he had definition in the public's mind on social issues, it came not from his powerful rhetorical defense of personal and family responsibility in his Memphis speech, but from the fight over gays in the military. Nor was he able to deliver a health care bill, which might at least have satisfied the Democratic Party's core constituencies and motivated Democratic turnout in 1994.

Just as revealing is where Clinton proved most successful. His largest achievements—free trade and deficit reduction—were, at bottom, *conservative* achievements. Yet they were conservative achievements that won him no political payoff among conservative constituencies. In pushing through his trade agreements, Clinton relied on Republican support and split his own party. This won him almost no support among corporate leaders who badly wanted both NAFTA and GATT. A 1994 *BusinessWeek* poll found that only 15 percent of the country's chief executive officers rated Clinton's handling of the economy as "excellent" or "pretty good," 85 percent rated it "fair" or "poor." Asked if they would support Clinton for reelection, only 9 percent of the CEOs said yes, 87 percent said no. On the other hand, the president's support for free trade cost him enthusiasm within the labor movement, and sharpened the attacks on him from further left and also from Ross Perot. What had been one of Clinton's most powerful issues, the insecurity created by the global economy, turned on him with a vengeance. Economically insecure voters who had rejected Bush now rejected Clinton, too. Writing after the 1994 elections, Jeff Faux, president of the Economic Policy Institute, noted that the Clinton Democrats might inadvertently have aggravated those insecurities and frustrations by repeating over and over that workers would have to work harder, retrain themselves, switch jobs. Many workers, Faux observed, did not like this new treadmill and resented being told that they weren't working hard enough—"that *they* are the problem." No wonder the Republicans' claim that there was nothing wrong with America that couldn't be solved by a tax cut sounded so soothing.

Embracing deficit reduction, in the meantime, brought Clinton and the Democrats almost no credit, either in the electorate or among deficit hawks. The polls suggested that few voters believed that Clinton had reduced the growth of the deficit. They saw only that the deficit was still there. Voters did, however, remember that the president had junked the middle-class tax cut. And because the deficit put such pressure on all new initiatives, Clinton had little to show in the way of promising new programs. Many of them were there—the school-to-work job apprenticeship program, some new job-training programs, some reforms in education. But they were funded at levels so modest that voters could be forgiven for not seeing them at all.

At the same time, the Democrats were simply not ready for the renewal that the party required and the discipline that governing demanded. Congress continued to operate under essentially feudal rules that ceded control of various patches of policy to long-serving committee and subcommittee chairs. The party's various factions struggled to defend particular regional, group and programmatic interests for reasons that had nothing to do with philosophy. This made the task of reordering the federal budget a nightmare. Conservatives in the party argued that Clinton's transformation did not go far enough: They attacked his health plan, even though it made many concessions to the market, and even though national health insurance had been one of the oldest Democratic commitments. Liberals, on the other hand, feared that the Clinton renovation was going much *too far:* They accused the president of attacking welfare recipients, of embracing draconian criminal penalties, of spending too much on the Pentagon and too little on "domestic needs." Some also assailed his embrace of free trade and the priority he had given to deficit reduction. As one Clinton adviser lamented after the 1994 voting, "The only thing the Democratic Party needs is a *Party.*" He was not calling for a bacchanalia; he was saying that Democrats lacked the unity of purpose and the internal discipline to support the claim that they actually were a political party, a coherent political institution with a chance of governing the country. In the 103d Congress, the Democrats were dysfunctional.

The argument presented here can be read, in part, as an assertion that the problem with Clintonism was that, in the administration's first two years at least, it was never really tried. The policy mix that Clinton proposed in the campaign—of social moderation, of active but renovated government, of programs embodying both compassion and personal responsibility, of a federal establishment engaged in the struggle of so many Americans with the rigors of the new economy—kept disappearing from view. New Democrats around the Democratic Leadership Council would say over and over that Clinton had not governed as he had run. They were right, but in ways more complicated than their own analysis would admit. It was not that Clinton had gone from being a New Democrat to being a big government Democrat. He went from being a leader who satisfied the party's various wings to a politician who satisfied none of them. An adept juggler of policies and positions aimed at appealing to the many different kinds of Democrats, he began to drop all the balls at once.

But the deep problems inside the Democratic Party would have made the juggling close to impossible for anyone. At least as important as Clinton's troubles was the failure of the Democratic Congress to treat the various planks of his program as something resembling a "contract" (it had, after all, been the party's electoral platform). Clintonism could work only if all (or at least most) of its parts could be put in place at once: if welfare reform could be *balanced* by health care reform; if deficit reduction could be *balanced* by new investment programs; if relief for gays in the military could be *balanced* by tax relief for middle-income families with children; if freer trade could be *balanced* by intensive efforts at job placement and retraining. When Republicans began blocking programs one by one, they knew exactly what they were doing. Clinton, though a compelling personality, would not make his mark in personal terms, since so many voters held aspects of his personal life against him. He would not do so in foreign policy: Clinton was never fully trusted in foreign affairs, and the almost necessarily hit-and-miss quality of even the best-executed post–Cold War foreign policy making would not galvanize a nation. For Clinton to triumph, he needed to enact his carefully calibrated domestic policies whole. The Republicans prevented this and inherited the Congress.

The fundamental failure of the Democrats, in Congress and in the White House alike, lay in their refusal to take their own campaign rhetoric seriously. The 1992 campaign had been fought explicitly around the country's deep sense of crisis. Over and over,

Clinton spoke accurately about the hard transition the United States was passing through, thoughtfully about the ways in which government action could make the transition easier, movingly about the suffering that would take place in the absence of creative government. The mission that Clinton and the Democrats had undertaken was nothing short of a reinvention of the Progressive tradition, an effort to apply its principles and insights to an era quite different from the times of Progressivism's earlier triumphs, first at the turn of the century and then during the Great Depression. But Democrats, including the administration itself, rarely understood their project in these large terms, or acted with the boldness and clarity required. The renovation effort fell short.

The Republicans, in the meantime, were undertaking their own effort at revival. For most of 1994, the Republicans had little positive to say. Their answers seemed to be mostly old bromides repeated endlessly: low taxes, small government. But in fact, Newt Gingrich and a group of Republican intellectuals thought they did have a response that would work, not only electorally but also philosophically. Beneath all the negativism, the Republicans were undergoing a quiet revolution.

REINVENTING OLD ANSWERS:

The Republicans' Quiet Revolution

IN THE HEAT of the 1994 health care debate, with Republicans ripping President Clinton's plan as a big government monstrosity that would destroy freedom of choice, the Republican National Committee aired a series of television commercials that could not have been more moderate, upbeat or compassionate. The message of the ads was that Republicans, too, cared about those who feared losing their health insurance if they switched jobs or lost them. Flashing from one leading Republican to another, the ads cast the Republicans as the avatars of bipartisan activism.

"Working together, Republicans and Democrats can fix health care," said Oklahoma Republican Senator Don Nickles.

"Without a big new bureaucracy," added Republican House leader Bob Michel.

"Let's get it done," concluded Senate Republican leader Bob Dole.

As short-term politics, the ads were successful. They helped to dilute criticism of the Republicans as heartless obstructionists while casting Clinton as the partisan aggressor. This overall approach worked brilliantly for the GOP. They killed health care, placed the blame on the Democrats—and proceeded to win the 1994 elections.

But the ads, unintentionally to be sure, pointed to a fundamental problem confronting the Republicans in the 1990s: They can, indeed, win cheers and votes by talking against "big government." Americans, as we have seen, have become deeply skeptical about whether government *can* solve the problems that worry them —whether it's capable of doing anything right. But Americans also continue to *wish* that government might be effective and fix a social contract they sense to be broken. So even Republicans have to concede now and again that the federal government may have to do some things. In the health care ad, Republican Senator Trent Lott of Mississippi insisted that to help those worried about losing health insurance, "Congress simply needs to change the law so you can change jobs and keep continuous coverage." When you think about it, that's a breathtaking promise from the party of free markets and a small federal government: *Congress will solve your health insurance problems with a law passed in Washington.* So spoke the anti-government Republicans!

Yet it is undeniable that while the Republicans were helped immensely by Democratic failures, they also engaged in a brilliant effort at reconstruction after George Bush's disastrous 1992 defeat. In only two years they transformed the political landscape and tilted the terms of the debate heavily in their favor. A climate supportive of government activism—fostered by Bush's perceived indifference to domestic problems and the "let's do it" mood that dominated both the Clinton and Perot campaigns—was quickly replaced by an anti-government spirit that was, according to some polls, even stronger than it was in the Reagan years. Potentially deep splits within the Republican coalition, particularly between well-to-do social moderates and less-well-off religious conservatives, were papered over. Divisive issues, notably abortion, were played down.

Republican candidates won votes by using old social issues, especially crime and welfare, and new ones, notably immigration. In 1994 many among the economically hard-pressed, normally a natural target group for the Democrats, either dropped out of the electorate in frustration or voted Republican in protest. To a large degree, cultural explanations for the severe social problems associated with poverty were more convincing to more voters than the economic explanations that Democrats tended to offer. The very poor were seen as being in trouble not primarily because of discrimination or bad economic trends—a shortage of jobs and opportunities—but because of their own behavior. Public attention was increasingly focused on the rise in illegitimacy, the number of "unsocialized" fatherless male children living in female-headed families, and a general decay of values, ambition and discipline.

Most of the mass movements of the mid-1990s were on the right. The best-organized groups included the Christian conservatives and the gun owners. There was also much organizing around movements to limit taxes, shut down immigration and punish illegal immigrants, and impose term limits on politicians. By contrast, the mass movements associated with Progressivism or the Democrats— trade unions, civil rights groups, big-city Democratic organizations—were in decline. And the Republicans moved deliberately and skillfully to harness the anti-Washington, anti-politician sentiment associated with the Perot constituency.

The Republicans reached this point without fundamentally challenging the underlying assumptions of "the Reagan Revolution." On the contrary, their new ascendancy was based on the idea that what voters most wanted was the completion and expansion of what Ronald Reagan had started. But the limits of Reaganism were manifest, and admitted by many conservatives and Republicans. Reagan did not reduce the size of the federal government. The federal deficit ballooned, and the reaction to Republican fiscal policies destroyed Reagan's electoral coalition in 1992 as deficit hawks who had voted Republican for twelve years swarmed to Ross Perot's banner. Reagan's tax cuts for the wealthy, never really popular, did not survive the first year of a Democratic presidency—and indeed, they were already eroded during the Bush years. Republicans, fearful of a populist backlash, did not offer much of a public defense for lower taxes on millionaires. Attacks on government in general remained popular, and that is mostly what Republicans offered. When House Republicans unveiled their "Contract with America" before the 1994 elections, their program came under sustained attack, even from some within conservative ranks, for proposing tax cuts and an amendment to the Constitution requiring a balanced budget without offering any specifics about where they would find the money to achieve their ends. As Republican economist Herbert Stein put it later, the contract "was strong on the need for a balanced budget amendment but very weak on suggesting expenditure cuts to bring the budget into balance." It was not surprising that Democrats pounced on the program as warmed-over Reaganomics (an attack that did them precious little good). More significantly, deficit hawks in both parties denounced the contract for being precisely like the policy that had produced huge budget deficits in the first place. The plan's failure to show how the government might be made appreciably smaller suggested that the Republicans were still far from confident that Americans were nearly as opposed to government as their own rhetoric suggested.

These issues were rejoined when Republicans proposed a balanced budget amendment in the new Congress. House Republican majority leader Dick Armey effectively admitted that political support for deep budget cuts would not be automatic when he argued against a Democratic demand that Republicans outline their path to fiscal balance *before* passing their amendment. "Once members of Congress know exactly, chapter and verse, the pain that the government must live with in order to get a balanced [budget], their knees will buckle." In other words, this was a great idea until people looked at what it really meant.

Moreover, when it served their purposes, the Republicans were quite willing to rely on big government—and not just, as in the ad cited at the beginning of this chapter, rhetorically. In the 1994 crime debate, as we have seen, the Republicans assailed Democratic social spending on crime "prevention" programs. But they also called for a series of tough new federal penalties, many of them for crimes that had traditionally been dealt with solely by state and local authorities. They also proposed creation of new federal prisons to house state prisoners and wanted to mandate that states could use the new facilities *only* if they agreed to tough new federal rules about how prisoners were sentenced. In other words, the party of states' rights and no federal "mandates" was willing to spend a pile of federal money in order to tell states what to do with criminals. Republican Senator Alfonse D'Amato of New York even argued that the federal role on crime should be even *more* far-reaching: "I would like to see this go further . . . to take even greater authority."

Similar inconsistencies tore at the Republicans on the welfare issue. At the beginning of the 1995 congressional session, the Republicans were badly split between those who wanted to send welfare programs back to the states and those who wanted tough rules imposed from Washington *before* any devolution took place. The House welfare bill, cast as an effort to give states more authority, was full of limitations on the states, requiring them to toughen their welfare systems. To Bob Dole's consternation, the Republicans in the Senate were torn among their moderate, conservative and very conservative constituencies over how far to push the welfare system, and where.

This chapter and the next will explore the Republican response to the defeat of 1992. It begins with a brief review of the problems inherent in the conservative ideology that became dominant among Republicans in the late 1970s. It then looks at the modifications Republicans made in their doctrine—and, at least as importantly, in their presentation of it—after Bush's defeat.

What is striking is that until the 1994 elections, the Republicans rejected a wholesale reassessment of their position and sought instead to fashion a kind of neo-Reaganism that would apply to the 1990s essentially the same ideas that had dominated the late 1970s and the 1980s. In broad terms, the Republicans continued to preach that less government and low taxes were the answer to most of the nation's problems. They linked this to a critique of the cultural breakdown allegedly fostered by liberal programs. That sounded familiar enough.

But beneath the surface, important changes were taking place. Even Republicans most insistent on the tactical and philosophical correctness of the Reagan vision understood that divisions in the party over social issues—especially abortion and, more generally, the role of religion in public life—threatened its ability to construct a majority coalition. The response of conservative strategists was to move the party slowly away from some of the more absolutist stances of the religious right and toward a far more libertarian vision. Even strong opponents of abortion, including Ralph Reed of the Christian Coalition, conceded that it was unlikely in the near future that a majority of Americans would support measures to make abortion flatly illegal. So they proposed instead a "gradual" approach that would push for some relatively popular limitations on abortion rights (for example, banning late-term abortions and requiring minors to get permission from their parents before having abortions) while leaving the battle for absolute prohibition to another day. Many advocates of this position did so not from mere political calculation, but on the old-fashioned conservative theory that transforming cultural attitudes was a precondition for transforming government policy. But in this case, principle and political expediency reinforced each other.

Yet Republicans could not afford to ignore the cultural issues and risk alienating the Christian conservatives, perhaps the most important grassroots force in their party. The new strategists, led by William Kristol, Bill Schambra and Michael Joyce, therefore proposed a return to one of the core principles of the original conservative revival in the 1940s and 1950s: the use of libertarian means to traditional ends. Rather than urge massive new forms of government intervention on behalf of conservative values, these neo-Reaganites suggested that the best thing that could be done for traditional ideas and institutions was to *tear down* federal programs and union-dominated city bureaucracies. These they accused of fostering permissive attitudes, dependency, family breakup and all manner of other evils. Their program included shipping welfare (and as many other assistance programs as possible) back to the states. It suggested educational voucher programs to break up the big-city public school systems. It proposed that local governments and school systems be given more leeway to promote values, including religious values, to whatever extent local citizens thought appropriate. As a short-term tactic, this approach worked brilliantly, submerging fundamental differences within the Republican electorate. Anti-tax, anti-government conservatives could embrace the agenda without fearing that the religious right was about to impose its worldview through the powers of the federal government. The harder-edged far right opposed to all forms of gun control, federal environmental regulation and virtually anything else Washington did could also identify with this approach. The religious right, in the meantime, was more than happy to rally to a critique of liberal, big-government "permissiveness." Republicans formed what conservative activist Grover Norquist called the "leave us alone" coalition.

But if the neo-Reaganites were very effective in finding language to address the country's sense of moral crisis, they lacked an effective response to the insecurities created by the global economy and technological change. Promising a leaner government sounded good and had the potential of rallying significant support from an electorate reacting against Democratic failure. But leaner government, on its own, offered no solution to the problems that worried the great share of the electorate in the Anxious Middle.

The more radical message came from Newt Gingrich and his House Republicans. Gingrich, as we shall see in Chapter Seven, broke in important ways with the consensus of the Reagan period (even while paying homage to Reagan). For Gingrich, it was not morning in America. Rather, he emphasized an America "with twelve-year-olds having babies, with fifteen-year-olds killing each other, with seventeen-year-olds dying of AIDS, and with eighteen-year-olds ending up with diplomas they can't even read." Gingrich described what he saw as a crisis in American "civilization." And he took the issues of technological change and the new global economy head-on, arguing that they were not the problem but the solution. For Gingrich, the goal was not to slow down change or take the edge off it, but to *accelerate* the transition into what he called, after the writings of Alvin and Heidi Toffler, "the Third Wave" of civilization, an information age economy.

To an extent unexpected by their critics, the new Republicans in Congress also took on the deficit early, in 1995, proposing to eliminate it in seven years. In doing so, they sought to answer one of the most telling critiques of Reaganism: that it was fine at cutting taxes, lousy at cutting government. True, the bulk of the cuts the Republicans proposed were in health care programs, thus offering a kind of retroactive legitimacy to Clinton's claim that deficit reduction was impossible in the absence of health care reform. (The Republicans, of course, proposed cuts without extending health coverage.) Many of the rest of the cuts came from programs for the poor. Despite problems in the Republican budgets—the House budget cut taxes while, in classic 1980s fashion, postponing the hardest spending cuts to the end of the seven-year period—there was a boldness here absent from either the Reagan or Bush programs. In the mid-1990s the Republicans seemed intent finally on proving Reagan's claim that if the government's "allowance" were cut off through tax cuts, smaller government would inevitably follow.

But in taking the deficit plunge, the Republicans effectively admitted that much of what they had said in the 1980s was wrong: that it was not possible to cut taxes, maintain popular federal programs and balance the budget all at the same time. They forced themselves to face up to decisions they had largely postponed for fifteen years. In important ways, they radicalized conservatism. In so doing, they pushed the country toward decisive choices over how to

deal with the four crises in American politics and how to weather
the great economic transformation.

II

The conservatism that came to dominate the Republican Party
in the Reagan era and after was an amalgam of ideas, a brilliant
philosophical cut-and-paste job aimed at satisfying the various
groups that might come together to produce a national majority.
After World War II two sets of ideas emerged that came to be known
as conservative. On the one side was traditionalism, rooted in an
old-fashioned reverence for family, neighborhood, the values
passed on through generations. This conservatism was pessimistic,
or perhaps realistic, about human nature. It was, in any event, without illusions about the destruction human beings could unleash,
absent the guidance of religion and the constraints imposed by
families and communities.

Traditionalists were critical of modern liberalism because of
what they saw as liberalism's veneration of the national state over
localism, its excessive optimism about human nature and its willingness to let social experimentation run roughshod over settled
values. This traditionalist conservatism, therefore, often supported
free market economics as a better alternative to centralized state
power. Markets could encourage certain virtues honored by traditionalists—prudence, thrift and work. But traditionalists did not
revere the market and could be critical of its workings. Markets
alone did not create values, virtue or social order. "Not many conservatives would be happy to enlist under the banner of one abstraction, Capitalism, against another abstraction, Communism,"
declared the traditionalist Russell Kirk, "or to die, absurdly, for 'a
higher standard of living.' " For traditionalists, those conservatives
who said that adults should be free to trade pornography or vile
videotapes in the open marketplace could not be genuine conservatives. They did not value the truly important things.

The other school of conservatism that arose after the war made
the contrary assertion. These libertarian conservatives were animated less by worries over the destruction of old values than by a
fear of the overweening modern state. For these libertarians, the

market was everything, or almost everything. Some on the right might defend the welfare state as a stabilizing and thus a conservatizing force, but the libertarians would have none of it. For them, the welfare state was simply the early stage of a process that would lead inexorably to the Leviathan of Hitler or Stalin. The surrender of some power to the state in the interest of winning a bit of security was, in the libertarian's view, just the first of many such surrenders. Friedrich von Hayek, the great prophet of modern libertarianism, argued that when democracies attempted central economic planning, they were taking the first steps down the terrible path toward totalitarianism. Planning inevitably centralized power in the hands of a small group claiming special powers based on alleged expertise. For the libertarians, not reverence for tradition but the rights of the individual occupied the hallowed place in politics.

The simultaneous rise of these two fundamental critiques of New Deal liberalism after World War II represented the first cracks in the hegemony of liberalism. Liberalism's popularity had been built on the collapse of the laissez-faire economy in the Great Depression, which discredited conservatism for a generation. The successes of liberal national government in bringing relief during the Depression and in winning World War II assured its ascendancy. By the early 1950s, liberalism was hegemonic, and conservatism was due for a revival.

The contradictory strains of conservatism were able to come together because they shared a common enemy in New Dealism and the large national state it had built. The job of conservative journalists and philosophers was to paper over the intellectual differences between the two sides. This was done brilliantly by the writers whom William F. Buckley Jr. gathered around *National Review,* particularly by Frank Meyer, who coined the term "fusionism" to baptize the linking of traditionalism and libertarianism. Meyer's basic insight saw the United States as, at heart, a traditionalist society. Thus, American conservatives, in what became a talismanic formulation, could use libertarian means to traditionalist ends. If the central government just got out of the way, the basic, traditionalist, commonsense decency of Americans would assert itself. To dismantle big government was to empower family, church and neighborhood.

It's important to note that the "fusionism" backed by Buckley and Meyer did not satisfy all on the libertarian right. The central passion of *National Review*–style conservatives was anti-communism, and this led them to a decisive break with the old-style conservatism associated with the late Senator Robert Taft and other opponents of a global role for American power. The old right, the isolationists of the 1930s, were as skeptical of the military as they were of the rest of government. They saw the aggressive internationalism pioneered by Franklin Roosevelt and later adopted by the conservative Cold Warriors as strengthening centralized state power far more effectively than anything ever undertaken by the New Deal. For Buckley and his allies, this was a secondary consideration: If the world were not saved from heavily armed bolshevism, liberty itself would die. All the conservative and libertarian agitation would become a mere footnote to a horrible and bloody history of Soviet triumph. This break sent many on the libertarian right into the political wilderness for two decades. It was Buckley's synthesis that came to dominate conservative Republicanism. It carried conservatives right through the Reagan Revolution and defined Ronald Reagan's basic assumptions.

It is notable that Reagan's own practice of conservative politics was remarkably free of the resentments and angers that characterized significant segments of the right wing, represented by Joe McCarthy, George Wallace and (depending on what face he was putting on his politics) Richard Nixon. There was no "paranoid style" to Reagan's approach and surprisingly little baiting of his enemies. It was as if he had bought Meyer's optimism about the American people whole and saw little need to appeal to darker impulses. Fusionism worked for Reagan and the conservative movement as long as there was a visible liberal enemy to rout, a national government seen as both a meddler and a purveyor of bad values. It continued to work for a while under Reagan as long as the economy grew and produced "morning in America." That much-derided campaign theme in fact represented much of what fusionism was about. The happy television commercials showed people hard at work, caring for their kids, getting married—prosperity underwriting tradition, or at least what passed for tradition in the 1980s.

But fusionism—Reaganism—finally ran up against terrible limitations. As a philosophy, it posited a happy synthesis and therefore never forced believers to confront the hard questions. In the end, did liberty matter more than virtue, freedom more than tradition? Or was it the other way around? What about abortion? Was this an issue about personal liberty, as so many libertarians would have it, or about right and wrong, as traditionalists opposed to abortion insisted? Where were conservatism's real priorities? In the Reagan years, tax cuts took priority over school prayer and a host of other traditionalist causes. The defense buildup was more important than smaller, more frugal government. If it was a choice between deficits and a bigger military, the Reaganite answer seemed to be: Damn the deficit, build the torpedoes, spend. Winning elections also took priority over seriously trimming the welfare state. If Social Security and Medicare were the price of victory, then the government's two biggest domestic programs would be allowed to grow and grow. And what if the American people weren't as traditional as Meyer thought them to be? What if illegitimacy kept rising under conservative rule, as it did in the Reagan years? What if violent crime went up, as it also did? And how could this increasingly fractured synthesis hold together if economic times went bad, as they eventually did after George Bush took over? What was left of fusionism, of Reaganism?

Some conservatives sought refuge in the oldest of comforts for believers: Their problem was that their ideas had been betrayed. The fact that Reaganism blew up not under Reagan but in George Bush's presidency led conservatives to the obvious strategy—Blame Bush first. This was certainly easy on the issue of taxes. In 1988, searching for an emotive issue to use against Michael Dukakis, Bush realized that the fear of taxes could reunite most of the old Reagan constituency, certainly enough of it to carry an election. Thus the infamous sentence, written for Bush's acceptance speech at the 1988 Republican National Convention by former Reagan speechwriter Peggy Noonan: "Read my lips, no new taxes." Dukakis himself had been careful not to run, as Walter Mondale had, on the promise of new taxes. He simply wouldn't rule them out. Bush had to go to Dukakis's right, and did. The strategy worked brilliantly, but this was a classic instance in which the imperatives of campaigning were at odds with the imperatives of governing. In the period before Bush delivered the infamous "read my lips" lines, Richard Darman, who would become Bush's budget director, desperately tried to excise

Noonan's evocative words. It appeared that Darman knew in advance that the realities of the deficit might force Bush to raise taxes at some point in his term (as, indeed, even Ronald Reagan had done during his). Noonan carried the day with the cogent argument that her words were a way of saying "I really mean this." The problem, of course, was that Bush didn't mean it—or stopped meaning it once he confronted a slowing economy and rising deficits.

But Bush did not create the problems for which he was blamed. The budget deficit was a creation of the *Reagan* years, the product of Reagan's own inability to slash government spending. David Frum is one of the few conservative commentators to admit this outright. Because Frum is so candid, it's worth quoting him at some length. "Conservatives," he wrote in his 1994 book, *Dead Right,* "have lost their zeal for advocating minimal government not because they have decided that big government is desirable, but because they have wearily concluded that trying to reduce it is hopeless, and that even the task of preventing its further growth will probably exceed their strength." He went on:

> However heady the 1980s may have looked to everyone else, they were for conservatives a testing and disillusioning time. Conservatives owned the executive branch for eight years and had great influence over it for four more; they dominated the Senate for six years; and by the end of the decade they exercised near complete control over the federal judiciary. And yet, every time they reached to undo the work of Franklin Roosevelt, Lyndon Johnson and Richard Nixon—the work they had damned for nearly half a century—they felt the public's eyes upon them. They didn't dare, and they realized that they didn't care. Their moment came and flickered.

Frum concluded that "the conservatives who had lived through that attack of faintheartedness shamefacedly felt they had better hurry up and find something else to talk about."

The core problem for the Reaganites lay in the fact that the bulk of the welfare state they had spent so long denouncing—Social Security and Medicare—was deeply and broadly popular. Republican constituencies, from farmers to defense contractors, also benefited mightily from the expenditure of tax dollars. And so big government stayed big.

III

If those with hopes for a smaller government were disappointed at the end of twelve Republican years, so also were the virtuecrats who hoped that conservative rule might change the country's moral predispositions, cultural assumptions and religious values. The most ardent virtuecrats wanted government to take direct action to create a more moral society—to change the Constitution to restore prayer to the public schools, to shore up the "traditional family" and to pass laws to outlaw or discourage abortion, pornography, divorce and homosexuality. But the quest for virtue was by no means confined to the more extreme reaches of the Moral Majority. Many who understood the limits of government's ability to enforce tough moral standards nonetheless sensed that the search for virtue was a necessary component of conservative politics, not just for reasons of electoral strategy (i.e., for holding the votes of evangelicals and fundamentalists) but also as an answer to the moral problems created by the very market economy about which they enthused. Irving Kristol asserted that while liberal capitalism was in many ways a smashing success, "there is something joyless, even somnambulistic, about its survival." The conservative scholar Bruce Frohnen summarized Kristol's view: "Capitalism provides freedom and prosperity even as it undermines the values that make such freedom and prosperity worthwhile." So even without the religious right, conservatives would have to keep coming back to virtue. Capitalism wasn't enough, which is what the traditionalists kept trying to tell the libertarians for forty years.

The rhetoric of virtue was easy enough. The social costs of virtue's loss were visible everywhere: in the rise of teen pregnancy, in the growing number of children who grew up without fathers, in the crack epidemic, in the rise in violent crime, especially among teenagers. It became increasingly popular to say things that had been highly controversial as recently as the late 1970s: that there was a link between social problems and fatherlessness, that the number of single-parent families had to be brought down (somehow), that the moral education of children was as vital as their instruction in math and reading. This was no small change and might be counted as a genuine conservative victory. Once-derided "bourgeois values" were now seen as necessary virtues. The baby boom that had been at the heart of the cultural rebellion of the 1960s now found itself in middle age and raising children. Old verities sounded pretty good to rebels-turned-parents. The explosive popularity of William Bennett's *The Book of Virtues* was itself a sign of cultural change—or, perhaps more properly, of the partial reversal of earlier changes.

But it was one thing to talk about necessary virtues, quite another to turn them into a viable politics. For one thing, liberals in large numbers—and especially Bill Clinton—were as loud in promoting the old values as any conservative. After all, large parts of Clinton's well-received speech to the black ministers in Memphis in the fall of 1993 could have been written by Bennett himself. Indeed, Clinton began consulting with Bennett in the second half of his term. In 1994, Dan Quayle and Bill Clinton gave back-to-back speeches in the same week on the costs of single parenthood and the necessary role of fathers in rearing kids. Clinton was as tough as any conservative in talking about the costs of crime; he was as passionate as anyone in speaking up for "personal responsibility." Clinton's critics could sneer at his personal life, but they could not fault his analysis of social breakdown because it overlapped considerably with their own.

But going beyond Clinton's rhetoric and the moderate pieties of Bennett's book posed large problems for conservatives. Many who endorsed the "bourgeois virtues" also enjoyed "bourgeois freedom." It was one thing to talk of the importance of enduring marital commitment, quite another to tighten up the divorce laws or criticize divorced conservatives, a point Bennett made, with some courage, to a gathering of the Christian Coalition. Bemoaning the number of abortions was easy; outlawing abortion was not. One could easily argue that religion had an important role to play in American life and that liberals were too eager to push religious people to the margins of the public square. But here again, this is an argument *liberals* themselves were starting to make—including, again, Clinton. The president drew on Stephen Carter's important book *The Culture of Disbelief* to make the case that religious people deserved to be heard and respected, and to play a role in the public debate. To the extent that moderates and liberals started occupying ground on this issue once comfortably held by conservatives, the right found itself forced to more dangerous terrain, having to hint that they would seek to expand religion's formal influence on government. The peril could be seen in the unpopularity of the religious right. The religious right was feared *not* because the country was irreligious—America remains one of the most religious countries in the world. Rather, a nation where no religious denomination comes close to holding majority sway is always inclined to look over its shoulder with trepidation when any one version of religious orthodoxy threatens to impose itself on everybody else. Pat Robertson could have his television channel—it was one among many. But nobody outside his regular viewership wants Robertson's "truths" imposed on the entire television band, or on the whole country.

Thus did Republicans develop a complicated approach-avoidance dance with the forces of the religious right. Republicans publicly sympathized with the religious right's worries about the decay of old values and certainly wanted its votes. But they had no interest in embracing the movement too closely, lest moderate voters—including many who went to church—come to fear Republicanism as an organized crusade to imprint a particular version of faith and morality on an entire nation. Ronald Reagan had always managed to get this balance just right. At their 1992 Houston convention, Republicans went over the edge.

The irony was large. George Bush was surely as moderate a cultural figure as could be found. Yet his very moderation made him suspect to the forces of the right, religious and otherwise. In an effort to appease these critics and to "nail down the base," as his managers put it, Bush overcompensated in his party's platform and in just enough of the convention's rhetoric. What might have been seen as an opportunistic effort to appease the forces of social conservatism became instead the Democrats' opportunity.

IV

One of the bits of Houston oratory later judged as right-wing overkill was the Patrick J. Buchanan speech that pushed Ronald Reagan himself out of prime time. This was not a case of Buchanan going off the schedule the Republicans had put him on. Rather, in what proved to be a large miscalculation, Bush's own managers decided to give Buchanan an excellent spot on the convention program because they wanted to reconcile him to Bush and—this dictated so much of what happened in Houston—to bring the Republican right home.

In placing so much emphasis on Buchanan himself, the Bush management misread the import of his 1992 primary challenge. The Buchanan insurgency had, indeed, been important. He won 37 percent of the vote in the primary in New Hampshire, with Bush managing only 52 percent—an astonishingly low result for an incumbent. Bush's numbers were pushed down not only by Buchanan but also by a large Republican write-in vote for Democratic candidates, especially Paul Tsongas, whose campaign against the deficit appealed to many Republican hearts.

Buchanan ran an unmistakably ideological campaign that represented not only a right-wing protest against Bush but also an effort to recast conservatism. In his announcement speech of 1991, Buchanan revived the pre–Cold War conservative slogan, "America First!" He avowed himself not simply a patriot but a nationalist opposed to Bush's "new world order." Buchanan had been one of a handful of conservative Republicans to oppose the Persian Gulf war. He had warned that the end of the Cold War would lead to a breakup of the old conservative coalition as nationalists of his stripe proudly returned to isolationism as the only proper alternative to "globaloney." He predicted that "the old Cold Warriors, Catholics and others who saw Communism as evil and a threat against our country will go back to our familiar point of view—let's tend to our own affairs." Buchanan's nationalism led him to dissent from what had been conservative orthodoxy on a slew of other questions, including trade. He pushed for protection and saw free traders as shirkers from the battle for the national interest just as surely as opponents of the Cold War had been. He spoke as harshly about Japan as he had about the old Soviet Union. He assailed Bush's internationalist economic policies, saying they had done wonders for Guangdong Province in China—at the expense of New Hampshire. Buchanan warned of the perils of immigration and saw new Americans from the Third World as threats to the country's tradition and character. In his views on immigrants, he differed markedly with economic conservatives (writers for the editorial pages of *The Wall Street Journal*, for example) who supported the free movement of people and labor, and also with Jack Kemp and William Bennett.

There is no doubt that Buchanan's substantial showings were a sign that Bush was in jeopardy and that many conservatives were in a restive mood. The mistake his managers made was to view Buchanan's vote as primarily ideological, as a sign of broad support for his particular brand of conservatism. While many of Buchanan's themes did, indeed, resonate with the public, as the history of the immigration issue was to show, his vote was not primarily about his issues at all. On the contrary, polls showed that he did as well or nearly as well among self-described Republican moderates and the few liberals left in the party as he did among conservatives. Buchanan voters were mostly *angry*—at Bush, at his performance in office, at the state of the economy and at their own position in it. Buchanan campaigned as if he knew this. While remaining uncompromising in what he stood for, he gave more emphasis to the suffering of the unemployed and to Bush's economic failures as the campaign went on. In so doing, he often sounded like a candidate in the *Democratic* primaries and underscored themes that both Ross Perot and Bill Clinton would use against Bush to such effect.

In agreeing to give Buchanan such a prominent stage for such a stridently ideological message, Bush's lieutenants thus misunderstood the message they should have drawn from the success of his insurgency. The Bush camp did not need Buchanan describing—or, as it sounded to so many, *declaring*—a "culture war." They did not need his gibes at Hillary Clinton or his chilling praise for the armed young men of the 18th Cavalry with their "M-16s at the ready" during the Los Angeles riots—men, he declared, who represented "force, rooted in justice, backed by moral courage." What the Bush camp *did* need was a better way of talking about economic problems and the pain of those at the Laconia, New Hampshire, unemployment office whom Buchanan mentioned in his convention speech and in just about every other speech of his campaign.

The truth is that Buchanan-style nationalism appealed to many non-Republican voters, but to only a limited segment of the organized conservative movement. Appeasing Buchanan was not thus going to appease "the right." Most of the leading organs of conservative opinion and most (though not all) of the conservative intellectuals rejected his views. The views of that leading popular spokesman for conservatism, talk show host Rush Limbaugh, run much more to traditional doctrine than to the Buchanan rebellion.

Nonetheless, Buchanan's rebellion did have broad implications for the Republican Party. In the Reagan era, as we have seen, nationalists and internationalists could march together in opposition to Soviet communism and in support of a strong, well-armed America. Buchanan's candidacy and rhetoric were symptomatic of the breakup of this alliance. And far better than the more establishment Republicans, Buchanan understood the festering resentments created by new economic conditions and popular fears of globalism. As an open nationalist, he could voice those fears in a way conventional, free-trading Republicans could not. Indeed, as his campaign progressed, it became clear that free market ideas did not matter nearly as much to him as his concern for the immediate economic interests *of* Americans *as* Americans. Buchanan tried, at first, to sound a Cold War sort of defense of American jobs, arguing that the loss of certain industries "vital to our defense" would amount to "unilateral disarmament." But as David Frum notes, Buchanan increasingly looked beyond the defense argument and argued frankly that certain big, important American companies deserved protection simply to make sure that America stayed "number one."

After the election Buchanan may have surprised himself by finding his way toward an alliance with Ralph Nader and organized labor in opposing both the North American Free Trade Agreement and the General Agreement on Tariffs and Trade. Right and left came together around the idea that both treaties undermined American national sovereignty in the name of helping multinational corporations gain a deeper hold in the world economy. Both sides argued that these megacompanies did not care a whit about what was in the American interest. The left might talk an internationalist language on behalf of all workers while Buchanan's nationalism specified that *American* workers were at the heart of his concerns. But they ended up in the same place.

Buchanan himself will neither break up the Republican coalition single-handedly nor take over the Republican Party for his style of nationalism. But some of the issues he helped bring forward, especially opposition to immigration, are destined to become more important. And Buchanan has particular appeal to working-class voters who signed on to the Republican coalition with Ronald Reagan but became restive in the 1990s. Ross Perot, who spoke a nationalist language when it came to trade, NAFTA and competition with Japan, picked up many Buchanan themes, and many of his voters. Buchanan understood that his candidacy helped pave the way for Perot's challenge. It was something of which he was not at all ashamed. And Buchanan, in turn, hoped to build on the Perot insurgency to create a nationalist movement in 1996 and beyond. When Perot gathered his movement together in Dallas in the summer of 1995, it was a speech by Buchanan—running a second time for president—that drew the most boisterous response.

V

For most mainstream conservatives, Buchananism constituted conservatism gone off the rails. They saw it as representing a repudiation of many of the central tenets of Reaganism: its optimism, its intellectual coherence in seeing that free markets and free trade necessarily go together, its rejection of nativism, its support for a United States deeply engaged around the globe. This mainstream, moreover, argued that it was hard to imagine a majority electoral coalition for conservatives that did *not* look something like Reagan's. The votes of the religious right remained crucial; so did the ballots of the young, who had been drawn to Reagan's upbeat style; so, too, did strong support in the upper middle class, where both the religious right and Buchanan-style nationalism went down badly. The answer to the end of Reaganism became—"neo-Reaganism."

But the shrewd among the mainstream conservatives knew that Reagan's would be a hard act to follow, that Reagan's failure to curb the size of government was a cautionary tale, that the absence of the Soviet threat robbed the conservative movement of a powerful series of themes that could hold together even the most fractious factions. The challenge for Republicans was well characterized by Adam Meyerson, the editor of *Policy Review,* the journal of the conservative Heritage Foundation. Conservatives, he argued, faced two imperatives. The first was "to combine the pro-growth, tax limitation message of Reagan Republicanism with a program to address the Perot people's concerns about long-term debt and eco-

nomic decline." The second was "to find a way to retain the enthusiastic support of conservative Evangelicals—an enormous asset for
the GOP—without antagonizing a majority of suburbanites."

So how was the party to reconstruct—or resurrect—a conservative political philosophy? The organizational redoubt of the neo-
Reaganites was a group called Empower America, formed after the
1992 election. It brought together some of the most important figures in the conservative movement. Its driving force was Jack Kemp,
who linked the old Reagan faith in tax cuts and incentives to "work,
save and invest" with an insistence that Republicans needed to
engage the problems of the inner-city poor, particularly African-
Americans. Considered coequal with Kemp was William Bennett,
whose concerns, as we have seen, run more to values than economics.

It was a sign of the ferment—or discord—on the right that
Kemp and Bennett, while striving for a common front, offered what
amounted to deeply divergent diagnoses for the ailments of the
inner city. Kemp, the optimist, insisted that there was nothing wrong
with the inner city that the right set of incentives couldn't cure. He
bristled at any suggestions that there was something wrong with the
people of the inner city or their values. Instead, Kemp saw them as
victims, trapped by a welfare state and a regulatory regime that
strangled opportunity. The only part of the American economy that
lived under socialism, he insisted, was the inner city, which is why
its failures matched those of the Soviet Union.

Kemp's free market war on poverty turned out to require a
rather significant investment of government money. He suggested,
for example, that residents of public housing projects be encouraged to buy their apartments and become homeowners. But a program to take some of the worst housing in America and make it
worth buying was not cheap. Purchasers required considerable subsidies, since American public housing tenants were, on the whole,
much poorer than their counterparts in Britain, which pioneered
the sell-off idea. Kemp also argued that welfare recipients suffered
from the highest "marginal tax rates" in America, since it was illegal
for them to have any significant amount in savings. And of course
there was Kemp's signature idea, "enterprise zones," which involved slashing or eliminating taxes and regulations in poor areas
by way of coaxing investors to move plants and jobs to where the

poor needed them. Ironically, it took the Clinton administration to enact a version of the enterprise zones idea. Once the idea had been embraced and modified by Democrats, it fell out of the Republican orbit. But the fact that many Clinton aides were sympathetic to Kemp and his rhetoric suggested the grave problems he faced inside the Republican Party: Kemp's compassionate conservatism was too compassionate and not conservative enough for many Republicans. Kemp himself seemed to understand this. When he announced in 1995 that he would not seek the Republican presidential nomination, he suggested that his own passions were out of sync with those of his party.

Bennett, on the other hand, was fundamentally a pessimist who believed that collapse in the inner city was largely the product of a collapse of families and values. All the incentives in the world could not be expected to lift up children who were born to teenage mothers, grew up without fathers and daily confronted the lawlessness and violence created by the fatherless kids a few years older. Although Kemp and Bennett repeatedly expressed faithfulness to each other's agenda—and shared strong commitments on civil rights and immigration—the differences between them were clear. Vin Weber, a former congressman and staunch Kemp ally, tried to hold things together at Empower America and bridge whatever differences existed between Bennett and Kemp. Significantly, both Bennett and Kemp emerged as leading sympathizers toward Colin Powell's presidential aspirations, a sign of their shared commitment to a more open and less rigid Republican Party.

Two of the leading intellectuals drawn to the organization represented important wings of Reaganism. Both were former Democrats, neoconservatives drawn rightward out of frustration with the liberalism of the 1960s. One was former United Nations Ambassador Jeane Kirkpatrick, who spoke for the Cold Warriors, the former followers of the late Senator Henry M. Jackson, stout anticommunists who could not abide McGovernites—or, as Kirkpatrick redubbed them, "San Francisco Democrats." The other was Michael Novak, a Catholic intellectual who had once written speeches for Sargent Shriver, George McGovern's 1972 running mate. Novak's drift to the right came not just from a reaction against liberalism but also from a rethinking of first premises. Once drawn to democratic socialism, he became a fervent supporter of what he called "dem-

ocratic capitalism." He defended capitalism not only for its efficiency but also for what he saw as its moral value. Capitalism
succeeded, Novak believed, because of its emphasis on individual
creativity and invention, and because of the accountability that competition imposed on individuals. In some ways, Novak's thinking
could be seen as an intellectual bridge between Bennett and Kemp,
much as Weber was the personal go-between. Novak shared Kemp's
inspirational approach to capitalism, but he saw democratic capitalist society as made up of separate moral and political spheres. It
was the obligation of the moral sphere to provide the values and
virtues on which competitive markets and free political systems
depend. A society without the economic base built by markets was
destined to collapse, but the market itself could be endangered
absent the solidarity and meaning created by the moral sphere.
Novak's formulation might be boiled down to the view that Kemp
and Bennett badly needed each other.

Initially, this band of conservatives confronted a large problem
in the immense adaptability of Clinton. The president accepted
large chunks of Bennett-style virtue-talk about the family and personal responsibility, and Bennett even came to the White House in
the spring of 1995 to address a conference on the subject. Clinton,
as we have seen, also adapted the conservative critique of the welfare state to his own purposes. He agreed wholeheartedly that the
welfare system had become dysfunctional, rewarding idleness over
work and encouraging family breakup. He embraced the view that
welfare benefits could not go on indefinitely, that welfare needed to
be seen as "a second chance, not a way of life."

Faced with this gambit, Bennett, Kemp and their allies saw no
alternative but to get to Clinton's right by proposing what Ronald
Reagan would not dare suggest: the total abolition of the federal
welfare system. Building on the radical ideas of social policy analysts Charles Murray and Robert Rector, they argued—to Kemp's
clear discomfort—that welfare had become the "enabler" of a whole
series of social pathologies. If teenagers knew that the mere act of
having a baby without getting married would provide them with a
degree of independence (housing, medical care, food stamps and a
check), why would they *not* bear children out of wedlock? The
welfare system put the government in the role once assigned to
fathers as providers. The Murrayite solution, adopted by Kemp and
Bennett, was to shut the system down and accept that a certain

amount of short-term suffering would be followed by the most socially helpful result of all: a sharp decline in out-of-wedlock births. Single mothers would be on their own, and would have to rely on families, friends and their own work to get by.

The fact that Murray's ideas on welfare had become acceptable enough to be adopted by serious conservative politicians was a sign of how far to the right—or, more properly, to the libertarian side— the social policy debate had gone. (This shift was later confirmed when the new Republican Congress moved to end welfare as a federal entitlement.) It was also symptomatic of the frustration bred by continuing inner-city deterioration. And it was proof of the extent to which Clinton had pulled large chunks of the Democratic Party to a new posture toward the welfare state. The rightward drift of the Republicans on welfare underscores the seriousness of the Democrats' error in failing to act on the welfare issue when they controlled Congress. The Democrats might have occupied a sensible middle ground and achieved substantial (and necessary) changes. Instead, they pushed the debate to the right and opened the way for the Republicans' radical departures.

But welfare—the Aid to Families with Dependent Children program—was in fact only a very small piece of an American welfare state dominated by two programs for the elderly, Social Security and Medicare. Few Republicans were willing to dismantle those. The question remained: How could Republicans present themselves as authentic advocates of a smaller government, given their failures to dismantle government in the past? How could they take a philosophy often condemned as a mean-spirited rationalization for the interests of the wealthy and demonstrate that it was, at heart, compassionate and humane? And how could virtuecrats and capitalists learn to live together in peace?

VI

The Republican success of 1994 should not be allowed to disguise the fact that these are not easy questions. In the immediate aftermath of 1992, many conservatives were deeply pessimistic about conservatism's future. For example, David Frum's brilliant analysis in *Dead Right,* published on the eve of the Republicans' great triumph, concluded on a deeply gloomy note:

When conservatism's glittering generalities, "you are over-taxed," turn into legislative specifics, "you must pay more to send your kid to the state university," we run into as much trouble in midsession as liberals do at election time. Twelve years of twisting and struggling to escape this snare have just entangled us more deeply in it. . . . Is there a way out? Only one: conservative intellectuals should learn to care a little less about the electoral prospects of the Republican Party, indulge less in policy cleverness and ethnic demagoguery, and do what intellectuals of all descriptions are obliged to do: practice honesty, and pay the price.

Frum, in other words, assumed that honesty on the part of conservatives about their goals would have high political costs. Frum, like Dick Armey, knew that small government sounded better in speeches than in practice.

Another pessimist was Weber. Writing even before the 1992 results were in, he declared that in his fourteen years in national politics, "I have never been so concerned about the future of conservative ideas." He went on: "What troubles me is that Republicans have failed to define a national agenda for leading the country. We have lost our emphasis on economic growth, such an important part of Ronald Reagan's achievement. We have failed to adopt a reform strategy for the unfinished business from the Reagan years—the state of our families, our schools, our cities." Weber, a compassionate conservative in the Kemp mode, also worried about the conservative response to poverty and the inner city. He wrote:

This country is never going to take a *laissez-faire* attitude toward the poorest people in our society. To do so would be contrary to our Judeo-Christian culture, and to all the values that America was built on. For conservatives simply to vacate the field on these issues, or to take a libertarian posture and say that the government has no responsibility here, is wrong and self-destructive.

Weber added that for conservatives to abandon the poor would mean "that the only response available to the American people is going to be statist, collectivist, redistributionist and paternalistic, which is what we've had now for generation after generation."

Finally, some Republicans, at least, saw that economic stagnation at the middle and bottom of the income structure had been a problem not just under Bush but also during the Reagan years. Adam Meyerson of *Policy Review,* for example, recognized that "single-income families have been on a treadmill for the past two decades." He continued: "The amazing growth in family income during the Reagan years came because more mothers and teenagers were working, not because wages were rising. The 'seven fat years,' as *Wall Street Journal* editor Robert Bartley has aptly described the Reagan boom, were lean ones for stay-at-home and single moms." Meyerson argued that on a whole range of issues of concern to the restive Perot voters—spending cuts, more efficient environmental regulation, litigation reform and job training—"conservatives, quite frankly, haven't done their homework. . . ." Meyerson, like Frum, was concerned that the Republicans would not be willing to accept the deep spending cuts that were needed to rationalize the lower taxes they had enacted in the 1980s. And he worried, too, about the impact of the absolutism of some on the religious right. He noted that the basic American impulse, which was also a good conserva-tive impulse, was to tell moral meddlers: "Don't tell me how to live my life" and "Don't impose your religion and morality on my chil-dren."

The Republicans also faced deep divisions on foreign policy. It was easy enough to criticize Clinton's handling of events in Bosnia, Haiti or North Korea. Going beyond criticism was harder. As foreign policy analyst Alan Tonelson noted, "What most observers still call 'American conservatism' seems split into no less than three princi-pal factions" on international issues, and even these factions "are only barely cohering." Tonelson distinguished among *conservative realists,* who favored an expansive American world role but were without illusions about the instabilities of the global system or the need to deal with less than perfect regimes; *democratic crusaders,* who saw the United States as having an interest and obligation to spread democracy throughout the world; and *conservative mini-malists,* such as Buchanan, who mistrusted engagement and inter-national organizations and hoped the Cold War would allow America to "come home." Splits among these Republicans were visible on virtually every controversial issue Clinton confronted with the exception of Haiti, where almost all Republicans opposed American intervention. These divisions endured after the Republi-can congressional takeover, when the party split over Clinton's economic aid package to Mexico despite support for the plan among most of the congressional leadership.

If Republicans were wary on foreign affairs, few of them (with the exception of nationalists such as Buchanan) had any interest in highlighting the challenges posed by the global economy. The basic Republican premise was that free trade, free markets and low taxes were the key to prosperity. Even conceding, as Meyerson was honest enough to do, that stagnating wages posed a serious problem was to admit the limitations and imperfections of the market economy. This would undermine the whole Republican case.

Given these fundamental problems, it is a near certainty that the 1994 Republican victories would have been impossible had the Democratic Congress and the Clinton administration not imploded. It was a sign of the conservatives' difficulties in formulating responses to the problems raised by Frum, Weber and Meyerson that the movement's intellectuals, politicians, talk show hosts and journalists spent far more time attacking Clinton and scandal-mongering on sex and Whitewater than in outlining what they would do in power. (The "Contract with America," it should be noted, was Newt Gingrich's attempt to respond to the wholly accurate perception that Republicans had done little to provide alternatives to Clintonism.) *The American Spectator,* a magazine that had offered serious conservative conversation and debate in the 1970s and 1980s, became the epicenter of tabloid-style assaults on both Bill and Hillary Clinton, publishing a running series of stories on the president's sex life, Whitewater and other tales. It certainly caught the angry anti-Clinton mood among conservatives: The magazine's circulation grew tenfold.

The right had a fundamental insight that proved correct: Clinton could not be allowed to succeed. Many conservatives believed privately that his program held great promise to legitimize government and the Democratic Party. It therefore had to be stopped. But there was a flip side to this insight: that conservatives should largely avoid the business of providing alternatives to the Clinton program that might become vehicles for compromise. In embracing some of the ideas offered by Kemp, Bennett, Bush Education Secretary Lamar Alexander and other Republicans, Clinton had proven himself adept at adapting the opposition's suggestions to his own purposes.

If conservatives allowed that some new government programs might indeed be necessary to deal with the country's economic uncertainties and the problems of the poor, they would only legitimize the Clinton project. It is significant that when a group of House Republicans led by Representative (later Senator) Rick Santorum proposed a welfare reform program that bore some similarities to Clinton's, they were criticized by Bennett, William Kristol and others for being accommodationists who had failed to go "far enough." That is when Bennett endorsed abolishing welfare altogether and Kristol suggested that the federal government's welfare role be ended and the whole mess shipped off to the states—views that proved decisive when the Republicans took over Congress. Clinton was often criticized for his failure to approach the Republicans in search of "centrist" solutions, and there were grounds for this criticism, especially where health care was concerned. But many Republicans were determined to make sure there was no center ground by turning the center into a free-fire zone. In 1993 and 1994, at every point that Senator John Chafee and other Republican moderates seemed to be moving toward a compromise with the White House on health care, they came under fierce assaults from commentators and politicians of the Republican right. As long as Clinton was president and the Republicans were in the congressional minority, government would not be allowed to work. Discrediting government remained at the heart of the Republicans' strategy. Democrats were so divided that they ended up complicit in this strategy. The Clinton administration did not understand until far too late how much it needed Republican moderates such as Chafee. This was a bonus the Republicans would not have dreamed of expecting.

VII

But more than the power of negative thinking was at work in the Republican Party. During the 1970s and 1980s a slow revolution took place within Republican and conservative ranks. While public attention focused on the rise of the Christian right, libertarianism was staging a strong comeback, intellectually as well as politically. Many baby boomers who had been seen as part of "the left" because of their opposition to the Vietnam War discovered that they were opposed not to capitalism but to *government.* They were anti-military and civil libertarian, anti-bureaucratic and in favor of individual freedom. This complex of views led not to socialism or to contemporary liberalism but to the libertarianism of the old right. Organizationally and intellectually, the forces of libertarianism began to gather strength, first through a well-orchestrated third-party presidential campaign in 1980 and ultimately through a Washington-based think tank, the Cato Institute, which turned out lucid and literate critiques of government activity in every sphere and at every level.

It is one of the ironies of conservative history that the religious right, which stood for much that the libertarians opposed, strengthened libertarianism enormously. Many Republicans decided they were libertarians when they began to analyze why they opposed the Christian conservatives. They came to the conclusion that unlike Jerry Falwell or Pat Robertson, they were consistent anti-statists, opposed to government meddling in the moral as well as in the economic sphere. Some Republicans, including important figures in the party such as House majority leader Dick Armey and Massachusetts Governor Bill Weld, began to offer public acknowledgment of their debt to libertarianism. When analysts started sorting out the views of the new Republican congressional class elected in 1994, they discovered that libertarianism was a dominant—perhaps *the* dominant—current in its thinking. When the House Republicans published *Restoring the Dream,* their sequel to the *Contract with America,* in the summer of 1995, its editor was Stephen Moore, the director of fiscal policy at Cato. Only a few years earlier, such a job would almost certainly have gone to someone at one of the more traditional conservative think tanks, such as the Heritage Foundation or the American Enterprise Institute.

But pure libertarianism would not sell in the ranks of the religious right, many of whose members came to politics not to oppose high taxes or government regulation but to moralize the country. Many of the religious right's supporters were still New Dealers in the modest sense—they saw nothing wrong with government helping people out through Social Security, Medicare and other programs. When they objected to various forms of government activism, they did so on *moral* grounds. Welfare was wrong because it promoted sloth and illegitimacy. Public school programs aimed at educating youngsters about sex and at promoting "tolerance" were opposed because they were seen as undermining traditional values and encouraging immorality and permissiveness. At the same time, the Christian conservatives were not at all averse to using the institutions of government to promote what they saw as the *right* values, whether through prayer in public schools, the teaching of "creation science," or laws banning abortion, outlawing pornography or—in the case of at least some in their ranks—making homosexual acts a crime.

Republican strategists and theorists thus had a hard problem to solve. They could not win without uniting the libertarians and the moralists. Yet when each camp pressed its views to their respective conclusions, there was no way for the two movements to remain on the same side. Clinton and the Democrats had understood this perfectly in 1992, which is why they sought to highlight the most extreme and controversial aspects of the Republicans' Houston convention. It was clear that a socially moderate country was no more enthusiastic about the "Houston Republicans" of 1992 than it had been about the "San Francisco Democrats" of 1984.

Moderate and liberal Republicans (and the staunchest libertarians) had a straightforward solution to this problem: Reject the religious right, embrace broadly liberal social attitudes and move forward. Many on the Christian right would have nowhere to go in any event—they could not vote for Clinton's Democrats. And what losses the party might suffer among the Christian conservatives would be more than made up for by gains among well-off, well-educated socially tolerant voters who favored smaller government and lower taxes. Many of these voters—especially well-educated women—were voting Democratic not out of loyalty to the New Deal or the Great Society, but to protect abortion rights, feminism's gains and civil liberties. Deprive such voters of their main reason for voting Democratic, and they would flock to the Republican Party. Or so the theory went.

But even Republicans sympathetic to this overall approach to the long term—Newt Gingrich's futurism was certainly congruent with this view—understood that the party could not afford in the near term to write off large chunks of the religious right. In fact, the religious right's basic theme of spiritual decay articulated well with the Republicans' need to cast the country's sense of moral crisis in cultural, not economic terms, in order to short-circuit demands for government intervention in the economic sphere. And at the level of principle, many conservative Republicans shared many of the Christian conservatives' concerns about social and moral break-down, even if they rejected some of their more radical solutions.

It fell to two political philosophers and the head of an important conservative foundation to sketch out the theory that might hold a potentially fractious coalition together. The most publicly visible of them was William Kristol, the son of Irving Kristol. Kristol the elder had been both the Marx and the P. T. Barnum of the neoconservative rebellion against liberalism. He had served as both the chief theorist of the new movement and the ringmaster of a slew of conservative organizations and foundations. Kristol the younger was his father's son in his energy and conservative disposition, but he essentially continued his father's journey by moving more firmly into the conservative camp and into the heart of Republican politics. The main influence on Bill Kristol's politics was the philosopher Leo Strauss, who viewed the whole project of Enlightenment liberalism as a horrible wrong turn. The proper grounding for political philosophy lay not in modern ideas, but in ancient ones: in Aristotle and the Greeks. What mattered most was understanding man's essential nature and natural laws that the modernists sneered at. For the Straussians, a paramount goal of government was to inculcate "virtue" in the citizenry. Kristol's Straussian disposition prepared him perfectly to understand the more populist approach to promoting virtue championed by the religious right.

Kristol began life in the academy, but was brought to Washington by William Bennett as a top aide in the Department of Education. During the Bush administration Kristol had an overview of all that went wrong from his perch as Vice President Dan Quayle's chief of staff. "Quayle's brain" he was often called. A job few would have wanted turned into a huge step forward for Kristol. His access to information and his willingness to talk made him extremely popular with the press, which (its supposed liberal biases notwithstanding) advanced him as a public figure. Quayle's office also became a center of dissent within the Bush administration, leaking warning after warning about the dangers the administration faced for abandoning its promise not to raise taxes and, more generally, for its lethargy on domestic affairs. Kristol was one of the first Republicans to take Bill Clinton's challenge seriously and one of the first to see that Bush's high poll ratings disguised potentially deep political problems.

After the election Kristol set out to establish the strategic and intellectual basis for rebuilding the party. He founded the Project for the Republican Future as a kind of personal think tank. Kristol added to his reputation during the first two years of the Clinton administration by issuing a series of widely publicized memos outlining tactical steps for the congressional party. His best-known missives were on health care. From the very beginning Kristol warned Republicans against accommodating Clinton or compromising in any way. The task of the party, he said, was to stop any health care reforms that had the effect of expanding government—which meant stopping anything that Clinton might have in mind. He explicitly challenged the Democrats' claim that the country faced a health care "crisis" at all. There was no crisis, claimed Kristol, just problems within a health system that in so many ways worked very well. It was a sign of his success that for some weeks in late 1993 and early 1994, the central issue in the public debate was not what should be done to fix the health system, but whether or not there was a "crisis." (The Republicans were to reverse field completely in 1995 when they insisted that there was a "crisis" in Medicare. Kristol, by then the founding editor of *The Weekly Standard,* a new conservative magazine, supported the Republican program.)

At a tactical level Kristol proved insightful. With Clinton having made health care the make-or-break issue of the first half of his term, Kristol concluded that it was essential that Republicans break him. The president was bound to get most of the credit for any reforms that were passed—even reforms that might be acceptable to many Republicans. Any success—and perhaps especially a *bipartisan* success—would suggest that Clinton had made good on his promise to break gridlock and make government work. Kristol, as we've seen, was at least as fearful that health care reform would *succeed* as that it would be a disaster. He did not want to give the Democrats a chance to convince the middle class that active government might actually be made to work on its behalf. That was the underlying meaning of another of his favorite arguments, that if a large new government health care program were passed, it would not be repealed. Kristol did not want health care reform to do for Bill Clinton's generation of Democrats what Social Security or the GI Bill had done for the Democrats of Roosevelt's and Truman's time.

Beneath the politics lay Kristol's fundamental commitment: that the task of Republicans in the next era was to limit (or "relimit") government. His overall approach was outlined in some detail in an important article, "The Future of Conservatism," published in *The American Enterprise,* the magazine of the American Enterprise Institute. "The agenda of American conservatism today," he declared, "can be defined as the construction (or reconstruction) of a politics of liberty and a sociology of virtue." Citing Robert Nisbet, a sociologist whose steady work established him as one of the central thinkers of postwar conservatism, Kristol argued that a commitment to the politics of liberty meant "to work tirelessly toward the diminution of the centralized, omnicompetent and unitary state with its ever-soaring debt and deficit." The sociology of virtue involved "strengthening the institutions in civil society that attend to the character of the citizenry," meaning families and churches, neighborhood associations and voluntary organizations.

Kristol, like David Frum, acknowledged that conservatives had "limited success in the 1980s in rolling back the huge expansion of government that took place in the 1960s and 1970s." He conceded that the "federal government is as big, as intrusive and as meddlesome as ever." He added: "Electing conservative or Republican presidents has not changed things very much."

But there was now a large opportunity to relimit government because of the voters' "deep mistrust of the federal government and its ability to do good." Kristol urged conservatives to embrace a series of popular initiatives—especially popular, it might be noted, with Perot voters—including a balanced budget amendment, term limits, "various taxing and spending limitations" as well as "the devolution and privatization of government functions." Kristol's arguments for supporting these proposals were quite different from the more populist rationales expressed by the electorate. The real reason for term limits, he said, "is not primarily an abstract belief that Congress will be a better institution if there is more turnover." Rather, he maintained, term limits could break "the Iron Triangle of the welfare state—the politicians, bureaucrats and interest groups who establish and benefit from its programs." Kristol went on:

The incentives for individual congressmen change once term limits are enacted. The seniority and committee system disintegrates. The balance of power within Congress and between Congress and the other branches of government, and even between Congress and the electorate, changes. That's the argument for term limits.

Implicit in this view was a desire to weaken Congress itself—perhaps because, at the time he wrote (in the summer of 1994), Democratic control of Congress seemed irreversible.

When he turned to "the sociology of virtue," Kristol distinguished it from older forms of traditionalism by arguing that simple "conservatism"—that is, "preserving our wasting moral capital from the depredations of modern life" and "shoring up old institutions that were under modernist assault"—was not enough. "The erosion has today gone too far for a merely 'conservative' approach," he argued. Many Americans were so alarmed by the decline of "virtue's moral capital" that they "have decided they can't wait for political victories to deal with these social problems." What was most needed to secure virtue, he said, was not government action but "a resurgence of efforts within the sphere of civil society." As examples of such nongovernmental successes, he cited "efforts of inner-city pastors to relegitimize and redignify fatherhood," the fact that "an authentic religious revival" was under way, and the work of the right-to-life movement "to convince women not to take advantage of a right they have won due both to the Supreme Court and political action." Even on the matter of crime, surely a direct government responsibility, many citizens were bypassing "ineffectual" government to organize their own communities against violence.

What is significant about Kristol's formulation is that he assigned the task of "liberty" to the political sphere and "virtue" to the sphere of society. This was an ingenious move, for it enabled him to pay homage to the importance of the religious right's agenda while insisting (with the libertarians) that much of its work would have to be done *independently of and apart from government.* The threat of fundamentalist preachers wielding state power thus receded.

Kristol then took his analysis one step further. He argued that his politics of liberty was actually essential to a resurgence of the sociology of virtue, precisely because a weakening of government would lead to a strengthening of the forces in civil society—families, churches and other character-building institutions. Rather than impose a new set of values on government bureaucracies, Kristol proposed ways of limiting or going around them. The task for conservatives was not to conscript the power of government on the side of *their* values but "the defense of sound social institutions from attempts by political institutions to suppress or reshape them."

On the matter of illegitimacy, for example, Kristol followed libertarian writer Charles Murray in arguing that "[w]e don't need more liberal social engineering to solve the problem, we need the state to stop interfering with the natural forces that have kept the overwhelming majority of births within marriage for millennia." Kristol cited other cases where libertarians and virtuecrats would find common ground:

> Many conservatives favor school choice on the grounds of liberty, because they like competition and want to break up government monopolies; others favor school choice because they believe that sound values will be taught in schools that parents have more control over.
>
> Similarly, when conservatives oppose government efforts to regulate day care, [and] try instead to provide vouchers to use in any private setting they want, we see a politics of liberty seeking to restrict the scope of the federal government and to keep the state out of the private sphere of civil society. But we also see a sociology of virtue in the sense that the quality of day care that families, relatives and private sector institutions offer will be friendlier to the values conservatives tend to favor than would be publicly provided day care.

This was a formula for peace between the wings of the Republican Party. If the libertarians tended to the politics of liberty by tearing down the state, the great beneficiaries would be the traditionalists who could battle for the sociology of virtue within civil society, unhampered by liberal-leaning bureaucracies.

Kristol was careful to acknowledge certain limits to this approach. He admitted that there was "some tension" between his politics and his sociology, between the partisans of liberty and the paladins of virtue. The two sides had much work to do together, but ultimately, some ground would have to be given to the virtuecrats.

"Our politics cannot simply be neutral between the sexual revolution and those who would resist it," he wrote, "and between radical feminism and those who would resist it." He argued that "the politics of liberty needs to accommodate the special status of the family, and the sociology of virtue needs political and legal support for the family as an institution." Kristol concluded that "the political sphere, whose primary goal is liberty, cannot be inattentive to the claims of virtue; and the social sphere, whose focus is virtue, requires some political support."

Potentially, this formula posed serious problems for both theory and practical politics. How much support was the political sphere to give to opponents of abortion? How far would "support" for the traditional family be extended when it came time to determine the legal status of homosexuality? What, exactly, could government do to roll back the sexual revolution or what Kristol called "radical feminism"? What would be the political costs—in terms of lost support among libertarians—of these various steps? And might not feminists—good Republican feminists—ask if Kristol was talking about liberty for men and virtue for women?

But such problems aside, Kristol's approach had huge attractions to the Republicans, and it became their de facto strategy. In a sense, Kristol could be seen as preaching to the religious right the need for a certain restraint. He was trying to convince them that they had much to gain from a broadly anti-statist agenda. Abortion might not be made illegal tomorrow and there might be limits on what the public schools could do to promote religious values. But by signing on to voucher programs and other strategies aimed at breaking up government institutions, the forces of conservative religion might ultimately find their own institutions vastly strengthened. Please, Kristol was saying to the Christian right, join us in battling the liberal, bureaucratic enemy. Once that enemy is routed, the harder questions could be confronted in a new context that would see the forces of virtue and religion vastly stronger.

Many of the shrewdest leaders of the religious right were already prepared to be convinced by Kristol's case. Ralph Reed, the savvy organizer and leader of the Christian Coalition, admitted that the religious conservatives' agenda was "policy-thin and value-laden, leaving many voters tuned out." In his 1994 book, *Politically Incorrect,* Reed argued that "[t]he American people need to know that we do not desire to exclude our political foes, only to gain our own place at the table." He went on: "They cannot hear too often that our objective is not to dominate but to participate, and that our vision of society includes protecting their right to speak and be heard as much as making our own voices heard." Reed said that while issues "such as abortion and opposition to minority rights for gays are important in building a winning coalition," even evangelical voters did not necessarily make such social issues their primary or only priorities. Supporters of the Christian conservative movement, he said, had to take account of the "startling" fact that "only 22 percent of *self-identified born-again evangelicals* (about 24 percent of the total electorate) listed abortion as an important issue." [Reed's emphasis.] And when it came time to listing a broader agenda for his movement, Reed's approach strikingly paralleled Kristol's "politics of liberty," emphasizing tax cuts for families and school vouchers as central goals. "It is utopian to think that we can save the family through legislative action," Reed wrote. "Our goal should be more attainable and immediate: to get government off the backs of families and out of their pocketbooks." He added: "Our first challenge is to restrict government and force its disengagement from the family, not to positively empower it to intrude further." Thus his recipe on taxes: "Cut the federal budget to find the revenue to supplement the family budget." Even the most secular of libertarians could have no quarrel with that.

Representative Dick Armey also noted the convergence between libertarians and religious conservatives in an essay, "Freedom's Choir," which argued that "social and economic conservatives are singing the same song." The religious conservatives, he said, had mobilized "not to impose their beliefs on others, but because the federal government was imposing its values on them."

It should be noted that both Reed and Armey were trying to put the least contentious spin on the religious right's goals. Armey's emphasis, for example, was on the rebellion against the *federal* government. When religious conservatives held power at the local level, they were quite prepared to use it on behalf of their own beliefs, especially in the public schools. Nor did the Reed-Armey formulas find any way of escaping the question of what government might do in cases where, whatever choice it made, it was picking a set of values. The most dramatic of these concerned whether or not the military should bar gays and lesbians from service. Nor could the abortion issue be wished away. Nonetheless, the very fact that Reed especially was inclining toward the Kristol formula suggested that the religious right—or at least some in its leadership—accepted the need to moderate its public stance by way of keeping the conservative coalition together.

If Kristol provided the short form of the new program, many of its intellectual underpinnings were being worked out by another thinker influenced by Strauss, William Schambra, who had spent some years writing on constitutional issues at the American Enterprise Institute before joining government. As chief speechwriter for Louis Sullivan, George Bush's secretary of health and human services, Schambra had written a series of addresses in which Sullivan highlighted the importance of personal responsibility as an essential component of any effort to ease social problems. Whether the matter at hand was family dissolution, drug abuse or the general physical health of the country, Sullivan argued, the issues at stake always came back to the individual. Individuals chose to become single parents, individuals said yes or no to drugs, individuals' habits helped determine how healthy or unhealthy they would be.

After Bush lost, Schambra went off to the Bradley Foundation in Milwaukee, which was headed by Michael S. Joyce. Joyce was frustrated at the behavior of "inside the Beltway" conservative think tanks, arguing that they had stopped looking at the world as grassroots conservatives did and had caught the Washington disease of thinking too much about national solutions to what were more appropriately seen as local problems. With Schambra, Joyce was seeking a new model for conservative political action that took seriously the responsibility of individual citizens and local communities.

The result of this collaboration was a series of essays by Schambra and a joint paper by Joyce and Schambra which sought to define "a new citizenship." They argued that the message of the 1994 elections was "unmistakable": "Government is too powerful. The citizen is powerless." The distinction was more interesting than it seemed because of their use of the word "citizen" (rather than a more neutral word, such as "individuals" or "people"). Democratic governments, after all, were supposed to be the creations of—and servants of—citizens. To cast "government" as being opposed to the interests of "citizens" was to suggest that the modern democratic state was no longer accomplishing its central end.

Moreover, standard conservative thinking, because it was skeptical of all government, harbored a certain quiet skepticism of the word "citizen." It was a word associated with the French Revolution and the powerful state. To emphasize citizenship, as against individuality, might be seen as lending legitimacy to the state. Joyce and Schambra, on the other hand, wanted to give the word "citizen" a new meaning, linking it more with the obligations of individuals in the *public* but *nongovernmental* sphere of neighborhoods and communities.

At the heart of their argument was a theme developed over many years by Schambra: that modern American liberalism had hijacked the word "community" for purposes inappropriate to its real meaning. Beginning with the Progressive Era's master thinker Herbert Croly, the author of *The Promise of American Life,* liberals had rejected the bonds of local community as "backward" and "unsophisticated." The liberal project, they argued, was designed to "construct within America's borders a great national community, which would summon Americans away from selfish interests and parochial allegiances, toward a commitment to an overarching national idea or purpose."

Joyce and Schambra acknowledged that the inspiration behind the Progressive project involved more than just a contempt for localism (embodied in extreme form in Karl Marx's well-known reference to "the idiocy of village life"). It was also based on an analysis that saw large forces conspiring to destroy even what was good in the local community. For theorists such as Walter Lippmann, John Dewey and Croly, and for public figures such as Theodore Roosevelt (and "to some extent" Woodrow Wilson), they wrote:

> the irresistible forces of modernity were beginning to sweep away the boundaries that historically had contained and preserved the island communities. Modern means of communication—telegraph, telephone, the high speed press—had breached the small town's borders with a relentless barrage of information about the larger world, ending its isolation. Great cities had sprung up, populated by aggregates of isolated, disconnected individuals, rather than by tightly knit neighbors.... In short, the forces of modernity had precip-

itated a crisis of community in America: the small town and
its civic virtues had been shattered.

The Progressives were especially concerned with the power of the
large new economic combinations that were replacing the small
shop and factory. They therefore called upon the central government "to tame through regulatory action those great and disruptive
concentrations of private wealth, the corporations, thereby turning
them into 'express economic agents of the whole community,' as
Croly put it."

Joyce and Schambra pointedly declined to join the central issue
raised by the Progressive and New Deal project: whether these large
concentrations of economic power needed taming if democracy
and some semblance of local community were to be preserved.
Instead, they carried the story forward through the New Deal and
the Great Society, arguing that Progressives had developed a cult of
"expertise," a devotion to centralized power and a contempt for
traditional local forms of civic life. As they saw the Progressives'
goals, "[e]xperts needed to replace civic and voluntary social
programs not only because those civil institutions represented backward, unsophisticated citizens hopelessly encumbered by retrograde values, but also because the social sciences understood how
to manipulate the powerful, subtle forces of modern society that in
fact had produced social problems in the first place." Americans—
citizens—were to be led to believe that the answers to their problems lay not at home, not in their neighborhoods and cities, but in
Washington, where a wise and benevolent federal government was
best equipped to deal with "the great economic questions."

For Joyce and Schambra, the revolt against this idea began in
the 1960s. Unusually for conservative theorists, they acknowledged
that not only conservatives but also the New Left came to reject the
centralizing, bureaucratic tendencies of the modern state and the
extent to which it sapped local energies, creating "loneliness, estrangement, isolation," as Students for a Democratic Society put it in
their founding document, "The Port Huron Statement." Joyce and
Schambra also acknowledged the importance of the backlash
against civil rights, especially in the old ethnic neighborhoods of the
big cities in the Northeast and Middle West. Seen from such places,
"the national government seemed to have launched a massive as-

sault—through cold, bureaucratic edict—against the traditional prerogatives of locality and neighborhood to define and preserve their
own ways of life."

Joyce and Schambra then offered a sweeping view of the country's political history after 1964. Since Richard Nixon's election, in
one contest after another, the victorious candidate had won by
avoiding forthright calls for a shift of power to Washington and
denouncing "centralized, bureaucratic government." This was not
only true of Republican candidates, they argued, but also of the two
Democrats to triumph in this period, Jimmy Carter and Bill Clinton.
Carter had spoken against "proliferating, wasteful, bloated bureaucracies." Clinton was more explicit in his support for government,
but even he declared repeatedly that "our problems go way beyond
the reach of government" and were "rooted in the loss of values,
the disappearance of work and the breakdown of families and communities." Clinton's emphasis on the importance of civil society and
local community, they argued, was quite different from the traditional liberal's call for "national community."

Yet repeatedly, America's call for less power in Washington was
frustrated, "solemn quadrennial promises to the contrary notwithstanding." This, said Joyce and Schambra, explained the "tsunami of
1994." Voters had "trudged . . . ever more angrily to the polls to vote
against centralized power, yet had found their wishes ignored."

Their conclusion flowed naturally from their historical analysis: that Americans had given up on big Washington-based dreams,
big government, big bureaucracies and a big class of big-headed
experts. Their concerns were more basic:

> that they are not safe from random violence in *this* house or
> *this* neighborhood; that they cannot send their children safely
> down *this* street to the local school; that they can no longer
> rely on *this* school to teach their children both rigorous,
> basic academics, and sound moral values in tune with *their*
> deepest spiritual and ethical commitments.

Thus is the rationale for their "new citizenship," designed to end
the rule of Washington-based "experts" and render power to citizens and the institutions they had built with their own hands and
hearts. "That positive agenda is once again to empower civic institutions, local governments, families and citizens genuinely to make

the public decisions and carry out the public tasks that really 'count,'" they wrote. Their analysis led them to the same place Kristol had discovered: the need to tear down government bureaucracies and "empower" citizens and community groups through vouchers. They urged this solution not simply for schools, but also as an approach to other social problems such as welfare. Instead of having the central government pass along money to the poor, why not send the checks to private, often church-based institutions that housed teen mothers and their children "in disciplined moral and spiritual environments"? The goal of the new citizenship, they argued, "would be to use public policy once more to encourage and cultivate, rather than to denigrate and undercut, the rich variety of vigorous civic, religious, ethnic and voluntary associations once central to American society...."

The importance of the Kristol-Schambra-Joyce approach lay in its promise of solving several conservative problems at once. As we have seen, it could ease the estrangement of the traditionalists and the moralists from the libertarians. All could agree on the need to battle against centralized state power and the bureaucracies, even if their motivations were different. Indeed, all could now celebrate "family values" with less fear that this slogan would entail the harsh use of government to impose a narrow or particular moral agenda. If social problems arose because of the decline of the family and the breakup of traditional institutions, the answers surely lay not with government but with strengthening these institutions *against* government. Libertarians had no problem with the idea that parents ought to be responsible for their own children. And especially in the hands of Schambra, the new agenda moved the Republicans away from their image as hardhearted accountants intent only on cutting budgets. "We must remind ourselves that to work for decentralization and the revival of civic institutions and values is not to turn our backs on community and compassion in the name of greed and self-interest," Joyce and Schambra wrote. "It is rather to reconstruct the most enduring forms of community that human beings and Americans have ever known—families, churches, neighborhoods, civic and voluntary associations." On top of this, Kristol's sense that reforms aimed at weakening Congress and other federal institutions would be good for conservatism gave the movement a strong bond with

the nonideological protest movements, and in particular with Perot's sympathizers.

Fundamentally, these theories underlay an attempt to reconstruct Reaganism on stronger ground. They gave Republican candidates in 1994 a set of arguments against the most effective liberal
and Democratic attacks. This conservatism, like the old, was for
smaller government and family values, but it also made *freedom* and
compassion partners in its creed, even if the new compassion would
do its work without government, or at least with as little government as possible. This conservatism spoke powerfully to the Anxious Middle's sense of alienation from government and to its
worries about moral crisis. In the short term, that was enough.

This conservatism also saw its goals in terms much larger than
those that had defined the Reagan Revolution. Reaganism was mostly
an effort to roll back the Great Society, but it broadly accepted the
New Deal project. Indeed, Reagan's repeated invocations of his own
past as an FDR supporter reassured many Democrats-turned-
Republican that they were breaking not with their basic political
commitments but with an aberration from those commitments represented by the politics of the sixties counterculture and the New
Left.

The new conservatives of the 1990s, on the other hand, were
waging war on the whole Progressive tradition going back to Croly,
Theodore Roosevelt and Wilson and continuing through Truman. It
became commonplace in conservative circles to refer to the 1994
elections as "the end of the New Deal," and many wanted to rip the
New Deal out from the roots, which meant attacking Progressivism
itself.

Significantly, Joyce and Schambra's paper was the centerpiece
of a conference organized by the conservative Hudson Institute in
December 1994 around the theme "The New Promise of American
Life," a play on Croly's 1909 Progressive manifesto, *The Promise of
American Life*. The thesis of virtually all the papers delivered at the
conference, including a keynote address by Republican presidential
candidate Lamar Alexander, was that the time of Croly and the
Progressives had passed. While treating Croly respectfully, the participants argued that the long-term impact of his ideas had been to
centralize power, aggrandize government and create what Chester
E. Finn Jr. called "the culture of governmentalism."

Finn, a professor at Vanderbilt University and a former Bush administration official, argued that the Progressive dream ended in a nightmare involving "vast government bureaucracies that brim with delay, red tape, frustration and constraint" and "widespread dependency—both the material and behavioral kinds—on government for the wherewithal of daily life." Finn, Alexander and the rest of the participants contended that the future lay in an entirely different direction: toward decentralization and devolution of authority from Washington. Local communities, not Washington-based experts, offered the wisest counsel on the solution to social problems. Even if the centralized state inspired by the Progressive vision had been necessary to solve the problems created by the Great Depression and to win the battles against Nazi Germany and the Soviet Union, it was needed no longer now that the Cold War was over. Thus did the new conservatives claim not simply to be right, but also on the right side of history.

VIII

The neo-Reaganite (or, perhaps, anti-Progressive) formula did not solve all the problems of conservatism. Like the *National Review*'s earlier efforts at "fusionism," it had the potential of flying apart whenever one wing of the movement pressed its demands too strongly. It could suppress many differences within the right, but as Bill Kristol acknowledged, it could not eliminate them. Ultimately, issues such as abortion, public school prayer, gay rights and feminism would have to be faced. Ralph Reed's efforts to push his constituency toward "the politics of liberty" could go only so far, as Reed knew well.

Many who came to the Christian Coalition were motivated not by abstract theory but by a deep anxiety over what they saw as the moral decay of the country. The messages Reed put forward often clashed sharply with those of the man who had founded the Christian Coalition, Pat Robertson. To listen to Reed's press conferences and then either to Robertson's broadcasts or to many of the movement's activists was to become aware of two very different worlds. "Will the real Christian Coalition please stand up?" asked James Guth, a professor of political science at Furman University, speaking

at a conference organized by the generally conservative Ethics and
Public Policy Center. "Is its true nature more like that of its executive director, Ralph Reed, or of the activists I heard at the Coalition's national convention, responding . . . in ways that I thought did
not reflect the broadened and more moderate policy stand?"

When the coalition's candidates triumphed in election contests,
particularly for control of local school boards, their programs—
whether on creationism or sex education or promoting "proper values"—inevitably unleashed a powerful backlash not only among
liberals but also among more moderate conservatives and Republicans. Those who might agree with the coalition on some of what it
was fighting *against* often disagreed with what it was fighting *for*.

Reed himself seemed to understand the delicacy of his situation. He was running ahead of his constituency in de-emphasizing
certain social issues and in laying heavy stress on free-market economics and low taxes—positions that were not particularly "bibli-
cal." Yet he knew that only such an emphasis held the prospect for
long-term peace in the Republican Party. Over the course of a single
weekend in February 1995, Reed underscored how difficult his
balancing act was by sending two quite different messages, one
clearly directed to his base in the evangelical movement, the other
to the broader Republican Party. On a Friday, Reed told the Conservative Political Action Conference meeting in Washington that
evangelical Christians and anti-abortion Catholics would refuse to
vote for a Republican ticket with a presidential *or* vice presidential
candidate who favored abortion rights. He complained that Christian conservatives were tired of being told "that the social issues are
losers, that we must downplay values and we must sublimate our
Christianity." *Washington Post* reporter Thomas B. Edsall noted that
for Reed, the speech marked "a shift from his past role as a concil-
iator" and "suggested that he has faced growing criticism within
Christian conservative ranks for his past willingness to postpone
some of the more controversial elements of the conservative
agenda. . . ."

Yet just three days later, there was Reed on the op-ed page of *The
Wall Street Journal* back to his conciliatory role. Having just declared
war against pro-choice Republicans, he asserted that "the much anticipated 'holy war' pitting moderates against religious people in the
GOP ended without a single shot being fired." He even picked up the

old Frank Meyer formula, writing that "in an essentially conservative society, traditionalist ends can be advanced through libertarian means." And he insisted that on issues such as abortion, it was possible for the discordant wings of the party to remain "civil." It's hard to believe that Reed regarded his threat of a few days earlier to bolt the party as lying within his definition of "civility." Rarely has a single individual so dramatically demonstrated the intellectual and strategic tensions within a political posture.

A further and even more profound problem arose when several journalists, notably Michael Lind in *The New York Review of Books,* reviewed the conspiracy theories contained in Robertson's 1991 book, *The New World Order.* Lind found remarkable parallels between Robertson's words and the contents of several anti-semitic classics. Robertson drained some of the old conspiracy theories of their most rabid anti-semitism, but still spoke of schemes by "German bankers," and said Paul Warburg and Jacob Schiff were part of the conspiracy. Both Warburg and Schiff were Jewish, and their names had appeared over and over in the literature of anti-semitism. Robertson vehemently denied any anti-semitic intentions. Reed, sensing danger, gave a powerful speech to the Anti-Defamation League of the B'nai B'rith. He did not mention Robertson by name, but did acknowledge that some in the Christian conservative movement had been insensitive to and insufficiently mindful of Jewish suffering in the Holocaust. Later, Robertson himself insisted that there was nothing anti-semitic in what he had written and said, and that he opposed anti-semitism.

Tensions emerged even among the different wings of social conservatism. These were most pronounced when the House took up its radical welfare reform bill in March 1995. The bill was designed to slash spending on the poor by $100 billion over seven years. The "pro-family" wing of the movement strongly favored measures to combat family breakup and to discourage the creation of single-parent families headed by teen mothers. They thus pushed hard for a measure in the House bill that would cut off all welfare assistance to children born to mothers who were under the age of eighteen. But this provision was anathema to the right-to-life movement, which argued that it would create strong incentives for teen mothers to abort their children. Representative Christopher Smith, a New Jersey Republican and a leading congressional spokesman

for the anti-abortion movement, labeled the provision "inhumane."
While the House Republican leadership eventually made enough
concessions to pull the party together, abortion foes came within six
votes of halting debate on the measure. Feelings were rubbed raw
during the battle. Smith, for example, reported that he had fought
fiercely with many pro-family conservatives—notably Gary Bauer, a
leading abortion foe and the president of the Family Research Council—who had been longtime allies.

These conflicts suggested the longer-term problems the neo-
Reaganites would face in trying to fashion peace within the conservative coalition. But Democrats were in a weak position to take
advantage of these shortcomings after their own failures in the first
two Clinton years. Compared to that failure, the new Republican
agenda sounded very good indeed. And no one liked talking about
it more than Newt Gingrich, who was busy fashioning an even
farther-reaching revision of conservative practice and doctrine.

WHY GINGRICH HAPPENED:

Old Waves, New Waves and Third Waves

"PEOPLE ARE NOT in general stupid," wrote Newt Gingrich in 1984, "but they are often ignorant. In their ignorance, they often tolerate ignorant news reporters who in turn tolerate ignorant politicians. The result is an ignorant politician making an ignorant speech to be covered by an ignorant reporter and shown in a forty-second clip on television to an ignorant audience."

Gingrich's central political mission is to stand athwart mass ignorance and shout, "Listen to me!" Nothing so defines his leadership style as a profound belief that he has unlocked the secrets of history and the meaning of the future. "I am a transformational figure," Gingrich declared shortly before the 1994 elections. "I think I am trying to effect a change so large that the people who will be hurt by the change, the liberal machine, have a natural reaction." Nor did he stop there. "I think because I'm so systematically purposeful about changing our world," he said, "I'm a much tougher partisan than they've seen . . . much more intense, much more persistent, much more willing to take risks to get it done." Gingrich spoke like that long before he was close to the real political power. "I have an enormous personal ambition," he said in 1985. "I want to shift the entire planet. And I'm doing it."

Gingrich's confidence, central to his ability to perceive a Republican opportunity that so many others missed, grows from a sense that he has developed the right critique of American culture, the right solution to the country's political impasse and the right strategy to advance the country's interests in the twenty-first century. At its worst, this intellectual certainty can convey itself as a remarkable arrogance impervious to outside views. But it also allows Gingrich to offer his Republican followers and the country a sense that he knows precisely where he is leading them.

Because Gingrich first came to wide public attention only in the late 1980s with his attacks on the ethics of House Speaker Jim Wright, it was widely assumed that his main purpose was bomb-throwing partisanship, that he was far more interested in disrupting the Democrats than in moving the country in any particular direction. But this was precisely wrong. For Gingrich, bomb-throwing was a means, not an end. By being confrontational, he once said, "you get attention; when you get attention, you can educate." And if Gingrich seemed ready to talk and talk and talk, that, too, was a method. "The trick is persistence," he asserted. "If you are prepared to talk about ideas long enough, the ideas filter out."

Gingrich's importance as a political strategist is obvious enough. But his greatest, if most problematic, contribution to the Republican cause was his effort to work out a set of ideas and goals that incorporated but moved beyond the neo-Reaganism of Kristol and Schambra.

In a sense, Ronald Reagan was simply bringing to center stage an older conservatism that had been routed by the New Deal but managed to regroup because of the exertions of the *National Review* crowd and the Goldwater movement. As often as not, Reagan could sound like the old pro-business conservatives of the anti-Roosevelt Liberty League, which declared in 1934 that its purpose was "to foster the right to work, earn, save and acquire property and to preserve the ownership and lawful use of property when acquired." Reagan could sound almost antique when he talked of the progressive income tax as a Marxist invention, and he dropped such rhetoric when it began to hurt him. (In 1995, though, some conservatives again began to talk of abolishing the progressive income tax altogether.)

Gingrich, on the other hand, gave conservatism a powerful forward-looking spin. The real purpose of dismantling government was not to foster old virtues or return to some golden day of free enterprise but to get bureaucrats out of the way of a new future, a future that was inevitable and irresistible and would certainly be better than the present. It was a future involving space and computers and fiber optics and unimaginable medical advances. Liberals, he insisted, were the enemies of this future and therefore had to be routed.

Within conservatism, Gingrich is one of the few leaders other than Buchanan willing to confront the meaning of the new global economy directly. Unlike Buchanan, Gingrich embraces the new economic order. For him, the central issue of politics is not to take the rough edges off the new economy or to ensure that its effects will be felt only gradually, but to push the country as rapidly as possible into the new age. Gingrich, the uncompromising partisan, surprised some Democrats with the eagerness and diligence he showed in working with the Clinton administration to pass the North American Free Trade Agreement and the General Agreement on Tariffs and Trade. But those who were surprised did not understand Gingrich's strategy or his fervor for economic change. NAFTA and GATT could only accelerate the economic transformation he was seeking. Anything that did this, he felt, would strengthen his cause in the long term. The more the United States was locked into the global market, the harder it would be for "reactionary liberals" to resist the imperatives of competition and change.

Much of what Kristol and Schambra said complemented Gingrich's own vision of a technologically oriented, individualist society where government would recede and private institutions would bear the burdens of philanthropy and moral uplift. But the roots of Gingrichism were radically different from the moral and intellectual inspirations behind the conservatism of Schambra and Kristol, Kemp and Bennett. Schambra and Kristol were moved morally and intellectually by the ancient philosophers, Kemp and Bennett by Christian sources. For Gingrich, inspiration came from futurists such as Alvin and Heidi Toffler and from management experts such as Peter Drucker and Edwards Deming. These differences in inspiration were not trivial. They pointed conservatism in very different directions.

II

Gingrich had worked out many—perhaps most—of the ideas that came to define him in the mid-1990s much earlier. His 1984 book, *Window of Opportunity,* is chock-full of concepts, notions, predictions and sermons that he was to repeat over and over again for the next decade. The specific policy recommendations in the book foreshadow many elements in the "Contract with America," and it is in many ways a more candid statement of Gingrich's view than his more cautious best-seller, *To Renew America.* Especially striking is that while Gingrich's agenda is routinely cast as "conservative," his own emphasis is quite the opposite—his strongest enthusiasms are futuristic and technological, and he often speaks and writes with disdain for those who warn of the perils and problems of change. In the first chapter of *Window of Opportunity,* Gingrich opens with page after page on how information technology, satellites, microelectronics, space exploration, advances in telephonic communication, biotechnology and "advanced health care" will transform the world for the better. He waits for twenty-seven pages before finding a moment to talk about conservative values ("old values"), and even then he links them to change. "Male and female roles will be redefined and old values rediscovered," he says. There is sociological detachment in Gingrich's discussion of religion; he speaks in large part of its social function and describes "the re-emergence of religion as a legitimate vehicle for explaining the world." Even when talking about faith, Gingrich cannot resist the high-tech angle. "Presently there will be religious software for home computers," he writes, "and a host of modern high tech efforts to spread a new, electronic gospel, an outreach building not only in Christianity today, but in Orthodox Judaism and Islam as well."

Gingrich's strongest criticisms of liberals focus less on radical or revolutionary tendencies in their creed than on their *resistance* to change, especially of the technological variety. "The forces of special-interest unionism and special-interest industries are combining with the Liberal wing of the Democratic Party to avoid change, to hide from competition, and to delay technology," he writes. "If they are successful, America's future becomes bleaker." Gingrich finds an anti-technological thrust in both the British and the American left which he traces to British writer John Ruskin's "romantic rejection of high technology." Again and again in his political pronouncements, Gingrich has returned to the idea that his main enemies are those who resist the drive for technological improvement and the coming of the "information age" economy. The left, he says, "has rejected any hope of salvation through technological innovation."

Salvation through technological innovation. Without question, this idea is central to the Gingrich creed. His fascination with outer space and the marvel of new worlds is underscored repeatedly in *Window of Opportunity,* beginning with the front cover, which notes that Gingrich is "Chairman of the Congressional Space Caucus." The preface is written by Jerry Pournelle, a science fiction writer, and another science fiction writer, David Drake, is listed as a coauthor of the book. Of its thirteen chapters, one is devoted to space exploration and describes space as "the greatest frontier." Two others are devoted to the importance of the "Star Wars" missile defense system, the only issue that gets two chapters of its own. Here is one area where Gingrich is all for large-scale government spending. He proposes giving the National Aeronautics and Space Administration funding equal to its "peak budget" of 1965, which would have been a large increase over 1984 levels. On the issue of space, as on so many other questions, Gingrich's sharpest attacks focus on the alleged refusal of the left to understand the enormous potential of technology. Accusing the left of helping to create "the anti-technology movement," he declares: "In a very real sense, our hippies overshadowed our astronauts and the anti-technology bias of the Left overshadowed the possibilities of the Computer Age." Citing C. P. Snow's essay on the distance between the culture of science and the culture of the humanities, Gingrich laments the aggressive articulateness of those who were skeptical of technological change. "Those who know how to speak and write have been technophobic," he says. "Those who understood technology's promise for the future have generally been inarticulate."

Gingrich's technological hopes lead him to a profoundly nonconservative critique of those who would resist the transformation that is coming. "Rather than whining that change is frightening (which it is), that change often disassociates us from our roots (which it does), and that change sometimes has undesirable side effects (which is true)," he writes, "our grandchildren will accept these caveats as facts of life." He adds: "They will ask their culture to teach them how to rise above these difficulties rather than hide from them." Gingrich here accepts in parentheses the theoretical legitimacy of some of the most powerful conservative impulses, but ultimately dismisses them as "whining."

It cannot be stressed enough that Gingrich's goal is not to avoid change but to speed it up, as he makes clear on the first page of *Window of Opportunity*. "The optimistic future will necessitate accepting the possibilities inherent in our emerging technologies and accelerating the transition to a high technology, information based economy," he writes. The key words here are "accelerating the transition." Gingrich's objective is to push the United States as rapidly as possible into "the Third Wave" of history, as described by his intellectual heroes, Alvin and Heidi Toffler. In 1994 the Progress and Freedom Foundation, the think tank founded by Gingrich the year before, brought out a ninety-seven-page booklet containing excerpts from the Tofflers' work under the title *Creating a New Civilization: The Politics of the Third Wave*. In a foreword to the book, Gingrich again underscores his impatience with "columnists and academics" who "all seem confused by the scale of change." Their problem, as ever, is that they are too worried about the costs of the Great Transition. Gingrich tries to cast his complaints in populist terms by claiming that critics of change are simply trying to protect falling elites. "There is an inevitable focus on the pain of those who have been dominant and the disorientation of those who have been powerful," he contends. "The agony of the past is outweighing the promise of the future." Neatly, Gingrich thereby moves attention away from the impact of the transition on those who are neither dominant nor powerful.

What must be understood about Newt Gingrich is that his sense of mission cannot be defined or limited by the Reaganite past. Other Republicans might be content to adopt a neo-Reaganite approach, to try to paper over internal party fights and philosophical differences in order to keep the old faith alive. Gingrich, however, brings an unusual mixture of ideas, visions and obsessions to the task of building a new Republican Party. He shares with Clinton an understanding that the United States is passing through a profoundly disorienting period of transition. His staple sound bite refers to "forcing the scale of change necessary to be successful in the twenty-first century." This might be dismissed as normal politician future-speak but for the telltale word "forcing." Politicians rarely speak openly about "forcing" anything to happen, usually preferring a language that emphasizes consensus and persuasion. Gingrich, however, does not shy away from this candid description of his style of leadership. Certain as he is about where the country needs to go, he is quite prepared to force it to get there.

Fundamentally, Gingrich envisions the Republican Party as representing the forces of the future—those who are doing well in the new economy, or expect or hope to, and are therefore willing to take the risk of accelerating the transition into "the Third Wave." His is the Republican gambit of William McKinley in 1896, and much about that strategy of a hundred years earlier appeals to Newt Gingrich. One of his heroes is Mark Hanna, the man who organized McKinley's triumph. The 1896 Republicans had made a fundamental choice: to represent the rising forces of industrialism, to organize the emerging captains of industry as the party's financial arm and to write off the country's "backward" rural sectors. It was left to William Jennings Bryan and a coalition of Democrats and Populists to speak for the hurt and the injustices the new order was inflicting on small farmers and small towns, the people losing out in the triumph of modern capitalism. The strategy worked well for McKinley and Hanna in 1896. The Republicans lost in the South, the farm states and the Rockies. But they swept the big industrial states of the Northeast and Midwest, with businessmen voting to defend their interests and industrial workers voting to preserve their jobs.

When Gingrich speaks of "the politics of the Third Wave," he is describing the 1990s version of the Hanna-McKinley strategy. Just as Hanna and McKinley embraced industrialism ("the Second Wave"), the new Republican Party needs to become the conscious agent of the new, global, information age economy. Its geographical base may be different: The Third Wave is surging through the Sun Belt and in the suburbs and exurbs, not in the big cities of the Northeast. But Gingrich, like Mark Hanna, believes he sees the future clearly, and he intends to organize and master it.

There are important substantive differences between Gingrich and Hanna (and, for that matter, between Gingrich and McKinley), notably that the 1896 Republicans were protectionist and that Hanna had considerable sympathy for government intervention and Progressivism. But the similarities between Gingrich's crusade and Hanna's are important for understanding both why Gingrich's proposals sound so radical and also why, despite their trappings in high technology and space, they actually mark a *reversion* back to the Republicanism of the pre-Progressive period, the particular form of conservatism that dominated the Gilded Age before the turn of the century. The radicalism of Gingrich's agenda lies in its effort to overturn the fundamental achievements of Theodore Roosevelt's Square Deal, Woodrow Wilson's New Freedom, Franklin Roosevelt's New Deal and Harry Truman's Fair Deal. At times, Gingrich made this quite clear, as when he embraced and repeatedly touted the social policy theories of Marvin Olasky. Olasky, the author of *The Tragedy of American Compassion,* argues that almost every trend in social policy since the emergence of Progressivism was wrong. In general, almost any forms of compassion that were sponsored by government were destined to atrophy into bureaucratized sustenance for bad values on the part of the poor. The only proper way to raise up the poor is through private efforts, mostly connected to churches, that can demand that as the price for charity, poor people have to live by very strict rules imposed by the charity giver. Olasky explicitly attacks reformers of the Progressive period for "utopian" efforts to routinize charity through government. Among other things, this undermined the private, mostly religiously based charities, reduced the "affiliation" and "bonding" between the poor and those who helped them, made it harder to "categorize" the poor to determine who was "worthy of relief," reduced the employment demands placed on the poor and, ultimately, cut the link between religion and uplift. Olasky admits that some government intervention might have been necessary to ease suffering during the Great Depression and sees the Work Projects Administration programs as better than most social programs. He also disassociates himself from (and criticizes) turn-of-the-century "social Darwinists" such as William Graham Sumner, who scorned charity as a useless interference in a "natural" process through which the fittest survived and prospered. But Olasky's broad conclusion is that the bulk of government-led social welfare efforts in the twentieth century were failures, and that the lessons that most needed to be learned were those from the voluntaristic charities of the 1800s. "It's time to learn from the warm hearts and hard heads of earlier times, and to bring that understanding into our own lives," he concludes. Olasky later joined Gingrich's Progress and Freedom Foundation, and Gingrich repeatedly praised Olasky's book, declaring flatly: "Olasky has the right sense of where we have to go as Americans."

Even more importantly, Gingrich, at least implicitly, embraces a version of the philosophical materialism of Gilded Age conservatism. He asserts that a natural evolutionary process (represented by "the Third Wave") is inevitable, that it will bring with it enormous technical progress, and that those who resist the change are sentimentalists ("the anti-technology movement"). That was exactly how conservatives who championed "Second Wave" industrialism felt about social reformers, agrarian rebels, church leaders and others who challenged the authority of the industrial giants. They, like Gingrich, were concerned with removing the barriers to industrial innovation and achievement, and did not shy away from such steps even if they led to economic concentration or significant inequalities. In the long run, they argued, the process of change would immensely strengthen the country since countries, too, went through their own "natural" patterns involving rise and fall. "What is true," said Sumner, "is that there are periods of social advance and periods of social decline, that is advance or decline in *economic power, material prosperity* and *group strength for war.*" Compare this with Gingrich's celebration of

> a new generation which reasons that *if* we are the most creative society on the planet, *if* we have the most advanced technology, *if* we continually shoulder the monetary burdens of other nations, *if* we provide the umbrella under which the freedom of others are protected, and *if* we disproportionately finance the United Nations, then maybe other countries ought to listen to us at least as closely as they expect us to listen to them.

Gingrich elaborated on this position in a speech to the National Association of Manufacturers in May 1995:

> We want to communicate a vision of America which is the decisive economic power on the planet, which is the most competitive nation, which is capable of leading the human race and which has reestablished here at home a culture that works and has reestablished physical safety so that people get up in the morning knowing they have a terrific opportunity to pursue happiness and an economic structure that works and a neighborhood that's safe. Now that's our general positive vision.

It should be noted here that Gingrich's formulation of Republican goals has the potential to speak powerfully to some who are drawn to Pat Buchanan's nationalism. Gingrich's vision is also a nationalist conception, seeing the United States as "the decisive economic power on the planet" and "capable of leading the human race." But unlike Buchanan, Gingrich rejects protectionism, seeing the rigors of world competition as good for a United States amply capable of dominating the new information age. Their difference in approach is fundamental and has deep historical roots. Buchanan is in some ways closer to the protectionist nationalism of McKinley and Hanna, Gingrich to the fiercely competitive nationalism espoused by Sumner. But both Buchanan and Gingrich repeatedly use strongly nationalistic language about the United States' destiny to be the planet's premier power.

Sumner was unapologetic about the need to achieve his ends by rewarding the most powerful and productive. "If we should set a limit to the accumulation of wealth," he writes, "we should say to our most valuable producers, 'We do not want you to do us the services which you best understand how to perform, beyond a certain point.' It would be like killing off our generals in war."

Gingrich is equally willing to allow those with the wherewithal to invest to set many of the terms, not only in economics but in politics itself. Gingrich declares frankly that his goal is to make the United States more attractive to investors who are searching the globe for low taxes, few regulations and few lawsuits. In his speech to the manufacturers, for example, Gingrich declared that he would ask Congress's Joint Economic Committee to pose the following question to the heads of multinational companies: "Tell us under what circumstances you'd put the next thousand high value-added jobs in the U.S. What do we need to do to regulation, taxation, litigation, education, welfare, the structure of the bureaucracy? You tell us how to make this the best place on the planet to invest." Rarely has a politician been so explicit in laying out the meaning of the old phrase "the business of America is business." Critics of Gingrich's view could reasonably see it as involving a wholesale surrender to the forces of the global marketplace. What kind of democracy leaves its policies on "regulation, taxation, litigation, education, welfare, the structure of the bureaucracy" to the dictates of multinational investors? But Gingrich, following the Gilded Age view, sees the alternative involving government regulation and government-sponsored welfare as weakening society and the natural process of competition. "The fatal problem of the welfare state," Gingrich once said, is that "the welfare state creates losers." He went on:

> You didn't have losers in immigrant America of the 1800s. You had future winners. You had people who worked extra hard and they sent their kids to school and they took two or three jobs and they saved like crazy and it was very hard. But within a generation, they were winning. And we've replaced that with a system that says we're going to help you so much your grandchildren are going to be exactly where you are.

Gingrich, of course, would deny any affiliation with nineteenth-century social Darwinism, and he could cite his own strongly stated opposition to racism, along with his affection for Olasky, in support of this claim. But the core similarity between Gingrich and the main line of Gilded Age conservative thinking, including social Darwinism, is clear and well captured by Robert McCloskey in his brilliant book, *American Conservatism in the Age of Enterprise*. In Gilded Age conservatism, McCloskey wrote in 1951, "Civilization was equated with industrialization, and progress was defined as the accumulation of capital and the proliferation of industrial inventions." Change "industrialization" to "the Third Wave" and "industrial" to "high-tech," and one has a fair description of the Gingrich creed. McCloskey also understood how radically this view transformed traditional American notions of democracy and personal liberty. "Classical economics and the concept of organic evolution," he wrote, "conspired to change the old doctrine of the moral improvement of man into a theory of material progress."

Gingrich, with considerable subtlety and intelligence, is proposing a drastic rewrite of a social contract that is a hundred years old. But beneath his talk of the new are some very old ideas that were, until very recently, thought obsolete. Gingrich's "revolution" might just as properly be seen as a counterrevolution built on an old evolutionary materialism that many conservatives themselves have rejected. Gingrich does bow to "traditional values" and is certainly aware of the importance of the Christian conservatives to his coalition. But what most interests him about cultural questions are not "traditional values" as such, but whether the United States can build a culture that could function on behalf of the information age. As he told the manufacturers, he wants "a culture that works."

At times Gingrich's obsessions lead him to sound like a parody of himself, as when he proposed what he admitted was the "nutty idea" of providing a tax credit so poor people could buy computers. But beneath the high-tech jargon lies a sophisticated strategy that seeks to transform the Republican Party into the advance guard of the economy, and leave the Democrats to defend the "obsolete" sectors. This time those sectors represent not rural America but decaying big cities, unionized manufacturing and other institutions, and groups destined, in Gingrich's view, to be swept aside by "the Third Wave."

For the most part, Republicans have ignored Gingrich's Third Wave talk as a personal eccentricity and have chosen instead to admire his raw political acumen. At an operational level, he puts his emphasis on those issues most likely to create a sustainable Republican coalition. Thus he speaks incessantly about replacing the "welfare state" with "an opportunity society," knowing that the word "welfare" is now associated in the public mind with dependency, sloth and illegitimacy. His rhetoric is built around a careful study of the impact of words and their reception by the public. He issued a well-publicized list of "good" and "bad" words in public discourse, calling on his allies to associate themselves with "good" words (such as "reform") and their opponents with "bad" ones (such as "corrupt"). When he compared the "liberal welfare state" with the "conservative opportunity society," each word in each phrase amounted to a pair. "Liberal" was contrasted with "conservative" (there are more self-identified conservatives than liberals), "welfare" with "opportunity" (no contest between those two), and "state" with "society" (because, echoing Schambra's arguments, he wants to move attention away from government's role and toward the social forces outside government). He identifies all government with the word "bureaucrats" and seeks to cast all choices about spending and taxes as a decision between giving money to those "bureaucrats" or letting citizens use the money themselves.

Gingrich constantly ties himself back into the conservative tradition, of course, paying regular tribute to Ronald Reagan as the founder of the great movement of which he is part. But in truth, Gingrich likes most of all to describe himself as a "revolutionary," and his message, in the end, is more that of a revolutionary than the talk of a conservative. ("When Newt says he is a revolutionary," Alvin Toffler once remarked, "take him seriously.") The dialectics of Marx (or, perhaps more accurately, Hegel) are never far from Gingrich's lips. "I see us at a point where the old thesis is now collapsing and there's an opportunity to launch a new thesis, not just to be the antithesis but to launch a new thesis," he once said.

III

Inspired by both Hanna and Hegel, Gingrich has long had a genius for thinking and plotting systematically, of finding ways to sow disorder in the opposition while strengthening the bonds within his own coalition. He has never been shy about talking of his long-term objectives, yet he has never confused vision with tactics or strategy, and he has always understood that in the absence of tactics and strategy, a vision is lifeless and without effect. So he does not allow his vision for tomorrow to cloud his view of what needs to be done *today,* to assemble the votes and political support to pursue his objectives.

Gingrich's rise to power can be seen as passing through four stages. His earliest years in Congress, from his election in 1978 to the mid-1980s, were spent on developing a long-term view, a critique of the existing Republican congressional leadership and a strategy that would link the two. The vision was outlined in *Window of Opportunity* and in a series of speeches and lectures—notably in his own college course. The critique was developed in practice, rooted in Gingrich's earliest political campaigns and sharpened in response to Republican failures, particularly in the 1982 midterm elections.

The second stage involved his frontal assault against the Democrats, epitomized by his success in bringing down House Speaker Jim Wright on charges of corruption. In the third stage, Gingrich consolidated his hold on the House Republican Party, culminating in his unopposed selection as party leader, all of his potential competitors having been driven from the field of battle. In this stage, Gingrich was willing to divide his own party in order to conquer it and to confront a Republican president, even at the risk (eventually realized) of bringing his president down.

Finally, Gingrich sought to assemble a program that could both unite a majority coalition behind Republican candidates at election time and provide the party with a guide to action once in power. The "Contract with America" was the centerpiece of this effort, but it was only part of a broader plan.

If Gingrich's vision, as we have seen, was based on a hard, cold analysis of the future, his critique of the Republican Party and its habits was at least as tough-minded. John M. Barry, the author of an excellent book on the Jim Wright affair, describes Gingrich as possessing "the coldness of raw intellect, of absolute zero." Barry cites a speech Gingrich gave in 1978 to a college Republican group, recruiting volunteers for his first successful congressional campaign:

> One of the great problems we have had in the Republican Party is that we ... encourage you to be neat, obedient, and loyal and faithful, and all those Boy Scout words which can be great around the campfire but are lousy in politics. ... A number of you are old enough to have been a rifleman in Vietnam. This is the same business. You're fighting a war. It is a war for power. ... Don't try to educate. That is not your job. What is the primary purpose of a political leader? To build a majority. ... If [people] care about parking lots, talk to them about parking lots.

Unlike many politicians, Gingrich was unapologetic about the need to address voters where they were, with what they wanted to hear. "Politics is about public opinion and gathering public support," he told *The Washington Post*'s Dan Balz and Charles Babcock after the 1994 elections, defending his use of polls. "It's like saying, isn't it pandering for Wal-Mart to stock everything people want to buy?" And the Gingrich who was proud not to be a Boy Scout was to be on frequent, often outrageous, display, ever willing to condemn the Democrats for espousing "Woody Allen" values, as he did in 1992, or to suggest on the eve of the 1994 elections that Democrats were somehow complicit in a gruesome, well-publicized murder case involving a mother who killed her own children.

Running in the mid-1970s against a Georgia Democratic Party that had utterly dominated state politics, Gingrich understood the power of the corruption issue to forge the majority he was seeking. It would become his version of parking lots. In his very first campaign for Congress in 1974, he began using the word "reform." Waging war on corruption was not simply a broadly popular thing to do; it also had the potential of splitting the opposition, drawing reform-minded moderates and liberals, including many Democrats, to the Republican side. It was an especially valuable issue to Gingrich in his first two campaigns against John Flynt, a conservative, segregationist Democrat much hated by liberal Georgians. In both 1974 and 1976, Gingrich ran with substantial liberal support. Only when Flynt retired and the national tide began moving toward conservatism did Gingrich, an admirer of Eisenhower and a former supporter of Nelson Rockefeller, move substantially to the right. Still, he did not forget the value of the corruption issue.

In his first year in the House, he led a Republican effort to get Representative Charles C. Diggs, a Michigan Democrat, expelled. Diggs had been convicted of diverting $6,000 from his congressional payroll to his own use. It was a preview of how Gingrich would use the ethics issue to overturn the entire House Democratic establishment. But what dominated his early years in the House was his effort to formulate an alternative to the "go-along-to-get-along" strategy that had failed House Republicans for years. Gingrich liked to say that he operated on a "planning model" that involved a hierarchy of values, topped by "vision" and followed by "strategies," "projects" and "tactics." In his first years in Congress, he concentrated on "vision" and "projects."

Immediately after his election, he was given an unlikely task for a freshman by Representative Guy Vander Jagt, the chairman of the National Republican Congressional Committee: to formulate a plan to convert the Republicans into a majority party. It was, in a sense, the task that was to dominate Gingrich's political life. The Republicans took a huge step forward in 1980 with Ronald Reagan's victory and gained thirty-three House seats. But the 1982 elections, held in the middle of a deep recession, wiped out almost all of the Republicans' gains. A discouraged Gingrich met with Richard Nixon, who shared Gingrich's pessimism about the state of the party. Nixon told Gingrich the Republicans needed to be "more interesting, more energetic, and more idea-oriented." Gingrich was inspired to form what became the Conservative Opportunity Society, his group of Republican rebels. In a sense, the group embodied Gingrich's quartet of goals, "vision, strategies, projects, tactics." Its broad purpose was to lay out a more comprehensive vision than even Reagan himself had managed, the administration having run out of steam long before the 1982 election returns were in. The COSers embraced Jack Kemp's imperative that the Republican Party needed to convey a far more optimistic approach to the future, embodied in the word "opportunity." Gingrich and his close working partner, Representative Vin Weber, were to emerge as two of Kemp's important supporters. The COS was the launching ground for Gingrich's vision-spinning for a high-tech future. But the group was also fiercely dedicated to projects and tactics meant to harass the House Democratic leadership and draw public attention to its flaws.

Gingrich and his allies were among the first members of Congress to realize the potential use of C-Span's broadcasts of congressional sessions to reach sympathetic voters and potential activists out in the country. (In *Window of Opportunity,* one of Gingrich's suggestions to conservative activists was that they try to convince their local cable company to carry C-Span.) COS members regularly used the time at the end of the congressional day, given over to individual speeches known as "special orders," to give highly partisan addresses, usually to an empty House chamber. The empty chamber, of course, was not the target audience; listeners out in the country were. Since the camera focused only on the speaking member, viewers had no idea that almost no members of Congress were listening. In 1984 their speeches so infuriated House Speaker Tip O'Neill that he ordered House cameras to pan the floor, just so viewers could know that no one in the House was listening. COS members had taken to the floor to denounce Democrats for a "Dear Commandante" letter to Nicaraguan Sandinista leader Daniel Ortega. Gingrich had called the Democrats appeasers who had a "pessimistic, defeatist and skeptical view toward the American role in the world." Days later O'Neill took the floor to denounce Gingrich for launching his assault when those under attack were not even present to defend themselves. "You deliberately stood in the well before an empty House and challenged these people when you knew they would not be there," he said. "It's the lowest thing that I have ever seen in my thirty-two years in Congress."

Not all the conservatives who started out with Gingrich stayed with him. Representative Dan Coats, a staunchly conservative Indiana Republican who was later elected to the Senate, was one who decided to pursue other political options. "Newt's belief that to succeed you almost had to destroy the system so that you could rebuild it ... was a kind of scary stuff for new people coming in," Coats recalled. "I ultimately came to the conclusion that the style in which COS was operating was not compatible with my personal style, so my involvement diminished."

Gingrich was not one to rest with just one approach to change. In 1986 former Delaware Governor Pete du Pont asked him if he wanted to take over GOPAC, an organization that helped Republicans with state and local offices, especially seats in state legislatures. GOPAC substantially broadened Gingrich's horizons, giving him a chance to head an organization dedicated to rebuilding the Republican Party at the grass roots. The way Gingrich used GOPAC was revealing of his ability to understand how organization, fund-raising and intellectual entrepreneurship could reinforce one another. He transformed the group from one that largely gave out money to Republican candidates into a vehicle for motivating Republican activists. Gingrich himself was the motivator and he sent around what were, for Republicans at least, inspirational tapes in which he lectured on practical politics and preached on Republican purposes. He dubbed GOPAC the Bell Labs of Republican politics.

GOPAC also afforded Gingrich his first large-scale opportunity to try to match the skill of the Gilded Age's Mark Hanna in forging a financial base for a revitalized party. Because GOPAC gave most of its money to state and local candidates, the vast majority of its contributors were not covered by federal laws limiting the size of campaign contributions or requiring that the names of contributors be disclosed. Gingrich could therefore supplement GOPAC's other fund-raising efforts by cultivating a relatively small group of very wealthy people for very large contributions. He did this with skill and thus built the foundations of a political empire that came to be known popularly as Newt Inc. Gingrich was to expand his realm by starting the Progress and Freedom Foundation in 1993, effectively his own think tank. Progress and Freedom, like GOPAC, was free to raise anonymous donations—and contributions to the foundation were also tax deductible, since it is a not-for-profit and, theoretically at least, nonpartisan organization. Among the foundation's projects was Gingrich's college course, which was to draw ethics complaints from congressional Democrats. In keeping with Gingrich's gift for high-tech promotion of himself and his ideas, videotapes of the course were sold, and it also ran on a cable television network. The interlocking nature of Newt Inc. and charges that he used GOPAC illegitimately if indirectly on behalf of his efforts to elect Republicans to Congress later played a central role in Democratic ethics complaints against him.

For all his concerns for developing a "positive" and "optimistic" message, Gingrich never forgot that he would accomplish nothing unless he brought down the entrenched House Democratic leadership. Thus he began the attack that first made him well known, against Speaker Wright, in 1987. Gingrich not only understood the power of the corruption issue; he also perceived, correctly, that Wright shared with him an instinct for power, even if Wright fatally lacked Gingrich's mastery of modern media. Wright, Gingrich thought, was dangerous. "If Wright survives this ethics thing," said Gingrich in 1987, "he may become the greatest Speaker since Henry Clay." On another occasion, he stated: "If Wright consolidates his power, he will be a very, very formidable man. We [have] to take him on early to prevent that." For two years Gingrich carried out his battle, at first with little support (and some hostility) from the Republican leadership. He once again demonstrated his skill at going around traditional Washington power centers, often traveling the country to drum up stories about Wright in local newspapers. Eventually, the mainstream press and other Republicans, then many House Democrats and finally the House ethics committee came to take Gingrich's charges against Wright seriously. In April 1989, an ethics committee report concluded that bulk sales of a thin book of Wright's speeches to lobbyists and others violated House rules, since the book sales amounted to a way of getting around limits on the speaking fees members of Congress could accept. The committee also challenged Wright's financial dealings with a Texas friend. Wright resigned and the Speakership was assumed by Tom Foley, a Washington Democrat who was highly respected by his peers, but lacked either Wright's or Gingrich's gift for gaining and consolidating power.

Democrats frequently asked how Gingrich, who had made "corruption" such a large issue against them, could so willingly play close to the edge of the ethics rules in financing his own political empire. Rank hypocrisy was the usual answer from Gingrich's partisan foes. Gingrich, said his critics, was prepared to see anything that helped the "Democratic machine" in the House as automatically corrupt.

Putting aside the fact that the core of Gingrich's charges against Wright were sustained by the ethics committee, there was another answer. Gingrich had never objected to the influence of money on politics as such. Indeed, his central political effort was to establish a new era in which a limited government would be unapologetically friendly to the interests of business groups and the productive wealthy. To finance his political movement, Gingrich, like Hanna, was more than willing to turn to wealthy interests for help—and to pressure them *not* to give to the Democrats, which in Gingrich's view was to work against their own best interests. Once he took over the Speakership, Gingrich was therefore unembarrassed (except, perhaps, for public relations reasons) when it emerged that lobbyists for interests that had given heavily to the Republicans' campaign were deeply involved in writing the party's deregulatory legislation. He was frankly and energetically in favor of deregulated capitalism, and saw this as in the public interest. How could business leaders who would benefit *not* be involved in crafting legislation to that end? And why would they *not* contribute to Republican campaigns? In his view, money to the Democrats bought special favors from a government whose power stemmed from its ability to impose excessive regulation. Gingrich was not selling government piecemeal; he was proposing to undermine the regulatory state itself, openly and aggressively. This view of political money might seem odd and dangerous to traditional reformers, and to many in the Perot movement and elsewhere in the Anxious Middle, but it was another sign of Gingrich's embrace of Hanna's Gilded Age conservatism. The prejudice against money's influence on politics had been a Progressive prejudice or, as Gingrich might put it, a "socialist" prejudice. He was not about to be constrained by it.

The Wright battle had made Gingrich well known. His GOPAC exertions provided him with an independent financial network and, along with C-Span, a grassroots following. The Conservative Opportunity Society gave him a base among members of Congress. His intellectual efforts and his concern for developing positive Republican themes won him respect even among party moderates who disagreed with many of his views and his style. Gingrich's election as House whip in 1989 should thus not have surprised as many people as it did. The opening itself was an example of the sort of unexpected good fortune of which successful political careers are made. When John Tower lost his battle to be confirmed as George Bush's defense secretary, Bush went for a safe choice, naming Dick Cheney, the popular Republican whip, whom many saw as the obvious successor to minority leader Bob Michel. Although he had never held a leadership position, Gingrich jumped into the race to succeed Cheney. His opponent, Representative Edward Madigan of Illinois, was the favorite, but also the perfect foil for Gingrich—a well-liked pal of Michel's, he embodied the old Republican way of doing business that Gingrich had been attacking for years. Gingrich started out with his hard core of conservative supporters and expanded his coalition to include moderate Republicans who were weary of minority status and saw in Gingrich a chance for delivery. He won by two votes.

IV

The Bush years proved to be a nightmare for the Republican Party, but they were the making of Newt Gingrich. If anything showed Republicans that in the absence of a vision a party perishes, it was the Bush presidency. If any single event demonstrated that the Republicans had few options but to be the anti-government party, it was Bush's calamitous (if in many ways courageous) decision to raise taxes. If any movement showed that a substantial body of American voters might be open to more radical approaches, it was Ross Perot's. And if anyone underscored the importance of working out a policy agenda that was carefully calibrated to put together a victorious coalition, it was Bill Clinton in 1992. Newt Gingrich knew all these things and took full advantage.

Although it suffered from fewer highly publicized mishaps than the early Clinton presidency, George Bush's administration was in no way a smoothly running machine. On the contrary, Bush inherited a listlessness in the Republican Party and a sense of drift in the conservative movement that had set in during the final years of the Reagan presidency. While theoretically leading a unified party, Bush was more the unthreatening sovereign presiding over a large group of contending fiefdoms. His administration thus lacked a unifying purpose and was badly torn among advocates of competing strategies and tactics.

The greatest difference was over whether the Bush presidency's central objective was to consolidate and rationalize Reagan's achievement or to push the "Reagan Revolution" even further. Bush's instinct, and that of his budget director, Richard Darman, was clearly to be a consolidationist. Reagan's major achievements in foreign policy were to be preserved. American power in the world was to be maintained and, where feasible, expanded. In the domestic sphere, the consolidationists reasoned that Reaganism had gone roughly as far as it should. Indeed, for some Reagan veterans such as Darman, Bush's task was to undo the fiscal mistakes of the Reagan period by cutting the deficit, even if that meant accepting tax increases. The idea was to save at least some of the Reagan reductions in taxes on income and investment; move, if possible, toward more consumption taxes; and advocate further spending cuts but also leave some room for program innovations in areas such as education and the environment. Especially when judged in light of subsequent Republican departures, Bush's instincts on issues such as the environment and civil rights were decidedly moderate. In an important speech Darman signaled a significant redefinition of Republican goals, attacking what he called the culture of "now-nowism." The country, he said, needed to deal with long-term problems involving fiscal and economic balance and to eschew short-term thinking and short-term benefits. In some ways Darman's views paralleled those of Clinton, Gingrich and Robert Reich in sensing that the United States was in the midst of an era of transformation. But his solutions were, on balance, more similar to those of Clinton and Reich than to Gingrich's. Chief of Staff John Sununu, a Darman ally who was a conservative both by conviction and (unlike many conservatives) temperament, was skeptical of too many policy innovations, seeing them as antithetical to an administration whose major task was to conserve the Reagan legacy.

But the administration, especially at the second and third echelons, was full of convinced conservatives who felt that a failure to push the frontiers of the conservative agenda forward would inevitably cede the initiative to liberals and Democrats. As we have seen, Bill Kristol was often a supporter of the rebels, many of them conservative idealists in their twenties or thirties. Housing Secretary Jack Kemp was their inspirational leader. Jim Pinkerton, a young domestic policy adviser, became one of their most visible champions, especially after Darman publicly ridiculed Pinkerton's repeated calls for a "new paradigm" in public policy that would emphasize decentralization and the dismantling of bureaucracy.

In important ways the Bush rebels foreshadowed both the new conservative synthesis that Kristol and Schambra would put forward and Gingrich-style "Third Wave" conservatism. Their causes included an absolute opposition to tax increases, Kemp's market-oriented proposals to revitalize the inner city, and school vouchers to allow poor children to attend private schools. Some of them, like Pinkerton, were fascinated by the potential of cyberspace and high technology, and consciously saw themselves as "post-modern" conservatives. That meant, among other things, that they did not pretend that the promised land lay back somewhere in the 1950s, and they embraced rather than rejected much of what contemporary culture had to offer. In a sense the Bush rebels were as much about a style and an orientation—toward activism, confrontation and change—as about policy. True, there were potentially deep contradictions in their policy views. Combining an activist agenda on the Kemp model with either no tax increases or tax cuts would only deepen the deficit, which conservatives were committed to cutting. This explained some of Darman's impatience with them. Yet there was also something powerfully appealing about these younger conservatives, particularly their energy, social tolerance and willingness to admit domestic problems and try to deal with them.

Most congressional leaders would be expected to work with and support a president of their own party and to defend his agenda. Gingrich was initially quite ready to do this. Indeed, a striking change came over him after he was elected Republican whip. He reveled in attending White House meetings and seemed at times amazed that after years in the wilderness he was now seated at the councils of power. The rebel seemed on the verge of embracing the establishment.

But in the end, the logic of his own position seemed to trump whatever short-term excitement Gingrich found at being on the inside. During the lengthy negotiations with House Democrats over a deficit reduction agreement in 1990, Gingrich sat at the table and negotiated alongside Darman, Sununu and the Republican congressional leaders. When a deal was cut involving a tax increase, the other Republicans assumed that Gingrich was honor-bound to go along.

Gingrich, it turned out, did not feel that way—much to Bush's bitterness—and led a most unusual rebellion against the Bush budget plan. With some of the most conservative members of Congress joining with some of the most liberal (they opposed the package's regressive consumption taxes and some of its budget cuts), the House voted down the initial budget agreement. In the short term this proved a terrible defeat for the conservative cause. A new package had to be negotiated and, to achieve its deficit-reduction targets, it would have to contain some tax increases. With the conservatives insisting they would vote "no" on *any* taxes, Bush had to negotiate with the liberals, and the final tax package was more progressive than the first, eating further into the Reagan income-tax reductions. The fiasco hurt the Republicans in the 1990 midterm elections and badly hurt Bush, who faced endless repetitions on the television news of his "read my lips" pledge against taxes.

Gingrich's stance could be read as the crassest kind of personal politics. It was clear that his own political base in the House among conservatives was resolutely against the tax increase. Had he supported the Bush plan, his strongest supporters would have branded him a sellout who had "gone establishment" and walked away from many of the things he had preached for a decade or more. It could thus be argued that the most practical political choice for Gingrich was to go with his supporters and against his president. When Gingrich declared of Bush that "he has sold Ronald Reagan's inheritance for a potter's field," the response from the Republican right—in Congress and around the country—was thunderous.

Gingrich's decision certainly enhanced his reputation for ruthlessness and created a deep rift with Darman—Gingrich later called for his resignation. But it was also clear that Gingrich perceived a logic to conservative politics that many in the Bush administration rejected. In electoral terms Gingrich understood that opposition to taxes was the one issue with the power to hold together a highly diverse Republican constituency. Bush, after all, had turned to the tax issue when he was desperate in 1988 and it had worked. More broadly, Gingrich shared with the Bush administration's rebels the

view that if attitudes toward government returned to "normal"—
that is, a rational and sober argument over whether this or that
program was better, *how much* government could do about a particular problem, whether a given program needed reform—the
drift of politics would inevitably be back to the liberal side. In
general, the public turned to Democrats when it wanted government to solve new problems. The entire Progressive tradition that
Democrats had come to embody was based on a rationalist's view of
government as a necessary balance wheel in a complicated society,
intervening where the market was failing, solving problems that the
market could not deal with. To the Bush administration rebels and
to Gingrich, Bush had confined himself to the role of conservative
tinkerer. That meant broadly accepting the legitimacy of the governmental enterprise. Such an approach would inevitably energize
liberals, who would always be willing to do at least a bit more with
government for at least a few more people. Critics of conservative
accommodationism could note that even Dwight Eisenhower, in
most ways a highly successful president, did not manage to build a
long-term majority for his party through his own version of practical, moderate governance. Only by continuing the assault on government, taxes, regulation and bureaucracy—only by waging a kind
of permanent revolution—could conservatives hope to keep the
initiative, hold their own coalition together and keep the liberals off
balance. This was Gingrich's order of battle.

Thus began the radicalization of conservatism, with Gingrich
playing the central role. Bush's defeat, far from giving Gingrich and
his allies pause, only confirmed their view that the party needed to
embrace a radical, mostly libertarian conservatism that would destroy the liberals' power base in government. Initially, as we saw
earlier, this strategy took the form of opposition to virtually all of
Clinton's initiatives. This strategy neatly accomplished several ends
at once. Above all, it prevented Clinton from being effective. It
continued to discredit the federal government and the Democrats
by throwing Washington into disarray. And it put the Clinton program, not the Republicans' intentions, at center stage. Thus the
Republicans could run advertisements such as the one cited at the
beginning of Chapter Six saying that they, too, wanted to reform
health care—a seemingly moderate, reasonable approach. The fact
that the logic of the Republican strategy, as conceived by Gingrich,

led inevitably to far less government action—on behalf of health care or anything else—went largely undebated until after the Republicans took over Congress. Until 1995 the Republicans could have their anti-government rhetoric without paying the price of saying exactly how they would dismantle government.

Having established himself as the Republicans' chief tactician, strategist and visionary, Gingrich inevitably emerged as the House Republican leader, and he won that job unopposed. Triumph only emboldened Gingrich to broaden his policy of confrontation to cover even issues such as crime or congressional reform where common ground could easily have been achieved. Indeed, as we have seen, Republicans blocked some of the very reform proposals that they later included in the "Contract with America," such as requiring Congress to live by the regulations it passed for others. Gingrich, who had always prided himself on taking risks, was more than willing to risk charges of obstructionism. What he was obstructing, after all, was the Democrats' ability to govern.

Gingrich's radical approach increasingly became the lodestar of Republican strategy, and even more conventional Republicans came to embrace it. At the beginning of the 103d Congress, for example, Senate Republican leader Bob Dole supported health care reform in principle and cosponsored Senator John Chafee's rather far-reaching bill. But as the debate turned against Clinton, Dole withdrew his support for Chafee and eventually allied himself with those who would stop all action on health care. Dole shared Richard Nixon's ability to sense wherever the center of Republican gravity was at a given moment, and he knew where things were moving. He was to move even further right in the new Congress. A deficit hawk who had once been a critic of excessive tax cuts, Dole was not about to let an upstart conservative senator such as Phil Gramm outmaneuver him on the right as both competed for the 1996 Republican presidential nomination. Dole, the critic of supply-side economics, began to sound like a longtime supporter of the doctrine. His twists were the definitive demonstration of how much the party was moving Gingrich's way. Dole and Gingrich had despised each other in the Reagan years. Gingrich had once attacked Dole as "the tax collector for the welfare state." Dole was no more restrained in his view of Gingrich and his allies; he had once referred to Gingrich's Conservative Opportunity Society allies as "the young hypocrites."

He had declared after the 1984 Republican Convention: "They think they can peddle the idea that they've taken over the party." Dole added: "Well, they aren't the Republican Party and they aren't going to be." But a decade later they were. Dole, desiring the presidency, was fully prepared to acknowledge the fact.

V

Gingrich had an entirely legitimate complaint about the coverage of the 1994 elections: that the "Contract with America" was not taken as seriously as it should have been. But instead of complaining, he should have been grateful, for the contract was an important clue as to how much he was proposing to radicalize his party, and in ways that the electorate might *not* have found appealing had it known more. The Democrats contented themselves with criticizing the contract's approach to tax and budget issues, arguing that the Republicans could not possibly keep their promises without deep cuts in popular programs such as Medicare. That, it turned out, was entirely true. But what may have been even more important about the contract was the extent to which it showed that the new Republicans were prepared to go far beyond Ronald Reagan in their efforts to dismantle government. Gingrich approvingly cited a column by Charles Krauthammer after the 1994 elections to make the point that "you have the most explicitly ideologically committed House Republican Party in modern history." More accurate words were rarely spoken by a politician.

It's true, as noted earlier, that the contract included a series of promises that were highly popular with the interest and voter groups that the Republicans needed for assembling their majority. Its various tax cuts (unmatched by specific spending cuts) were bound to appeal to those whom they would benefit. But the parts of the contract that drew little attention—other than from those who might benefit from them—proposed to strip away the federal government's authority in area after area. The contract showed that Gingrich was quite serious in his promise to construct a regulatory and litigation regime that was entirely congenial to business. It showed as well that he was serious in his promise to repeal the "liberal welfare state." Its requirement that regulators complete a "regulatory impact analysis" covering "23 specific criteria" on every major new rule promised to tie regulatory agencies in knots. Its proposal that property owners receive compensation for "any reduction in the value of their property" from new regulations had the potential of either opening federal coffers to tens of thousands of claims (one Republican critic called it "a new entitlement for property owners") or of stopping regulators cold. If that did not do it, the Republicans' call for a moratorium on new regulations certainly would. And when deliberations began on the budget, House Republicans opened yet another front in their deregulatory war, proposing to delete all the money needed by regulatory agencies to enforce sixty-two specific regulations on matters ranging from motorcycle helmets to endangered species. "The laws would remain on the books, but there would be no money to carry them out," said Representative David McIntosh, an Indiana Republican. "It's a signal to these agencies to stop wasting time on these regulations." "Signal" was a rather mild word for what the Republicans were up to.

In the area of litigation the contract was unabashed in responding to the business community's desire to get out from under consumer lawsuits—even if that meant violating the party's stated commitment to "states' rights" by overturning state laws in the matter. Among other things, the contract proposed imposing a "loser pays" rule, which would require those who brought lawsuits and lost to pay the legal costs of those who were sued (up to a certain point). This would be, as intended, a powerful deterrent to litigation. The contract also proposed to cap punitive damages in consumer suits, another powerful deterrent to litigation.

On welfare, the Republican contract proposed to let states opt out of the Aid to Families with Dependent Children program, and when it came time to legislate the House Republicans repealed the program altogether and replaced it with a "block grant." The block grant included no requirement that states keep up with their current payments to welfare recipients to qualify for federal funds. That created strong incentives for states to cut their welfare payments. The House version of the proposal pushed further in this direction by including requirements barring various groups from receiving welfare. It promised to require welfare recipients to work, but included no money to pay for training, work and day-care programs that might make work possible. Indeed, the House bill actually cut spending over time, raising the question of how states would enact work programs absent large new spending of state tax money.

The point here is *not* that all of the problems identified by the Republican contract were phony. The imperative to reform welfare was felt across much of the political spectrum. Even advocates of a rather liberal regime on lawsuits acknowledged problems with an explosion in litigation, product liability suits and excessive punitive damages. Even staunch environmentalists accepted that "command-and-control" regulation could at times be inefficient or unfair. It was hard for anyone not to sympathize with the problems faced by a land-owner of modest means who woke up one morning to discover his property had lost a good deal of its value because it had been de-clared a "wetland."

Rather, what was striking about the contract was its eagerness to throw out twenty years' worth of protections for consumers and the environment. It was plausible to argue that consumers could be adequately protected by regulations and that strong regulation might reduce the need for lawsuits. Similarly, it might be reason-able to suggest that if consumers could win adequate redress in the courts, it might be possible to scale back regulation in certain areas. But the contract seemed determined to limit consumer and envi-ronmental redress through *either* the courtroom or the regulatory agency. The House Republicans continued their war on regulation once they took over by proposing, among other things, a drastic hemming in of the Clean Water Act. This was a long way from George Bush, who declared he would be the "environmental pres-ident" and who made good on that by supporting a strong new Clean Air Act and by appointing William Reilly, a moderate friend of environmental groups, as head of the Environmental Protection Agency.

But the full extent of the revolution within conservatism was made clear only in the spring of 1995 when Republicans in both houses finally adopted a goal (again, one largely set by Gingrich) to balance the federal budget within seven years without tax increases—indeed, *with* a tax cut. This was truly a bold move. It was by no means inevitable, even after the 1994 elections. Indeed, Sen-ator Pete Domenici, the Senate Budget Committee chairman and as firm a deficit hawk as could be found, doubted at the beginning of the 104th Congress that it would be possible to do more than make a significant down payment on deficit reduction. But here again, the logic of the Gingrich strategy had its own imperatives.

The decision must first be contrasted with what happened not only in George Bush's administration but also in Ronald Reagan's. In 1981, Reagan had been unable to hold his conservative congressional coalition together long enough to balance his tax cuts with spending cuts. And Reagan himself made the task of reaching balance extremely difficult by insisting on very large increases in defense spending. In 1982, Reagan actually agreed to a substantial tax increase—mostly a restoration of some of the taxes cut in 1981—to keep the deficit from getting worse. In the middle of his administration Reagan killed a serious effort sponsored by Dole to further reduce the deficit with potentially unpopular cuts in Social Security. And then there was Bush's deficit-reduction effort that relied on tax increases. In other words, the core Republican assumption after 1981 was that the effort to close the big deficit gap opened in 1981 would be a slow and steady slog. Implicitly, if not always at campaign times, many of the leading Republicans accepted that some mix of tax increases and spending cuts would be required. For all their anti-government rhetoric, Republican leaders implicitly accepted limits on how much government could be cut—one of the reasons a libertarian-leaning writer such as David Frum could criticize them so severely. In 1995 those constraints were thrown overboard.

The Republicans may also have hemmed themselves in by their sponsorship of an amendment to the constitution requiring a balanced budget, to take effect in seven years. Democrats made much of the fact that Republicans had proposed an amendment requiring balance without a plan to get there. "The proposal looked like a free ride, enabling its proponents to get credit for wanting to balance the budget without actually having to do it," wrote economist Herbert Stein. In arguing for the amendment, Stein noted, the Republicans insisted repeatedly "their determination and ability to balance the budget by 2002." After that, Stein continued, "failure to follow through with at least Congressional plans to do that would have been viewed as total hypocrisy. And while hypocrisy is acceptable, total hypocrisy is not." Stein concluded that had the balanced budget amendment actually passed in Congress in 1995, the pressure on Republicans to achieve real balance might have been *less,* since "they could have basked in their accomplishment as budget balancers, without having to do anything more for a while." Gingrich understood this clearly, since he began promising to reach balance in seven years during the battle over the amendment.

Finally, it was clear to the Republicans that while achieving balance would force them to take on the Medicare issue and thus risk alienating a broad range of voters, many of the rest of the cuts could be found by reducing or eliminating programs, especially for the poor, that had few Republican constituents. As long as Republicans held taxes steady or tried to cut them, and as long as they limited cuts in programs that benefited core Republican groups (which they did), the party could sharply limit the political price it would pay for trying to go to balance. As Bill Kristol was honest enough to admit, since most of the constituencies that relied on government help leaned toward the Democrats, Democratic voters, not Republicans, would necessarily end up paying the largest price. In all events, final balance was to be achieved not only long after the 1996 election but also after the millennial election of 2000. A lot could happen between 1995 and then. Republicans could get credit for boldness while spreading some of the political costs over time.

In forcing the budget debate in this direction, Gingrich revolutionized factional politics within the Republican Party. Before 1995 the party had been badly torn between "deficit hawks" such as Dole and Domenici, who favored balanced budgets even if they might require tax increases, and "supply-siders," who cared far more about tax cuts than balanced books. Gingrich essentially threw the conservative supply-side wing over to the side of balanced budgets by insisting that if the budget were cut deeply enough, there would be no need for tax increases and some room for reductions. The "deficit hawks," having argued for years in favor of balance, found themselves forced to march down Gingrich's road. In some ways, they welcomed the chance to do so—if cuts could balance the budget, why not? But in doing so, they also bought into a set of assumptions far more radical than any they had ever held about how much could be cut, and how quickly. For Gingrich, the move held huge promise, whether the Republicans won the budget fight or not. One of his long-term goals, after all, was a smaller federal government. What better way to achieve this than to use the desire deeply embedded in much of the Washington establishment (including many parts of the Democratic Party) for an end to deficits?

For years Democrats had chided Republicans for creating the large deficit. Yet they had many reasons, rooted in both politics and principle, for opposing the Republicans' specific cuts. Gingrich was trying to build a trap for Clinton and the Democrats. If they opposed his cuts, they would seem to be defending deficits "as far as the eye could see," as the Republicans liked to put it. If they supported the cuts, they would be breaking their own coalition. Within the Republican Party, in the meantime, Gingrich was trying to end the war between its conservative wing and its more moderate anti-deficit wing. Conservatives would happily join the moderates to cut the deficit, since the broader purpose of the exercise—a smaller federal government—embodied a central long-term goal of the conservative movement. This strategy went well beyond the specifics of a single year's budget fight. It could be used in one political campaign after another. And it could be used not simply to further the party's electoral interest, but, more importantly, to push Gingrich's broader purpose of rolling back the state. "You know one team favors bigger government, larger bureaucracy and higher taxes," Gingrich said. "The other team favors smaller government, less bureaucracy and lower taxes. Now I'm fairly comfortable giving the American people in the '96 election that choice." Indeed, he was.

VI

Gingrich's achievement has been discussed mostly in electoral terms, and the Republican takeover of the House in 1994 was a monumental accomplishment of practical politics. But Gingrich's long-term impact will go well beyond one election. In decisive ways he is seeking to reshape the Republican Party, American conservatism and the choice facing the American electorate.

He has done so by trying to resolve many of the contradictions within contemporary conservatism on the side of a radical vision. This vision sees American progress as depending upon a large-scale dismantling of the federal apparatus, including functions related to welfare and income support, consumer and environmental protection, economic regulation and management. He is, as a matter of principle, unconcerned about rising income inequality created by the new economy because he is as unabashed as his nineteenth-century conservative forebears were in seeing rewards for the wealthy, the productive and the innovative as the key to technological advance and economic improvement. By tearing down governmental barriers to change, Gingrich believes he will accelerate the arrival of a high-tech information age with unparalleled possibilities for American society. By building a disciplined and highly competitive society, Americans will be able to leap into the global marketplace and fulfill their destiny to be "leaders of the human race."

Understanding the next phase of American politics depends on understanding how radically Gingrich is seeking to transform the nature of the decisions American voters will be asked to make. In the Reagan and Bush years, even very conservative Republicans accepted the need to preserve institutions bequeathed them by the Progressive and New Deal eras. There was a reluctance to tamper with welfare, food stamps, Medicare and other basic components of the social safety net. There was much deregulatory rhetoric, and the regulatory agencies were led by administrators with a more sympathetic view to business; but for all that, the necessity of government intervention, especially on behalf of the environment, the elderly and the poor, was broadly accepted. The deficit itself stood as testimony to conservative reluctance to take on the task of a radical dismantling of the federal government.

The new Republicans, pushed by Gingrich, have no such reluctance. Theirs is unabashedly a revolt against the New Deal and Progressive traditions—and it is a revolt not limited to partisans of Gingrich's Third Wave. On the contrary, as we saw in the last chapter, it is also part of the neo-Reaganite synthesis put forward by Bill Kristol, Bill Schambra and their allies. The revolt against Progressivism is becoming the dominant political project of the Republican Party.

It is the central argument of this book that this attack, far from routing Progressivism, is a precursor of its renewal. For two decades, Progressives have been timid in defending their project, and distracted by cultural politics. The Gingrich Revolution gives them no choice but to battle to preserve Progressivism's achievements and renew its program. And as support for the Republican Congress dropped in the autumn of 1995, it became clear many voters were, indeed, looking for more from government than Gingrich wanted to offer. *Especially* if Gingrich is right about the vast technological changes that are coming, it is highly unlikely that the central thrust of American politics will be toward dismantling the buffers that ease change and the social protections that ease suffering. By moving American conservatism toward a rendezvous with nineteenth-century laissez-faire doctrines, Gingrich and his allies will force their opponents to grapple with the task of constructing the twenty-first-century alternatives to laissez-faire.

It is nonetheless true that the radical anti-government politics that came to dominate the Republican Party in the mid-1990s is a logical response to a series of changes in American political life over thirty years. The invigoration of an intellectually serious libertarianism in the late 1960s and 1970s created the substantive ground on which the new conservatism was built. Anti-government ideas had a broader audience still because of popular disillusionment with government that began in the Vietnam years and grew during Watergate and the Carter administration.

In the meantime, the nature of the debate itself did almost everything possible to deepen voter cynicism about the political enterprise and inspire mistrust about the possibilities of government. The assault of negative thirty-second advertisements on television at campaign time did nothing to promote public confidence that politics might be an ennobling enterprise. The politics of moral annihilation led partisans of virtually all points of view to assume that their adversaries were fundamentally corrupt and evil, and to paint them that way for the broader public. The increasing expense of political campaigns led voters to assume that anyone involved in governing them had been bought off long in advance of the election.

And then there was journalism. In theory, the reporters, commentators and radio talk jockeys were the referees of the political contest. In fact, they were very much in the fight, though in the case of "objective" news outlets, not always of it. The growing popularity of conservative talk radio not only suggested that there was an audience for a steady diet of attacks on government; the talk radio spokesmen and spokeswomen of the right also reinforced the anti-government message. If politicians—especially liberals—were indeed as foolish as your best friend on radio told you day after day, week after week, then the entire twentieth-century tradition of using government to solve problems was itself foolish. As for the mainstream media, they were no longer certain what their position was. Their practitioners felt challenged (as they should have) by the rise of militant talk radio. What were the radio men and women doing that the mainstream media weren't? Yet the mainstream press and television news outlets also had a skepticism of government all their own, based on their experiences with government officials who had lied and cheated. Mainstream journalists, however, rebelled against the ethic of at least some on talk radio that "the facts" were less important than commitment to a set of ideas. If "the facts" no longer mattered, what in the world was a journalist to do? It is to the travails of the modern media—and to the media's complicated role in political disconnection and disillusionment—that we turn next.

☐ 8 ☐

NO NEWS IS GOOD NEWS:

Why Americans Hate the Press

THE CLASSIC MACHINE politician's definition of a public official's "political base" is "the people who are with you when you're wrong." By that definition, the press is rapidly losing its base. Increasingly, *all* sides in the political debate are ready to stand against the press. Few outside journalism support reporters in times of controversy, and reporters themselves have emerged as their own profession's fiercest critics.

The unpopularity of the news, gossip and opinion businesses can be measured by the lumping together of the entire enterprise under what has become an epithet, "the media." That term is used to cover everything from the major newspapers to the evening news shows to Rush Limbaugh and *Oprah* and *Hard Copy.* The proposition that "the media" are complicit in the public's disenchantment with politics and its cynicism about democratic government is so widely accepted that it is barely debated.

It's surprising that it took so long for the challenge to the norms of contemporary journalism to arise. This may be a tribute to the accuracy of Timothy Crouse's observation in his classic account of campaign reporting, *The Boys on the Bus,* that "journalism is probably the slowest-moving, most tradition-bound profession in America. It refuses to budge until it is shoved into the future by some irresistible external force." Although the media world

231

changed enormously with the birth first of radio and then of television, the rules followed by radio and television journalists—emphasizing fairness, accuracy and speed—were little different from those of their colleagues in newspapers. It can be argued, in fact, that politicians became aware of the huge transforming power of the broadcast media before journalists themselves did. This was demonstrated by Franklin Roosevelt with his mastery of radio and John Kennedy with his dominance of television. Early on, politicians and their advisers proved to be among the best media analysts and media critics, understanding that television especially had fundamentally altered the relations between politicians and voters. Consider this 1967 memo to Richard Nixon from Ray Price, one of his top advisers:

> *We have to be very clear on this point: that the response is to the image, not to the man,* since 99 percent of the voters have no contact with the man. It's not what's *there* that counts, it's what's projected—and, carrying it one step further, it's not what *he* projects but rather what the voter receives. It's not the man we have to change but rather the *received impression.* And this impression often depends more on the medium and its use than it does on the candidate himself. [Price's emphasis.]

What might be thought of as "Price's Law" has now become the received wisdom of political campaigns. Equally shrewd in his analysis of the media (though rather less than effective in dealing with it when he was in the White House) was Lyndon Johnson. David Halberstam recounts a casual conversation between Johnson and a CBS News producer in 1971 during which the producer asked Johnson to describe the changes that had taken place in political life over the previous three decades. "You guys," Johnson replied. "All you guys in the media. All of politics has changed because of you. You've broken all the machines and the ties between us in Congress and the city machines. You've given us a new kind of people."

Indeed, the media were disrupting the patterns of politics, not for explicitly political purposes but just by doing what they did. But the media themselves were also changing. Strangely, the press and television were becoming both more powerful and less influential at the same time.

The increased power of news coverage to affect events is undeniable. Again and again, wide press attention to any particular scandal—whether at the House bank, at the United Way or in Little Rock—has produced large political effects. If the press decides to make a famine in Somalia or genocide in Rwanda big news, it can force the United States government to respond with its armed forces. As James Hoge, the editor of *Foreign Affairs,* has noted, television was so "sufficiently underdeveloped" in 1962 that Defense Secretary Robert McNamara did not even turn on a TV set during the two weeks of the Cuban missile crisis. Now, policy makers are forced to respond almost instantaneously as news of a new crisis is broadcast, since "friend and foe have come to expect signals instantly, and any vacuum will be filled quickly by something."

The power of television was visible in other ways. A single debate on *Larry King Live* between Vice President Al Gore and Ross Perot was for many Americans their *only* experience with real public argument about the North American Free Trade Agreement. The subjective tone of the news coverage, especially on television, can have more effect on a president's popular standing than "objective" events or experiences, such as the state of the nation's economy. Media analyst Robert Lichter demonstrated not only that most of the routine television news commentary about President Clinton was negative during his first year and a half in office, but also that the president's poll ratings were closely correlated to just how negative the news commentary was. When the commentary about Clinton was favorable (as it was in the period after his NAFTA victory) his poll standing went up; when the commentary was particularly harsh his drop in the polls was severe.

True, newsmakers, particularly political candidates, are increasingly inclined to "go around the media," especially when they have the resources to do so. Ross Perot did this by spending huge sums on his half-hour lectures-with-charts during the 1992 campaign. His efforts to discuss the issues and fill people's heads with numbers about the deficit were almost a mocking commentary on journalism itself. Perot seemed to be asking his viewers: How many times have you gotten this much detail from your average news broadcast? Wealthy candidates followed Perot's model in 1994 whenever they could. Republican Michael Huffington was the subject of a series of stinging news stories and magazine articles which ultimately undermined his candidacy. But given the amount of money Huffington was pouring into television commercials, voters saw the same message over and over. "People don't read *Vanity Fair* six or seven times, but that TV commercial comes on six or seven times," said Ken Khachigian, his campaign manager. (Huffington, however, lost.) Less-well-to-do candidates (such as Clinton in 1992) also got their message across outside the traditional news formats—on MTV, *Donahue* and the late-night shows, among other places.

Clinton, like Perot, was consciously seeking to break professional journalism's hold on the political debate (and by extension, its power to affect his own fate). He said that he no longer took the press "seriously as our sole intermediaries to the voters of this country" and added that "anyone who lets himself be interpreted to the American people through these intermediaries is nuts." Clinton went on: "Since the President is hired by all the people, he should perhaps go to where the folks *are*. I don't think there is anything undignified about a President going on *Larry King* or the right kind of MTV program." He later put it more colorfully at the 1993 radio and television correspondents' dinner. "You know why I can stiff you on press conferences?" he asked. "Because Larry King liberated me by giving me to the American people directly." Clinton became, as Stephen Hess of the Brookings Institution put it, "the first president to conclude that he didn't need White House reporters, that it was not necessary to be filtered through the press corps."

It turned out that Clinton's conclusion was wrong, that he *did* need the press corps, that the great media revolution had not happened quite as he thought it had. Jonathan Alter of *Newsweek* noted that the administration had suffered from the "Jurassic Park syndrome," the conviction "that the traditional White House press corps was a bunch of dinosaurs." He added: "The White House learned that dinosaurs can still bite your head off." Clinton and his lieutenants returned to a much more traditional approach to the media, instituting more frequent formal news conferences and acknowledging the importance of the evening news shows.

But the failure of the Clinton administration's Jurassic Park strategy was a tribute more to its inartful execution than to the permanence of current media arrangements. Challenges to those arrangements—whether from presidents, millionaires like Perot or talk show hosts like Rush Limbaugh—were arising everywhere. For all their power, journalists enjoy increasingly less influence and standing with average citizens. Polls show that the press's credibility with the public is declining—journalists win about as much esteem as members of Congress. Moreover, individual journalists and news organizations can no longer think of themselves as fully the masters of their own house, since no one can control the definition of news. A scandal floated on a tabloid television show or in a supermarket weekly can overwhelm all other news. No matter how intense the desire of any given newspaper or news show to "stick with issues" or "stay away from gossip," personal scandals develop a momentum of their own. The "respectable" press often backs into the story by reporting on its "impact" or the "ethics" of breaking such a story in the first place. Then it's off to the races. As Howard Kurtz, the media critic for *The Washington Post,* put it: "Even false rumors, if the names are big enough and the whispering grows loud enough, float into print on the flimsy rationale that they are 'out there' and therefore must be dissected and analyzed by the press."

The influence of mainstream journalism is also being challenged by other sources of information and opinion, including talk radio. Newspapers, as Kurtz noted, "are losing ground to C-Span and pay-per-view, to home computers and fax machines, to direct mail and specialty magazines and home shopping clubs and books on tape and a hundred other leisure pursuits." The network evening news, though far more powerful than Clinton realized, does not enjoy the same monopoly it held in the 1950s and particularly the 1960s.

It is not surprising that public disaffection with politics has evolved into dissatisfaction with the media. When the public's problem is with the content of the political debate, it is natural that the main medium through which that debate is carried out should also come under challenge. This has happened before. The current structure of the media is the product of the last great overturning of political institutions during the Progressive Era. We are now in the middle of a new revolt against the journalistic order.

II

The problems of the media are systematic. They are not merely the result of technological change or new fads, although both obviously play an important role. In a literal sense we journalists no longer know what we're doing; there is no consensus on what the goals of journalism really are, nor is there agreement as to whom or to what we are obligated. I speak here especially of political journalism, broadly defined to include not just the coverage of elections but also reporting on major public issues and controversies.

When asked what they do, journalists can offer all sorts of answers. At times we'll say we're there to provide information, to report on an ongoing debate, to "keep the people informed." At other times we'll say we exist to be "watchdogs" on the people in power—to make sure they don't abuse it or lie or steal. Sometimes we'll say our main obligation is to "fairness" and "balance." Other times we'll say our goal is to push politicians beyond their normal back-and-forth and challenge their assumptions, their facts (or nonfacts) and the hidden purposes behind their rhetorical gambits. Sometimes we speak in grand terms about our obligations to "the people" or "democracy" or "free speech." Other times we'll speak mainly in terms of professional ethics, focusing on our obligations to live by certain rules and well-worked-out conventions. Sometimes we'll revel in our stance as the friends of the underdog, defining our role as involving "comforting the afflicted and afflicting the comfortable." Other times we'll vehemently deny bias in favor of the down-and-out and insist that we are thoroughly fair and accurate in assessing the good and the bad in even wealthy and powerful institutions. Sometimes we'll acknowledge that the media have commercial purposes—we make our money, after all, by winning large audiences and selling them to advertisers. Therefore, we often have to entertain as well as inform. Other times we'll argue passionately that money does not affect what we do, that we report the news without fear or favor and don't care whom we might offend.

It can be argued, of course, that each of these statements is true as far as it goes. Many news organizations, for example, can worry desperately about the bottom line and still pursue stories that enrage advertisers. It happens all the time. It can be further argued that modern journalism is enriched by the fact that some journalists do some of the things just described, while other journalists set themselves other tasks on this list. Movie critics and sportswriters and recipes attract certain readers who don't give a damn what happens at the Federal Trade Commission. Yet without the audiences (and income) brought in by the movies, sports and food, there wouldn't be the money to pay the reporter at the trade commission. (Other people, of course, care desperately about government, yet never read the sports pages and couldn't read a recipe.) News organizations now routinely separate the functions of "political" and "investigative" reporters. The political reporters can cover the give-and-take among politicians that is supposed to be the stuff of politics when it's on the level. The investigators try to peer under the surface to see if a politician is up to more (or less) than meets the eye.

It can all work splendidly, and often does. Yet journalists themselves, when not under fire, readily concede that there are some real contradictions in their own rationales for what they do. The argument of this chapter is that those contradictions are deeper than they have been for decades.

Between the nineteenth and twentieth centuries American journalism went from one coherent purpose, partisanship, to another, "objectivity." Newspapers in the 1900s were mostly party organs that spoke to and for partisan constituencies. Before and during the Progressive Era newspapers adopted a new goal: to attract readers of all political persuasions and offer them "objective" information that served no partisan purpose. The current upheaval in journalism owes to the fact that the news media are now neither one thing nor the other. Overt partisanship is still unacceptable. Reporters cringe when they are accused of being "in the tank" for a cause, a politician or a party. Thus the "nonpartisan" ideal of the Progressive Era is still, theoretically, intact. Yet "objectivity" has in fact been rejected as an impossible goal, a fact underscored when journalists speak of having an "adversarial" relationship to politicians. The adversarial ethic can be defended as necessary and useful. But it is not the same as "objectivity" or even "fairness." Such an ethic is inherently mistrustful of politics and thus makes certain assumptions about what politicians do.

In pursuing the adversarial ethic, journalists can often find themselves serving partisan purposes even when they act in a "nonpartisan" way. *The Washington Post* and a conservative magazine such as *The American Spectator* may find themselves reporting the same negative stories about President Clinton's past business dealings. The *Post* will no doubt subject its reports to tougher standards of accuracy—it may not report these things as readily or gleefully as a partisan organ. The *Post*'s purposes will not be the same as the *Spectator*'s which frankly wants to destroy the Clinton presidency. Yet a negative story in the *Post* will still have a direct political impact, effectively achieving the *Spectator*'s political objectives. If anything, the nonpartisan *Post*'s reports are likely to have a *larger* political impact than those of the highly partisan *Spectator,* precisely because average readers are less likely to dismiss the bad things the *Post* might report about a Democratic president. (Similarly, a negative *Post* report about a conservative politician would likely have a larger impact than the same report appearing in a highly partisan liberal magazine.)

The point here is that the press has an overwhelming *political* impact even if it insists on defining its role in a consciously *nonpolitical* way. It still harbors remnants of the old ethic of "objectivity" but knows things don't quite work that way. Journalists seek "impact" while often denying they have goals larger than simply "doing their jobs." Journalists think we can balance all these ideas at the same time. We can say that our goal in investigating Clinton or Clarence Thomas is to expose "wrongdoing" and to present "the facts" without any intention of moving the political debate in a particular direction. But our ability and standing to make that claim is now under question.

III

To understand how we got here, it's worth examining the last great revolt against the media order at the turn of the century. What is striking about the current disaffection with the press is how closely it parallels—in form and purpose, if not in substance—the last great journalistic revolt around the turn of the century. When the Progressives in that period assailed the way politics was conducted, they directed some of their sharpest fire against the news business. In the end, they revolutionized it.

From the 1830s until the turn of the century, newspapers were, for the most part, the organs of political parties. There was no ideal of "objectivity." On the contrary, the purpose of the newspapers was to mobilize support for parties all year round. But during the Gilded Age, as Christopher Lasch has pointed out, parties got a bad name. Reformers who looked for "professionalism" (as against "bossism") in politics eventually turned to seeking "professionalism" in journalism. Walter Lippmann led the way to a redefinition of journalism's role and the journalist's responsibilities. The notion that newspapers should be "objective" rather than partisan was the product of his admiration for the scientific method, his skepticism of ideology—and, his critics would argue, his less than full-hearted faith in democracy. Lippmann had noted with horror the breakdown of journalistic dispassion during the frenzy of World War I. Newspapers had appointed themselves as "defenders of the faith" and this resulted in a "breakdown of the means of public knowledge." The purpose of the press, as he saw it, was to disseminate accurate information, not to appeal to partisan feelings or foster argument.

Writing at the end of the Progressive Era in 1920, Lippmann linked the problems facing democracy with the problems of the news business. Could democracy survive when "the manufacture of consent is an unregulated private enterprise"? He argued that "men who have lost their grip on the relevant facts of their environment are the inevitable victims of agitation and propaganda. The quack, the charlatan, the jingo and the terrorist can flourish only when the audience is deprived of independent access to information." The Lippmann formulation of journalism's goal, which became so influential, came to the idea of "objectivity" because that is what the scientist prized in his work. Lippmann sought for journalism the scientist's "unity of method," which was "the unity of the disciplined experiment." A journalism based on scientific "standards of measure," Lippmann believed, could cut through "entangling stereotypes and slogans," the "threads of memory and emotion." He went on:

> The cynicism of the trade needs to be abandoned, for the true patterns of journalistic apprentice are not the slick persons who scoop the news, but the patient and fearless men of science who have labored to see what the world really is. It does not matter that the news is not susceptible of mathematical statement. In fact, just because the news is complex and slippery, good reporting requires the exercise of the highest of the scientific virtues.

Lippmann declared that his fight was against the tendency of the "news" to be experienced as "episodes, incidents, eruptions."

It would be hard for anyone to have a more elevated view of journalism's importance than Lippmann did. "Insofar as those who purvey the news make of their own beliefs a higher law than truth, they are attacking the foundations of our constitutional system," he wrote in *Liberty and the News* in 1920. "There can be no higher law in journalism than to tell the truth and shame the devil." And if a reference to journalism's constitutional role was not enough to make his point, Lippmann reached to the Scriptures, declaring that "the newspaper is in all literalness the bible of democracy, the book out of which a people determines its conduct." He sought to turn the "newspaper enterprise from a haphazard trade into a disciplined profession."

The agent of the transformation of journalism toward "objectivity" and "professionalism" was Joseph Pulitzer, who endowed the Columbia School of Journalism in 1904. "I wish to begin a movement that will raise journalism to the rank of a learned profession," Pulitzer wrote, "growing in the respect of the community as other professions far less important to the public interest have grown."

But more was going on with the Pulitzer/Lippmann revolution than a shift in philosophy. As Paul Weaver points out in his provocative book *News and the Culture of Lying,* Pulitzer had revolutionized journalism long before he helped establish a journalism school. He not only helped move journalism away from political parties, but more generally away from public affairs as defined by the major public institutions of his day. "Pulitzer was taking events out of their official context and framing them in stories with sharp dramatic focus that suggested intense public interest," Weaver writes. He continues:

> He achieved this effect by incorporating into journalism the elements of drama. What previously had been a sober, eye-witness account of an institutionally defined event now acquired character, action and plot. There were villains and heroes. Stories had beginnings, middles, turning points, endings. . . . In sum, Pulitzer's strategy for attracting readers boiled down to creating materials that immediately interested a lot of people and that created the further suggestion that the whole world was watching. . . .

Weaver goes on to note what a truly radical innovation Pulitzer's journalism represented. Before, newspapers had been primarily political, and partisan at that. Pulitzerian journalism was not only nonpartisan; it was fundamentally nonpolitical. It, Weaver says, "stood the old journalism on its head."

> It addressed, not the citizen and constitutionalist and partisan, but the private pre-political human being. Where the old journalism had invited its readers to step into, and renew their commitment to, constitutional and political processes, the new Pulitzerian journalism was inviting people to turn away from formal institutions and focus instead on the community evoked by the storytellers of the newsroom.

One of the main effects of this change, Weaver concludes, was to transform newspapers from a "reader-focused, reader-driven business into an advertiser-focused, advertiser-driven business." Newspapers turned from serving a limited community of like-minded readers—much as opinion magazines do now—to trying to build mass audiences to sell to advertisers. And this proved immensely profitable. As Michael Schudson notes in his excellent history of newspapers, "Most leading newspaper proprietors of the late 19th century were businessmen rather than political thinkers, managers more than essayists or activists." By being nonpartisan and "objective," newspapers did not offend half or more of their potential audience. Republicans, Democrats, Socialists and Independents could all find what they were looking for in one newspaper—and patronize its advertisers. "The journals which pay best in this country," exulted *The Kansas City Star* in 1884, "are those which are absolutely free from all external influences, and which are conducted as legitimate business enterprises on strict business principles." Historian Michael McGerr cites Whitelaw Reid's loving description of independent journalism as "passionless ether," which inadvertently also suggested the problems caused by the decline of the partisan press. It was not much noted at the time that a decline in the press's partisan passions might also have *negative* effects on democratic politics. As Lasch has argued, the Lippmann/Pulitzer approach pushed the press away from its classic democratic function, the promotion of argument among citizens. For Lippmann, writes Lasch,

the relationship between information and argument was an-
tagonistic, not complementary. He did not take the position
that reliable information was a necessary precondition of
argument; on the contrary, his point was that information
precluded argument, made argument unnecessary. Arguments were what took place in the absence of reliable information.

The transformation of American journalism was not a neat or
straight-line affair, but the combination of the Progressive impulse
and the incentives of the market created a new form of journalism
that would seek broad audiences and avoid partisanship. In Lippmann's terms, newspapers would appeal not to the passions but to
the intellect, not to the desire of readers to have their opinions
confirmed but to their thirst for accurate information.

It's true, of course, that journalism has never fully lived up to
such ideals. During the New Deal newspaper proprietors were as
passionately opposed to Franklin Roosevelt as most working journalists were on his side. Even in the heyday of the idea of "objectivity," journalists themselves acknowledged that the idea was more an
ideal than a realistic possibility. Schudson notes that in the mid-1930s
the social scientist Leo C. Rosten asked seventy reporters whether
they agreed or disagreed with the following statement: "It is almost
impossible to be objective. You read your paper, notice its editorials,
get praised for some stories and criticized for others. You 'sense policy' and are psychologically driven to slant your studies accordingly."
Among the reporters Rosten interviewed, forty-two agreed with the
statement, twenty-four disagreed and four were uncertain.

But however contested "objectivity" might have been as a
philosophical principle, it did not come under sharp practical challenge until the 1960s. Journalism was no less susceptible than other
institutions to the dissenting currents of that time and—despite
Crouse's comments on journalism's "tradition-bound" character—it
may have been more so than most. The critique of allegedly "apo-
litical" journalism that arose then is summarized nicely by Schudson. Journalists, in this view, were inevitably "political," even if
"unwittingly or even unwillingly." He goes on:

> Their political impact lay not in what they openly advocated
> but in the unexamined assumptions on which they based
> their professional practice and, most of all, in their confor-

mity to the conventions of objective reporting. In this view, objectivity was not an ideal but a mystification. The slant of journalism lay not in explicit bias but in the social structure of news gathering which reinforced official viewpoints....

Schudson sees the basis for this revolt against objectivity both in the rise of a "critical culture" (or, as the neoconservatives called it, an "adversary culture") and as a reaction to the perfection of "news management" techniques by government and large institutions. Absent a reexamination of journalistic rules and conventions, news outlets were destined to report not "facts" and surely not "truth" but rather versions of events manufactured by those with the power to do so. In *The Image,* his extraordinarily prescient account of the new world of journalism and public relations written in 1961, Daniel Boorstin notes that news was heavily dominated not by events but by "pseudo-events" manufactured for the sole purpose of winning news coverage for a particular point of view, person, product or company.

The growing self-consciousness among journalists that the news was not always what it seemed fundamentally changed the relationship between journalism and politics in other ways. A revolutionary event was the publication of Theodore H. White's *The Making of the President 1960*. No journalist before him had penetrated behind the scenes of a campaign to the extent he had. White not only reported brilliantly on the personalities of the candidates and the state of the country. He also offered inside accounts of why campaigns had done what they had done and how. If Boorstin warned journalists about pseudo-events, White explained how they were organized and came to pass, and what they meant. As Crouse notes in *Boys on the Bus,* campaign coverage would never be the same after White. In fact, White did much more than report from "the inside." His books also took the words and ideas of politicians very seriously, and analyzed them judiciously. He also used elections as a taking-off point for brilliant dissections of the state of the country. But Albert Hunt, the longtime Washington bureau chief for *The Wall Street Journal* and a White admirer, spoke for many reporters when he discussed the "one negative by-product" of White's work. "The press gets so caught up in trying to report the story behind the scenes," he wrote, "that major speeches or position papers or the substances of a campaign receive relatively little attention." Indeed, several excellent campaign books took advantage of the post-White obsession with "the inside story" by arguing that journalists' incessant interest in tactics and strategy often blinded them to the real reasons that people voted as they did. Jeff Greenfield, now of ABC News, argued in his book *The Real Campaign: How the Media Missed the Story of the 1980 Campaign* that "the flow of ideas and the underlying political terrain" had far more to do with Ronald Reagan's victories than all the twists and turns of campaign strategy. The conservative writer Richard Brookhiser consciously revolted against the White tradition with a book, *The Outside Story,* which paid attention mostly to what Ronald Reagan and Walter Mondale did in public in 1984. Brookhiser said that you didn't need to understand the work of the media meisters and pollsters to know why voters did what they did. All you had to understand was where each candidate stood and how his views articulated with the voters' ideas and aspirations. But Greenfield and Brookhiser notwithstanding, reporters knew they would not be rewarded for missing the inside stuff—and few did.

In defense of reporters, it should be said that a refusal to take things as they seemed to be on the surface was not the fruit of some blind cynicism. As Schudson points out, the concern with "news management" took on considerable urgency during the Vietnam War. It became more important still during Watergate when the officialdom's "covering up" of important facts was a matter not simply of journalistic inconvenience but of criminal behavior. In light of Watergate, it was inevitable that "investigative reporting," a rebirth of the "muckraking" tradition of the Progressive Era, would take on a new and respected role in conventional journalism. But this put the press in a situation of unprecedented tension with both government and politicians. Challenging official versions of events meant that reporters began to produce their own. They went beyond questioning authorized accounts and toward an examination of subjects the powers-that-be didn't even want to talk about. In a quite literal sense, investigative reporting meant that reporters were prepared to "set the agenda" for government. The scandals unearthed by reporters became the matters that government officials had to deal with, whether they liked it or not. It should surprise no one that politicians hated this—and so did their supporters—because in fundamental ways, the rise of investigative reporting shifted the balance of political power away from politicians and toward reporters. By pursuing the Watergate story, *The Washington Post* helped bring down a presidency, for which many Republicans never forgave it. By reporting incremental developments on the Whitewater story week after week in early 1994, the press slowly dragged down Clinton's approval ratings and forced the administration to spend inordinate amounts of time strategizing on Whitewater—to the detriment of many things, including its efforts on behalf of health care reform. (Some Democrats who loved the press during Watergate began to have second thoughts.) The press could argue that it was simply being "fair-minded," challenging incomplete or misleading official accounts in the interest of "the truth." But its critics saw it as pursuing a single-minded agenda aimed at destroying political leaders who had been freely chosen in democratic elections. "No one elected the press," its critics would say, which was, of course, quite true.

The press also confronted more specific challenges. The conservative revolt against journalism's alleged "liberal" bias (which we'll turn to in more detail in the next section) created pressure on newspapers and, especially, on television networks to provide some form of "balance." This was an intriguing development. Conventional journalism, after all, insisted on its own "objectivity," or at least "fairness." Yet it had enough of a guilty conscience (or felt enough pressure) that it moved to appease the critics. Conciliation—or capitulation—took the form of offering the "balancing" views of conservatives. The era of journalistic compensation during and after the Nixon era promoted the careers of some of the country's most talented conservative commentators (notably William Safire), who began to appear on op-ed pages and on television. The importance accorded such conservative voices was the beginning of a much larger trend toward rehabilitating the role of "opinion" in contemporary journalism.

Finally, the 1980s saw the rise of a new emphasis on "analysis" and "edge" in both television and newspaper reporting. For newspapers especially, analysis became important as they lost their franchise to be "first with the news" to television and radio. To survive, newspapers had to add value, and one clear way of adding value was to put events into context, to explain "why" something had happened, to get "behind" events.

This, then, is journalism's mishmash in the 1990s. Journalism has never entirely lost its Lippmannite aspirations to fairness, even if the word "objectivity" went out of fashion. Reporters still believed they should not be partisan, should present "both sides" of a controversy and thereby allow the readers or listeners to make up their own minds (or to hold fast to their preconceptions). Yet journalism was operating under a whole series of contradictory rules and imperatives—to be neutral yet investigatory, to be fair-minded and yet have "edge," to be disengaged from politics and yet have "impact." None of this was easing the estrangement between citizens and public institutions. Nor did it seem to be promoting a more engaging public debate. If politicians hated the press, so, it seemed, did the public.

IV

Over the last three decades the media have confronted three lines of criticism, all of them challenging the way newspapers and television were playing their roles as institutions vital to a democratic society.

The most familiar critique came from political conservatives who charged the press with extreme liberal bias. The conservatives argued that most reporters were liberals—and the polls did show that reporters were more inclined toward Democratic candidates than the rest of the country. To hear the conservatives talk, it was impossible for those whose convictions inclined rightward to get their message to the American people through conventional media channels (although this did not seem to stop them from winning a great many elections). The result was an onslaught on the media from both conservative political figures—former Vice President Spiro Agnew was the first in a long line—and conservative organizations and commentators.

The press has been unpopular with the political right since at least the 1960s. The conservatives' uneasiness with the press began with the important (and heroic) role it played in highlighting the evils of segregation through extensive and accurate coverage of the struggles of the civil rights movement. Civil rights leaders of the early 1960s were the country's first political activists to understand the power of television pictures. Broadcasts depicting innocent, nonviolent black people being beaten in the streets of southern cities powerfully affected the national mood on civil rights and paved the way for the great legislative victories of 1964 and 1965. For many southern conservatives, the press had been complicit in ending a "way of life" that they had found quite congenial. This was not soon forgotten.

The right's mistrust of the press only deepened during the Johnson and Nixon years. The war in Vietnam was the first televised war, and it became increasingly difficult to prosecute because it was televised. Wars, even just and popular wars, are always gruesome. Terrible pictures of suffering, fed into homes night after night, cannot help but reduce the public appetite for combat. The impact was all the greater as the public became increasingly uncertain about the purposes of the war and began wondering if it had to be fought at all. The overall tenor of the coverage shifted decisively to the negative side in 1968, especially with the Tet offensive. When Richard Nixon came to power, he inherited not only a war but also an insurrectionary mass media, which had never liked him in the first place.

The second set of attacks arose during the 1980s, especially after the 1988 presidential campaign and particularly in the academy. Analysts such as Thomas Patterson and Kathleen Hall Jamieson argued that the media had played a large role in the trivialization of politics. Jamieson took the media to task for doing little to challenge the way political consultants (especially George Bush's in 1988) sought to shape the debate. Reporters, she argued, were slow to call Bush and his lieutenants to account for a campaign built on "flags and furloughs." The assumption was that the media could and should demand a higher standard from candidates and see to it that campaigns reflected more closely the "genuine" concerns of the electorate. The media were criticized for ignoring issues, highlighting conflict and writing obsessively about the "horse race" aspects of campaigns—that is, who was "up" and who was "down." Sociologist Todd Gitlin argued that the press's emphasis on the horse race was a technique of evasion. Since reporters were not supposed to express their views on vital matters, they sought refuge in covering the political contest because reporting on who did what to whom and how well it was working meant never having to make value judgments. "In the absence of a vital polis," he wrote, "they take polls." The media were, indeed, good at understanding the internal dynamics of campaigns, Gitlin said. But mostly, they reported on what campaigns were doing "to" voters, rather than on the decisions the voters themselves made. Voters were thus encouraged to become "the cognoscenti of their own bamboozlement." Voters themselves talked less and less like citizens and more and more like the commentators they saw on television. A voter interviewed by *The Boston Globe* after the October 1994 debate between Senator Edward M. Kennedy and Mitt Romney, his Republican opponent, knew the jargon perfectly. Romney, the voter said, "didn't do what he needed to do." Kennedy was "confident, forceful, comfortable. He did what he needed to do. Romney tried to do that in an attack format, but ended up being simplistic and defensive." And it was no wonder that voters saw it all as a game. In Patterson's telling, conflict and passing controversy were all for the media. The press, he said, generated "a politics of shifting standards and fleeting controversies, with no identifiable core."

The third line of attack related to the first two: that the media were interested only in bad news and bad stories about people in power. Conservatives assumed that the terrible things written and broadcast about Richard Nixon, Ronald Reagan, Oliver North and Clarence Thomas—among many others—were motivated by ideological bias. Liberals and Democrats challenged this view when the press began paying so much attention to controversies involving President Clinton's love life and the Whitewater land deal. Frequently in private and occasionally in public, Clinton challenged the negativism of the news media and its tendency to ignore what his administration was doing and focus on racy stories about the past—especially his own. He won strong support from academic critics of the press such as Patterson, who argued that the media assumed that politicians were liars. Politicians' keeping their promises was a nonstory—even though, as Patterson accurately noted, what politicians said at campaign time actually bore quite a close relationship to what they did in office. The media assumed that politicians only broke their promises and spent much energy trying to prove that thesis.

These three critiques of the media—bias, trivialization, excessive negativism—made some important assumptions about the obligations of reporters. The most obvious of these was that reporters were supposed to be "fair-minded" or "objective." This could be interpreted as assigning journalists a rather passive role in the political process. Politicians were supposed to "make news." Journalists were supposed to "report news." The difficulty, of course, lay in the fact that journalists not only bridled at this "stenographic" function, as it came to be known derisively in the 1970s; they also began to question whether this approach reduced them to reporting lies. The wide coverage the press gave to Joseph McCarthy's claims about who was a "Communist" led to a crisis of faith among reporters who later regretted reporting McCarthy's allegations without challenging them. During the Vietnam War many reporters came to question official accounts that asserted the war was going well when it seemed obvious to them that it wasn't. For many reporters, being "fair-minded" or "objective" came to mean, as we have seen, *challenging* official versions of events that were obviously neither.

There is, it must be said, a strong "whose ox is being gored" quality to much of this debate, especially as it related to the question of "fairness." The very same people who thought the press was demonically irresponsible in the way it reported on Justice Clarence Thomas's private life cheered (and encouraged) reports about Bill Clinton's love life. On the other side, many who loved every moment of the Watergate coverage that brought down Richard Nixon accused the press of hyping the Whitewater story and giving it far more attention than it deserved. These views are not automatically inconsistent. It was possible, even reasonable, to believe that Whitewater was not remotely the scandal that Watergate was. It was plausible to argue that the evidence about Clinton's personal life was more convincing than the testimony about Thomas's. But in this sort of discussion, the principles proclaimed with great certainty often turned out to be, on inspection, rather conditional and heavily influenced by which side of the political spectrum is being put on the rack.

There was also a fundamental contradiction between critics who thought the press too passive and those who assailed its "edge." When the press was criticized for *not* challenging the nature of George Bush's 1988 campaign, it was being told its edge was gone. In her book *Dirty Politics,* Jamieson argues that journalism "allowed itself to be shaped by polls and manipulated by the more artful political consultants." Yet the press was *also* being accused of giving political stories so much "edge" that candidates were never allowed to answer the voters' most basic question and to explain what they believed, or would do. "Candidates have been given steadily fewer chances to speak for themselves through the news," writes Patterson in his book *Out of Order*. He goes on: "The candidate's words are now usually buried in a narrative devoted to expounding the journalist's view. . . ."

Which was it, that the press was too respectful or insufficiently respectful? Of course it's possible to say that *both* Jamieson and Patterson are right by arguing that the press is assertive at the wrong times and in the wrong ways. But this, in turn, suggests that while critics of the press may focus on the flaws of particular techniques, their uneasiness is really not about technique at all—something Jamieson and Patterson themselves emphasize, since their main concern is whether the democratic system is working. Lurking beneath the widespread criticism of the media is the sense that something is deeply defective in the public debate itself and that the press is not taking on a role that it ought to embrace: to make that debate more accessible, coherent and honest.

V

One of the central problems that has emerged in the contemporary press is figuring out just what is meant by words such as "journalism" and "the media." There is huge confusion over just what constitutes "reliable" journalism (presuming there is such a thing). With the rise of politically neutral journalism in the Progressive Era, the country as a whole developed a common source of information through the radio networks and the wire services that served most of the country's papers. It was news reported according to a fairly consistent set of rules. Of course this was not the only source of "information." Newspapers and radio had their gossipmongers; in cases such as Walter Winchell's, they could be quite powerful and sometimes quite destructive. Radio also had its subaudiences, including a vast network of religious programs that prefigured the televised church of later years. And there were powerful spokesmen for causes, such as Father Charles Coughlin, who used the airwaves to raise themselves and their views to fame, much as Rush Limbaugh would do later. Nonetheless, until at least the end of the 1960s, there was a strong trend toward homogeneity which had both weaknesses (it limited the range of the political conversation) and strengths (it created a common conversation carried out according to certain reasonably well-understood rules).

Beginning in the mid-1980s, the trend toward homogeneity was reversed by the explosion of media outlets created by cable television, the rise of new magazine-style and tabloid television formats, the growth of talk radio, and the increasing importance of commentary and analysis. The rise of all these formats has democratized the media conversation in important ways. In theory, at least, a range of strongly held points of view is now given a chance to be heard, reviving the nineteenth-century tradition of opinionated commentary. The new media, especially during the 1992 campaign, also gave voters unprecedented access to the presidential candidates and greater opportunities to hear them unmediated by "professional" journalists. The new media could be seen as "democratic" in another sense: There was absolutely no deference to politicians, even presidents. When it came to reporting their foibles and weaknesses, almost anything went. A president's love life was no longer secret, nor even the kind of underwear he wore.

Yet for average listeners, readers and viewers, it became even more difficult to distinguish between information and rumor, fact and opinion. This was not because news consumers were stupid, but because the rules followed by the different media were so different. Highly opinionated commentators such as Rush Limbaugh or Pat Robertson could sound just as authoritative as the average news anchor, and their supporters put great faith in what they said. But of course neither Limbaugh nor Robertson was constrained by the rules of conventional journalism. They literally could say anything, and often did—spreading, in Limbaugh's case, unsubstantiated reports that Clinton aide Vince Foster had been killed when every official investigation ruled his death a suicide. In the national debate on President Clinton's health care plan, it became increasingly difficult to separate fears from facts. Perfectly valid critiques of the plan relating to how much it might cost were intermingled with fantastic claims that its adoption might make seeking a second medical opinion a jailable offense. Given the plan's complexity, it was difficult even for the exceptionally well informed to figure out what it would do. Many chose to suspect the worst.

A particularly dramatic instance of the power of the conservative talk show hosts involved the killing of a lobby reform bill at the end of the 1994 congressional session. Urged on by Newt Gingrich, then the House Republican whip, Limbaugh and Robertson derailed a bill that had seemed on its way to easy passage. The measure surely ought to have been popular with many in Limbaugh's Congress-bashing audience—and with the vast majority of the public. It was a direct assault on standard (and highly questionable) congressional practices, including free meals and gifts from lobbyists, among them those well-publicized "charity" golf and tennis trips that amounted to interest group–financed free vacations. But Limbaugh and Robertson argued that the bill might force even those who wrote to their congressman to register as lobbyists and also endanger the freedom of religious groups to make their views known. The first charge wasn't even remotely connected to what the bill actually did. The second referred to a provision requiring fuller disclosure of spending on so-called grassroots lobbying campaigns that arose not from the grass roots but from the labors of paid, Washington-based lobbying firms. (They were popularly known in Congress as "AstroTurf" campaigns because of their artificial quality.) In fact, the bill contained some careful language designed precisely to protect the rights of religious groups to make their views known. But this didn't matter to Limbaugh or Robertson, whose highly tendentious reading of the bill became gospel to their listeners. Capitol Hill was suddenly inundated with calls against the bill.

Fred Wertheimer, president of Common Cause, a group that lobbied hard for the bill, argued that the episode was a remarkable example of "the extraordinary distortions that come into play when modern communications resources are linked up to a certain kind of advocacy." Those who can command large audiences on television or radio, he said, can "lie, distort and mislead . . . and there's no way that anyone can catch up and compete with that." Representative John Bryant, a Texas Democrat who was one of the bill's principal authors, spoke of the strange powers of the new opinion outlets. "The astonishing thing," he said, "is how a network of talk shows can turn a total fabrication into a serious line of argument."

The confusion of fact and opinion in public debate was the focus of a powerful 1994 essay in *The New York Times* by Michiko Kakutani.

"Throughout our culture," she wrote, "the old notions of 'truth' and 'knowledge' are in danger of being replaced by the new ones of 'opinion,' 'perception,' and 'credibility.' " She argued that "as reality comes to seem increasingly artificial, complex and manipulable, people tend to grow increasingly cynical, increasingly convinced of the authenticity of their own emotions and increasingly inclined to trust their ideological reflexes. . . ." In such a situation there are no arguments in the sense of an engagement over ideas and evidence but simply a clash of assertions. In this climate, said Kakutani, "the democratic idea of consensus is futile." We are witness to the creation of "a universe in which truths are replaced by opinions."

Kakutani points to a crucial aspect of the media's problem. In abandoning standards of "objectivity" or "fairness" and embracing a certain style of controversy, the press and television may have produced livelier formats without actually enlivening the public debate. The liveliness is, in some sense, artificial. It involves people tossing epithets and one-liners at one another as weapons. Combat between gladiators is not the same as an argument between citizens. Genuine argument involves a real exchange of views and information. In real argument, as Christopher Lasch nicely put it, "we have to enter imaginatively into our opponents' arguments, if only for the purpose of refuting them, and we may end up being persuaded by those we sought to persuade. Argument is risky and unpredictable and therefore educational." Arguments are not won, Lasch noted, "by shouting down opponents." Rather, "they are won by changing opponents' minds—something that can happen only if we give opposing arguments a respectful hearing and still persuade their advocates that there is something wrong with those arguments."

Lasch referred back to debates during the 1920s between Walter Lippmann and the philosopher John Dewey. Dewey insisted, against Lippmann's skepticism, that democracy was a practical as well as a noble system of government. Dewey did so in part because he had enormous faith in the educational functions of free and open debate in a democracy. Where Lippmann believed that facts and information were more important than argument, Dewey believed, as Lasch put it, "that our search for reliable information is itself guided by the questions that arise during arguments about a given course of action."

The problem for the media in the current day is that they may be losing the benefits of old-style journalism, designed mostly to convey information, without actually gaining the advantage of a journalism of controversy, which would seek to promote genuine, reasoned and engaging debate. Without either information or reasoned debate, there is—cynicism.

The real issue confronting modern journalism is thus a paradoxical one. On the one hand, there is a need to resurrect a concern for what's true—to draw clearer distinctions between fact and opinion, between information and mere assertion, between flip predictions and reasoned analysis. At the same time, there is an urgent requirement that the media take seriously their obligation to draw people into the public debate, to demonstrate that the debate is accessible and that it matters. Journalism, in other words, needs to be conscious simultaneously of its traditional "professional" imperatives and of its obligations to making democracy work. And it needs to do so in an economically competitive climate, one in which public disaffection with politics is so deep that television executives and editors are tempted to conclude that there is less demand than ever for *any* coverage of public issues. What is needed, in other words, is both a strengthening of the older professional ethic involving accuracy and balance and a new engagement with the obligations of journalists to democracy. No one elected the press, yet the press is now an intimate part of everything having to do with elections. The press is not there to make political decisions, yet everything the political press does shapes those decisions. The press does not exist to represent the citizenry, yet in fact reporters do believe they represent citizens (or at least their interests) when they probe and question and analyze and pontificate. The press, radio and television have no obligations to Democrats or Republicans. But they do have a powerful obligation to worry about their role in the functioning of a democratic republic.

VI

If the media have an obligation to promote democratic debate, it's worth asking: Does not a figure like Rush Limbaugh perform exactly such a role?

In fact, Limbaugh can be seen simultaneously as part of the solution and part of the problem—or, perhaps, as the wrong answer to the right question. He represents a new form of highly opinionated commentary that harkens back to the partisan press before the Progressive Era. His purpose is not to inform by way of neutrality and objectivity. Indeed, as his critics have noted, he often does not let the facts get in his way at all. Rather, his purpose is to engage, enrage, entertain and mobilize a constituency that comes to him precisely for those purposes. He can, when he wants, generate thousands of phone calls to members of Congress (or to journalists or to the White House). He has almost certainly created converts to Republican and conservative causes, and has strongly reinforced the views and attitudes of those already on his side. For the minority of Limbaugh listeners who disagree with him, his monologues no doubt mobilize them, too, reminding them of why they are liberals.

To the extent that one agrees with Lasch's assertion that one of the causes of political demobilization and democratic decay is the rise of the nonpartisan, "objective" press, the emergence of Rush Limbaugh and his imitators can be seen as a positive development. Here, after years of arid "fairness," is someone whose goal is to get people mad and active. He exists to tell scattered members of the community of political conservatives that they are not alone, that they have friends and allies, including an important one sitting behind the mike. This is a man whose whole purpose is to engage in political argument.

So what's the problem with Limbaugh? Many Democrats and liberals, including President Clinton himself, have attacked Limbaugh as a pernicious force. Obviously, they dearly wish that Limbaugh were less effective on behalf of conservative causes. But his critics also make a substantive case. They argue that he fills the political bloodstream with half-truths or worse. They see him making claims that he is replacing the mainstream media when he is doing nothing of the sort. Journalists of the traditional school, no matter how strongly held their views, are forced to live by certain rules that sharply limit their ability to invent "facts." Most journalists work for large institutions which impose a series of checks and balances; many journalists would be fired or disciplined for making some of the mistakes Limbaugh does. Moreover, Limbaugh's large audience allows him to create immediate constituencies for whatever causes he decides to put into play, whether his claims about an issue are true, doubtful or demonstrably false.

A second line of attack against Limbaugh looks not so much to the factual content of his work as to its tone. Endless invective and mockery, these critics argue, is antithetical to genuine debate. Limbaugh, they contend, is not interested in rational argument with his opponents and is dragging the quality of the whole political debate down. It's true, of course, that mockery has a long and distinguished tradition in political speech and writing. But these critics make the plausible point that invective is surely not something American politics needs in larger quantity.

Finally, Limbaugh's critics see him as promoting a kind of passive hostility that is, over the long run, inimical to a healthy democratic system. Limbaugh's listeners are just that—*listeners*. They might occasionally call in to vent their anger or express their views. But there is no clear link between Limbaugh and political action, as there was in the case of the partisan press of the nineteenth century.

The truth is that Limbaugh has come under all these attacks in large part because he has, so far at least, been a one-of-a-kind phenomenon. There are many talk radio hosts, but no one enjoys an audience of his size or loyalty. If there were several talk show hosts with comparable national audiences—say, a radical Limbaugh, a liberal Limbaugh and a moderate Limbaugh—the radio's marketplace of ideas would be seen as more balanced and Limbaugh's enemies would not be complaining so loudly. This, of course, begs the question of *why* there is no comparable liberal figure. Some have suggested that liberals are chronically "on the one hand, on the other hand" sorts of people. They seem more inclined to listen to the fine reporting on National Public Radio than to a liberal version of Limbaugh. But it is also possible to argue, as Limbaugh himself sometimes does, that conservatism now enjoys a mass popular appeal that liberalism does not. The mass movements of liberalism, in the labor and civil rights movements, for example, are in decline, while popular movements on the right, such as the Christian conservatives and the pro-gun movements, are on the upswing. Certainly the managers of local radio stations seem to find that conservative programs are a larger draw than more moderate or liberal programs.

For all of their shortcomings, the popularity of Limbaugh and the other talk radio jockeys transcends the matter of ideology. Their success reflects a public thirst for debate and argument that goes beyond the confines usually imposed by conventional definitions of news. The lesson Limbaugh offers—both to his critics and to the conventional media—is not that all should copy his style of argument, but that argument itself is much in demand. For the established media, this will mean going back to the original debate between Walter Lippmann and John Dewey. *The objective should be to salvage Lippmann's devotion to accuracy and fairness by putting these virtues to the service of the democratic debate that Dewey so valued.*

This means, in turn, that journalism needs to be concerned about far more than its professional rules and imperatives. It is not enough to create an image of balance—for example, by being as rough on Newt Gingrich's personal failings as on Bill Clinton's. Nor is it enough to report in a desultory style that there are "two sides" to a given question. (There are often more than two sides.) And it is surely less than useful to have so much time and attention spent on who is winning and who is losing to the exclusion of the issue of who is fighting for what and for whom, and how the parties to the argument are making their case.

In broad terms, the media need to help Americans recover what Christopher Lasch called "the lost art of argument." Journalism has to do far better than it does now in demonstrating the connections among facts, arguments and political action. Journalism was right to delve into what was going on behind "the media events." But simply demonstrating that manipulation happens and describing how the process works does nothing to advance the political debate. Journalism's task now is to look not just behind "the spin," but also behind the public arguments put forward by politicians. It is not enough to report them and "fact check" them for errors. What really matters to citizens are the underlying assumptions and goals of those putting forward various positions. And there also needs to be much more attention paid to whether a given *policy* would actually solve the *problem* it is addressing. Most citizens care more about solving problems than about abstract policy. What is needed is what might be called an investigative reporting of *ideas.* Its purpose would be to take what politicians actually say and do very seriously—to report more fully than is now the rule on the words as well as the actions of politicians, and then to look more carefully at the underlying implications of their ideas and proposals. Journalists would examine not simply what a particular proposal might

do to individuals or particular groups, but also how various proposals fit into a politician's long-term goals for the society. The key
is to understand how a set of proposals are linked to a set of ideas,
and how those ideas would shape the day-to-day lives of citizens.
What is true of a style of history well described by Robert Wiebe
should also be true of journalism: that it should be "situated at the
intersection between beliefs and actions." It's important to examine
carefully not only what politicians say and do, but also what they *say*
about what they do—and what they *do* about what they *say*. The
point of such a journalism would be to make clear that the words
and actions within the political realm matter, and to take seriously
the ability of average citizens to sort out which words and actions
matter most.

Lippmann was skeptical of democracy because he believed that
the citizens making the decisions had little information and little
interest in acquiring it. Dewey had a more positive view of democracy precisely because he believed that the public debates democracy fostered helped to create a more enlightened public. As Lasch
puts it, following Dewey, "it is only by subjecting our preferences
and projects to the test of debate that we come to understand what
we know and what we still need to learn." Lasch concludes:

> If we insist on argument as the essense of education, we will
> defend democracy not as the most efficient but as the most
> educational form of government, one that extends the circle
> of debate as widely as possible and thus forces all citizens to
> articulate their views, to put their views at risk, and to culti-
> vate the virtues of eloquence, clarity of thought and expres-
> sion, and sound judgment.

Lasch, of course, is describing an ideal to which democracy should
strive, not the day-to-day workings of democracy in the United
States. But nurturing the educational spirit that ought to lie at the
heart of democracy is surely a central task of journalism in a free
society. Journalism ought to be where facts, convictions and arguments meet.

With the country passing through a series of crises, journalism's primary task ought to be to engage citizens in the quest for
paths forward. That will involve understanding the alternatives and
weighing them for their faithfulness not only to the facts but also to

the values and moral commitments that supposedly underlie them. It involves debate experienced not simply as combat but also as conversation. In this telling, journalism's role of providing information is only the *beginning* of its task. As James Carey puts it, "The press, by seeing its role as that of informing the public, abandons its role as an agency for carrying on the conversation of our culture." The press and television must find ways of keeping the public informed without shutting the conversation down or closing it off to all but the most inside of political insiders.

VII

After the 1995 bombing of the federal building in Oklahoma City, the nation's newspapers and television programs brimmed with contradictory but revealing analyses of what that awful event might say about the state of American society and politics. There was a good deal of loose talk about "angry white men," but also more careful attention to the political and economic worries that had bred such frustration well beyond the confines of a race or a gender. There was useful reporting on the rise of armed right-wing militias and on how Americans who wanted nothing to do with gunmen shared some of their anger and skepticism toward the federal government. There was as well much said about the work done daily by the sorts of federal workers who labored inside that Oklahoma building, work aimed at helping people to get their Social Security checks, veterans benefits, Medicare coverage, farm payments and student loans. The possibility of competence and compassion on the part of government workers was underscored after the bomb went off by the work of rescue teams, firefighters, police, and federal law-enforcement agents. Suddenly, "bureaucrats" became human beings. Also much noted was the spontaneous response of the citizens of Oklahoma City. Beyond their fury over an inexplicably gruesome deed, there was an instant and continuous outpouring of help and support for neighbors, friends and strangers. Churches and every other kind of voluntary organization moved quickly, supplementing what the government was doing and providing forms of personal support that even the best government could not hope to offer.

Finally, there was a fierce debate over whether the rage expressed by the bombers of the federal building might not be telling
us a great deal about what was wrong with the public debate within
the political mainstream. "People should examine the consequences of what they say," President Clinton declared, "and the
kinds of emotions they're trying to inflame." He called on Americans to resist and condemn "the purveyors of hatred and division"
and "the promoters of paranoia." Clinton and the sentiments he
expressed were in turn condemned by conservatives, who argued
that liberals were using McCarthyite smear techniques to implicate
legitimate conservatives in the actions of crazed fanatics. "It is gro-
tesque," said Newt Gingrich, "to suggest that anybody in this country who raises legitimate questions about the size and the scope of
the federal government has any implication in this."

But of course the issue was not one of implicating Gingrich or
any other mainstream conservative in a despicable act. The issue
rather was whether conservative politicians in the mainstream might
not at times have tolerated and perhaps even encouraged an ex-
tremist response to political problems by promoting a hostility toward the federal government that went well beyond "legitimate
questions" about its size and scope. As Republican economist Herbert Stein asked shortly before the Oklahoma attack, was there not
something dishonest and demagogic about casting "the government" and "the people" as enemies locked in fierce struggle when
the government in question was democratic and when "the people," as they demonstrated in 1994, had every capacity to change it?

The issue here involved far more than the pronouncements of
conservative politicians or talk show hosts. The militias represented
in extreme form the great gulf that had grown between Washington
and many in the rest of the country. They symbolized the popular
sense that the day-to-day talk of politics had little to do with what
Americans actually worried about. The impatience with the nature
of political talk could lead to extremism, but it also embodied a
longing for what the political philosopher Glenn Tinder has called
"the attentive society." The attentive society as he conceives it is a
place that sees freedom as being of infinite value. But freedom is
understood by Tinder "as a pathway, not a destination." Understanding freedom in this way explains much of the impatience with
so much of public speech—in journalism, in advertising, on televi-

sion and in politics. "One reason freedom is degraded today," writes Tinder, "is that serious speech, which is *speech in search of truth,* is relatively rare. Freedom of speech is most energetically and conspicuously used for advertising and electioneering—for activities based on the assumption that speech is an expedient in the service of profits and power and that truth is an extreme outer limit rather than central purpose."

Applying Tinder's rigorous test—*speech in search of truth*—to day-to-day talk and writing in politics and journalism would have a revolutionary impact. Tinder, like Lasch and Dewey, sees public life not simply as a realm of combat but also as the ground on which citizens can engage in a common search for understanding. "A society in which people listen seriously to those with whom they fundamentally disagree—an attentive society—is the proper setting for freedom," Tinder believes. "An attentive society would provide room for strong convictions, but its defining characteristic would be a widespread willingness to give and receive assistance on the road to truth."

Politics, in the Tinder formulation, is not simply about struggles for power and the defeat of adversaries. It is, in democratic countries at least, a continuous and ongoing effort to balance worthy but competing values, to mediate conflicts, to resolve disputes, to solve problems. For good or ill, politics shapes the context in which individuals must make choices. It establishes the rules under which people will work, compete, raise their families, help their neighbors. If politics goes well, it engages citizens in the kind of debate that Tinder has in mind. It thus establishes rules that are seen broadly as fair and reasonable, partly because they have arisen out of an open dialogue, and partly because they are always subject to challenge and change. The result is a dynamic society. But if politics goes badly, the rules under which citizens must live come to be seen as unjust and distant from the values the society claims to espouse. Citizens come to doubt the legitimacy of political and economic systems that preach one thing and reward another.

Politics, in other words, will be at the center of the country's efforts to navigate through the current moral and economic crises. There is no escaping politics because there is no escaping the fact that the rules established in government, the marketplace, the workplace and the neighborhood will powerfully influence what even the most individualistic souls will be able to do. Some rules will make it easier for families to raise their children; others will make that task more difficult. Some will make it easier for individuals to seize opportunities for education and advancement; others will get in the way. Some rules will encourage charity, generosity, community-mindedness; others will discourage them. Getting the rules right, the task for which Tinder's attentive society is well suited, is the precondition for creating a dynamic society.

Journalism, all by itself, is ill suited to creating a new society— or, for that matter, any kind of society. But good journalism, thoughtful commentary, engaging argument are all essential to the attentive society Tinder has in mind. The mass media can enlighten or distract, engage or sedate, treat serious matters thoughtfully or trivialize them. Journalism is under such sharp attack now precisely because the public (and most journalists) suspect that it is not promoting a level of public debate that matches the seriousness of the choices the country confronts. The country is now engaged in one of the great arguments in its history, an argument in which many of the most basic questions—about definitions of morality, the role of government, the shape of the economy—are in play. If Americans in large numbers sit out this great debate and decide that politics has nothing to do with the problems at hand, and nothing to do with them, the whole political class—and perhaps *especially* journalists—will have failed.

Part Three

THE PURPOSE

SHOWDOWN:

*The Republican Challenge
and the Progressive Promise*

THE NEW RADICALISM in American politics means that the debate in 1996 and beyond is not simply a contest between political parties. It is a confrontation between fundamentally different approaches to economic turbulence, moral uncertainty and international disorder. American politics has been unsettled in recent years because most Americans sense that the country has not adapted well to these changes, and because they are ambivalent about them. They see enormous potential in technological change and the global economic revolution, but also know that both carry high costs, challenge old values and threaten the living standards of many. Like most people facing comparable choices in other times, Americans would like to reap their gains from the new era and minimize the costs it will impose. The central political question is whether such a trade-off can be managed, and how.

It is Newt Gingrich's genius to be the first major Republican politician to pose many of these questions explicitly. His strategy would make technological change itself the priority and push government aside. "We do have an economic game plan," said the House Republicans in their post-contract manifesto, *Restoring the Dream,* "and its central theme is to get bureaucratic government off of America's back and out of the way." Third Wave conservatism posits that virtually all the constructive changes in the next era will take place in the private marketplace. Thus, as *Restoring the Dream* puts it, the way to create a "first rate, globally competitive" economy is to free it from the "iron shackles" of "taxation, regulation and litigation."

This new conservatism harks back not to Ronald Reagan but to the Gilded Age of the 1890s. "Today," declares Paul Starr in *The American Prospect,* "the forces of the nineteenth century are laying siege to the accomplishments of the twentieth century in the name of the twenty-first." The new conservatives would resolve the country's political crisis by shrinking government. They would resolve the economic crisis by accelerating the economic transition. Denying any link between economic developments and the country's moral state, they would leave the solution of the moral crisis to traditional institutions, limiting the government's charitable endeavors in the hope that this would revive religiously based programs for social and personal uplift. All this would resolve the international crisis by transforming the United States, in Newt Gingrich's memorable phrase, into "the decisive economic power on the planet, which is the most competitive nation, which is capable of leading the human race and which has reestablished here at home a culture that works."

The new conservatism will fail not because it isn't bold—it is *very* bold to try to restore nineteenth-century doctrines—but because it seeks to define away almost all the problems that Americans want politicians to grapple with. The new conservatism is premised on the idea that there is no trade-off in the new era, that if only economic change goes forward unfettered, everyone will be better off. But most Americans don't believe that. Nor do most Americans define the moral crisis simply in terms of the misbehavior of others and presume that more and better preaching will solve the problem. They experience the moral crisis in their own lives, in worries about whether their own work will be rewarded and how they will raise their children in a culture that can make that task difficult. There is overwhelming distrust of government, but this does not translate into the overweening confidence in the corporate sector that so characterizes the new conservatism. The popular anger at government reflects not simply an impatience with bureaucrats but also a disappointment at government's failure to help citizens who are working their way through a difficult economic period. Americans want some protection from *both* the government and the market to preserve space in which families, voluntary associations, churches and the other institutions of civil society can thrive. If the old liberals seemed too eager to have the government usurp the authority of those institutions, the new conservatives appear blissfully unaware of how the economic marketplace can encroach on their prerogatives. Government, but never the market, is to blame. There is an irony here: that conservatives who tout the decisive roles of the private sector, cultural norms and community institutions often find themselves arguing that government, all by itself, has caused virtually every social problem. "Conservatives," said liberal writer Guy Molyneux, "have far more faith in government's ability to do harm than liberals ever had in its ability to do good."

The central evasion in the program of the new conservativism is its effort to deny that even the most conservative government will constantly be making rules—through tax laws, regulations or trade agreements—and that these rules have consequences. The new conservatism speaks the language of a joyful anarchism. In fact, it is, like most conventional political movements, simply reshaping government to serve particular purposes and interests. If in the name of "deregulation" the government weakens environmental protections, the new rules it creates will powerfully affect how individuals and companies treat the environment. Repealing worker safety rules changes the incentives for employers who face enormous pressures from the marketplace to cut corners—even when they would prefer not to. If income from investments is treated more favorably for tax purposes than income from employment, the government is making a powerful statement about the relative importance of investment and labor. Trade agreements affect the lives and job prospects of millions. Even agreements promoting freer trade are thousands of pages long, containing scores of new rules that reshape the economy.

Thus the new conservatism's emphasis on a battle between "big government" and "small government" is a misleading and false choice because it disguises what is at stake: not merely the *size* of government but the *direction* of government policy—the incentives government will be offering and the values that will dominate policy making. The central issue in American politics in 1996 and beyond is thus not *whether* new rules will be written but *what* those rules will be and the extent to which they will make it easier or harder for average Americans—and especially those in the Anxious Middle—to prosper in a new era.

There is a final difficulty with the new conservatism that goes largely undiscussed: *Its program has been tried before and found wanting*. That is the importance of realizing that the new laissez-faire is simply Gilded Age conservatism dressed up in the finery of a high-tech age. Both doctrines cast all worker protections as "socialism" and any effort by government to write rational rules for a new style of competition as an attack on property rights. Throughout this century American voters knew better. They understood that a free market economy could not function properly in the absence of rules, workers' rights, government spending on public goods and continuing public investment to enhance the skills and opportunities of the workforce. This understanding was not confined to liberals or Democrats. It was accepted also by most Republicans. It was Dwight Eisenhower, after all, who sponsored the Interstate Highway System, one of the great public works in American history, and supported the first student loan program to help poor and middle-class Americans go to college. Much of the American business community eventually came to welcome government's role in preventing chaos in the marketplace and redressing social wrongs. This understanding of politics, drawn from America's Progressive tradition, defined the center of gravity in *both* parties.

The logic of the new high-technology era demands not the dismantling of this tradition that is now under way in Congress, but its revival and renewal. Not since the industrial transition at the turn of the century and the mass dislocation of the Great Depression have Americans felt a greater desire for creative approaches to governing.

Contemporary liberals have failed to meet this demand, and Americans have paid a high price for their loss of imagination. It is visible in the political fatalism of millions of working Americans who once looked to Washington as an ally in their efforts to achieve self-sufficiency. In casting ballots for Roosevelt and Truman, Kennedy and Johnson, these Americans sensed they were part of a historic, and effective, political movement. Now, politics lies discredited and with it the hope that democratic government can respond effectively to change. The responsibility for this failure is widely shared. It encompasses "New Democrats" who said they would revitalize government, traditional liberals who claimed to speak for "average Americans," moderate Republicans who now face a choice of being isolated in their party or capitulating to its new disposition, and a left that lost its way in the controversies surrounding multiculturalism and deconstruction and often gave up on democratic politics.

But the game is not played out. Indeed, it is just beginning. The demand for a new Progressive project will not go away, and all these groups have an opportunity to help shape it.

II

The need for this project will become increasingly obvious as the weaknesses of the new conservatism become clearer. Much as the right gained strength from liberalism's failures, so will Gingrich's revision of conservative doctrine create disaffection. His revolt is aimed not only against liberalism and Progressivism but also against many parts of the *conservative* tradition.

Gingrich's embrace of the theories of Alvin and Heidi Toffler means that he has broken with some of the fundamental assumptions of traditional conservatism. On issues related to the family, the views of the Tofflers could not be more at odds with those of Ralph Reed and his followers in the Christian Coalition. "The family system," the Tofflers write, "has become demassified: the nuclear family, once the modern standard, becomes a minority form, while single-parent households, remarried couples, childless families and live-alones proliferate." In writings published by Gingrich's foundation, the Tofflers explicitly criticize the "family values" movement by arguing that its conception of the family is rooted in old thinking. "The irony," they contend, "is that many 'family values' advocates, without knowing it, are not pushing toward a stronger family when they urge a return to the nuclear household; they are trying to restore the standardized model of the Second Wave." Note here that the sort of family that religious conservatives see as ordained by God and that other traditionalists view as ratified by time and nature becomes, in the Tofflers' conception, simply "the standardized model."

It's true, of course, that Gingrich might admire the Tofflers without agreeing with them on every issue. (The Tofflers have made clear that they feel that way about Gingrich.) And aspects of the

Tofflers' analysis of the rise of an information age contain insights that can be accepted by people of a wide variety of political views. But the most important idea Gingrich draws from the Tofflers is a belief that history now has a certain logic. It is a logic asserting that a particular kind of change is coming, that it is inevitable and that resistance to it is both futile and stupid. Elites who fail to "flow with the Third Wave," the Tofflers warn, are only asking for disaster—for themselves and for their societies. "If these groups prove to be as shortsighted, unimaginative and frightened as most ruling groups in the past, they will rigidly resist the Third Wave and thereby escalate the risks of violence and their own destruction."

This broad, deterministic argument is the antithesis of the conservative tradition with its emphasis on (and respect for) small communities, its belief in slow and gradual change, its skepticism of sudden innovation, its admiration for old moral habits. The Tofflers speak of a "collision of constituencies." In proposing a particular resolution to conservatism's contradictions, Gingrich's Third Wave approach is bound to create such a collision within his movement, sharpening the conflicts between traditionalists and libertarians and creating new lines of division that will become clearer as Gingrich's objectives become more explicit. "Accelerating the transition" and "forcing the scale of change necessary to be successful in the twenty-first century" entail a faith in technology, a willingness to accept substantial social costs and a disdain for traditional arrangements. All are antithetical to so much that is basic to conservatism, a point made in very different ways by Buchanan's economic nationalist supporters and by abortion opponents uneasy with attacks on programs for the poor.

Even some among Gingrich's admirers and allies have expressed doubts about his worldview. Bill Kristol argues that "insofar as it substitutes for a debate over the merits of certain social policies the claim that 'we are the future and you are the past so you are discredited,'" Gingrich's Third Wave vision is "intellectually wrong and bad for our political discourse." Kristol goes on: "We should make arguments that our way of proceeding is better for people than the liberal way of proceeding, rather than saying history has been on our side, which has been an argument of the left." Columnist Charles Krauthammer also noticed the peculiarity of Gingrich's conservatism. "At root, the problem with Gingrichism is not its belief in technology, but its belief in revolution," Krauthammer notes. "Technology is just the means. Revolution is the end—and for conservatism, a very odd end."

Moreover, despite Gingrich's fervently hopeful view about the direction of history and his capacity for eloquence on alleviating suffering in the inner city, his brand of conservatism differs from the optimistic stream of contemporary conservative thought exemplified by one of his heroes, Jack Kemp. Gingrich's emphasis on Olasky's thinking about the role of private charity and his support for deep cuts in federal spending on the poor suggest that he is less sanguine than Kemp on government's role in helping the poor. There is also a hard edge to Gingrich's analysis of what ails American society that contrasts sharply with Kemp's warmhearted ebullience. In a speech shortly after the 1994 elections, Gingrich spoke of "the pursuit of happiness" and noted that the phrase included "an active verb." He went on: "Not happiness stamps, not a department of happiness, not therapy for happiness. Pursuit." His conclusion: "This is also a muscular society and we've been kidding ourselves about it. The New Hampshire slogan is 'Live free or die.' It's not 'Live free or whine.' And so we will have to think through what are the deeper underlying meanings of being American and how do we reassert them." Whatever Gingrich meant by this, it is clear that he has in mind a fiercely competitive world that takes no prisoners. Kemp, by contrast, often speaks of a compassionate, "Good Shepherd" brand of conservatism.

Gingrich is right to call himself a "revolutionary." But by its very nature, as Krauthammer notes, conservatism is *not* a revolutionary creed. Traditional conservatism tempers its hopes with a skepticism about what passes for "progress." It does not believe that technological change can guarantee the good society. Wary of all forms of materialism and historical determinism, it sees the values of the citizenry as being more important to the creation of a decent society than either the great technologies of the private sector or the great plans of the public sector. It not only understands the limits of government, but also the limits of limited government. For example, when William Schambra speaks of the need for government to provide help for single mothers through intermediary institutions such as the churches, he is implicitly accepting a substantial government role in financing social welfare policy. He is not pretending that a conservative welfare state will be costless. While neo-Reaganism shares Gingrich's enthusiasm for the market economy, its emphasis is less on economics than on society's cultural and moral values.

The Kristol-Schambra synthesis is less doctrinaire than Gingrich's and more inclusive of conservatism's traditionalist insights. Schambra is not only more explicit than Gingrich in accepting a government role in shoring up local communities and traditionalist institutions; he also speaks openly and fondly of the conservative tradition. His is a conservatism that feels affection for old social forms and small communities even if they do not pass the strict scrutiny of marketplace logic or obey the iron laws of technological progress. If contemporary conservatism continues to shuck its communitarian traditions in favor of a more radical individualism, many conservatives will find themselves falling by the wayside and in search of political alternatives.

The differences between Gingrich and the neo-Reaganites are subtler versions of a larger gulf within the conservative movement. For all of Gingrich's brilliance in constructing a new synthesis, mass conservatism—at the level of the ballot box—remains a coalition of well-off economic libertarians, middle-class Christian conservatives and a growing far right that has come to identify "power in Washington" with the threat of "one world government" and the global market. In the 1994 elections, attacks on Washington sufficed to hold this alliance together. They satisfied low-tax libertarians who opposed almost anything Washington did, Christian conservatives who despised Washington's "countercultural liberal elites" and many on the far right who feared the federal government's power— especially its power to impose restrictions on firearms.

But this alliance runs up against a hard political fact: *that many of the anxieties of the cultural conservatives and the far right are rooted in the very changes that the economic conservatives applaud.* The social conservatives are oriented to family, community and locality, which are disrupted by the economic progress that the free marketeers hail. The social conservatives may or may not go along with cuts in the capital gains tax, but rewarding capital is not the cause that motivates their commitment to politics. Their commitment is to reward virtue as they understand it. In a particularly striking example of the inherent contradictions in contemporary conservatism, Senator Bob Dole won loud applause in mid-1995 when he criticized

Time Warner, the entertainment giant, for producing movies and music that "cultivate moral confusion." Sounding much like Ralph Nader, he asked of the company's executives: "Must you debase our nation and threaten our children for the sake of corporate profit?" Yet within weeks Dole was leading the Senate in passing a telecommunications bill whose deregulatory provisions promised a great increase in the profits of large entertainment companies—and particularly Time Warner. Thus did conservatism's cultural messages run explicitly counter to their economic commitments.

The new conservatism's problem and challenge is that many on the cultural right—as well as many drawn to the far right—are part of the Anxious Middle in fearing for their living standards and mistrusting the state and the market alike. When partisans of the militias and the radical right speak of the threat of "world government" or spin conspiracy theories around the interests of distant bankers and global economic institutions, they are expressing rage at economic changes that have disrupted their lives. Many drawn to the militias in Montana and Idaho, for example, come from regions where once-prosperous logging and mining industries have fallen onto hard times. For now, militia members and their more mainstream allies may associate this transformation with the rise of environmentalism and Washington's excesses. Many of them are thus willing to throw in their lot with anti-Washington conservatives. But a conservative politics that does not address the underlying economic anxieties of these voters will, over time, deepen their disappointment and rage. One conservative who understands this is Pat Buchanan, and his economic nationalism and attacks on "the new world order" are winning a wider audience than many conservatives had anticipated.

The new conservatism refuses, on principle, to address the link between economic change and the moral unease of so many Americans. Recall, for example, the Schambra-Joyce critique of the turn-of-the century Progressives. Schambra and Joyce acknowledged that economic change was the driving force behind its rise and that Progressivism's call for a more active federal government was a direct response to the "crisis of community" created by industrialism and urbanization. They noted as well that the purpose of the Progressives was "to tame through regulatory action those great and disruptive concentrations of private wealth, the corporations." But Schambra and Joyce chose *not* to discuss what might have happened if the Progressives had *failed* to address the issue of concentrated economic power—first at the turn of the century, and then during the New Deal—and had failed to offer communities and individuals some protection from the full effects of economic change. The conservative critique of Progressivism, in other words, tries to ignore Progressivism's central achievement, the effective use of democratic government to temper market outcomes, and to accomplish things that the market could not have achieved on its own.

The new conservatism is not wrong in defending the economic market in its proper sphere. It *is* wrong in trying to apply a market model to almost all aspects of human life. Bob Dole acknowledged as much in his critique of Time Warner: The market does not produce families and children and does not always serve them well. As David Broder, the dean of American political columnists, argued in *The Washington Post* after Dole's speech, "the morality of the marketplace does not in itself guarantee a good society. Seeking profits is not synonymous with being responsible." Broder went on to argue that "too much of contemporary conservatism has simply become an apologist for corporate power. The complex workings of healthy civil society have been reduced to a few banalities: Profits good. Taxes bad. Business builds. Government obstructs."

To have one of the leading moderate voices in the American political debate speak up in this way underscores the radicalism of the new conservative disposition—and the widespead doubt this radicalism has created.

There were other signs of ferment suggesting that the turn taking place in American politics was not toward the right but rather toward a new era of reform. Recall, for example, that when the Republicans ran their 1994 campaign, they assiduously avoided talk about how they would balance the federal budget. They were especially circumspect about saying anything that would imply their willingness to cut popular programs for the elderly such as Medicare. Once they did mount their effort to cut and reshape Medicare, the response in the country was far from positive. Gingrich was extremely shrewd in negotiating with all the groups affected by his program, and visible opposition took a long time to build. But build it did, and confidence in the Republican Congress dropped steadily as the year dragged on. Yes, Americans wanted fiscal prudence, and they even had some admiration for the Republicans' boldness. But they were very wary of dismantling the basic elements of the social safety net, particularly those parts designed to protect the elderly. The Republicans themselves admitted as much when they kept insisting that their plans on Medicare were designed merely to "save" the program.

The Republicans also faced growing disaffection over their failure to move early on reforms in the political system. In the fall of 1995, when Ross Perot announced his plans to begin a third party, his main cause was reform of the campaign finance and lobbying laws. Up to that point, Republican leaders, particularly in the House, had sidelined efforts by both freshmen and veteran reformers to push these issues higher on the party's agenda. Most Republican leaders had also shrugged off the news reports about the important role that industry lobbyists (and campaign contributors) had played in writing the party's legislation on such matters as the environment and deregulation. But the voters had not, and even the Republican leadership was forced to notice. When Americans told the pollsters that the Republicans had not moved quickly enough to change Washington, party ideologues presumed this meant that government hadn't been cut enough. In fact, the surveys suggested that voters were *critical* of many of the Republicans' proposed cutbacks. What they were most upset about was the sight of "business as usual." Again, the public was reformist, not conservative.

Clinton himself gained ground in the polls precisely because of this. All through 1995, the Republicans' once substantial advantages over Clinton on their core issues—the budget, the deficit and taxes—declined or disappeared entirely. Some Republicans (as well as some liberal Democrats) complained that Clinton had coopted Republican themes with his new "centrist" approach to governing. Clinton had, indeed, moved to the right of where he had been, particularly on the welfare issue. But Clinton's approach also involved sharp attacks on the Republicans in those areas where they were seeking to dismantle the core of the Progressive achievement—in health care, the environment, regulation and education. A country fully convinced of the wisdom of the new conservative disposition would not have responded to Clinton as it did. The White House was resigned to further volatility in Clinton's personal popularity before the 1996 elections. But the vulnerability of the Republican agenda was clear.

There were doubts even within Republican ranks. Some conser-

vatives looked with dismay at the broad interest Colin Powell's potential candidacy engendered before Powell announced he was not
running. Many conservatives feared Powell could derail Gingrich's
revolution and might represent a revival of Eisenhower-style Progressive Republicanism. The fact that some on the Republican right
attacked him so harshly suggested that they themselves were not so
sure that the party's rank and file was firmly in the right-wing camp.
In the meantime, conservatives who supported Powell—notably Bill
Kristol—seemed to sense that the electoral revolution of 1994 was
less far-reaching than its architects claimed and that someone of Powell's stature and moderate credentials was thus needed to confirm
the Republican shift; a more conservative candidate might not be
able to do it. Powell himself noted when he withdrew that the response to his potential candidacy suggested that many of the Republican faithful were not as radical as the party's public positions
suggested. "I think there is more moderation there than one might
believe from some of the rhetoric," he said.

Outside Washington, there were rumblings of Progressive resurgence. A successful rebellion within the AFL-CIO and the embrace
of a reform program by both the old and new guards signaled new
life in a labor movement that had been struggling for decades. Betty
Friedan, the intellectual founder of contemporary feminism, sought
to push the movement to organize around the issues of work, family
and economic security, a departure that held the promise of building
new alliances across old dividing lines. Opposition to deep cuts in
assistance to the poor galvanized many in the churches that were
outside the orbit of the religious right. The Catholic Church was especially outspoken, but so were many other religious groups, both
Christian and Jewish. And there was a proliferation of community
service programs—similar to the development of settlement houses
during the Progressive years—that drew particularly on the commitment of the young and marked a new popular engagement with social problems. Finally, the Republican surge stalled out in the
elections of November 1995. The Democrats held the governorship
of Kentucky with a campaign that explicitly targeted Gingrich, Bob
Dole, the Republicans' Contract and their Medicare cuts. In Virginia,
one of the most conservative states in the union, the Republicans had
expected to capture the state legislature with an anti-tax, anti-
government program that was an explicit copy of the Contract with

America. Instead, to the Republicans' shock, the Democrats held the legislature by highlighting the importance of public investment in education—a campaign that won Democrats surprising support from many business leaders.

And there was a searing reappraisal of the country's state in the wake of the O. J. Simpson verdict and the Million Man March in Washington. The response to the verdict was so polarized across racial lines and the angers the case aroused were so deep as to render foolish any claim that the country could comfortably or happily remain on the same course. The March was experienced by many as a moving call to personal and family responsibility, but it was marred by the demagogic and anti-semitic leadership of Louis Farrakhan. Both the Simpson experience and the March heightened the country's longing for a rediscovery of racial harmony and underscored the need for a biracial project of social reconstruction.

Finally, the heirs to the Progressive tradition were rediscovering their own connections to it. The turn-of-the-century Progressives had, after all, been strongly opposed to the political reaction and social injustice of the Gilded Age, but they also resisted the efforts of some Populists to stop the transition to the industrial era cold. The earlier Progressives, noted the journalist Paul Starobin in late 1995, "were civic-minded reformers who stood to prosper in the new economy but were appalled by the corruption of big city governments and the squalor of raw industrialism. And they worried about the political stability of unregulated capitalism." In our era, the New Progressives are those who accept the need to make another large economic transition, but know that the transition will be successful only if government acts creatively, and with a strong concern for social justice. As Starobin put it, "the political masters of economic change are those who manage to give soul, sustenance and hope to the new order of things."

That defines both the spirit of the Progressive project and the yearning of the Anxious Middle. Most in the Anxious Middle are wary of the economic change now under way but skeptical of efforts to turn the process back. They are dissatisfied with the responses that have come from government so far, but are worried about their prospects in an economic order in which government withdraws and removes basic social protections. They are, potentially, the core constituency of a New Progressivism. But Progressives will not cre-

ate an effective competing vision unless they learn from past liberal
mistakes, speak with genuine conviction about government's purposes and reexamine the tradition from which they spring.

III

It is now a commonplace that Democrats and liberals have lost
their intellectual coherence and their sense of the future, but the
conservative writer David Brooks explored this idea with particular
insight in a 1995 essay in *Commentary* magazine. Liberalism, he
argued, has gone through so many bouts of redefinition that it no
longer has a distinctive character. "The trouble," he wrote, "is that
30 years of shuffling have blurred the creed, so that liberalism now
resembles a person who has undergone 27 face-lifts; the natural
contours have disappeared." Whatever their own troubles, conservatives had at least argued through the tenets of their creed to the
point where there is now "built into the movement a sense of
solidarity with the effort as a whole." For liberals, by contrast, "endless redefinition has erased any sense that certain issues are settled,
that certain guiding policies are constant."

Brooks traced "the Clinton administration's inability to define
a clear policy direction" to the fact that "mainstream liberalism . . .
has become vaporous." Liberals have become so obsessed with
redefinition, he wrote, that liberalism "is increasingly divorced from
the immediate concerns of people who do not spend their lives
trying to redefine liberalism—in other words, most people." He
went on: "Unable to devise policies the electorate would buy, they
came up instead with plans for coalitions, and only then with policies that might bring these coalitions together. But coalitions are
unplannable." It's policy and direction, said Brooks, that count.

Those who would embrace a new Progressive project need to
take Brooks's critique seriously. So many of the contemporary efforts to redefine liberalism have failed because they either sought to
fudge fundamental disagreements to create temporarily successful
electoral alignments, or they tried to impose issues particular to one
group of progressives as the dominant agenda for an entire movement—and to excommunicate those who refused to bow to the
particular interest. In the process, broader purposes disappeared
from view.

The troubles of the Clinton administration and the Democratic Congress can be traced to both problems. As we have seen, there was coherence to what Clinton tried to do in his campaign and during his first two years in office. Health care reform, political reform, welfare reform and reforms in job-training and education programs could in principle have laid the basis for a successful term and an alternative political vision. But rather than win credit as someone seeking to do large things, Clinton was too widely seen instead as a figure who shifted and pandered. And his party in Congress failed to understand the urgency of coherent action.

Part of the problem was a constant fiddling with labels: Clinton was not to be a "liberal" (a word that fared badly in the polls) but insisted that he was a "New Democrat." But being a New Democrat meant many things to many people—and different things at different times to the same people. For most conservative Democrats, especially southerners in Congress, being a New Democrat simply meant being more like the Republicans. Clinton disappointed them because many of them had hoped that he would be a conventional, moderately conservative president who would deal with the budget deficit, welfare reform—and not much else.

But the intellectual spirit behind the New Democrat project as conceived by its authors in the Democratic Leadership Council had been not conservative but *progressive* in spirit. The DLC named its think tank the Progressive Policy Institute precisely to make clear its allegiance to the tradition of the Roosevelts and Woodrow Wilson. In its policy papers if not always in its political pronouncements, the DLC argued consistently for more activist government in areas such as job training, welfare and national service. Its call for an end to corporate tax subsidies put it to the "left" of many in the party. Yet the enmity between the DLC and many in the party was such that neither side felt part of a shared project. In the health care battle, for example, the shared commitment of "newer" and "older" Democrats to universal medical coverage became less important than their disagreements over the relative role of markets and government in providing the guarantee. In the fight over welfare, liberals accused the New Democrats of being "too punitive," even though both sides favored putting *more* resources into jobs and education for the very poor.

By seeming to straddle the New and Old Democratic strategies, Clinton made enemies on both sides. Al From, the DLC's president, became so frustrated with the administration's direction that he emerged as one of the most vocal *critics* of a president he had worked so hard to put into office. Yet Clinton was also assailed from the party's liberal and left wings—and he made matters far worse for himself in late 1995 by seeming to disown his own earlier approaches to taxes and welfare. Some liberals accused him of being insufficiently constant on what they saw as core liberal social and cultural commitments—by backing down on gays in the military, for example. Economic liberals argued that far from being a traditional Democrat, Clinton had made his strongest commitment to such New Democratic causes as free trade, through NAFTA and GATT, and a balanced budget. Clinton's centrist and conservative critics gave him little credit for achievements that were very much theirs. His liberal critics, in turn, cut him little slack for what he actually did on behalf of *their* causes (much more progressive taxes on the wealthy, a family leave law, tax cuts and wage subsidies for the working poor) or tried to (the initial battle for gays in the military and, of course, health care reform).

Looked at one way, it was easy to see why Clinton and his loyalists were so frustrated: The competing wings of the Democratic Party blamed him for everything they disliked about what he had done, while rarely praising him when he landed on their side. And having made so many enemies, Clinton was nonetheless persistently attacked for a lack of political "courage"—and an *unwillingness* to "make enemies."

But the fact that Clinton found himself in this fix reflected systematic problems in his own approach—his back and forth on welfare and taxes enraged liberals but won him little new support—and in that of his constituency. At work here in part was David Brooks's observation that liberals and Democrats had become so obsessed with finding ways to build *coalitions* that they had subsumed ideas and policy to the coalitional arts. In the summer of 1995, for example, From argued that the key to Clinton's chances for a political revival depended on his willingness "to take on the party's base." The failures in the first part of his term, From maintained, were rooted in the extent to which Clinton "became defined by the very forces in the party that he had come to Washington to change." On the contrary, said Jeff Faux, president of the liberal Economic Policy Institute, Clinton's core problem lay in his desire to *flee* traditional Democratic constituencies and in his failure to defend their interests. Faux saw the 1994 elections as proving that the "right wing of the Democratic Party has little mass base" and "is primarily a collection of conservative politicians and business lob- byists held together by a centrism calculated to appeal to the estab- lishment press." The "liberal-labor constellation of forces is the only sector of the party that has a capacity to field a grass roots challenge to the right," he said, and concluded: "Exposed and un- sheltered, the core constituencies of the party must regroup, reor- ganize, and pursue a disciplined, independent path to the next election to revitalize themselves as a political force."

As Brooks would point out, this argument buried the broader matter of the party's substantive purposes beneath a battle over which constituencies mattered most. Winning, said From, required *taking on* the base. No, said Faux, it required *strengthening* the base.

Clinton's difficulties can be measured by the fact that From and Faux were having this argument three years *after* the 1992 election. Then, Clinton had managed to unite the forces for which both From and Faux spoke by arguing that there were substantive reasons for the two sides to come together. Clinton's case, after all, was that From's insistence on the politics of "opportunity and personal re- sponsibility" went together with Faux's call for an economic pop- ulism on behalf of average workers. But once elected, Clinton failed to make a convincing argument to *either* wing of his coalition that his administration would embody that coherence. Instead, many of the news accounts of his presidency focused on the constant feud- ing between "centrist" and "liberal" or "populist" strategists. Clinton fostered this perception by seeming to move from one group of political advisers to another—from the "populism" of a James Carville or a Paul Begala to the "centrism" first of David Gergen and then of Richard Morris. Clinton's failure to get credit for his successful policies reflected his failure to frame his administra- tion's work in larger terms. His purpose had been to use many of the means proposed by the New Democrats to secure the ends—of social justice and improved living standards—supported by tradi- tional Democrats. But neither side in the internecine wars saw things that clearly, because the White House didn't seem to, either.

In fairness—both to Clinton and to the adversaries inside his coalition—the problems here embody more than politics and per- ception; they also had substantive roots. The two issues that con- stantly tore at the Clinton coalition, setting business-oriented centrists and labor-oriented liberals against each other, were trade and the budget deficit. In the past, Democrats had always been able to turn to trade and budget issues to overcome divisions on matters involving race, culture or morality. Trade and the deficit were devastating precisely because they turned economic matters, traditionally the ground of unity, into a new battlefield.

The battle over trade, as we saw earlier, is about far more than arcane rules over imports and exports. At root, it is a conflict involving deeply held convictions toward the global economy—on the one side, the view that the increasingly global nature of commerce will lead to rapid growth and enhance American living standards; on the other, a fear that it will result instead in a downward spiral of wages and benefits. Many critics of free trade are animated by a fundamental worry: that the global marketplace will mean the end of any effective democratic control of economic policy, since democracy operates only inside national borders. Supporters of free trade are animated by the opposite fear: that countries which try to escape the global market will ultimately destroy their own living standards and condemn themselves to shrinking, statist economies.

No one understood better than Clinton the need to find ways around this argument as much as possible, as long as possible. That is why he presented himself in his campaign as both a free trader and an economic nationalist. He evaded taking a stand on NAFTA until the campaign's end, and even his final position was a finesse: for the treaty, but with new side agreements to protect the environment and the rights of workers. "It was the sort of split decision," writes Elizabeth Drew, "that critics saw as a sign of his trying to please everyone and others saw as evidence of his high political acumen."

Paradoxically, Clinton's "political" solution was effective precisely because it was based on a substantive approach that held promise for settling at least some of the disputes between the warring trade factions. Clinton was saying in effect that the global market itself was a given; no country could expect to escape it. But he was also acknowledging that critics of free trade had a point about democracy's writ within the global trading system. Trade agreements governed only the transfer of goods. They did not govern *how* goods would be produced—what rules would apply to the rights of workers or the protection of the environment. Clinton's NAFTA compromise thus took the free traders' arguments about the benefits of open markets and added the caveat that global markets needed rules similar to those that already applied within national borders. The president also insisted that free trade would enhance living standards only if it was accompanied by aggressive government policies to improve the skills of workers.

Unfortunately, Clinton's formulation of this question was—and remains—far easier to execute rhetorically than in practice. The labor and environmental agreements negotiated as part of NAFTA were extremely mild; the administration pulled back from anything stronger for fear of losing Republican votes for the treaty. The president's education and job-training initiatives, as we have already seen, were far less comprehensive than what had been proposed in the 1992 campaign. A potentially promising approach was thus never fully realized.

The budget deficit, a problem created by conservative Republicans, proved to be a continuing nightmare for liberals and Democrats. As the political scientist Theodore Lowi put it, Ronald Reagan "left all of the . . . liberal state intact but made it almost impossible for it to work. Drastic tax cuts coupled with maintenance of defense and welfare commitments effectively killed governmental capacity." Conservatives, at least, knew what the point of the exercise was. By cutting government revenues, wrote Irving Kristol in 1982, they had "put the welfare state in a moderately tight straitjacket." Liberals chafed inside the straitjacket, but were sharply divided over how to get out of it.

Liberals had a fundamental problem: Historically, they had no principled objection to deficits. The secret of Keynesian economic policies had been to run up the deficit during economic downturns to boost demand and speed recovery. Keynesian deficits, however, had a purpose. Keynesian theory looked to balancing the government's books in times of prosperity. The Reagan era deficits were chronic.

For Progressive deficit hawks, there was no choice but to bring the books into long-term balance. Otherwise, government would be forever blocked from undertaking serious new initiatives. Critics of deficit reduction as a priority argued that balancing the books was not nearly as important as government investment programs to create jobs, improve the country's physical plant, train workers and lift living standards. Clinton's first swipe at the deficit had already put it on a downward path as a percentage of the nation's economic output, the deficit doves argued. In international terms, the deficit was low. There was no reason to do more.

Clinton himself was torn by this debate throughout his presidency. "What you have to understand is that no one enjoys deficit reduction," he once said. "While we may have to do it, it's not a good thing." But the urgency of resolving the intra-Progressive dispute over fiscal policy was underscored by the Republicans' takeover of Congress and their subsequent moves to shrink the debt. It was no longer possible to cut deals with more moderate Republicans involving trade-offs between some program cuts and some new revenues. The new conservatives took taxes off the table entirely and proposed cuts that no Progressive, and few Democrats of any stripe, could accept. Moreover, by making a balanced budget their goal, the Republicans robbed Democrats of their easiest battle cry, against "borrow-and-spend" Republicans as "fake" conservatives. Now, Democrats would have to come to terms with the deficit issue itself. Were they in fact for balance, or were they willing to defend modest deficits over many years? Were they willing to save programs by proposing new revenues, a.k.a. taxes, or at least by closing tax loopholes? Were they willing to make steeper cuts in the military?

Clinton himself, under Republican pressure, finally moved in mid-1995 toward his own path to balancing the budget. He urged a balanced budget in ten years, rather than in the seven proposed by the Republicans. This eased the need for sharp spending cuts and allowed Clinton to offer spending increases in areas such as education. But the initial reaction of many congressional liberals to Clinton's new budget was white anger. They felt the president's reductions in Medicare, although more modest than those offered by the Republicans, undercut the congressional party's attack on the Republicans' plans for the elderly. In fact, the division between the White House and congressional liberals transcended such immediate tactical concerns: Many Democrats in Congress feared a Clinton deal with the Republicans that would abandon the party's values, especially after Clinton criticized his own tax increase and, implicitly, his own party. The president's defenders retorted that only by offering his own alternative approach to balance would he be able to challenge the Republicans on the broader question of what government should do.

The entire episode was yet another reminder of how foul the deficit had made the atmosphere within the Democratic Party and among Progressives generally. It was clear that chronic deficits were not viable either as policy or politics. Indeed, to the extent that the deficit was the central matter under debate, it reduced politics to a battle among accountants. Larger purposes would be lost in the arithmetic of fiscal feuds. Democrats needed finally to confront a choice they had largely evaded: whether to accept and defend deficits as reasonable for financing certain aspects of government, or to create instead their own path to budget balance, including a defense of new taxes.

The deficit has combined with the rising costs of pensions and health care to create a further problem: The federal government now has less and less room in its budget for innovation and useful investment. The government is reduced to a caretaker role. Its dynamic role in promoting growth and change is lost. No wonder conservatives accuse Progressives of being interested only in "redistribution." Government now has little chance to do much else.

This is a huge change from America's historical pattern, and it helps explain frustration with government. In the past, the federal government literally helped to build America—with roads, bridges, canals and other "internal improvements" of the pre–Civil War era; with federal help to the land grant colleges established by Lincoln; with large public works such as Roosevelt's TVA; and, after World War II, with the interstate highway system, federal help for school and hospital construction and investment in space and high technology.

Government needs to rediscover its dynamic role as an investor in growth. One approach to encouraging this comes from Robert Shapiro and other economists who argue that the federal government should divide its budget between "consumption" and "investment" spending. Except during sharp economic downturns, it makes good sense to balance the consumption budget. Debt is most useful as a way of financing necessary investments that pay off in the long term—which is why cities and states float bond issues for roads, schools, highways and environmental projects, and why businesses sell bonds to build plants and buy equipment. The current deficit argument is a dead end because it treats all government spending as the same, much as if an individual treated the purchase of expensive restaurant meals and investments in a home or a business as being equivalent uses of money. Progressives will not prosper unless they come to terms with the deficit issue in a way that preserves both government's solvency and its capacity to invest.

With government under such sharp assault, those who believe

in its potential efficacy can no longer evade the imperative of defending its role if they ever hope to convince voters to give Washington enough revenue to achieve larger purposes. Here again, following David Brooks's admonitions, the need is not simply for a new marketing strategy or a new approach to coalition-building. What is required is a fundamental, philosophical defense of the promise of democratic government.

IV

Those who believe in government's possibilities cannot pretend that they share the new conservatism's view of the state. At the heart of the new conservatism is the belief that government action is not only essentially inefficient but also inherently oppressive. Democratic government, in this telling, has interests all its own that have nothing to do with what the voters want. What's especially important about this idea is that it ultimately sees no *fundamental* distinction between free government and dictatorship. The differences are only a matter of degree, not of kind: The more limited democratic government is, the better; the more active democratic government is, the more it begins to approach the evils of Nazism or communism. "Behind our New Deals and New Frontiers and Great Societies," writes House majority leader Dick Armey, "you will find, *with a difference only in power and nerve,* the same sort of person who gave the world its Five Year Plans and Great Leaps Forward—the Soviet and Chinese counterparts." [Emphasis added.]

This is an extraordinary and radical claim, effectively equating Roosevelt, Kennedy and Johnson with Stalin and Mao. If the problem is stated like this, then there is only one choice: Preserving freedom means having government do as little as possible. A government that might levy taxes to provide health care coverage for all or pensions for the old is seen as marching the people down "the road to serfdom," in the evocative phrase of the libertarian economist Friedrich A. Hayek. Better, in this view, to have no health care and no pensions than to have the government embark on this terrible path. Environmental regulations are seen not as preserving streams and forests for future generations; they are viewed as ways of interfering with the free use of private property. Work safety regulations are no longer ways of providing employees with some protections against hazardous machines or conditions; they are seen as "interference in the right of contract."

This sort of thinking is now so common that it has been forgotten how radically different it is from the tradition on which the United States was founded—a tradition to which contemporary liberals, moderates, conservatives and libertarians all trace their roots. As the political philosopher Stephen Holmes has argued, the entire project of freedom going back to America's founders rests not on *weak* government, but rather on an *energetic* government, government strong enough to protect individual rights. Free government is different in *kind* from despotic regimes because its fundamental purpose—to vindicate the rights of individuals—is different.

Imagine on the one side a dictatorship that has no government-provided social security, health, welfare or pension systems of any type. It levies relatively low taxes which go almost entirely toward supporting large military and secret police forces that regularly jail or kill people because of their political views, religious beliefs—or for any other reason the regime decides. Then imagine a democracy with regular open elections and full freedoms of speech and religion. Imagine further that its government levies higher taxes than the dictatorship to support an extensive welfare state, generous old-age pensions and a government health system. The first country might technically have a "smaller government," but there is no doubt that it is *not* a free society. The second country would have a "bigger government," measured as a percentage of gross domestic product, yet there is no doubt that it *is* a free society. This point might seem obvious, but it is in fact obscured by the presumptions that underlie the conservative anti-government talk now so popular. The size of government is an important issue, but it is not as important as—and should not be confused with—the *kind* of government a society has.

Because the anti-government ideology of the new conservatism views almost all forms of government intervention (beyond basic police protection) with suspicion, it misses entirely the fact that democratic governments can intervene in ways that *expand* individual liberty. At the extreme it took a very strong national government (and very forceful intervention) to end slavery and literally free four million Americans from bondage. It's worth remembering that supporters of slavery saw abolitionists as "enemies of liberty" interfering with the "property rights" of slaveholders and imposing the federal government's wishes over "the rights of states." Similarly, it took a strong federal government to end segregation in the 1960s and vindicate the right of African-Americans to vote. Such actions were well within the liberal tradition of free government which, notes Stephen Holmes, accepted that there were occasions when "only a powerful centralized state could protect individual rights against local strongmen and religious majorities."

In the current cacophony of anti-government sloganeering, it is forgotten that the ever-popular slogan "equality of opportunity" was made real only by extensive government efforts to offer individuals opportunities to develop their *own* capacities. As Holmes points out, Adam Smith, the intellectual father of the free market, favored a publicly financed, compulsory system of elementary education. After World War II the government's investment in the college education of millions through the GI Bill simultaneously opened new opportunities for individuals and promoted an explosive period of general economic growth. As Holmes puts it: "Far from being a road to serfdom, government intervention was meant to enhance individual autonomy. Publicly financed schooling, as Mill wrote, is 'help toward doing without help.' " John Stuart Mill offers here a powerful counter to those who would insist that government intervention always and everywhere increases "dependency."

Government also fosters liberty by doing something so obvious that it is little noticed: It insists that certain things cannot be bought and sold. We do not, for example, believe that justice in the courts should be bought and sold. We presume that votes and public offices cannot be bought (even if expensive political campaigns raise questions about the depth of our commitment to this proposition). We now accept, though we once did not, that it is wrong for a wealthy person to buy his way out of the draft during a time of war. And, of course, we do not believe that human beings can be bought and sold.

But these do not exhaust the instances in which a free people might decide to limit the writ of money and the supremacy of the market. As the political philosopher Michael Walzer has argued, one of the central issues confronting democratic societies concerns which rights and privileges should not be put up for sale. As an abstract proposition, we reject the notion that a wealthy person should be able to buy extra years of life that a poor person cannot, since life itself ought not be bought and sold. Yet the availability of health care affects longevity, and by making health care a purely market transaction, we come close to selling life and death. This was the primary argument for Medicare and remains the central moral claim made by advocates of national health insurance. Similarly, we do not believe that children should be deprived of access to food, medicine or education just because their parents are poor. As Holmes puts it, "Why should children be hopelessly snared in a web of underprivilege into which they were born through no fault of their own?"

The current vogue for the superiority of markets over government carries the risk of obscuring the basic issue of what should be for sale in the first place. In a society characterized by growing economic inequality, the dangers of making the marketplace the sole arbiter of the basic elements of a decent life are especially large. Doing so could put many of the basics out of the reach of many people who "work hard and play by the rules." The interrelationship between the moral and economic crises can be seen most powerfully in families where the need to earn enough income forces both parents to spend increasing amounts of time outside the home. One of the great achievements of this century was "the family wage," which allowed the vast majority of workers to provide their families with both a decent living and the parental time to give their children a decent upbringing. The family wage was not simply a product of the marketplace. It was secured through a combination of economic growth, social legislation and unionization. If the marketplace becomes not simply the main arbiter of income, as it will inevitably be, but the *only* judge of living standards, then all social factors, including the need to strengthen families and improve the care given children, become entirely irrelevant in the world of work.

Two questions are frequently confused in the current debate: whether marketplace *mechanisms* might be usefully invoked to solve certain problems, and whether the solution of the problems themselves should be left *entirely* to the market. This confusion afflicts Progressives and conservatives alike.

On the one hand, applying marketplace logic to government programs can be highly useful. One of the most telling criticisms of government is that it does not live by the disciplines of the market, and can thus—in theory at least—deliver services as shoddily as it chooses, with as large a bureaucracy as it wishes. This argument can become a parody of itself, denying that there are, in fact, good public schools, fine police forces, excellent public parks, great public libraries and the like. But the argument does point fairly to certain limits on the government's capacities. David Osborne, author of *Reinventing Government,* argues that government's logical response to this problem is to mimic the marketplace wherever it can in order to foster competition for its goods and services, while also creating a more productive set of incentives for public employees. This idea lay behind the Clinton administration's "reinventing government" project. There *are* instances when it is more efficient for government to give each citizen a voucher to purchase services in a competitive marketplace than to provide the services directly. The GI Bill, for example, did not prescribe where veterans would go to college. It let them choose and gave them the means to pay for the education of their choice. Clinton's housing secretary, Henry Cisneros, proposed scrapping federal subsidies for local public housing *agencies* and turning federal aid into housing vouchers that would go directly to poor people. If a given public housing project was so crime-infested and run-down that poor people would choose not to live in it, it could be closed and sold off. An abstract fear of marketplace logic should not impede experiments of this sort.

But supporting market-oriented solutions to problems is *not* the same as suggesting that the market itself, left to its own devices, will solve all problems. If the government had not given the education vouchers to the GIs, many of them would never have gone to college. The market can break down, recessions can throw people out of work, families can lose their health insurance, poor people can lack the money to buy food and shelter for their children. The answer to the most rabid free-market advocates is that the free market is a wonderful instrument that also creates problems and leaves others unsolved. To assert as a flat rule, as Representative Armey does, that "the market is rational and the government is dumb" is to assume that it is rational to accept problems created by unemployment, low wages, business cycles, pollution and simple human failings; and dumb to use government to try to lessen the human costs associated with them. Mr. Armey might believe that; most Americans do not.

The difference between this era's conservatives and the American Progressive tradition lies in the distinction between two phrases, "freedom from" and "freedom to." Free market conservatives are very much alive to the importance of what the philosopher Isaiah Berlin called "negative liberty," defined as freedom *from* coercion by the state. American Progressives and liberals share this concern for negative liberty, which is why they accept with the conservatives the need for limited government. Historically, however, Progressives have been more alive to the promise of "positive liberty" and to free government's capacity for promoting it. To be the master of one's own fate—a fair definition of liberty—means not simply being free from overt coercion (though that is a precondition); it also involves being given the means to overcome various external forces that impinge on freedom of choice and self-sufficiency. It means being free *to* set one's course.

From the beginning, therefore, the Progressive project has involved the use of government to give men and women the tools needed for achieving positive liberty, beginning with free elementary and secondary education and moving in the Depression and postwar era to Social Security, unemployment compensation and access to college and to health insurance. (The Progressives, beginning with women's suffrage, were also at the forefront in expanding the realm of freedom for women.) Herbert Croly, the intellectual founder of American Progressivism, argued that "wholesome democracy" should seek to guarantee "a certain minimum of economic power and responsibility." Croly maintained that government action to assist the "workingman to raise his standard of living" would "increase the amount of economic power enjoyed by the average laborer" and "make the individual workingman more of an individual." Significantly, Croly did not see such a program as involving class warfare. On the contrary, he hoped that recognizing the dignity of the worker would "diminish his 'class consciousness' by doing away with his class grievances."

In expressing these views, Croly reflected a revolution within free-market liberal theory taking place on both sides of the Atlantic. Toward the end of the century in Britain, a school of "New Liberals" led by T. H. Green and Leonard Hobhouse sought to convince friends of the free market that the intervention of democratic government into economic affairs "not only involves no conflict with the true principle of personal liberty," as Hobhouse put it, "but is necessary to its effective realization." Green argued that "the ideal of true freedom is the maximum power of all members of human society to make the best of themselves."

In our era, conservatives have monopolized the concept of liberty and given it a particular and largely negative definition. Progressives have been cast—and have sometimes foolishly cast themselves—as defenders of coercion and bureaucracy, of government for government's sake. The imperative for Progressives is to rediscover their own tradition as the party of liberty. In a free society *all* parties to the debate should be arguing about the best ways to enhance and advance human freedom. For Progressives, that is and always has been the central purpose of government.

V

But at the end of the century, Progressives find themselves in trouble not merely because they have been misunderstood—or because they have misunderstood themselves. The new conservatism was also born out of the real failures of contemporary liberalism, some of them rooted in problems within the Progressive tradition itself. A new Progressivism will arise only if liberals address them.

Some of these difficulties have been underscored with great clarity—if also with some exaggeration—by the conservative critics of the Progressive tradition. As Joyce and Schambra argued, some Progressives showed contempt for local institutions and the "backward, unsophisticated citizens hopelessly encumbered by retrograde values" that they allegedly represented. This, contended Joyce and Schambra, led to the Progressives' faith in centralization and to their call for a greater role in government by "experts." Along similar lines, Chester Finn asserted that Herbert Croly's brand of Progressivism had bred a "cult of governmentalism" that created a vast federal apparatus. This, he said, "made us lazy and dependent while taking vast sums out of our pockets" and overturned the tradition of "subsidiarity" which held that "problems should be solved as close to home as possible."

Less partisan critics of Progressivism also detected centralizing, anti-democratic tendencies that encouraged the sapping of power from local and traditional institutions. In his brilliant book *Self-Rule,* historian Robert Wiebe noted that while the Progressives were committed to expanding popular participation through initiative, referendum and recall, the effect of the Progressive period was to diminish mass involvement in politics. "If most progressives did not set out to keep the poor from the polls," Wiebe wrote, "they had little invested in bringing them there." Wiebe went on to note that "what mattered most to the progressives was not getting out the vote, but getting things done, priorities that produced a good deal of impatience with unresponsive citizens, hostility toward locally oriented political parties, and praise for streamlined administrative solutions to broad public issues." Wiebe concluded that "reforms that originated in a desire to make governments more responsive to people's needs ended up making them less responsive to people's voices."

Some sympathetic observers of Progressivism located the source of this problem in the theory of Progressivism itself. For example, the historian Michael McGerr said that in light of Herbert Croly's "preoccupation with strong government, strong leaders and strong nationalism, it is hard not to question his commitment to democracy." For McGerr, Croly "made explicit what was implicit in middle class culture at the turn of the century: a subtle but significant loss of faith in traditional democratic norms." Many in the middle class, wrote McGerr, "doubting individualism and fearing the working class, were clearly redefining—and limiting—the meaning of democracy."

The historian Christopher Lasch described a related problem in the attitude of some of the Progressive reformers toward family life. The turn-of-the-century reformers, he said, saw themselves as "the guardians of public health and morality" who "insisted that the family could not provide for its own needs without expert intervention." He went on: "Some of them, indeed, had so little confidence in the family that they proposed to transfer its socializing function to other agencies; others wanted merely to improve the quality of family life through ambitious programs of 'parent education,' marriage counseling and psychiatric social work."

The Progressive movement, it must also be noted, arose in the wake of the Supreme Court's 1896 decision ratifying "separate but equal" treatment of African-Americans, a decision that sealed the end of Reconstruction and marked the triumph of Jim Crow. With a few exceptions, the Progressives did not stand up for African-American rights. Indeed, the presidency of one great Progressive, Woodrow Wilson, was marred by the deepening of segregation. Wilson had been elected with the support of important black leaders such as W. E. B. Du Bois. In office, as the historian Arthur Link noted, while Wilson may have "stood firm against the cruder demands of the white supremacists, . . . he and probably all of his Cabinet believed in segregation, social and official." As Wiebe observed of even some of the most culturally open Progressives, "there were no people of color in their cultural orchestra."

The Progressives' project was sufficiently complex and the Progressive constituency sufficiently diverse that most of these criticisms—though not the ones relating to race—need to be qualified. What Wiebe says about the net effect of Progressive politics on participation is true, and certain strains of Progressive thought were, as McGerr argues, decidedly skeptical of democracy. But Progressivism also embodied a radically democratic strain that appeared in the thought of John Dewey, who saw democracy not simply as a form of government but a "way of life." Lasch is right in detecting among middle-class Progressives an intense desire to "improve," through state action if necessary, the family lives of the lower classes. Yet as the historian Morton Keller observed in his fine history of Progressive social policy, the Progressives operated with considerable restraint in family matters, resisting legislation at the national level and operating cautiously even at the state level. "Public interest in family issues clearly grew in intensity, due no doubt to the rise of an urban-industrial, culturally polyglot society," Keller writes. "But the belief persisted that the active state was as likely to weaken as to foster the autonomy of the individual, the sanctity of the family, the supremacy of the husband and father. The result: heightened public concern, conflicted and relatively static public policy."

Nonetheless, Progressivism's critics have identified critical flaws in Progressive thought that have haunted the liberal project through to the Great Society and the present day. The Progressives were right in seeing government action as necessary to securing certain ends. But Progressives often confused reasonable defenses of government's necessary role with arguments that seemed to see expanding government as worthy for its own sake. This confused the means with the ends. As we have seen, one of the central purposes of active government is to enhance the individual's capacities for autonomy. Such a project cannot be based on a skepticism of the capacities of average Americans that McGerr identifies correctly as an important strain within upper-middle-class Progressivism at the turn of the century. Rather, it grows from a conviction that "average" and "ordinary" people are capable of doing extraordinary things, given the opportunity to do so. To the extent that liberals aped the conviction of those of their Progressive forebears who doubted this, they invited—one might say demanded—attacks on them as "elitist." This hurt Progressives both substantively and politically, allowing the political right to win a near monopoly on the rhetoric and symbols of American populism, as the historian Michael Kazin has shown.

This problem was deepened by the tendency of some partisans of Progressive liberalism to turn it into an ideology that preferred government action over *all* other approaches to solving social problems. To the extent that Progressives cast the choice in this way, they lent support to some of the most telling criticisms offered by their conservative adversaries. If given a choice between "government" or "private" solutions to social problems, many Americans instinctively opt for the "private." But in areas of social concern, they do not use the word "private" to refer to the free market or business; they mean instead the voluntary institutions that communities establish for themselves. They mean, in a term that has rightly become popular, "civil society." As the philosopher Benjamin Barber put it, "Civil society, or civic space, occupies the middle ground between government and the private sector." He went on: "It is not where we vote and it is not where we buy and sell; it is where we talk with neighbors about a crossing guard, plan a benefit for our community school, discuss how our church and synagogue can shelter the homeless, or organize a summer softball league for our children. . . . Civil society is thus public without being coercive, voluntary without being privatized."

By casting "government" and "the market" as the main mechanisms of social organization, the conventional political debate thus leaves out the most important institutions in people's lives—family, church, neighborhood, workplace organizations and a variety of other voluntary institutions ranging from sports clubs and youth groups to privately organized child-care centers and the loose fellowships created at taverns like Cheers of television fame. All are places where, as the theme song of *Cheers* tells us, everybody knows your name. The great flaw in the binary choice between government and the market was described brilliantly by the sociologist Alan Wolfe in his book *Whose Keeper?*: "The opposition between individual freedom and state authority that guides so much of contemporary political theory . . . is a false opposition. [C]ivil society, not the individual, is the better alternative to government in modern society." Wolfe noted that while "believers in laissez-faire complain that the state has grown at the expense of individuals, and advocates of a stronger state sometimes bemoan individualism, the truth is that the decline of obligations once associated with civil society strengthens both individualism *and* governmental authority."

Conservatives, both new and old, have done a good job of reminding us of the Progressives' sometimes excessive eagerness for replacing the mechanisms of private charity and communal responsibility—family, church and mutual assistance societies—with the often clumsier mechanisms of government. What conservatives, especially the new conservatives, refuse to recognize is the extent to which these organizations are effective precisely because they do *not* operate according to the logic of free markets, but according to an older moral logic that predated capitalism. As Wolfe points out, economic exchanges between friends are not the same as economic exchanges within the larger market—"friends can rely on their knowledge of one another and the trust they have developed to smooth over economic transactions." On the other hand, "if we organize all our social relations by the same logic we use in seeking a good bargain, we cannot even have friends, for everyone else interferes with our ability to calculate conditions that maximize self-interest." Wolfe argues that capitalism has been successful so far because "it lived its first hundred years off the precapitalist morality it inherited from traditional religion and social structure."

Following Wolfe, one can begin to see how the moral crisis Americans are experiencing grows not simply from the "countercultural" or "permissive" ideas that developed in the 1960s. Its roots lie deeper, in a society built on individualistic and market values that steadily cut away the bonds of solidarity, morality and trust. If profit is all that matters, filmmakers or music producers will not think twice about filling the marketplace with products that foster amoral or dysfunctional values among the young. If all personal ties between employer and employee are deemed to be "irrational" or "sentimental" when compared to the competitive needs of the marketplace, employers need not think at all about how work schedules might affect the ability of employees to rear their children or how cutbacks in medical coverage might affect their employees' lives. And if government gives no protection for those many employers who *do* care about such things, it risks forcing them out of business as they are undercut by competitors for whom cost and price are the only factors in business decisions. As David Broder has pointed out, one of the terrible ironies of the health care battle is that the *minority* of employers who do not offer health insurance took control of the political debate from the vast *majority* of businesses that do. A debate that might have been over how businesses and individuals might fairly share the obligation of providing help for the sick became instead a fight over government "compulsion," as if government itself had created the need for health insurance.

The central irony of our time that so many of the new conservatives wish to avoid is this: *A capitalist society depends on non-capitalist values in order to hold together and prosper.* Adam Smith certainly recognized this. It is what Daniel Bell has referred to as "the cultural contradictions of capitalism." More recently, Francis Fukuyama has written of "the social virtues" behind "the creation of prosperity."

If the problem is cast this way, the purpose of Progressivism is not to use government to undermine the free market, but precisely the opposite: to create the social conditions in which the market can work well in its proper sphere. Progressives, as the experience of Franklin Roosevelt showed, have historically been assigned the task of saving capitalism precisely because they were willing to be its critics. The Progressive's goal is not to strengthen government for government's sake, but to use government where possible to strengthen the institutions of civil society. Those institutions need protection against the state, but they also need protection from market forces. How, for example, can families be liberated from some of the pressures of the marketplace—through more "family-friendly" tax laws, through better rules on parental leave, through incentives to create more flexible workplaces so parents feel less conflicted between the obligations of work and home? How can government policies strengthen rather than weaken the voluntary sector? Can the poor who live in public housing projects be given more control of their surroundings and a larger stake in their communities? Can rules be written so that employers who feel a sense of loyalty and obligation to their employees will not be punished by the marketplace? Given that the American charitable sector prospered for years on the unpaid labor of women volunteers, how can it be revitalized now that so many women both want and need to work for wages and salaries?

As the communitarian thinker Philip Selznick puts it, the welfare state, like the market, can become "a bloodless repository of moral virtue." But "[t]he alternative is not a rejection of government." Instead, he maintains, "it is for the architects of the welfare state to transform their vision of how governments fulfill their responsibilities. . . . If the government will pay more attention to communal values and civil society, it will more clearly perceive and more adequately protect the needs of individual persons." And if supporters of adequate welfare provision seek less bureaucratic approaches, they could make the welfare state "more limited, more accountable and more humane."

Progressives—liberals—thus need to embrace a politics of liberty and community. They cannot leave the definition of liberty to their conservative adversaries. They need to contest the negative definition of liberty as incomplete. Yes, individuals need to be protected against omnipotent, abusive government. But they also have a right to look to government for help in defending their autonomy and expanding the possibilities of self-reliance. Government should not weaken the bonds of civil society. But government *can* step in to strengthen civil society and protect it against the disruptions created by the normal workings of the economic market. Surely anyone who claims to believe in "family values" should want to relieve families of some of the pressures placed upon them by work and economic distress. As Theodore Roosevelt put it: "No man"—he could have added women—"can be a good citizen unless he has a wage more than sufficient to cover the bare costs of living, and hours of labor short enough so that after his day's work is done, he will have time and energy to bear his share in the management of the community, to help in carrying the general load." Long before "civil society" was a fashionable phrase, TR understood its meaning.

A New Progressivism based on these principles would take seriously Bill Kristol's talk about "the politics of liberty and the sociology of virtue." But it would contest the effectiveness of the new conservative program supported by Kristol and his allies, arguing that liberty and virtue require not only freedom from government coercion, but also the active support of a government that understands not only its limits but also its obligations. It is not enough to preach virtue to a family that finds its living standard falling despite its own best efforts to work, save, invest and care for its children. Such a family surely deserves some support for its own efforts to expand its opportunities—and, at the least, some insurance against the worst economic catastrophies that might befall it.

Alternatives to the new conservatism will thus arise simply because the voters will demand them. One can see in the responses to Pat Buchanan's nationalism and to Ross Perot's anti-Washington pronouncements the rumblings of an Anxious Middle prepared to be radicalized by economic frustrations, moral unease and impatience with government's failures. The emergence of such movements betrays the failure in our day of the heirs to America's Progressive tradition, but also defines their challenge. In the past, the practical application of Progressive ideas subsumed the ideas of more radical movements in broad and moderate reform campaigns. Theodore Roosevelt and Woodrow Wilson inherited important pieces of the Populist and Socialist programs and constituencies. TR and Wilson alike understood that industrialism neither could nor should be rolled back, but that government could prevent monopoly, protect the environment, safeguard the consumer and enhance the rights of labor. Franklin Roosevelt quelled opposition to his left and also on the angry far right with the boldness of his "Second New Deal" program—it included, among many other things, Social Security—and his warnings against the power of "economic royalists." Harry Truman faced down opposition to his left and right by holding firm to his anti-communist foreign policy while also embracing an aggressive program on behalf of labor, civil rights and the New Deal legacy, and also by assailing the Republicans for "trying to fool the people into voting for the interests of the few."

Truman thus became, as one of his midwestern supporters put it, "the common man's common man."

Many of the social, political and economic forces operating at the end of the 1990s are different from those of 1912, 1936 or 1948. No effort to produce exact replicas of the achievements of the two Roosevelts, Wilson or Truman can hope to succeed. But the basic inspiration behind the Progressive project remains relevant—a belief in the use of government to expand individual choice and protect communities, an effort to improve living standards across the society, and an understanding that a democratic society works best with a broad and thriving middle class. Progressives do not seek absolute equality or anything like it; but they also know that rising inequality can be dangerous for democracy.

VI

The tragedy of President Clinton's term, especially his first two years, is that he raised many of the right issues without producing either the results he hoped for or a set of political alliances that could carry on a long-term project of social reconstruction. He did not encourage New and Old Democrats to work together; if anything, rifts in the party seemed to widen. He did not draw in moderate Republicans, many of whom still have impulses shaped by their own party's progressive tradition. He did not convince the left that he shared its goals of social justice and social equality. And he did not succeed in nurturing a progressive wing within the business community that accepted the need for government action to solve problems that the free market neither would nor could solve on its own. Clinton's most obvious failure was personal: that none of the wings of this potential Progressive alliance fully trusted him. It was a personal failure that had repercussions across almost every area of policy.

Yet precisely because Clinton was on the right track in the questions he asked and in some of the solutions he offered, many of the issues of the Clinton term will need revisiting—perhaps by Clinton himself if he draws the right lessons from his own difficulties. Clinton's response to the 1994 elections was a mixture of the shrewd and the cautious. He sought to recapture the center ground, especially on issues of cultural unease and moral breakdown. He correctly sensed that the country would ultimately see the Republican Congress as far too radical, too pessimistic about the potential of government and too little engaged with the electorate's fundamental concerns about falling living standards. Polling in the fall of 1995 suggested that disillusionment with the Republican Congress had already set in as voters began to wonder whether the Republicans were not simply serving a new set of special interests. Support for third-party challenges began to rise again, and Ross Perot reappeared on the scene. Senator Bill Bradley's suggestions that he might run an independent campaign for the presidency were seen as a challenge to Clinton, which they were. But their resonance—along with the interest in Colin Powell—was at least as symptomatic of the failure of the highly ideological Republican Congress to reverse voter cynicism and disillusionment.

But repositioning or trimming will not be enough for Clinton if he sees his task as recapturing the promise of his 1992 campaign. Fulfilling the earlier hopes he aroused would entail providing a coherent Progressive alternative to the new conservatism and convincing voters that this time around, the alternative could reach fruition. Above all, he—or anyone else who takes up this task—will need to demonstrate a commitment to the large purposes and to take on the Republican attack against the Progressive tradition. This will require action in four spheres: enhancing individual economic security and opportunity; strengthening families and communities; finding more productive approaches to trade and economic cooperation among the democracies; and revitalizing democracy at home.

Providing economic security will mean, first, a renewal of the battle for universal health coverage of some sort, almost certainly involving a mix of government assistance and the use of the existing private insurance system. The pressure for health care reform will rise again, not only because of the cost of health care to government (a lesson the Republicans finally learned), but also because inevitable cost-cutting by businesses will steadily reduce the coverage enjoyed by many workers. The rise of health maintenance organizations and their efforts to cut costs have already pushed new issues onto the public agenda. When it was learned that some HMOs forced doctors to discharge the mothers of newborns from hospitals as quickly as possible, states began passing legislation requiring all insurers to give new mothers at least two day stays. Questions of this sort will come up again and again across the health system and spur public demands for other forms of government intervention—perhaps through a "bill of rights" for the users of HMOs—to protect health care consumers.

Similarly, the need to rethink, consolidate and expand the federal government's education and job-training programs, as suggested by Labor Secretary Robert Reich, will become increasingly pressing. It's important to recall that President Clinton's most popular and evocative pledges, during his 1992 campaign and after, involved his call for universally available retraining of displaced workers and his insistence on forging stronger links between high schools, community colleges and the world of work opportunities. Training is not a cure-all. There must be jobs for trained workers to take. But the absence of aggressive government efforts to assist workers in making the transition to a high-technology economy will worsen inequalities and lessen opportunities. One promising approach would link the unemployment insurance system directly to a new training insurance system. Workers could move into training as soon as they lost work and speed their return to the workforce.

In this era an essential element of economic security for most families is confidence that their children will be able to afford college. Over the years the country has moved back and forth on the proposition that a lack of money should not block any qualified student from higher education. Student loan programs have, by turns, expanded and contracted, with the new Republican Congress trying to cut them back again. The better alternative is a comprehensive and predictable program through which students could attend college and repay their loans without burdening themselves with huge costs immediately upon leaving school. The Clinton administration took some important steps in this direction by allowing students to repay their loans as a percentage of their post-college incomes. Students who do well financially repay faster, which is fair to the taxpayers who lent them the money. But students with lower after-college incomes are allowed to pay back more slowly. This is fair, too, and has the additional advantage of providing graduates with incentives to enter fields (teaching and police work, for example) where the tasks they perform are vital, but where the pay is not high. Clinton had proposed a related approach, to allow students to repay a portion of their loans through work in community

service. He won approval for only a relatively modest service program, and it, too, was attacked by the Republicans. But the principle
was sound—and popular.

There will also be a need for a candid debate about public
elementary and high school education. The inequalities of educational opportunity are stark, along class as well as racial lines. It is
true, as conservatives have said, that money alone does not determine the quality of a child's education. But money helps, which is
why some of the finest suburban school districts in the country also
have some of the highest per-pupil costs. In many big cities, public
schools have become almost entirely black or Hispanic; white children—as well as many in the black and Hispanic middle class—
have fled them. A real debate over public education should, if it is
honest, be uncomfortable for liberals and conservatives alike. Conservatives need to face up to the inequalities. Liberals need to confront the failures in public institutions. Teachers unions in particular
should be prepared to join this debate as allies, not obstacles to
change.

It's true that teachers are blamed for all manner of difficulties
within the schools over which they have little control. Family breakdown has forced teachers to assume more and more responsibilities that ought rightly be handled in the home. It's also true that
bashing public employee unions is often an easy way for politicians
to evade their own responsibilities. Nonetheless, teachers and their
unions should be ready to embrace—as some of them already
have—experiments such as "charter schools," new, competitive institutions within the public school system. Within the poorest neighborhoods with the poorest public schools, there ought also to be a
willingness on the part of both teachers unions and liberals to
experiment with private school vouchers. The unions and the liberals are right in asserting that vouchers are not a cure-all for what
ails public education, and voucher experiments should be confined
to the lowest-income students; vouchers should not become a co-
vert way of destroying the entire system of public education. But
surely Progressives, with their long history of favoring public innovation, ought at least to be open to some experiments along these
lines. Public education is also an issue that can be addressed with
some hope. Recent studies suggest that in response to the reforms
spurred by the agitation around the schools in the 1980s, students

are getting better educations, taking harder courses and earning better test results. Progressives need to assert what has too long been denied: public institutions *can* be improved.

Progressives must also address themselves candidly and unapologetically to rising inequality in wealth and income. Inequalities are rising for many reasons, not the least being the decline of the labor movement. Organized labor's troubles have weakened the bargaining power of wage earners within the whole economy. A revitalized union movement could help rectify this balance. It is remarkable that productivity increases no longer seem to translate into higher wages. This goes against the implicit pact that has up to now allowed Western capitalist economies to prove Marx quite wrong about the relationship between capital and labor—labor up to now has shared in the general improvement in economic conditions. If the link between economic growth and improved living standards is broken, the basic American bargain will be in danger.

In the short term, government must be conscious of the problem of falling wages. Its goal would not be massive income redistribution. On the contrary, its purpose should be to *prevent* a massive redistribution of income and wealth *away* from the middle class and the poor. At the moment, the conservative vogue is for "flat" taxes or national sales taxes. But these approaches would cut taxes on the wealthiest Americans and raise them on the middle class and the poor. They would only worsen economic trends that are already crimping the standard of living of many in the middle. If upper-income people continue to make substantial economic gains while the standard of living of many in the middle class continues to stagnate, it makes sense to try to reduce taxes on those whose incomes are not growing and to have those making significant gains pick up a bigger share of the load. Even more importantly, the tax code needs to be wrung of the tens of billions in subsidies that even conservatives have taken to calling corporate welfare. These distort the free market, reduce government's tax revenues and force a bigger burden onto middle income individuals.

Finally, government should be in the advance guard in pointing to future problems that, if not dealt with early, will become nightmarish over time. One such problem is pensions. Under the system of work established after World War II, a large percentage of the nation's workers could count on spending all or much of their lifetimes with a single firm, which provided not only decent pay and benefits, but also decent pensions for retirees. Growing job mobility will endanger that system, and even prosperous pension funds could face problems when the baby boomers retire. The Social Security system works well because so many workers are in a position to supplement its benefits with their own. A social catastrophe looms if private pension coverage is allowed to atrophy.

But economic problems are not the only issues that trouble the country. America's sense of moral crisis, as we have seen, is not a set of worries invented by conservative politicians and the religious right. It is a real crisis based on real concerns—crime, family breakup and a general decline in public civility. Progressives are right in asserting that the moral crisis has an economic dimension that conservatives are wont to deny. But Progressives will not make their arguments effectively if they try to reduce all moral questions to economics. Both the moral and the economic dimensions need to be taken seriously.

Nonetheless, the government's efforts to strengthen families will be most effective in the spheres of economics and work. These include changes in tax laws to help families with children, especially moderate-income families with preschool children. These families could use some relief from the pressures to work outside the home. Here, the Republican Congress was onto something, but it spoiled its program by not extending tax breaks to lower-middle-class workers and by trying to cut tax credits to the working poor. Laws and incentives encouraging changes in work rules to give families with children more flexibility would also be helpful. American society has undergone only half a revolution. Women have entered the workforce in large numbers and are there to stay, both because they want to and because their families need their incomes. But remarkably few adjustments have been made to accommodate this reality in a way that does justice to the task of rearing children. Many families are unhappy with the choices they now have for child care. Some would work less outside the home if they felt they could. Others want better day care than is now available. Many women (and some men, too) would like to take some years off or work part-time for a while when their children are very young. But they worry about the impact of such decisions on their long-term career prospects. Society—and government—should be looking for ways to make such choices, which clearly serve the common good, easier. A society that cares as much about children as ours claims to needs to bring these issues into the open and debate them not as ideological propositions but as practical problems that many families are trying to solve. "Family values" are too important to leave to ideologues, direct-mail specialists or thirty-second spots.

Similarly, there must be honest talk about the costs to society of the rise in fatherless families—and equally honest talk about the difficulties in fashioning government policies to deal with the problem. As David Blankenhorn argues in his important book, *Fatherless America,* there is simply no way a society can feel at ease when some 40 percent of its children will live a major portion of their childhoods without their fathers. The issue here is not the incapacity of single mothers to care for their children, but the responsibility of men to share in a task in which their role is crucial. Government cannot force men to love their children, but it can at least require them to pay child support. It can also use its capacity for public education to strengthen the already growing sense that something is awry in the way many Americans are discharging their family responsibilities. Public education has already changed popular attitudes toward smoking, drinking and drug use. The same sort of public campaigning could reinforce the need for individual responsibility about parenthood.

There is an equal need for candor about what can be done to help families that cannot be put back together. The welfare debate that unfolded in the new Republican Congress was an example of exactly what should *not* happen. Many Republicans pushed for cutting off welfare payments to mothers under the age of eighteen, on the theory that removing the welfare check would vastly change the incentives to have a child out of wedlock. There might be some reduction in births—though the evidence for this conclusion was scant even as the risks to children were large. In any event, as conservatives themselves have argued repeatedly, the problem here is as much cultural as economic. The conservatives were unable to answer the question: What would happen to poor children in the absence of the welfare check? "Conservatives needlessly risk the well-being of children," writes Kathleen Sylvester of the Progressive Policy Institute. "Ignoring the inadequacy of the welfare system, they would break up families with no alternative safety net in place. Ignoring the reality that the welfare system was designed to help families whose fathers are absent, they would reform it by absenting mothers as well, substituting institutions such as orphanages for real parents."

Sylvester proposes not to defend the existing system, but to search for alternatives. She calls for federal help to local communities to build a national network of "second chance homes," which would be "a new version of the homes that once provided community support for unmarried mothers." Young mothers could live with their children under adult supervision, "while meeting their social and personal obligations for receiving welfare support." Such homes, she says, could offer mothers "nurturing and support, structure and discipline, and socialization" while also "removing children from dangerous environments" in which they might be abused or neglected, or simply be "shuffled from foster home to foster home."

Sylvester's proposal embodies precisely the spirit a New Progressive project needs to embrace. It accepts the seriousness of moral concerns and does not pretend that the problems confronting poor children are only economic. It accepts the need for innovation. At the same time, it embraces government's responsibility to assist those who need help and who would be unlikely to find it if government did not act.

A similar logic can be applied to the broader task of welfare reform. Here again, the link between economics and values cannot be avoided. The broader society rightly upholds a work ethic that sees every adult as responsible for providing for his or her own support. The welfare system, by encouraging dependency, violated that principle. But the economic circumstances of inner cities and many rural areas are such that it is a fantasy to presume that simply cutting benefits will move thousands off the welfare rolls and into jobs, since the jobs are often not there. Further, the decline in the minimum wage and the decline of benefits associated with low-paying jobs has reduced incentives to work. A broad social bargain is clearly within reach, even if it has been ignored in the legislative efforts of the new Congress. It would involve work requirements for welfare recipients, in exchange for a decent level of public support and the creation of work where private jobs were lacking. Such a program could be linked to a continuing effort to raise the pay and living standards of the working poor.

Father Philip Murnion, the director of the National Pastoral Life Center, offered a powerful insight from the time he spent as a child on welfare after his father died. In his day, he said, poor children could count on three basic forms of support: some money from government, love and nurturing within the family, and moral guidance from churches and from neighbors who lived in relatively safe and orderly communities. Now, he argued, poor children are under threat in all three spheres: Government help is in danger; many of the poorest children live in difficult (and at times dangerous) family situations; and the moral order and physical safety of many neighborhoods has collapsed. The next phase of social policy requires attention to each of these problems: economic support, a concern for family life, and serious efforts to strengthen community institutions and to restore public order. All are essential to the pursuit of social justice.

The third area in which Progressives need to act involves the impact of technological change and the global economy on living standards. We've already seen, in the NAFTA and GATT battles, how deeply divisive this issue is for Democrats and liberals. Clinton's effort to patch over this difference failed in the short term. In the longer term, two ideas must be brought into harmony: that the global market will not go away and that all countries will have to accommodate to it to one degree or another, but also that these accommodations will invite social havoc if they occur without any attention to the living standards and livelihoods of those threatened in the new economic order.

Trade agreements can thus no longer confine themselves to narrow rules about who will sell what. They will need to embody shared commitments by democratic governments to protect environmental and labor standards. The purpose of open trade, after all, is to "level up" living standards, not to level them down. World prosperity could be seriously threatened if the purchasing power of middle-income workers is steadily reduced. And without some international environmental standards, companies will come under pressure to evade potentially costly environmental measures in the developed countries by producing goods in cheaper "rule-free" zones in the Third World.

The original Progressives dealt with a world in which an economy that had largely operated locally became national in scope. It was thus natural—and, given the existence of a federal government, relatively easy—to create new national rules for economic entities that crisscrossed state lines. Now, the economy is global, yet there are no global democratic structures; democracy operates only within nation-states. Democratic nations face two choices: to withdraw from the global economic system, an impractical idea, or to maintain democratic influence on the economy by reaching agreements among themselves. This is what the European Community has sought to do, especially by way of its "social charter." The world's wealthy nations already engage in a loose coordination of their economic policies. More serious efforts at cooperation could give democratic governments what they now lack: the capacity to keep their promises to their own electorates for economic growth and a degree of social justice. The paradox is that those rightly concerned about the national sovereignty of individual democratic nations will preserve that sovereignty only in cooperation with other democratic nations. Those who would argue for a new American nationalism will find that it must come to pass by way of a new internationalism among the democracies.

Advocates of free trade need to be mindful of the rise of economic nationalism throughout the wealthy countries. This is the utterly unsurprising response of citizens whose living standards are threatened. If the grand bargain for shared prosperity that took hold after World War II is not renewed, calls for protection will gather popular force. After World War II, it needs to be remembered, the United States led the way to a series of international agreements that strengthened democracy, set off a long era of economic growth and created a social bargain that revolutionized the living standards of average citizens—first in the United States itself, then in Western Europe and Japan, and later in other parts of Asia. The logical response of the developed nations to a drastically transformed world economy is to reach for a new bargain on behalf of democracy, the prosperity of their market economies and the well-being of average citizens.

The final sphere for Progressive action involves democracy itself. The discrediting of democratic politics, the popular impatience with political argument, the decline of political civility, the sense that politics has nothing to do with the improvement of people's lives—all are signs of a decay in the U.S. civic culture. The responsibilities of citizens go beyond their requirements as producers and consumers of goods. To hold together, a society needs citizens who will not only defend their own interests, but also take a broad view of what those interests are and perceive the interests they hold in common with the rest of their own society. "The government and the market are not enough to make a civilization," said Senator Bradley in a powerful speech in 1995. "The language of mutual obligation has to be given equal time with the language of rights that dominates our culture."

Democracy is, in the end, more than just periodic elections and the formation of shifting majorities. The United States has always embodied a stronger view that saw democracy, as John Dewey did, as "a way of life." It was a way of life in which citizens constantly learned from one another—in their own arguments and discussions in the taverns and the churches, and not just from someone else's talk on television or radio. Democracy requires citizens who respect one another as equal under the law and as civic equals in a deeper moral sense. Democracy entails the belief that citizens, through common action, can improve their own lot and their society, and create new means of practical cooperation. In a functioning democracy, problems are not simply argued about, but solved.

At the national level, it's easy enough to list some minimal steps that need to be taken to rebuild popular confidence in government. These include serious reforms in the way campaigns are financed, to decrease money's role in the political process, as well as stricter limits on what lobbyists can give to legislators and greater openness about how the lobbying works. Many in the Anxious Middle rightly complain about the influence of special interests on Washington. The battles over health care, environmental regulation, taxation and legal reform all showed that the interests who finance political campaigns can win large and unfair advantages in shaping legislation, and also in blocking it. Ultimately, political reform—particularly in the financing of campaigns—is the precondition of all other serious reform. But private institutions and individual politicians also need to act. We've already seen how the modern media shape the public debate. Television, radio and newspapers must find better ways of drawing citizens into the political argument. This does, indeed, include talk radio, which is creating opportunities for citizens to make their voices heard. But it must also include an effort by mainstream journalism to highlight the importance of the democratic debate and to draw more citizens into it. Above all, those media that have traditionally been serious about reporting and commenting on politics and government cannot use the public's current dismay with politics as an excuse to abandon their responsibilities to give serious coverage to the democratic enterprise.

Finally, as Bradley pointed out, there are opportunities for communities themselves to create what he called "quality civic space." He noted for example, that the "most underutilized resource in most of our communities is the public school, which too often closes at 4 p.m., only to see children in suburbs return to empty homes with a television as their baby sitter, or, in cities, to street corners where gangs make them an offer they can't refuse." Ultimately, democracy will always come "from below," from communities themselves taking responsibility for themselves. If America is to experience a rebirth of its civic culture and democratic values, it will occur because citizens decide to create their own civic space and force onto the political system a seriousness and civility it now lacks.

VII

In an otherwise brilliant dissection of the great economic and political transformations of our era, the social thinker Peter Drucker asserts flatly that "if this century proves one thing, it is the futility of politics." He argues that the most important changes of the twentieth century had nothing to do with "the headline-making political events" and everything to do with social and economic changes that operate "like ocean currents deep below the hurricane tormented surface of the sea." These, he says, have had "the lasting, indeed the permanent, effect."

Drucker goes on to describe with great clarity the agricultural revolution, the declining role of agricultural employment, the rise of industrialism and the emergence of the blue-collar worker, "the first lower class in history that could be organized and could stay organized." He speaks of urbanization and the fact that cities in this age, unlike cities in earlier ages, actually *improved* public health. This was, he writes, primarily because the factory produced higher living standards, but also because of "new public health measures: purification of water, collection and treatment of wastes, quarantine against epidemics, inoculation against disease." The new era, with the rise of the "knowledge worker," Drucker concludes, will demand "social and political innovations"—particularly in education, because the new period will put a premium on "the quality of knowledge and the productivity of knowledge."

What is so striking about Drucker's view is that his detailed and insightful analysis of developments in commerce, science and society flies in the face of his insistence on "the futility of politics." *That is because he takes democratic politics for granted.* The truth is that almost none of the advances Drucker describes could have happened absent the victories of democracy and free government. The freedom accorded by democracy allowed the innovators to experiment, the scientists to discover, societies to create forms of organization appropriate to their needs. Social protections, through government and private organizations, allowed prosperity to be shared under conditions of social peace. Industrialization did *not* have that same bracing effect in other places where it went forward rapidly, notably the Soviet Union, largely because the political conditions were different.

Moreover, Drucker's entirely accurate assertion about the effective organization of blue-collar workers is a statement about politics itself. The twentieth century turned out for the better in significant part because ordinary people were able to use politics in free societies to do extraordinary things—first to organize themselves and then to demand and win improvements in their living standards, create opportunities for their children and insist on a basic social equality that is the essence of democracy as a way of life. This century, far from proving the futility of politics, is a history of the triumph of *democratic politics*. At the end of the century, the central problem confronting the democracies is not excessive government or a lack of economic and technical inventiveness, but a decay in the sort of social and political inventiveness and organization that gave power to ordinary citizens, shaped the economy into an engine of mass prosperity and strengthened democracy.

The overriding need in the United States and throughout the

democratic world is for a new engagement with democratic reform, the political engine that made the industrial era as successful as it was. The technologies of the information age will not on their own construct a successful society, any more than industrialism left to itself would have made the world better. The industrial age needed to be rescued from those who thought that technology on its own could save the human race. Now the information age must also be saved from the cyberutopians. Even the most extraordinary breakthroughs in technology and the most ingenious applications of the Internet will not save us from social breakdown, crime or injustice. Only politics, which is the art of how we organize ourselves, can even begin to take on such tasks.

Politics and government cannot raise children, write love songs, create computer languages, invent the technology after the microchip or discover a cure for cancer. But politics and government do shape the conditions under which such acts of creativity are made easier or harder, more likely or less likely. Politics has everything to do with building a more just, more civil, more open society. Those who rallied to Progressivism, the cause of those who believe that democratic government has the capacity to improve society, always understood this. Their time has come again.

Notes

CHAPTER ONE: *Why Politicians Don't Get Respect Anymore*

21   "You need someone with a substantial gut . . .": Quoted in Michael Weisskopf, "The Professionals' Touch: Role of Political Consultants Keeps Growing," *Washington Post* (November 8, 1994), p. 1.

22   North and Robb ads described by Kent Jenkins and Peter Baker, "On the Air," *Washington Post* (November 14, 1994), p. A4.

22   Gaylord described and quoted in Phil Kuntz, "Joseph Gaylord, Newt Gingrich's 'Eyes and Ears,' Is Expected to Play a Major Role in Washington," *Wall Street Journal* (December 8, 1994), p. A20.

23   But more than liberals may realize . . . : My point here was a philosophical one: that a foul political atmosphere works against supporters of government, usually meaning liberals and Democrats. Since I wrote that sentence, a useful and detailed academic study has been published showing that this point also has application at the most practical level of what works in campaigns. Stephen Ansolabehere and Shanto Iyengar conclude that "negative campaign commercials . . . are much less effective than positive advertisements at reinforcing the preferences of the Democrats' own partisans. . . . Republicans, by contrast, have a strong incentive to attack. . . . The principal implications of the findings here is that, whatever the ultimate reason, negative advertising gives Republicans a considerable electoral advantage." Ansolabehere and Iyengar, *Going Negative: How Attack Ads Shrink and Polarize the Electorate* (New York: The Free Press, 1995), esp. pp. 95–96. As the title suggests, they also conclude that negative ads push down turnout, drive away independent voters and increase voter apathy.

23   "Listen to Rush Limbaugh . . .": David Frum, *Dead Right* (New York: A New Republic Book/Basic Books, 1994), p. 2.

23   The ads against Chiles and Cuomo are described in Howard Kurtz, "Ads Use

Crimes' Pain for Candidates' Gain," *Washington Post* (November 2, 1994), p. 1.

23–24   Engler ad described and commented upon in Howard Kurtz, "Slash Attacks Remain a Big Hit in Televised Political Advertising," *Washington Post* (September 26, 1994), p. 7.

24   I draw here on Frum's excellent analysis of Reagan's budget policies in *Dead Right*, pp. 39–56.

26   The best account of the Atari Democrats (and a sympathetic one) is Randall Rothenberg, *The Neo-Liberals* (New York: Simon & Schuster, 1984).

26   For Tsongas on golden eggs and other economic ideas, see Paul Tsongas, *The Road from Here* (New York: Knopf, 1981), esp. pp. 30–48 and 127–53.

29   "the politics of displacement": On the loss of distinctions between public and private, see Jean Bethke Elshtain, *Democracy on Trial* (New York: Basic Books, 1995), p. 38.

30   "culture wars": James Davison Hunter, *Culture Wars* (New York: Basic Books, 1991).

CHAPTER TWO: *Politicians Adrift*

34–35   "Americans everywhere were crying out in scorn and despair": Robert Wiebe, *The Search for Order* (New York: Hill and Wang, 1967). The "Americans everywhere" quotation appears on p. 5, as does the reference to the "salary grab." The "reign of licentious extravagance" quotation appears on pp. 4–5; the reference to temperance appears on p. 56; "a hectic campaign to instill patriotism" on p. 57.

35   "There is something familiar...": Hugh Heclo, "The Progressive Impulse," *The Public Interest* (Spring 1995), p. 105.

37   Alan Reynolds on the U.S. economy: Reynolds, "Economic Foundations of the American Dream," in Lamar Alexander and Chester E. Finn Jr., eds., *The New Promise of American Life* (Indianapolis: The Hudson Institute, 1995), pp. 194–220. The figures on house sizes, air conditioners, etc. appear on p. 198.

37   "Here's how it could happen...": Bob Davis and Lucinda Harper, "Reason for Hope: Middle Class's Fears About Coming Years Might Be Misguided," *Wall Street Journal* (March 3, 1995), p. 1.

39   "the global hiring hall": Richard Rothstein, "The Global Hiring Hall," *The American Prospect* (Spring 1994), pp. 54–61.

39   Reich statistics and analysis from Robert B. Reich, *The Work of Nations* (New York: Knopf, 1991), esp. pp. 212–19.

40   "predators' ball": Connie Bruck, *The Predators' Ball: The Junk Bond Raiders and the Men Who Staked Them* (New York: Simon & Schuster, 1988).

40–41   The statistics on men, women and education are from E. J. Dionne Jr., "Speeches, Statistics and Some Unsettling Facts About America's Changed Prospects," *Washington Post*, Outlook section (January 26, 1992), p. C1.

41   Luntz on "underachievers": Interviews with the author during the 1992 New Hampshire primary and subsequently.

41   Data on 1993 income growth from Albert R. Hunt, "Clinton Opportunities," *Wall Street Journal* (December 15, 1994), p. A15.

41–42 Paul Krugman on technological change, see Krugman, "Technology's Revenge," *The Wilson Quarterly* (Autumn 1994), pp. 56–64, esp. pp. 60–62.

42–43 David Wessel, "Strong Growth Brings Jobs to Cedar Rapids, But Many Pay Poorly," *Wall Street Journal* (June 24, 1994), p. 1.

43 On the acceptance of inequality, see Derek Bok, *The Cost of Talent: How Executives and Professionals Are Paid and How It Affects America* (New York: The Free Press, 1993).

43 The "winner-take-all society": Robert H. Frank and Philip Cook, *The Winner-Take-All Society* (New York: The Free Press, 1995). Quotations here are from an earlier version of this argument, Robert Frank, "Talent and the Winner-Take-All Society," *The American Prospect* (Spring 1994), pp. 97–107.

44 "Television does not take the place . . .": Krugman, "Technology's Revenge," p. 63.

45 "There were no beggars . . .": Quoted in Wiebe, *The Search for Order*, p. 8. Interestingly, the congressman's name was Reagan.

46 Walter Russell Mead: See, for example Mead, "Saul Among the Prophets: The Bush Administration's New World Order," *World Policy Journal* (Summer 1991), pp. 375–420, and "The United States and the New Europe: American Grand Strategy After the Cold War," *World Policy Journal* (Winter 1989/90), pp. 35–70. Mead's brilliant writing on the postwar economic bargain has greatly influenced my thinking, as have several useful conversations with him.

48 On a new democratic *nomenklatura,* see Ralf Dahrendorf, "No Third Way," *Partisan Review* (Winter 1990), pp. 508–25. The reference to the democratic *nomenklatura* appears on p. 515.

49 Richard Rorty, "The Intellectuals and the End of Socialism," *Yale Review* (April 1992), pp. 1–16.

49 On the failure to predict a renewal of nationalism, ethnicity and regional separatism: One of the few people who actually saw what was coming was Nathan Glazer. See Glazer, "The Universalization of Ethnicity," *Encounter* (February 1975), pp. 8–17.

50 "the coarsening of the culture . . .": Contract with the American Family, quoted in E. J. Dionne Jr., "Monopolizing Family Values," *Washington Post* (May 30, 1995), p. A13.

50 "We have to say to the counterculture . . .": Gingrich speech of November 11, 1994, reprinted in Ed Gillespie and Bob Schellhas, eds., *Contract with America* (New York: Times Books, 1994), p. 191.

51 On children living without their fathers, see David Blankenhorn's valuable *Fatherless America* (New York: Basic Books, 1995), p. 18.

52 Representative Chris Smith on welfare: Interview with author in the spring of 1995.

53 For Hillary Clinton on "spiritual vacuum," see Michael Kelly, "Saint Hillary," *New York Times Magazine* (May 23, 1993), pp. 22ff.

53 "a working class with proletarian status . . .": Richard Cornuelle, "The Power and Poverty of Libertarian Thought," *Critical Review* (Winter 1992), pp. 1–10.

54 "gnawing conviction": The quotation is from Charles S. Maier, "Democracy and Its Discontents," *Foreign Affairs* (July/August 1994), pp. 48–64. The quotation cited appears on p. 54. This excellent article makes a case that all the industrial democracies are passing through a moral crisis. My analysis of the "four crises" in the United States parallels Maier's in certain ways, but Maier subsumes the crises I describe—political, economic, international—within a larger moral crisis and thus gives the word "moral" a broader definition than I do here.

57 Tarnoff quoted in Joshua Muravchik, "Clintonism Abroad," *Commentary* (February 1995), p. 37.

57 A sense of mission: Garry Wills, address to a conference on the press and the presidency organized by the Shorenstein Center, Harvard University, at the National Press Club in Washington (September 28, 1995).

61 "We might say that...": Muravchik, "Clintonism Abroad," p. 40.

63 "Our problem is not economic...": Bennett speech to the Christian Coalition, September 11, 1993.

CHAPTER THREE: *The Politics of the Anxious Middle*

67 "the Radical Middle" and "the anxious class": Both have been staples of the work, respectively, of Joe Klein and Robert Reich—Klein in his work in *New York* magazine and *Newsweek*, and Reich in a series of speeches as labor secretary. For the fullest expression of Klein's theory, see Klein, "Stalking the Radical Middle," *Newsweek* (September 25, 1995), pp. 32–36. I am grateful to both for extended conversations on many of the themes in this work.

69 "ambivalence toward the assertion of American values...": Quotation is from Al From, "Democratic Policy Review," *The Mainstream Democrat* (September/October 1989), p. 21.

69 The series of "We believe" statements is from the DLC's "New Orleans Declaration," reprinted in *The New Democrat* (May 1990), pp. 8–15.

70 "credibility on defense...": John Judis, "From Hell: The New Democrat Delusion," *The New Republic* (December 19, 1994), pp. 14–18. William Galston is quoted on p. 16. This article is the source of subsequent references to Judis's theories about the 1992 Clinton campaign.

71 Electoral analysis here and throughout is by the author unless otherwise indicated. Much of the important data on presidential voting, including county returns, can be found in *The World Almanac*. For a series of excellent essays on the 1992 election, see Gerald M. Pomper et al., *The Election of 1992* (Chatham, N.J.: Chatham House, 1993).

72 "now that the Democratic Party has revitalized itself": Perot quotation from *Congressional Quarterly* (July 18, 1992), p. 2131.

73 "The people are concerned...": and subsequent quotations are from "Ross Perot Reenters Presidential Campaign," *Vital Speeches of the Day*, vol. 59 (October 15, 1992), p. 15.

73 "A disturbing trend has emerged...": Perot quoted in Sean Wilentz, "Pox Populi: Ross Perot and the Corruption of Populism," *The New Republic* (August 9, 1993), pp. 29–35. The quotation appears on p. 34. Subsequent quotations and Wilentz's analysis are drawn from this excellent article.

74–75   Ruy Teixeira's telling analyses of the 1992 and 1994 elections appear in a series of papers available through the Economic Policy Institute, Washington, D.C. See especially *The Politics of the High Wage Path: The Challenge Facing Democrats* (Economic Policy Institute, Working Paper 110, October 1994); and Teixeira and Joel Rogers, "Who Deserted the Democrats in 1994?," *The American Prospect* (Fall 1995), pp. 73–77.

76   "lost the driving energy . . .": Jim Pinkerton, "Why Bush Lost," *The New Democrat* (January 1993), p. 12.

76   "one part Reagan, one part Perot . . .": Ronald Brownstein, "Republicans Must Negotiate Paradoxical Set of Pitfalls," *Los Angeles Times* (November 21, 1994), p. A5.

77   References to the Contract drawn from the House Republican Conference, *Legislative Digest*, September 27, 1994. The Contract with America, plus Republican commentary on it, was published as a book shortly after the 1994 elections by Times Books.

79   "whose sails were being carried . . .": Mitchell and Tony May quoted in a useful post-election analysis by Peter Landry, "Desire for Change Elected Wofford, Then Doomed Him," *Philadelphia Inquirer* (November 10, 1994), p. A23.

80–81   On the Republicans' 1994 gains in the South, an excellent analysis is Rhodes Cook, "Dixie Voters Look Away: South Shifts to the GOP," *Congressional Quarterly* (November 12, 1994), pp. 3230–31.

81–82   I am grateful to the National Republican Congressional Committee for sharing its post-election analysis, which offered many useful angles of vision on the voting, including a careful look at the closer races and at the relationship between recent presidential voting and the 1994 vote. Data on swing districts also come from the excellent analysis in Rhodes Cook, "Losses in Swing Districts Doomed Democrats," *Congressional Quarterly* (November 19, 1994), pp. 3354–57.

82   Michael Barone has expanded on his view of the Democrats' skills in training good candidates many times over many years in the indispensable volumes of *The Almanac of American Politics*.

82–83   "government spends too much . . .": Stan Greenberg's analysis of health care is from "The Revolt Against Politics," a paper prepared for the Democratic Leadership Council, delivered November 17, 1994.

83–85   Analysis of the exit polls is by the author, except the data focusing on the relationship of education to voting. Here I was helped enormously by the analyses of Ruy Teixeira of the Economic Policy Institute and Labor Secretary Robert Reich. My thanks to Dotty Lynch at CBS News, Keating Holland at CNN, Lissy Shapiro at VNS and Rich Morin at the *Washington Post* for help with data. The CNN polling is particularly helpful in figuring out who failed to vote in 1994.

87   For "business is seen also as a victim . . ." and subsequent quotations from Rogers and Freeman, see Louis Uchitelle, "The Rise of the Losing Class," *New York Times* (November 20, 1994), Week in Review, p. 1.

89   "In an astonishingly short time . . .": Reich's comments and data on health care are from Robert Reich, "The State of the American Workforce, 1994," address to the Center for National Policy, delivered August 31, 1994.

89–90   Robert Reich, "The Revolt of the Anxious Class," address to the Democratic Leadership Council, delivered November 22, 1994.

CHAPTER FOUR: *The Clinton Experiment*

96 and following   Where there are not specific references, the material presented is based on my own reporting. In gaining some perspective on what was going on inside the Clinton White House, I have been especially helped by running conversations and interviews over the last several years—some more extensive than others—with White House officials Melanne Verveer, Mary Ellen Glynn, Bill Galston, Bruce Reed, David Kusnet, Tom Donilon, Laura Tyson, George Stephanopoulos, Gene Sperling, Elaine Kamarck, Steve Kelman, David Gergen, Mack McLarty and Matt Cooper; with Labor Secretary Robert Reich; and with political consultants Paul Begala, Stanley Greenberg, Mandy Grunwald and Frank Greer. Not only are these people not responsible for the judgments I have drawn, but all of them will actively disagree with some of my conclusions and some will disagree with almost all of my conclusions.

96   Woodward, Drew and Maraniss: Bob Woodward, *The Agenda: Inside the Clinton White House* (New York: Simon & Schuster, 1994); Elizabeth Drew, *On the Edge: The Clinton Presidency* (New York: Simon & Schuster, 1994); David Maraniss, *First in His Class: A Biography of Bill Clinton* (New York: Simon & Schuster, 1995).

97–98   "The freedom to die before you're a teenager . . .": Clinton quoted in E. J. Dionne Jr., "Clinton's Bully Pulpit," *Washington Post* (November 16, 1993), p. A21.

99   "reinvent government": David Osborne and Ted Gaebler, *Reinventing Government* (Reading, Mass.: Addison-Wesley, 1992).

99–100   For Kuttner on reinvention, see Robert Kuttner, "Up from 1994," *The American Prospect* (Winter 1995), p. 11.

101   "most hostile to the image makeover": Ruy Teixeira, *The Politics of the High Wage Path: The Challenge Facing Democrats* (Economic Policy Institute, Working Paper 110, October 1994), p. 5.

105   "Unfortunately, for many Democrats . . .": Will Marshall, "Friend or Faux," *The American Prospect* (Winter 1994), pp. 10–11.

106   "indulge in the conceit . . .": Jeff Faux, "The Evasion of Politics," *The American Prospect* (Winter 1994), p. 16.

106   "a credible commander-in-chief" and other Faux quotations: Jeff Faux, "The Myth of the New Democrat," *The American Prospect* (Fall 1993), p. 24.

106–7   "Left-liberals" and other Marshall quotations: Marshall, "Friend or Faux," p. 11.

107   "those who invest" and other Faux quotations: Faux, "The Evasion of Politics," p. 17.

108   Kotkin: Joel Kotkin, "The Center Folds: High Noon for the New Democrats," *Reason* (February 1995), pp. 25–28. See also Joel Kotkin and Morley Winograd, "The New Constituency," *The New Democrat* (November 1994), pp. 15–19.

108–9   "jarring effects . . .": Marshall, "Friend or Faux."

109   "cut and invest": Shapiro's numerous papers on his "cut and invest" strategy are available through the Progressive Policy Institute in Washington, D.C. for an interesting defense of Clinton's original budget from a New Democratic point of view, see Shapiro, "Tax and Mend," *The New Republic* (March 22, 1993), pp. 19–24.

111   On Clinton resenting Tsongas's criticisms and Tsongas's popularity with editorial writers: This view was reflected by several Clinton staff members in background interviews during 1992 and again during the budget fight. See also Woodward, *The Agenda*, pp. 31–34.

112   "Bill Clinton knew where this deficit...": Woodward, *The Agenda*, p. 114.

114   On Kennedy economic policy, see James N. Giglio, *The Presidency of John F. Kennedy* (Lawrence: Kansas University Press, 1991), pp. 135–40. Kennedy's speech in support of his tax cut to the Economic Club of New York in December 1962 so upset Kennedy friend John Kenneth Galbraith that Galbraith referred to it as the most "Republican speech since McKinley" (p. 137).

CHAPTER FIVE: *The Failure of Reform*

119   Greenberg on Skocpol and Wilson: Greenberg refers repeatedly to the two in his writings. See, notably, Stanley B. Greenberg, *Middle-Class Dreams: The Politics and Power of the New American Majority* (New York: Times Books, 1995), pp. 279–85. I am grateful to Greenberg for many helpful conversations over the years, and for sending a steady stream of papers. Skocpol's views are summarized in "Sustainable Social Policy: Fighting Poverty Without Poverty Programs," *The American Prospect* (Summer 1990), pp. 58–70. For a fuller view, see Theda Skocpol, *Social Policy in the United States: Future Possibilities in Historical Perspective* (Princeton, N.J.: Princeton University Press, 1995). William J. Wilson's masterpiece is *The Truly Disadvantaged* (Chicago: University of Chicago Press, 1987). See also Wilson, "Race Neutral Policies and the Democratic Coalition," *The American Prospect* (Spring 1990), pp. 74–81.

120   "It will relegitimize middle-class...": Kristol's December 2, 1993, memo, "Defeating President Clinton's Health Care Proposal," is quoted in Greenberg, *Middle-Class Dreams*, pp. 282–83.

121   "the Republicans enjoyed...": Paul Starr, "What Happened to Health Care Reform?" *The American Prospect* (Winter 1995), p. 21. My view of the health care struggle—and thus the view presented here—has been greatly influenced by this important article. Subsequent references to Starr are from this article.

127   "an intermediary step to socialized medicine": Dick Armey's comments are in a symposium in *Policy Review* (Winter 1993).

128–29   On business and health care, see John Judis, "Abandoned Surgery: Business and the Future of Health Care Reform," *The American Prospect* (Spring 1995), pp. 65–73. All liberals, progressives and businesspeople should read this piece for an understanding of how support from at least some segments of the business community is indispensable to the success of progressive reform.

130–35   My view of the welfare battle has been informed by numerous conversations and interviews with David Ellwood, Bruce Reed, Robert Greenstein and his able colleagues at the Center on Budget and Policy Priorities, notably Sharon Parrot, and also Paul Offner, Representative Robert Matsui, Bill Galston, Will Marshall and John Carr. I thank them for their help. The views expressed here are mine, not theirs, but they all influenced them.

132   On Ellwood's views, see David Ellwood, *Poor Support* (New York: Basic Books, 1988), and Mary Jo Bane and David T. Ellwood, *Welfare Realities: From Rhetoric to Reform* (Cambridge, Mass.: Harvard University Press, 1994). An impor

tant view of the whole welfare debate is offered in Mickey Kaus, *The End of Equality* (New York: A New Republic Book/Basic Books, 1992).

133 "My goal is to make sure that . . .": The Matsui-Ellwood exchange is quoted in Eric Pianin, "Similarities, Conflicts Arise at Welfare Reform Hearing," *Washington Post* (July 28, 1994), p. A9.

134–35 The poll cited here is reported in Geoffrey Garin, Guy Molyneux and Linda DiVall, "Public Attitudes Toward Welfare Reform: A Summary of Key Research Findings," paper issued by Peter D. Hart Research Associates (January 1994).

139–43 My view of the campaign finance reform debate was informed by conversations and interviews with Fred Wertheimer of Common Cause; former Representative Karen Shepherd; Senators Paul Wellstone, John McCain and Russ Feingold; and former Representative Eric Fingerhut. Peggy Connolly, formerly of the Democratic Congressional Campaign Committee, provided a useful perspective on the place in its heyday. Here, as on welfare, the views are mine, but all these people had a large role in shaping them.

140 Brooks Jackson, *Honest Graft* (New York: Knopf, 1988).

141 On Thomas E. Dewey and the PAC issue in 1944, see Steven Fraser, *Labor Will Rule: Sidney Hillman and the Rise of American Labor* (New York: The Free Press, 1991), pp. 526–38.

142–43 PAC donations to Republicans reported by Craig Karmin, "In Reversal, Corporate PACs Flock to GOP," *The Hill* (May 31, 1995), p. 1.

143–46 Conversations with Cynthia Hogan, the chief counsel at the Senate Judiciary Committee before the 1994 elections, with Bruce Reed of the Clinton administration and with Representative Charles E. Schumer were helpful for this chapter, though they are not responsible for its conclusions.

144 a *compendium* of brain-dead notions: Joe Klein, "Robert Kennedy's Last Campaign," *Newsweek* (August 8, 1994), p. 23.

147 The poll of business leaders: "Why Business Hates Clinton," *BusinessWeek* (October 10, 1994), pp. 38–40.

147 "that *they* are the problem": Jeff Faux, "A New Conversation," *The American Prospect* (Spring 1995), pp. 35–43. The specific quotation appears on p. 38.

CHAPTER SIX: *Reinventing Old Answers*

151 Tape of health care ad made available by the Republican National Committee.

153 On decline of mass movements associated with Progressives: I am grateful to my friend Harold Meyerson for underscoring for me the importance of this development in American politics. He has made this point frequently in *Dissent* and in the pages of the *LA Weekly*, and will make it forcefully in a forthcoming book, tentatively entitled *The Disorganization of America*.

153 "was strong on the need . . .": Herbert Stein, "What Happened?" *Wall Street Journal* (May 31, 1995), p. A16.

154 "Once members of Congress . . .": Dick Armey, quoted in George J. Church, "Hard Going for the Easy Part," *Time* (January 1, 1995), p. 35.

154   Al D'Amato quoted in Albert R. Hunt, "Federalism Debate Is as Much About Power as About Principle," *Wall Street Journal* (January 19, 1995), p. A19.

155   A principled case for the gradualist approach to abortion has been offered by George Weigel, Mary Anne Glendon and William Kristol. See, for example, George Weigel and Bill Kristol, "Life and the Party," *National Review* (August 15, 1994), p. 53; and Mary Anne Glendon and George Weigel, "Catholic Politicians Must Fight Abortion," *Newsday* (May 8, 1990).

156   "leave us alone" coalition: Norquist, conversation with author.

157   "with twelve-year-olds having babies . . .": This is a staple Gingrich line. See, for example, Gingrich speech reprinted in Ed Gillespie and Bob Schellhas, eds., *Contract with America* (New York: Times Books, 1994), p. 182.

158–61   For a fuller treatment on the rise of contemporary conservatism, see E. J. Dionne Jr., *Why Americans Hate Politics* (New York: Simon & Schuster, 1991), esp. chapters 6 and 7. By far the best account of the intellectual origins of the postwar right is George H. Nash, *The Conservative Intellectual Movement in America Since 1945* (New York: Basic Books, 1976). Also insightful, from a different perspective, is Theodore J. Lowi, *The End of the Republican Era* (Norman: University of Oklahoma Press, 1995). David Frum offers useful observations on the history of the right throughout *Dead Right* (New York: A New Republic Book/Basic Books, 1994). Although Frum and I have quite different political commitments, his overall analysis (and critique) is similar in many ways to my own in *Why Americans Hate Politics*, particularly on the contradictions within contemporary conservatism and the rebirth of the libertarian impulse.

159   Hayek's classic is *The Road to Serfdom* (Chicago: University of Chicago Press, 1944; reprint 1976).

159   On "fusionism," see Nash, *The Conservative Intellectual Movement,* pp. 154–185, and Dionne, *Why Americans Hate Politics*, pp. 157–69.

162   "Conservatives have lost their zeal . . .": Frum, *Dead Right*, p. 3.

163   "there is something joyless . . .": Irving Kristol, *Reflection of a Neoconservative* (New York: Basic Books, 1983), pp. 40–41. This passage is cited in Bruce Frohnen, *Virtue and the Promise of Conservatism* (Lawrence: University Press of Kansas, 1993), p. 191, where Frohnen's comment also appears. Frohnen's is a poetic and powerful defense of traditionalist conservatism, which deserves attention both on its merits and because it sees conservatism from a vantage point quite different from that of conservatism's current political leadership.

164   the explosive popularity: William Bennett, *The Book of Virtues* (New York: Simon & Schuster, 1993).

164   The president drew on Stephen Carter's important book: Carter, *The Culture of Disbelief* (New York: Basic Books, 1993).

167   "M-16s at the ready": Buchanan quoted in E. J. Dionne Jr., "Buchanan Heaps Scorn on Democrats," *Washington Post* (August 18, 1992), p. A18.

168   On Buchanan's growing economic nationalism, see Frum, *Dead Right*, pp. 136–42. Having covered Buchanan during much of the 1992 New Hampshire primary, I can testify that Buchanan's emphasis changed from a balance between conservatism on the one side and nationalism and populism on the other to an increasingly full-throated version of the latter. My impression was that Buchanan

was affected by the economic distress he saw—and also realized that his best chance of beating Bush was with the protest votes of those angry about their economic status.

169–70 "to combine the pro-growth...": Adam Meyerson, "Between Little Rock and a Hard Place: What Conservatives Should Learn from Defeat," *Policy Review* (Winter 1993), p. 2.

171–72 "democratic capitalism": For the best recent statement of Novak's views, see Michael Novak, *The Catholic Ethic and the Spirit of Capitalism* (New York: The Free Press, 1993). See also Michael Novak, *The Spirit of Democratic Capitalism* (New York: Simon & Schuster, 1982).

172 Building on the radical ideas: Charles Murray's classic text is *Losing Ground: American Social Policy, 1950–1980* (New York: Basic Books, 1984). Also extremely influential—and discussed seriously by President Clinton as well as by conservatives—is Murray's "The Coming White Underclass," *Wall Street Journal* (October 29, 1993), p. A14.

174 "When conservatism's glittering generalities...": Frum, *Dead Right*, p. 205.

174 For "I have never been so concerned..." and following, see Vin Weber, "Mandate for Leadership: The Idea Vacuum in the GOP," *Policy Review* (Summer 1992), pp. 34–35.

175 "single-income families have been on a treadmill...": Meyerson, "Between Little Rock and a Hard Place," p. 3.

175 "What most observers still call 'American conservatism'...": All references here are drawn from Alan Tonelson, "Beyond Left and Right," *The National Interest* (Winter 1993/94), pp. 3–18. His taxonomy of conservatives appears on pp. 9–13.

177 On the rise of libertarians, see *Why Americans Hate Politics*, chapter 10. For an excellent recent look at the libertarians, see Nina J. Easton, "Red, White and Small," *Los Angeles Times Magazine* (July 9, 1995), pp. 12–30.

178 When the House Republicans published: Stephen Moore, ed., *Restoring the Dream* (New York: Times Books, 1995).

182–85 All quotations drawn from William Kristol, "The Future of Conservatism in the United States," *The American Enterprise* (July/August 1994), pp. 32–37. Kristol also published a version of this paper as "The Politics of Liberty, the Sociology of Virtue," in Lamar Alexander and Chester E. Finn Jr., eds., *The New Promise of American Life* (Indianapolis: The Hudson Institute, 1995), pp. 120–28.

186 "They cannot hear too often that our objective...": Ralph Reed Jr., *Politically Incorrect* (Dallas: Word Publishers, 1994), pp. 222–23; "only 22 percent," p. 225; "Our goal should be," p. 226; "Cut the federal budget," pp. 256–57. Dick Armey quoted in Reed, *Politically Incorrect,* p. 18.

187–93 This section draws from Michael S. Joyce and William A. Schambra, "A New Citizenship, a New Civic Life," in Alexander and Finn, eds., *The New Promise of American Life*, pp. 139–62. The roots of Schambra's thinking can be found in an essay that also clearly influenced Kristol. It is the foreword to a new edition of Robert Nisbet's *The Quest for Community* (San Francisco: Institute for Contemporary Studies, 1990), pp. vii–xix. I am personally grateful to Schambra for some useful discussions over the years and for his consistently open spirit.

193   "vast government bureaucracies...": Finn quotations from Chester E. Finn Jr., "Herbert Croly and the Cult of Governmentalism," in Alexander and Finn, eds., *The New Promise of American Life*, pp. 27–46.

193–94   "Will the real Christian Coalition please stand up?": James Guth in Michael Cromartie, ed., *Disciples & Democracy: Religious Conservatives and the Future of American Politics* (Washington, D.C.: Ethics and Public Policy Center/Eerdmans, 1994), p. 37.

194   For Reed on anti-abortion candidates and Edsall comment, see Thomas B. Edsall, "GOP Warned Not to Forget Family Values," *Washington Post* (February 12, 1995), p. A27.

194–95   "the much anticipated 'holy war'...": Ralph Reed, "Conservative Coalition Holds Firm," *Wall Street Journal* (February 13, 1995), p. A14.

195   "German bankers": Michael Lind, "Rev. Robertson's Grand International Conspiracy Theory," *New York Review of Books* (February 2, 1995), pp. 21–25, and "On Pat Robertson: His Defenders," *New York Review of Books* (April 20, 1995), pp. 67–68. Reed speech to B'nai B'rith: See Laurie Goodstein, "Christian Coalition Leader Extends an Olive Branch to American Jews," *Washington Post* (April 5, 1995), p. A3.

195–96   Representative Christopher Smith, comments to author. For Bauer's perspective, see Gary Bauer and Phil Gramm, "Why Pro-Lifers Should Support Welfare Reform," *Wall Street Journal* (August 30, 1995), p. A10.

CHAPTER SEVEN: *Why Gingrich Happened*

197   "People are not in general stupid...": Newt Gingrich, *Window of Opportunity: A Blueprint for the Future* (New York: Tom Doherty, 1984), p. 263.

197   "I am a transformational figure...": Gingrich quoted in Dan Balz and Charles R. Babcock, "Gingrich, Allies, Made Waves and Impression; Conservative Rebels Harassed the House," *Washington Post* (December 20, 1994), p. A1 and quote box. The *Post*'s series on Gingrich was superb, and it will be a basic point of reference for all future writing on Gingrich, as it has been for me here. My observations are also based on extensive conversations with Gingrich in the years before he became Speaker, particularly from 1986 to 1992. I am grateful for those chats, interviews and arguments.

198   "you get attention...": John M. Barry, *The Ambition and the Power* (New York: Penguin, 1990), p. 166. Barry's book is essential for anyone with an interest in Gingrich.

198   "The trick is persistence": Kenneth J. Cooper, "In Classroom and Town Meeting, Gingrich Spreads the Word at Home," *Washington Post* (February 20, 1995), p. A11.

198   "to foster the right to work...": Liberty League statement of purpose quoted in Clyde P. Weed, *The Nemesis of Reform: The Republican Party During the New Deal* (New York: Columbia University Press, 1994), p. 58.

200   a more candid statement: Most of what appears in Gingrich's best-seller is anticipated in *Window of Opportunity,* but *Window* is the more far-reaching—or perhaps less politically cautious—book. Newt Gingrich, *To Renew America* (New York: HarperCollins, 1995).

200–201   "advanced health care": Gingrich's utopia is laid out in *Window of Opportunity*, pp. 1–39. Interestingly, some of what Gingrich says sounds like Robert Reich. "No society as wealthy as ours should allow people to suffer simply because they took the wrong job; or the right job one year became the wrong job a decade later..." (p. 21). The "re-emergence of religion" quotation appears on p. 32, as does his reference to "religious software." His reference to "special-interest unionism" appears on p. 91; "anti-technology movement" on p. 57, and his comments on C. P. Snow on p. 58.

201   For a critical view of Gingrich on space and a look at his fascination with science fiction, see Thomas M. Disch, "Newt's Futurist Brain Trust," *The Nation* (February 27, 1995), pp. 266–70.

201   "Rather than whining that change...": Quotation in Gingrich, *Window of Opportunity*, p. 19.

202   Alvin and Heidi Toffler, *Creating a New Civilization: The Politics of the Third Wave* (Washington, D.C.: Progress and Freedom Foundation, 1994). Gingrich's comments appear on p. ix.

202   "forcing the scale of change...": Katharine Q. Seelye, "As a Model, Gingrich Takes Presidents, Not Predecessors," *New York Times* (April 11, 1995), pp. A1, A22.

204   All references to Olasky from Marvin Olasky, *The Tragedy of American Compassion* (Washington, D.C.: Regnery Publishing, 1992); "utopian," pp. 116–33; attacks social Darwinism, pp. 60–79; conclusion, p. 233; Gingrich quote from the cover of the 1995 edition. For a thoughtful critique of Olasky, see Alan Wolfe, "What Ever Happened to Compassion," *Critical Review* (Fall 1993), pp. 497–503.

205   "What is true...": Sumner quoted in Robert Green McCloskey, *American Conservatism in the Age of Enterprise* (New York: Harper Torchbooks, 1951), p. 46. This fine book deserves to be rediscovered in light of contemporary political events.

205   "a new generation which reasons that...": In Gingrich, *Window of Opportunity*, p. 38.

205   "We want to communicate...": Gingrich, remarks to the National Association of Manufacturers meeting in Washington, D.C., delivered May 18, 1995.

206   "If we should set a limit...": Sumner quoted in McCloskey, *American Conservatism*, p. 50.

206   "Tell us under what circumstances...": Gingrich speech to Manufacturers Association, delivered May 18, 1995.

207   "You didn't have losers...": "The World According to Gingrich," *Washington Post* (December 19, 1994).

207   "Civilization was equated...": McCloskey, *American Conservatism*, p. 12.

209   "When Newt says he is a revolutionary...": Quoted in Kim Masters, "Inside Newt's Brain," *Washington Post* (December 12, 1994), p. B1.

209   "I see us at a point where the old thesis...": Quoted in Thomas B. Edsall, "Can the GOP Survive Its Class Struggle? From Christian Right to Futurist, the Big Tent Begins to Tear," *Washington Post*, Outlook section (February 19, 1995), p. C1.

210   "the coldness of raw intellect...": Barry, *The Ambition and the Power*, p. 162.

210   "One of the great problems...": Quoted in Barry, *The Ambition and the Power,* p. 162.

210   "Politics is about public opinion...": Quoted in Balz and Babcock, "Gingrich, Allies Made Waves and Impression."

211   "more interesting, more energetic...": Balz and Babcock, "Gingrich, Allies Made Waves and Impression."

213   "Newt's belief...": Quoted in Balz and Babcock, "Gingrich, Allies Made Waves and Impression."

214   "If Wright survives this ethics thing...": and "If Wright consolidates his power...": Quoted in Barry, *The Ambition and the Power*, pp. 760 and 162, respectively.

217   For accounts of the Bush White House from the rebels' point of view, see Charles Kolb, *White House Daze: The Unmaking of Domestic Policy in the Bush Years* (New York: The Free Press, 1994), and John Podhoretz, *Hell of a Ride: Backstage at the White House Follies 1989–1993* (New York: Simon & Schuster, 1993). For the political views of the rebels leading theoretician, see Jim Pinkerton, *What Comes Next: The End of Big Government and the New Paradigm Ahead* (New York: Hyperion, 1995). Pinkerton's is a fascinating and insightful view of American politics that embodies some of the insights of Kristol, Gingrich and the libertarians but gives Republican politics a spin all Pinkerton's own.

219   "he has sold Ronald Reagan's inheritance...": Quoted in James Ceaser and Andrew Busch, *Upside Down and Inside Out: The 1992 Elections and American Politics* (Lanham, Md.: Littlefield Adams, 1993), p. 34.

222   "They think they can peddle...": Quoted in Balz and Babcock, "Gingrich, Allies Made Waves and Impression."

222   "you have the most explicitly ideologically committed...": Gingrich speech to the Washington Research Group Symposium, delivered November 11, 1994, reprinted in Ed Gillespie and Bob Schellhas, eds., *Contract with America* (New York: Times Books, 1994), p. 182.

223   "regulatory impact analysis": Quotations appear in Times Books version of the *Contract*, pp. 134–35.

223   "The laws would remain on the books...": McIntosh quoted in Christopher Georges, "House GOP Hopes to Cut Funding Used to Enforce Dozens of U.S. Regulations," *Wall Street Journal* (June 1, 1995), p. A16.

225–26   "The proposal looked like a free ride...": Stein's comments are in Herbert Stein, "What Happened?," *Wall Street Journal* (May 31, 1995), p. A16.

CHAPTER EIGHT: *No News Is Good News*

231   "journalism is probably...": Timothy Crouse, *The Boys on the Bus* (New York: Random House, 1972), p. 303.

232   *"We have to be very clear*...": Price quoted in Robert Schmuhl, *Statecraft and Stagecraft: American Political Life in the Age of Personality* (Notre Dame, Ind.: University of Notre Dame Press, 1992), p. 18.

232   "You guys...": Johnson quoted in Schmuhl, *Statecraft and Stagecraft*, p. 14.

233   "sufficiently underdeveloped": James Hoge, "Media Pervasiveness," *Foreign Affairs* (July/August 1994), p. 137.

233   Lichter analysis of Clinton: Robert S. Lichter, "They're No Friends of Bill: TV News Coverage of the Clinton Administration," *Media Monitor* (July/August 1994), pp. 1–6.

234   "People don't read *Vanity Fair* . . .": Howard Kurtz, "Unconventional Challengers Build Immunity to Shots from Press," *Washington Post* (October 15, 1994), p. A10.

234   "seriously as our sole intermediaries . . .": Diana Owen and Michael Robinson, "1992 Heralds Electronic Populism," *The World and I* (February 1993), p. 119.

234   "You know why I can stiff you on press conferences?" and "the first president to conclude . . .": Stephen Hess, "President Clinton and the White House Press Corps—Year One," *Media Studies Journal* (Spring 1994), p. 4.

234   "Jurassic Park syndrome": Jonathan Alter in "Assessing the Press and Clinton in the New Media Age: An Expert Roundtable," *Media Studies Journal* (Spring 1994), p. 29.

235   "Even false rumors . . ." and "are losing ground . . .": Howard Kurtz, *Media Circus: The Trouble with America's Newspapers* (New York: Times Books, 1993), pp. 143 and 5, respectively.

237   Between the nineteenth and twentieth centuries: An excellent analytical look at the history of American journalism is Michael Schudson, *Discovering the News: A Social History of American Newspapers* (New York: Basic Books, 1978).

239   But during the Gilded Age, as Christopher Lasch has pointed out: Lasch, *The Revolt of the Elites* (New York: Norton, 1995), pp. 166–68.

239   "defenders of the faith": Quoted in Lasch, *The Revolt of the Elites,* p. 168.

239–40   "men who have lost their grip . . ." and "unity of method": Walter Lippmann, *Liberty and the News* (New York: Harcourt, Brace and Howe, 1920), pp. 54, 67; "standards of measure," Lippmann quoted in Lasch, *The Revolt of the Elites,* p. 169; "The cynicism of the trade needs to be abandoned . . . ," Lippmann, *Liberty and the News*, p. 82; "episodes, incidents, eruptions," Lippmann, *Public Opinion,* quoted in John Patrick Diggins, *The Promise of Pragmatism* (Chicago: University of Chicago Press, 1994), p. 332; "Insofar as those who purvey the news . . . ," "the newspaper is in all literalness . . . ," "newspaper enterprise . . . ," Lippmann, *Liberty and the News,* pp. 13, 47, 78.

240   "I wish to begin a movement . . .": Pulitzer quoted in Schudson, *Discovering the News*, p. 153.

240   "Pulitzer was taking events . . .": Paul H. Weaver, *News and the Culture of Lying* (New York: The Free Press, 1994), pp. 36–37.

241   "stood the old journalism . . .": Weaver, *News and the Culture of Lying*, pp. 40–41.

241   "reader-focused . . .": Weaver, *News and the Culture of Lying*, p. 46.

241   "Most leading . . .": Schudson, *Discovering the News,* p. 98.

241   "The journals which pay best . . ." and "passionless ether": Quoted in Michael

E. McGerr, *The Decline of Popular Politics* (New York: Oxford University Press, 1986), pp. 119–20, 121.

242 "the relationship between...": Lasch, *The Revolt of the Elites*, p. 161.

242 "It is almost impossible...": Rosten study cited in Schudson, *Discovering the News*, p. 155.

242–43 "Their political impact...": Schudson, *Discovering the News*, pp. 162–63.

243 Daniel Boorstin, *The Image* (New York: Atheneum, 1962).

243 A revolutionary event: Theodore H. White, *The Making of the President 1960* (New York: Atheneum, 1961).

243–44 "one negative by-product": Albert R. Hunt, "The Media and Presidential Campaigns," in A. James Reichley, ed., *Elections American Style* (Washington, D.C.: The Brookings Institution, 1987), p. 57.

244 "the flow of ideas...": Jeff Greenfield, *The Real Campaign: How the Media Missed the Story of the 1980 Campaign* (New York: Summit, 1982); Richard Brookhiser, *The Outside Story* (Garden City, N.Y.: Doubleday, 1986).

244 "news management...": Schudson, *Discovering the News*, pp. 160–94.

247 Jamieson took the media to task: Kathleen Hall Jamieson, *Dirty Politics: Deception, Distraction and Democracy* (New York: Oxford University Press, 1992).

248 "In the absence of a vital polis...": Todd Gitlin, "Blips, Bites and Savvy Talk: Television's Impact on Politics," *Dissent* (Winter 1990), pp. 18–19.

248 "didn't do what he needed to do": Quoted in "What Voters Thought of the Romney-Kennedy Debate," *Boston Globe* (October 26, 1994), p. 22.

248 "a politics of shifting standards...": Thomas Patterson, *Out of Order* (New York: Knopf, 1993), p. 206.

249–50 "allowed itself to be shaped by polls...": Jamieson, *Dirty Politics*, p. 10.

250 "Candidates have been given steadily fewer..." and following: Patterson, *Out of Order*, pp. 73–74, 75.

251 On Limbaugh et al. spreading unsubstantiated rumors about Foster's death, see Susan Schmidt, "Family Asks End to Foster Scrutiny," *Washington Post* (July 21, 1994), p. A5, and Diane Rehm, "We Need a Truth Detector," *Washington Post* (June 30, 1994), p. A31.

252 "the extraordinary distortions...": Fred Wertheimer, interview with the author, October 1994.

252 "The astonishing thing...": John Bryant quoted in Charles Babcock, "Democrat Challenges Gingrich on Lobby Bill Defeat," *Washington Post* (October 30, 1994), p. A7.

252–53 The confusion of fact and opinion: Michiko Kakutani, "Opinion vs. Reality in an Age of Pundits," *New York Times* (January 28, 1994), pp. C1, C27.

253 "we have to enter imaginatively...": Lasch, *The Revolt of the Elites*, pp. 170–71.

257 "the lost art of argument": Lasch, *The Revolt of the Elites*, p. 161.

258 "If we insist...": Lasch, *The Revolt of the Elites*, p. 171.

260   "People should examine the consequences of what they say . . .": Clinton quoted in E. J. Dionne Jr., "A Time for Politicians to Look Within," *Washington Post* (April 25, 1995); Gingrich quoted in Dionne.

260–61   the attentive society and subsequent quotations: Glenn Tinder, "The Spirit of Freedom: To Live Attentively," in Richard John Neuhaus and George Weigel, eds., *Being Christian Today* (Washington, D.C.: Ethics and Public Policy Center, 1992), pp. 152–53.

CHAPTER NINE: *Showdown*

265–66   "We do have an economic game plan . . ." and "first rate": Stephen Moore, ed., *Restoring the Dream* (New York: Times Books, 1995), pp. 143, 144.

266   "Today, the forces of the nineteenth century . . .": Paul Starr, "Who Owns the Future?" *The American Prospect* (Spring 1995), p. 7.

267   "Conservatives have far more faith . . .": Guy Molyneux, conversation with author. Molyneux is also a Democratic polltaker.

269   "The family system has become demassified . . .": Tofflers quoted in Thomas B. Edsall, "Can the GOP Survive Its Class Struggle?" *Washington Post*, Outlook section (February 19, 1995), p. C1.

269   "The irony is that many 'family values' . . .": Alvin and Heidi Toffler, *Creating a New Civilization: The Politics of the Third Wave* (Atlanta: Turner Publishing, 1995), p. 87. This is the more widely available reprint of the book published by the Progress and Freedom Foundation.

270   "If these groups prove to be as shortsighted . . .": Toffler and Toffler, *Creating a New Civilization*, p. 105.

270   "collision of constituencies": Toffler and Toffler, *Creating a New Civilization*, p. 72.

270   "insofar as it substitutes . . .": Kristol quoted in Edsall, "Can the GOP Survive Its Class Struggle?"

270–71   "At root, the problem with Gingrichism . . .": Charles Krauthammer, "A Critique of Pure Newt," *The Weekly Standard* (September 18, 1995), p. 57.

271   "the pursuit of happiness": Gingrich speech reprinted in Ed Gillespie and Bob Schellhas, eds., *Contract with America* (New York: Times Books, 1994), p. 191.

273   "cultivate moral confusion": Bob Dole quoted in E. J. Dionne Jr., "Dole v. Hollywood," *Washington Post* (June 6, 1995), p. A18.

273   Many drawn to the militias: See Marc Cooper, "Montana's Mother of All Militias," *The Nation* (May 22, 1995), pp. 714–21. Cooper has done some of the best and most insightful reporting on the militia movement.

274   "the morality of the marketplace does not in itself . . .": David Broder, "Cries of Conscience," *Washington Post* (June 11, 1995), p. C7.

275   On the decline of the Republicans and the resurrection of Clinton, see Ann Devroy, "Opponents' Issues Drive Political Recovery," *Washington Post* (October 9, 1995), pp. A1, A14.

277   "were civic-minded . . .": Paul Starobin, "The Politics of Anxiety," *National Journal* (September 30, 1995), p. 2406.

278 "The trouble is that 30 years of shuffling..." and following: David Brooks, "What's Left of Liberalism?" *Commentary* (May 1995), pp. 63–65.

280 "to take on the party's base" and following: Al From, "Leftovers Again?" *The New Democrat* (July/August 1995), pp. 27–28.

280–81 "right wing of the Democratic Party..." and following: Jeff Faux, "A New Conversation," *The American Prospect* (Spring 1995), p. 36.

282 "It was the sort of split decision...": Elizabeth Drew, *On the Edge: The Clinton Presidency* (New York: Simon & Schuster, 1994), p. 288.

283 "left all of the... liberal state...": Theodore Lowi, *The End of the Republican Era* (Norman: University of Oklahoma Press, 1995), p. 93.

283 "put the welfare state in a moderately tight straitjacket": Irving Kristol, *Reflections of a Neoconservative* (New York: Basic Books, 1983), p. 255. Reprint of January 11, 1982, *Wall Street Journal* article.

284 "What you have to understand...": Clinton quoted in Drew, *On the Edge*, p. 70.

285 On creating separate consumption and investment budgets, see Robert J. Shapiro, "Cut and Invest," Progressive Policy Institute Policy Report 23 (1995), and "Enterprise Economics," in Will Marshall and Martin Scram, eds., *Mandate for Change* (New York: Berkley Books, 1993), ch. 2.

286 "Behind our New Deals and New Frontiers...": Dick Armey, *The Freedom Revolution* (Washington, D.C.: Regnery Publishing, 1995), pp. 15–16.

287 rests not on *weak* government: Stephen Holmes, *Passions and Constraint: On the Theory of Liberal Democracy* (Chicago: University of Chicago Press, 1995), pp. 18–23.

288 "only a powerful centralized state...": Holmes, *Passions and Constraint*, p. 20.

288 "Far from being a road to serfdom...": Holmes, *Passions and Constraint*, p. 23.

288 As the political philosopher Michael Walzer has argued: Walzer, *Spheres of Justice: A Defense of Pluralism and Equality* (New York: Basic Books, 1983), esp. pp. 97–108, 3–10, 64–94.

290 *Reinventing Government*: David Osborne and Ted Gaebler, *Reinventing Government* (Reading, Mass.: Addison-Wesley, 1992).

290 "the market is rational and the government is dumb": Armey, *The Freedom Revolution*, p. 316.

291 "negative liberty": Isaiah Berlin, *Four Essays on Liberty* (New York: Oxford University Press, 1969), pp. 118–72.

291 various external forces that impinge on freedom of choice....: This definition is essentially a summary of Berlin, *Four Essays on Liberty*, p. 131.

291 "wholesome democracy" and "a certain minimum...": Herbert Croly, *The Promise of American Life* (Boston: Northeastern University Press, 1989; reprint of 1909 edition), p. 205; "workingman to raise his standard of living" on p. 452; "make the individual workingman more of an individual" and "diminish his 'class consciousness'..." on p. 416.

291–92   "New Liberals": T. H. Green and Leonard Hobhouse quoted in Edward A. Stettner, *Shaping Modern Liberalism: Herbert Croly and Progressive Thought* (Lawrence: University Press of Kansas, 1993), pp. 52–53. I am grateful to Michael Lind for calling this very helpful book to my attention, and for preaching on the importance of Croly and Croly's version of liberal nationalism. For Michael Lind on Croly, see Lind, *The Next American Nation* (New York: The Free Press, 1995), p. 301. I am also grateful to Michael Lacey for preaching on the importance of the "New Liberals." For other helpful looks at Croly, see John B. Judis, *Grand Illusion: Critics and Champions of the American Century* (New York: Farrar, Straus & Giroux, 1992), pp. 23–45, and John Morton Blum, *Liberty, Justice, Order* (New York: Norton, 1993), pp. 89–99.

292   "backward, unsophisticated citizens . . .": Joyce and Schambra, "A New Citizenship, A New Civic Life," in Lamar Alexander and Chester E. Finn Jr., eds., *The New Promise of American Life* (Indianapolis: The Hudson Institute, 1995), p. 145; "cult of governmentalism," Finn in Alexander and Finn, eds., *The New Promise,* p. 38, and ". . . vast sums out of our pockets" on p. 43.

293   "If most progressives did not set out to keep the poor . . ." and following: Robert H. Wiebe, *Self-Rule: A Cultural History of American Democracy* (Chicago: University of Chicago Press, 1995), pp. 164–65.

293   "preoccupation with strong government . . .": Michael McGerr, foreword to Herbert Croly, *The Promise of American Life* (Boston: Northeastern University Press, 1989 edition), p. xi.

293   "the guardians of public health . . ." and following: Christopher Lasch, *Haven in a Heartless World* (New York: Basic Books, 1977), pp. 12–13.

294   "stood firm against the cruder demands . . .": Arthur S. Link, *Woodrow Wilson and the Progressive Era* (New York: Harper & Row, 1954), p. 64.

294   "way of life": On Dewey, see two excellent books, Alan Ryan, *John Dewey and the High Tide of American Liberalism* (New York: Norton, 1995), and Robert Westbrook, *John Dewey and American Democracy* (Ithaca: Cornell University Press, 1991).

294   "Public interest in family issues clearly grew . . .": Morton Keller, *Regulating a New Society* (Cambridge, Mass.: Harvard University Press, 1994), p. 37.

295   as the historian Michael Kazin has shown: Michael Kazin, *The Populist Persuasion* (New York: Basic Books, 1995), see esp. chapters 9 and 10.

295   "Civil society, or civic space . . .": Benjamin Barber, *Jihad vs. McWorld* (New York: Times Books, 1995), p. 281. See also what has become quickly the classic work on civil society, Robert D. Putnam, *Making Democracy Work: Civic Traditions in Modern Italy* (Princeton, N.J.: Princeton University Press, 1993).

296   "The opposition between individual freedom . . .": Alan Wolfe, *Whose Keeper?* (Berkeley: University of California Press, 1989), p. 126.

296   "friends can rely . . .": Wolfe, *Whose Keeper?,* p. 30.

297   "the social virtues": Francis Fukuyama, *Trust: The Social Virtues and the Creation of Prosperity* (New York: The Free Press, 1995).

298   "a bloodless repository of moral virtue": Philip Selznick, *The Moral Commonwealth* (Berkeley: University of California Press, 1992), pp. 512–13. If Selznick lays down a comprehensive theory for the communitarian movement, its manifesto

is Amitai Etzioni, *The Spirit of Community* (New York: Crown Publishers, 1993). On the importance of "community" to the Progressive idea, and some proposals, see E. J. Dionne Jr., "The Quest for Community (Again)," *The American Prospect* (Summer 1992), pp. 49–54.

298   "No man can be a good citizen . . .": Theodore Roosevelt, "The New Nationalism" (1910 speech in Osawatomie, Kansas), in Mario R. DiNunzio, ed., *Theodore Roosevelt, an American Mind: A Selection from His Writings* (New York: St. Martin's Press, 1994), p. 146.

299–300   "trying to fool the people . . ." and "the common man's common man": quoted in David McCullough, *Truman* (New York: Simon & Schuster, 1992), pp. 692, 715.

306   fatherless families: David Blankenhorn, *Fatherless America* (New York: Basic Books, 1995).

306–7   "Conservatives needlessly risk the well-being . . .": Kathleen Sylvester, *Second Chance Homes: Breaking the Cycle of Teen Pregnancy* (Washington, D.C.: Progressive Policy Institute, 1995). See also Sylvester, "A Second Chance," *The New Democrat* (September/October 1995), pp. 19–23.

308   Philip Murnion: conversation with author.

309   Those who would argue for a new American nationalism: The best statements of the new nationalist view are Lind, *The Next American Nation*, and John B. Judis and Michael Lind, "For a New Nationalism," *The New Republic* (March 27, 1995), pp. 19–27.

310–11   "The government and the market are not enough . . ." and "most underutilized resource . . .": Bill Bradley, "Civil Society and the Rebirth of Our National Community," *The Responsive Community* (Spring 1995), pp. 4–10.

311–12   ". . . the futility of politics" and other quotations: Peter Drucker, "The Age of Social Transformation," *The Atlantic* (November 1994), pp. 53ff.

Acknowledgments

It is at once a sobering and delightful discovery that if you write about politics, have a lot of thoughtful and generous friends and talk about political issues often and at length, it is impossible to do justice to all the personal and intellectual debts you owe. So when the time comes to thank all the people you should thank, you know you'll never do it right. I am thus certain that I have forgotten someone important and that I will not be detailed enough in explaining just how much the people I do mention have contributed to this book. Worries about similar problems led to a list of acknowledgments in my earlier book, *Why Americans Hate Politics,* that a friend jokingly referred to as "epic" in length. To save readers from an even longer list—but also to make clear that my obligations are deep and continuous—I thus ask all those who are mentioned in the acknowledgments of that earlier book (on pages 420–423 of the paperback) to consider themselves thanked once again. The notion that the people on that list or this one could possibly be held responsible for what is written here—given how much they might disagree with one another, let alone with me—is preposterous. On the other hand, I couldn't have written this book without them.

My particular debts for this book are large enough. I must thank first those who educate me every day, my colleagues on the editorial page staff of *The Washington Post*: John Anderson, Bob

335

Asher, Ken Ikenberry, Colby King, Martha McAteer, Peter Milius, Steve Rosenfeld, Amy Schwartz, Pat Shakow, Tim Ruane, Lou Marano, Fannie Zollicoffer, Julia Kennedy-White, Janet Rhuda and Kathryn Powell. I am particularly and deeply grateful to Meg Greenfield, the editor of the page, who brought me into this community and trusted me with a column on the *Post*'s op-ed page. Meg inspires all around her to challenge accepted views, to search for better words, to avoid humbug and cant, to think about those outside of the boundaries of the conventional political world and to remember that writing is a serious business that is also supposed to be fun. I must also again thank Ben Bradlee, Len Downie, Bob Kaiser and David Ignatius for encouraging me to join the *Post* in the first place. Thanks, too, to the smart and hardworking people at *The Washington Post*'s News Research Center.

I also thank Meg for granting me a leave, which I used to work at the Woodrow Wilson International Center for Scholars. What a magnificent place it is, and what great people work there. At a time when the world of ideas is increasingly organized along rigid ideological lines, the Wilson Center is a refreshing place. It is open to people of every imaginable view, and it encourages free exchange and serious argument within a framework of civility and fellowship. I am especially grateful to the Center's director, Charles Blitzer, for running such a fine program and for bringing me into the Center. I also owe a huge debt to Mike Lacey, who runs the Center's American program and knows so much more about the original Progressive Era than I do. Mike cannot have a chat without thinking of at least five good ideas and six important books or articles that bear on the subject at hand, plus a brilliant analysis of the underlying moral issues at stake in any debate. Thanks also to Mike Spleet, who was exceptionally resourceful and hardworking as a research assistant during my time at the Center. Thanks to George Wagner for many things, including rescue from computer catastrophe, and to everyone else on the staff, particularly Moira Egan, Christina Carhart and Laura Dowling. Needless to say, the Wilson Center is not even remotely responsible for the thoughts I offer here.

Many of my intellectual and journalistic debts are recorded, at times in some detail, in the notes at the end of the book. I have tried wherever possible to mention in the text all those from whom I have drawn ideas, insights and facts. But I need to say a particular thank you to Bob Kuttner, Paul Starr and the rest of the editors of *The American Prospect* for producing such a good magazine, and for letting me use so many of its ideas in these pages. A new Progressive Era will draw much inspiration from this journal's thoughtful efforts to revive, as its masthead puts it, "the liberal imagination." Thanks as well to Chester Finn of the Hudson Institute for organizing its conference on Progressivism and for letting me use so many of its fine papers—knowing in advance that I planned to take issue with them. And I should express my gratitude to several Washington think tanks for putting out work that has so obviously influenced my text and, in many cases, for helping me in more specific ways. A particular thank you to all the people at the Economic Policy Institute and the Progressive Policy Institute, which play an important role in these pages; and also to the Center for National Policy, the Brookings Institution, the Cato Institute, the Economic Strategy Institute, the Heritage Foundation and the American Enterprise Institute.

To those thanked in the earlier book, I add the following list of people in appreciation for their help: Paul Begala, Ron Brownstein, David Cohen, Joanne and Jack Deschauer, Nina Easton, David Ellwood, Noel and Anita Epstein, Paul Gigot, Mary Ellen Glynn, Cynthia Hogan, Marvin Kalb, Jill Lawrence, Michael Lind, David Maraniss, Larry Meyer, Harold Meyerson, Paul Offner, Sharon Parrott, Bruce Reed, Ralph Reed, Colette Rhoney, Cokie and Steve Roberts, Tim Russert, Dana Schwartz, Gerry Seib, Frank Sesno, Mark Shields, Allison Silver, Bob Stack, Lesley Stahl, Mo Steinbruner, George Stephanopoulos, Ruy Teixeira, Alan Tonelson, Cathy Mitchell Toren and Peter Toren, Melanne and Phil Verveer, David Von Drehle, Pete Wehner and Fred Wertheimer. The warmest possible thanks to every single member of the Boyle family, and to Brian and Caitlin for particular help. And with love I also thank my sister, Lucie-Anne Dionne Thomas, and Drew Thomas and Kim Thomas.

My friends Guy Molyneux and Amy Schwartz, and my wife, Mary Boyle, read the final manuscript with enormous care. They not only corrected many errors and misunderstandings, they also made what might have been a difficult process a joy by throwing themselves into it with complete engagement and much good humor.

My agent, Kathy Robbins, was, once again, enormously helpful and encouraging. Alice Mayhew, my editor at Simon & Schuster, is justly a legend. Those who cannot understand how she manages to edit so many books and win so much affection and respect from her authors have simply never met her. So it's not their fault, because only if you know her can you actually believe that God made a person with so much energy, warmth, intelligence, talent and fortitude. Roger Labrie, her assistant, combines intelligence and insight with patience and attention to all the important details—a rare and wonderful combination for which I am very appreciative. Many thanks also to Elizabeth Stein and Lisa Weisman.

My mother, Lucienne Galipeau Dionne, died in August of 1995, as this book was nearing completion. My debt to her is incalculable, and I miss her for so many reasons, not least because it was such a delight to learn from her always passionate, always deeply considered insights about public life and the responsibilities of individual human beings. She always met those obligations—to her community, to her friends and to her family—with loving commitment. All who knew her were blessed.

To my wife, Mary, and to my children, James and Julia, nothing I write here can be enough to do honor to the joyous surprise they bring to my life every day. St. Paul wrote that love believes all things, hopes all things, endures all things and never ends. St. Paul was right.

Index